Human-Computer Interaction Series

Human-Computer Interaction is a multidisciplinary field focused on human aspects of the development of computer technology. As computer-based technology becomes increasingly pervasive - not just in developed countries, but worldwide - the need to take a human-centered approach in the design and development of this technology becomes ever more important. For roughly 30 years now, researchers and practitioners in computational and behavioral sciences have worked to identify theory and practice that influences the direction of these technologies, and this diverse work makes up the field of human-computer interaction. Broadly speaking it includes the study of what technology might be able to do for people and how people might interact with the technology. In this series we present work which advances the science and technology of developing systems which are both effective and satisfying for people in a wide variety of contexts. The human-computer interaction series will focus on theoretical perspectives (such as formal approaches drawn from a variety of behavioral sciences), practical approaches (such as the techniques for effectively integrating user needs in system development), and social issues (such as the determinants of utility, usability and acceptability).

Author guidelines: springer.com > Authors > Author Guidelines

Also in this series

Gill, S.P., (Ed.)
Cognition, Communication and Interaction –
Transdisciplinary Perspectives on Interactive
Technology
ISBN 978-1-84628-926-2, 2008

Rossi, G., Pastor, O., Schwabe, D., Olsina, L. (Eds.)
Web Engineering – Modelling and Implemen-
ting Web Applications
ISBN 978-1-84628-922-4, 2008

Law, E., Hvannberg, E., Cockton, G. (Eds.)
Maturing Usability – Quality in Software,
Interaction and Value
ISBN 978-1-84628-940-8, 2008

Lieberman, H., Paternò, F., Wulf, V. (Eds.)
End User Development
Vol. 9, ISBN 978-1-4020-4220-1, 2006

Lieberman, H., Paternò, F., Wulf, V. (Eds.)
End User Development
Vol. 9, ISBN 978-1-4020-5309-2, 2006 (softcover)

Seffah, A., Gulliksen, J., Desmarais, M.C. (Eds.)
Human-Centred Software Engineering –
Integrating Usability in the Software
Development Lifecycle
Vol. 8, ISBN 978-1-4020-4027-6, 2005

Ruttkay, Z., Pelachaud, C., (Eds.)
From Brows to Trust – Evaluating Embodied
Conservational Agents
Vol. 7, ISBN 978-1-4020-2729-1, 2004

Ardissono, L., Kobsa, A., Maybury, M.T.
(Eds.)
Personalized Digital Television – Targeting
Programs to Individual Viewers
Vol. 6, ISBN 978-1-4020-2147-3, 2004

Karat, C.-M., Blom, J.O., Karat, J. (Eds.)
Designing Personalized User Experiences in
eCommerce
Vol. 5, ISBN 978-1-4020-2147-3, 2004

Ivory, M.Y.
Automating Web Site Evaluation – Research-
ers' and Practitioners' Perspectives
Vol. 4, ISBN 978-1-4020-1672-1, 2004

Blythe, M.A., Overbeeke, K., Monk, A.F.,
(et al.) (Eds.)
Funology – From Usability to Enjoyment
Vol. 3, ISBN 978-1-4020-2966-0, 2004
(softcover)

Blythe, M.A., Overbeeke, K., Monk, A.F.,
(et al.) (Eds.)
Funology – From Usability to Enjoyment
Vol. 3, ISBN 978-1-4020-1252-5, 2003

Schreck, J.
Security and Privacy in User Modeling
Vol. 2, ISBN 978-1-4020-1130-6, 2003

Chi, E.H.
A Framework for Visualizing Information
Vol 1, ISBN 978-1-4020-0589-2, 2002

Hartmut Obendorf

Minimalism

Designing Simplicity

 Springer

Hartmut Obendorf
University of Hamburg
22527 Hamburg
Germany
hartmut@obendorf.de

ISSN 1571-5035
ISBN 978-1-84882-370-9   e-ISBN 978-1-84882-371-6
DOI 10.1007/978-1-84882-371-6
Springer Dordrecht Heidelberg London New York

British Library Cataloguing in Publication Data
A catalogue record for this book is available from the British Library

Library of Congress Control Number: 2009921166

Printed on acid-free paper

Springer is part of Springer Science + Business Media (www.springer.com)

To Anne. For being there.

Foreword

The most important ideas are often quite simple ones. And the most important among these is simplicity itself. Simplicity has always been appreciated and understood best in the applied arts, such as design. To a distressing extent, it has been lost to modern science and engineering, supplanted by systematic methodologies that tackle practical problems by enumerating all possible cases, and then addressing each case in turn. The resulting gibberish is often not experienced as a design, is nearly unintelligible to thoughtful humans, and, at best, may function at only the most mediocre level of "correctness."

Fortunately, in many arenas of real life, scientists and engineers are kept away from actually designing anything of consequence. Agonizing, tedious and unilluminating task analyses and the cumbersome, inscrutable and marginally effective systems they help to define are created by scientists and engineers and for other scientists and engineers. There is sometimes justice in design!

I come to design work form science, superbly trained in the intellectual traditions that underwrite bloated and otiose designs. In the early 1980s, I was a scientist is IBM's Thomas Watson Research Center. Then, as now, science and engineering were enabling ever-faster processing of ever-larger datasets. Microcomputers were poised to turn secretaries and managers, teachers and school children, parents and grandparents into "users." Computer science, the computing industry, and the world's information were about to be transformed. You could feel it in the halls of the Watson Center. But something was wrong. The user interfaces and user support materials upon which all this possibility depended were arcane or, as we later termed it, unusable.

For me, the path to epiphany was a series of "thinking aloud" investigations of people asked to verbalize their interpretations, plans, and experiences as they tried to learn and use microcomputers and office applications. Being immersed fro many hours in these quite unhappy early examples of human–computer interaction sharped my outlook on technology, on learning, and on what people-as-users need, want, and do. It changed the course of my professional life.

My Colleagues and I come to realize that the failure of these early human–computer interactions was not due to inadequate motivation or knowledge on the part of users. It was not due to insufficient guidance in the user interface or support from online and paper documentation. Rather, we realized the people we studied were trying too hard to make sense of jargon-ridden nonsense. We came to see that the user interface and other support overwhelmed users with too much useless information and misleading guidance. Human beings are sense makers. But these early designs failed to recognize that, and they failed to leverage or support it. Our users were in effect penalized by these designs for trying and for thinking.

I am very pleased to see Hartmut Obendorf's book, *Minimalism: Designing Simplicity*. The specific challenges of user interface and information design that my colleagues and I wrestled with in the early 1980s are thankfully to a considerable extend behind us now. the solutions from that time have been embodied in designs that will go onward through standard mechanisms of technology emulation and evaluation. We called these deigns "minimalist" to emphasize that user interface and online information presentations should be simplified to their essence. Instead of the scientific and engineering design virtues of systematicity and comprehensiveness, we promoted the virtue of enabling self-directed exploration and sense-making through simplicity.

New categories of devices and new categories of human–computer interactions will always re-raise the fundamental challenge of creating design that effectively embody simplicity, designs that leverage and support human sense-making. It will fall to each succeeding generation of designers to discover and analyze what minimalism means in operational detail, and to implement it pervasively in the contexts of their own new design genres.

Designers, today and in the future, will be aided in this endeavor by incisive articulations of the foundations of minimalism. Indeed, such work is critical. For in technical design arenas, like human–computer interaction, the Zeitgeist of science and engineering is the majority culture. In such design arenas, the tension between systematic and comprehensive methods, on the one hand, and minimalism and simplicity, on the other, is an abiding dynamic. Obendorf's study is a significant contribution to articulating the foundations of minimalism in this contested space of design methods and values. I believe it will be an important text for designers of human–computer interactions for many years to to come.

John Carroll

Preface

I have only made this letter longer because I have not the time to make it shorter.
—Blaise Pascal

While writing this book, one question kept nagging me: Why explain minimalism at that length? What follows is my attempt at reducing the number of words:

Simple, powerful systems are an ideal of interaction design—and hard to find in the wild. Reduction is the path to simplicity, and minimalism describes paths to approach reduction. This book invites you to learn about minimalism and make sense of reduction—perhaps, unraveling some of the mysteries of simplicity. As the ultimate thought model, minimalism is a tool to think about the simple and to discover and instantiate patterns for designing simplicity.

If you choose to embark on this journey, you will encounter minimalism in the form of paintings and music that might be strange at first encounter and still hard to accept after long exposure as they take reduction to the extreme. You will find that many different ways of reduction coexist, some of which can be described using different types of minimalism. If you follow further, you will find how simplicity connects to minimalism and why simplicity may be one path towards successful products. In the end, I hope to convince you that understanding minimalism helps to understand and change the ways of design. This will need a few more words.

Who Should Read this Book?

As a book with both theoretical and empirical parts, different audiences can take different paths through the text. Practitioners, *software engineers,* *designers,* and *usability experts* are similarly targeted as those who are more interested in the theoretical framework, be it from the perspective of art or from human-computer interaction.

For all readers, the first chapter is designed as both introduction and synopsis. It starts with ideas leading to and defining this book but also introduces and discusses the four notions of minimalism that form the core of the argumentation. If there is only one chapter you have time for, read this.

The *usability expert* might find the discussion of norms, guidelines, and expert lore in terms of minimalism (Chapters 4 & 5) to provide some reflection of his/her own practical experience. Examples from analog and digital designs (Chapter 6) can help to form an idea of the different notions of minimalism used in this book (Section 3.3) and form the background for the design of development processes and roles (Chapter 7).

The *designer* might appreciate the discussion of real-world designs (Chapter 6) and will want to refer to the definition of minimalism (Section 3.3) later. The Minimal Design Game (Section 7.2) and—should he/she work with software—the other techniques discussed (Section 7.3ff) might provide inspiration for his/her design practice. The interaction of aesthetics and minimalism might be of most interest in the reflective part (Chapter 9).

The *software engineer* will want to parse the definitions of minimalism (Section 3.2), and then directly skip to the software development methods defined in this book (Chapter 7), perhaps stopping by some design rules (Chapter 5). He/She might then want to read more about the defined notions of minimalism in the closing discussion of design examples (Section 6.5) before jumping to the conclusions (Chapter 11).

Readers seeking a deeper understanding of the *minimalist standpoint* and its development will find manifold sources for the definition of minimalism in human-computer interaction in the discussion of the sources underlying this work in art and music history (Chapter 2). They will also want to follow the derivation of the notions of minimalism for human-computer interaction and understand the limits of this work (Chapters 3 & 10).

Readers who have become interested in minimalism and the evolution of different forms of simplicity might find value in the discussion of the four notions of minimalism and the changes to the original definition that were added by the discussion and application of minimalism in this book (Chapter 8).

The Structure of this Book

This book's content is divided into Parts I–V, where Part I, *Designing for an Age of Complexity*, delivers a *synopsis of minimalism* that briefly touches upon the perspectives proposed in this book and illustrates their application to the analysis of existing designs. Reading this part should provide you with an understanding of what minimalism refers to in this book without filling in the details.

Part II, *Defining Minimalism*, retraces the history of minimalism in art and music in Chapter 2; this chapter follows a historical rather than a conceptual order and aims not at a single definition of minimalism but instead tries to illustrate both the breadth of concepts underlying works characterized as minimal, and the recurrence of attributes of minimal art in different disciplines. Chapter 3 defines four kinds of minimalism for interaction design, namely functional, structural, constructional and compositional minimalism.

Part III, *Rethinking Minimalism*, connects the concepts developed in this book to the existing literature in human-computer interaction. In Chapter 4, norms, rules and guidelines are examined for similarity with minimalist concepts, and in Chapter 5, knowledge for interaction design that is based on practical experience is discussed in terms of reduction.

Part IV, *Applying Minimalism*, puts the four notions of minimalism to the test. In Chapter 6, different products of design are examined for their minimalistic qualities and possible problems created by reduction. While all examples—a mixture of research prototypes and commercial applications—apply reduction in some way and at some point, there is a surprising variation in results. Chapter 7 tries to find a more constructive approach to minimalism and discusses how reduction can both directly and indirectly be integrated in development processes; existing methods such as personas and scenarios, and methods based on agile development and participatory design are discussed for their contribution to reduction.

Part V, *Refining Minimalism*, finally aims to lead the discussion back to a more theoretical level. Chapter 8 revisits the notions of minimalism and re-evaluates the product and process threads for the changes they have brought about for the understanding of minimalism. Chapter 9 discusses the interaction of aesthetics and minimalism in design, and Chapter 10 marks down limitations and questions left unanswered. Finally, Chapter 11 follows the discussion with some conclusions.

Hamburg, Germany   Hartmut Obendorf

Acknowledgments

As this book took shape more than five years and grew with every encounter and experience, I am indebted to all who contributed and supported me: I would like to thank you all.

In reverse chronological order, some people have directly impacted the formation of this book: John Carroll, Beverley Ford and Helen Desmond did a great job of helping me reshape my thesis. Horst Oberquelle and Kaj Grønbæk connected my complex questions to an approach that finally led me to my PhD and I thank them for their time and enthusiasm. Susanne Bødker and Christiane Floyd influenced my perception of the discipline, and my colleagues in Hamburg and Århus kept extending it. Monique Janneck, Matthias Finck and Harald Weinreich helped me express my views in small doses and provided grounding when necessary. I have been fortunate to find a company that not only allowed me to consult on many interesting projects, but also not consult when the time was ripe for writing; this credit is due to Ute Zimmermann, Heinz Züllighoven, and Guido Gryczan. Dearest to me, however, is the gratitude I feel for my family for having and supporting me.

Thank you.

Contents

Part I
Designing for an Age of Complexity

Chapter 1
Minimalism: Introduction and Synopsis

Complex means having confusingly interrelated parts.

—Merriam Webster's Collegiate Dictionary, 10th ed.

In today's increasingly complex society, the "digital revolution", creating new tools and new ways of working, has contributed additional layers of complexity to our lives even though it set out to make work faster and simpler by building machines that help us calculate and even though mastering complexity through abstraction and systematization has been one of the constitutive goals of computing science.

New questions were raised by the dissemination of computer artifacts throughout society and, with the advent of informatics as a research discipline that complements computer and computing science, focus shifted from the engineering view of reducing complexity for the designing engineer to reducing complexity for the end user and ensuring his/her being in command of the procedures employed. Inseparably bound together, both complexities cannot be analyzed in separation; many problems that surface when systems are put into use are caused by engineering complexity adding to application complexity.

Reducing this complexity is the purpose of the use-centered design of interactive systems. Ideals such as "simplicity" play an important role in the self-conception of this discipline. Design aims to create interactive systems so simple they are no longer recognizable as systems, but fade into the background, quietly enhancing our abilities. What, however, *is* simplicity? The meaning of "simple" changes with both protagonist and subject, with both source and focus of perspective. Common to all notions of the simple is only their *relative* nature—they all refer to *some* type of *reduction*.

In this book, the notion of *minimalism* is proposed as a theoretical tool supporting a more differentiated understanding of reduction, and thus forms a standpoint that allows to define aspects of simplicity. Possible uses of the notion of minimalism in the field of human-computer interaction design are examined with both theoretical and empirical focus, yielding a range of results: Minimalism defines a radical and even potentially useful standpoint for design analysis. As the empirical examples demonstrate, it has also proven to be a useful tool for generating and modifying concrete design techniques.

H. Obendorf, *Minimalism*, Human-Computer Interaction Series,
DOI 10.1007/978-1-84882-371-6_1, © Springer-Verlag London Limited 2009

1.1 Motivations for Minimalism in HCI

The skeptical reader may ask, Who needs the notion of Minimalism? And is it necessary to examine and explain *simplicity*? In practice, simple systems can be created without the need for a theoretical conception: experience or even trial and error will eventually produce simpler, better solutions. Fieldwork, user modeling, and user testing can help to identify these, and successful engineering techniques exist to realize them.

It is not only the scientific interest of understanding simple design that motivated this book. Clearly, random hill-walking will get results, but would it be not only much more gratifying, but also far less expensive if simplicity could be planned for? The practitioner should be able to consciously choose his/her tools and make informed design decisions reflecting exactly those aspects of simplicity his/her design tries to achieve. To this end, this book defines an ideal for design, focuses on reduction as a technique, and draws on the notion of minimalism to differentiate understanding of simplicity (see Section 1.2 for spoilers). The resulting minimalist terminology helps to understand qualities of designs and how these qualities are created in design techniques and processes.

1.1.1 Machine Beauty = Power + Simplicity

There is a continuous and controversial argument about the relation and prioritization of usefulness and beauty in design and about the influence of aesthetics on usability or usefulness of artifacts. While the field of human-computer interaction has long been focused on "fitness for tasks", or functionality, the discussion currently seems to bend toward embracing "funology" or the anticipatory specification of use experiences (e.g. Norman, 2002).

David Gelernter introduced a concept that dissolves this constructed dualism: for him, "machine beauty" encompasses both the usefulness of an artifact and the joy its use will generate. Machine beauty is created through the combination of power and simplicity. Beauty, thus, is more than skin deep, more than a feeling to be measured; it is an explanation for the intrinsic quality of "tool"-ness that a "good" design emits (Gelernter, 1999). The term "machine beauty" also highlights the fact that the strength of great tools comes through a combination of abilities and their ease of access. While human-computer interaction methodology customarily used efficacy (or effectiveness) and efficiency as measures for usability, Gelernter stresses that machine beauty is created through more than power or simplicity in isolation.

A concentration on power and simplicity is nothing new in design: The Bauhaus school of design followed the motto of "form follows function" and aimed to abolish "superfluous" decoration. This led to an explicit focus on functionality. However, it turned out that this simply rephrased the design question as "what is function?", and the differentiation between decoration and function is seldom easy (cf. Section 5.5.1). A central objective of this book is thus the examination of the question "what is simple?" And due to the relative nature of simplicity, the question of degree—"how simple must it get?"—follows immediately on its heels.

1.1.2 Reduction—Give Up or Gain?

Less is more. This is a mantra that has been followed by many a designer. Yet, it does not answer the two questions given above, it does not tell *what exactly* should be less, and *how much less* is still more. And is not more sometimes more also ?

In this work, a method—or rather a procedure—for producing "machine beauty" is examined in more detail: reduction. It is important to keep in mind during the lecture in the following pages that the central proposition "less is more" should not be understood singularly as "simple is better". Although there may be some merit in this weaker statement, "less is more" also acknowledges the need for power, the quest for functionality that can be observed in almost any digital artifact. It should also be kept in mind that other methods and tools exist for the designer or the engineer; reduction is not always useful and some-times dangerous for the product. Yet again, while universal machines are theoretically elegant solutions, tools for the real world need not be Turing complete. While the Swiss army knife has many functions, it is inferior to specialized tools whose power often accrues out of limitation; in other words, not everything constructed by a computer scientist should be a computer, lest universal power be hidden by universal complexity.

Reduction, as such, often seems to be deceptively easy as the result of a reductive process appears to be simple and "less" than before; all one needs to do is strip off the superficial ornamentation, ask for less unnecessary interac-tion, concentrate on key tasks and thus provide less superfluous functionality, or introduce a service layer that conveniently defines away the underlying complexity of the service infrastructure.

However, reduction is almost always hard work: ornamentation is difficult to discern from "nice" design, established procedures must be followed for the sake of consistency, and breakdowns all too often expose the underlying infra-structure, making repair impossible as no interference with the hidden complex-ity is possible. And even the introduction of reduction as an ideal into the design process is extremely difficult: more pre-planning might be necessary, the benefit of spending extra money to perhaps lower hidden costs that would surface later is difficult to prove. Development processes are often driven by features, internally motivated by the developers—easily observable in open source projects— and externally by marketing demands—reduction is hard to sell as a feature.

1.1.3 Minimalism: Borrowing the Extreme from the Arts

Returning to the two questions a foray into reduction is confronted with, that of degree and that of direction, this work tries to arrive at a systematic viewpoint to explain why products and processes strive to reach "good design" through reduction; what exactly is the right target for reduction; what methods exist to find reducible aspects of a design, and where is the place to start the search.

To find some orientation support, the extreme was chosen as a model in this work: the phrase "less is more" is not only used in design, but also closely linked to the term minimalism, which initially referred to an art movement in the 1960s and was later successfully applied to music, literature, dance, architecture, design, and a multitude of other disciplines. Minimalism always denotes an extreme case of reduction, and a central proposition of this work is that we can learn from looking at these extremes.

Although simplicity as a value is widely accepted, simple systems are rare—most instead threaten to burst with complexity. Failing to understand why, this book sets out to find help for understanding this paradoxical state—in the liberal arts. The arts are understood as a sensitive arena where social and technical values are often displayed and discussed with extreme violence and clarity, long before they leap over to other disciplines. In the words of the director Peter Greenaway, "Today, many perceive painting as something that is both remote and insignificant. That is a tragical mistake. Painting is always ahead where sociological or philosophical developments are concerned. Look at the 20th century: all philosophical movements began with painting. Cubism, Surrealism, Minimalism, Structuralism, and so forth. A new way of thinking about the world manifests itself always in painting. For me, painting is leading all other arts" (Greenaway and Rauterberg, 2005, retranslation mine).

Art provides a manifestation of new ways of thinking about the world—definitions of perspectives from which things look different. Through its avant-garde nature, analyzing art can either help in scouting trends or make use of the longer experience that critics and historians have acquired examining a development. The latter approach is followed in this book: minimalism has been practiced and analyzed since the 1960s, enough time for a thorough analysis of the minimalist standpoint. Since then, many disciplines have adopted minimal terminology as a description for existing trends. This book aims to do the same for computer science, or more specifically, interaction design.

The approach taken tries to bring up answers that help identify and set the direction of reduction and illustrate trade-offs in degree. Minimalism is a better guide than simplicity as it is not necessarily desirable. It can produce boring, inadequate, even dangerous results. However, making use of the extreme as a model for design makes "extreme" traits visible in everyday products and allows designers to find the right degree of reduction.

1.2 Minimalism in a Nutshell

It took the better part of three years to develop and describe four notions of minimalism in this book. While a complete reading will take less time, this section presents a first overview of subject and method of this book to further shorten the waiting time for the reader. Details on the derivation of the four notions of minimalism are omitted, but an example tries to illustrate that they differentiate forms of simplicity.

1.2.1 Four Notions of Minimalism, Their Relationship, and Design

While the initial intention behind this work was to define a single, unified standpoint for "minimalism", the studies of the literatures in art and music history quickly made it clear that there existed no consensus about the signification of the term. Minimalism is a term used to describe art and music that is at the same time very similar and very different. Although this was disappointing at first sight, it became quickly clear that this multiplicity of perspectives is a virtue rather than a defect: it allows the disambiguation of different perspectives on minimalism, and thus of different kinds of simplicity.

Four different notions of minimalism that were observed to recur in the different literatures in art and music are introduced to the design of interactive systems. This transdisciplinary transfer is based on an extensive analysis of the critical discourse in both art and music that began in the 1960s and is still active today. Although the protagonists of minimalism are diverse in both their conception of reduction and their judgment of artistic qualities, five concepts repeatedly surface in the different literatures: a *minimality of means*, a *minimality of meaning*, and a *minimality of structure*, the *use of patterns*, and the *involvement of the recipient* in the work of art.

For the design of interactive systems, four notions of minimalism were identified drawing on these common qualities of the minimal. The four notions of minimalism focus on the *function, structure, architecture,* and *composition* of the *interface*. The choice of words is deliberate: the former two directly describe

Table 1 *The framework for analysis consists of four notions of minimalism.*

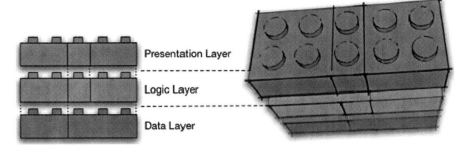

Fig. 1.1 The formal and the designer's perspective: discussion in this book focuses on the interface

aspects of the concrete design, while the latter two point towards more transient aspects of the design that are determined by the construction method and the introduction into the work context. Functional and compositional minimalism focus on the *use* aspect of the tool-in-context, while structural and architectural minimalism highlight how functionality is *accessed* by the user.

To illustrate the relationship of the minimalist terminology with existing terms in computer science, Fig. 1.1 reproduces a diagram often used to describe the architecture of software: a presentation layer handles interaction with the user, a logic layer does invisible processing and a data layer allows the storage and manipulation of data. Variations typically split one of these layers in two, e.g., the presentation layer to model lightweight distributed clients, or the logic layer to allow a distinction between presentation logic and data logic. In this book, neither "architecture" nor "structure" relates to the inner construction of a software system. Instead, the focus is on the interface of a design: assuming a designer's perspective, the design of the presentation layer is central for the use experience. Subjacent system layers become relevant only as they determine the design of the interface, and the concrete details of interfacing the different layers are not the central issue. Thus, the discussion explicitly avoids identifying different layers of a system, highlighting that even though the distinction between different layers is useful to engineer a product, some design decisions for the interface reach deep down into the conception of data and logic.

1.2.2 An Example Analysis Using Notions of Minimalism

A concrete example shall illustrate these rather abstract definitions, although it falls short of explaining them in depth—as the different notions of minimalism aim to highlight different aspects of a design that can be reduced, a single example will only partly match each area of minimalism. Nonetheless, the iPod Shuffle (Fig. 1.2), a music player introduced by Apple, offers a stunning

Fig. 1.2 The iPod Shuffle
(2005) has only few buttons,
and lacks a display.
Photograph courtesy of
Apple

example for how complex technological devices can feel simple (compare
Section 5.3.4).

Even at first sight, the iPod Shuffle is reduced in terms of *functionality*. That
does not mean it is not technically sophisticated: it is able to play a variety of
different media types and provides an audio signal of good quality. Its functional minimality refers to its use—except for the playing, it can only skip songs
and change the volume. Although its internal hardware would support a display, recording audio, and a radio function (Williams, 2005), the iPod Shuffle
does without them.

The interface *structure* of the iPod Shuffle is also reduced. There is no
display, and no menu system. Each function is mapped directly to an interface
element. This allows the user to immediately grasp control of the iPod Shuffle,
and even using it without looking becomes possible. In one of the two modes,
songs are simply shuffled as you press the next button. The other mode uses a
playlist and thus a source of possible complexity.

The functional simplicity of the iPod Shuffle is not the only reason that its
access structure is so simple. An important aspect of the iPod Shuffle is that it
was never designed to be used alone. Instead, the iTunes music player and library
manager was extended to provide functionality that competitors boast of
(Fig. 1.3). Apple had decided that a desktop computer with its large screen and
rich input channels is far superior for tasks such as selecting music tracks and
composing playlists. And thus, the responsibilities are shared between iTunes
and the iPod Shuffle: iTunes is used to select and arrange playlists, the iPod
Shuffle simply plays. This sharing of responsibility across different tools that

Fig. 1.3 iTunes software is used to compose and select playlists for the iPod Shuffle. Screenshot courtesy of Apple

combine to form the overall interface is referred to by *architectural minimalism*: the combination of several simple tools simplifies the handling of complex tasks.

Finally, the iPod Shuffle is also minimal in its *composition*. Again, this refers to its interface and does not mean that it is not engineered thoughtfully. Instead, compositional minimalism marks a maximization of possible uses that the iPod Shuffle can be put to. By designing a functionally minimal device, Apple does not restrict the use of the player, and except for the interaction of iTunes and the player itself, there is no strict workflow to follow. Its functionally, structurally, and architecturally minimal design helps the user feel in control. Thus, the iPod Shuffle offers itself to the user for appropriation. There are examples for constructive uses, such as the use of the player to rent e-books to library users (Stephens, 2005), or as an instrument for students to rehearse music pertinent to their studies—and for faculty as a first step towards new technology use (Calhoun, 2005). Other examples describe decorative uses—here, the users literally make the technology their own and recreate the design in a way that is appropriate for their specific use (Fig. 1.4).

The iPod Shuffle was simpler than its competitors and offered less features. On the market less than six months, it captured a 58% share among flash music players (Gibson, 2005). The short discussion here has tried to illustrate that the simplicity of the iPod Shuffle originates in a number of different aspects in its design, and although many more examples are necessary to sharpen the minimalist terminology used here, this brief example has demonstrated that the notions of minimalism are applicable to digital design.

Fig. 1.4 Examples for
decorative misuse of the
Apple iPod Shuffle

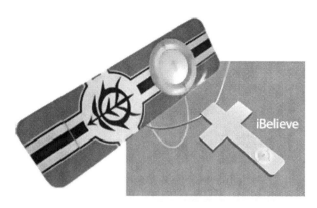

1.2.3 Minimalism, Products, and Processes

An underlying assumption for this book is that a wide range of products today already implicitly follow minimal values or are designed with reduction as a motive. While I know of no scientific study that might prove this argument, observation of current mature electronic products not targeted at the early adopter demonstrates a rise of "simplicity" and an increased stress on "usability" versus "abilities". Also, some support is lent by slogans like "sense and simplicity" (Philips, 2005) or new brands like "SIMply" (a network provider in Germany, see Pressebox, 2005) that advertise simplicity as a key "feature". And even software players like Microsoft use the simplicity brand heavily: more than 100,000 hits are found searching microsoft.com for simplicity.

Minimalism is used in this book to differentiate between possible meanings of simplicity. This is done first for design products, where minimal qualities are identified that match with one of the proposed four notions of minimalism. The products covered in the seventh chapter of this book include not only mass-market hardware products like the Nokia 3310 cell phone series and the Apple iPod family, but also current consumer software products that try to strip down full-featured products to fit the consumer market. From the personal experience of the author, the HyperScout web enhancement system and the CommSy CSCW system are examined. The application of the developed categories of minimalism to example products demonstrates the usefulness of minimalism as a standpoint for analysis, and it also helps to sharpen the theoretical framework as the abstract notions are connected with example qualities.

The book continues with a more constructive part, where the notions of minimalism are put to action in the creation of new designs; this was partly motivated by the personal involvement in the development and evaluation of designs that could have been simpler. Consequently, the question of minimalism in development processes is dealt with in more detail. The usefulness of minimalism as a construction tool is discussed for both a direct and an indirect approach: the Minimal Design Game, a design technique, is developed using identified minimal qualities. More subtly, different reductions in scope are ascribed to existing design techniques, determining their concrete use in projects. Iterative development and the genre of value-based design are discussed in terms of the shift from functional and structural minimalism to architectural and compositional minimalism.

1.3 Defining the Scope of Minimalist Terminology

A term as broad as minimalism evokes different interpretations, and while all of the following are legitimate, some are simplifications only useful in special contexts, while others are both different from the notion of minimalism quoted so far and difficult to apply to design. What follows are sketches of what this book does *not* understand as minimalism.

1.3.1 Minimalism—Mathematic Minimalism

> *Simplicity is prerequisite for reliability.*
> —Edsger W. Dijkstra (Dijkstra, 1982)

In mathematics, and also in theoretical computer science, minimalization of terms is an important and often-used method to create *readable* and *unambiguous* formulae (Cornell, 1997). Reducing the visual and functional complexity of terms, and thus increasing the readability of mathematical calculations, is central to manual mathematics. Reduction is used to unambiguously identify equivalent forms; for example, in the search for prime numbers or when computing the minimal polynomial of algebraic numbers—identical for complex conjugates— it eases the proof that numbers form a ring.

In more general terms, minimalism here denotes a principle that increases human understanding of formal notations: reduction is used to create simplicity and distinctness. This principle is long in use—it has become known as *Ockham's razor*,[1] the medieval rule of economy, that "plurality should not be assumed without necessity" (Britannica, 2003). This *Law of Parsimony*, as it is also called, suggests the simplest of two or more competing theories is preferable and that an explanation for unknown phenomena should first be attempted in terms of what is already known. Ockham's razor can be interpreted to relate closely to the functionalist understanding of minimalism—a single way of doing is sufficient. Its application to engineering, where it is often invoked to thwart unnecessary complexity, has become famous under the acronym KISS (keep it simple, stupid).

---

[1] This rule is often cited in Latin as "entia non sunt multiplicanda praeter necessitatem" (English translation in the text), and also referred to under the name "Occam's razor".

A different aspect of mathematical minimalism is the "elegance" of mathematics, suggesting an "inner beauty". Hardy (1940) famously argued in *A Mathematician's Apology*(1940, 63f and 85) that aesthetic considerations are sufficient to justify the study of pure mathematics—the same argument is ascribed to Poincaré: "The mathematician does not study pure mathematics because it is useful; he studies it because he delights in it and he delights in it because it is beautiful" (Poincaré "Science et Méthode" 1908, quoted in Huntley, 1970). An aesthetic experience of mathematics is shared by many experts; Dirac wrote that it is more important to have beauty in one's equations than to have them fit the experiment; Hungarian mathematician, Paul Erdõs, expressed his views on the indescribable beauty of mathematics when he said, "Why are numbers beautiful? It's like asking why is Beethoven's Ninth Symphony beautiful" (cf. Davis et al. 1995, 168–171). Aesthetics are also important for the inner workings of the discipline—proofs are being accepted partly based on aesthetic criteria; [2] however, the aesthetic dimension of a proof can sometimes be retraced to a better match with the essence of the problem: a proof is beautiful when it "reveal[s] the heart of the matter" (Davis et al., 1995, 299).

1.3.2 Minimalism—Linguistic Minimalism

Noam Chomsky, the main figure behind linguistic minimalism, has been heralding several shifts of linguistic research in the last 35 years. While "autonomous syntax" (e.g., Chomsky, 1968) gained immense popularity in the 1970s, the latest turn of his investigation of the human languages and their specific characteristics was given a new name and a stabler form with the publication of *The Minimalist Program*(1995). Its basic assumption is the existence of a single universal grammatical system for all languages, capable of generating different languages by following different choices made from pre-defined options within the system. The minimalist program is then defined as the perspective of how propositional thought is linked up with sound, the resulting research questions encompass (1) the function of language, given its cognitive and biological environment, (2) the construction of a system that fulfills the core functionality of language—the sort of machinery "a superbly competent engineer might have constructed, given certain design specifications" (Chomsky, 1997, 15) and (3) the comparison of actual human language with this ideal language system.

Chomsky's minimalist approach, dominating linguistic research for decades, was aimed at the construction of a perfect, minimal system. Thus, linguistic minimalism can be interpreted as an attempt to find regularities behind the rules that seem to govern language generation, introducing a more systematic and

---

[2] For a sample of beautiful objects in mathematics, see (Huntley, 1970; King, 1992; Lang, 1985; Rothstein, 1995; Chageux, and Connes, 1995).

analytic approach. This ambitious enterprise has, however, also been contested and was criticized as being largely unsuccessful, lacking empirical support and theoretical coherence (Seuren, 2004). Chomsky himself recently reverted to speaking of language as "expressing thoughts" (Chomsky, 1997, 1; Chomsky et al. 2002, 45), a notion "alien to the random-generator concept of grammar" (Seuren, 2004, 4) and consistent with the rivaling approach of generative semantics. Also, determining language as a "perfect system" (Chomsky, 1995, 1) is complicated by the evolutionary nature of the external systems that language interacts with, resulting in changing conditions for perfection; further-more, evidence exists that suggests language is often used in "distinctly anti-functional" ways (Seuren, 2004, 19).

1.3.3 Minimalism —Documentation Minimalism

> *Avoid missing ball for high score.*
> —instructions for PONG[3]

Of all reported uses of the term minimalism, John Carroll's minimalist approach to technical documentation, defined in *The Nurnberg Funnel*(Carroll, 1990) and refined in *Minimalism beyond the Nurnberg Funnel*(Carroll, 1998), is closest to the field of usability. Advocating the reduction of learning material, Carroll chose a learning style where "knowledge" is not presented in a pre-structured format and where users need to actively work on real tasks to acquire knowledge. The underlying proposition is that learning yields better results if the knowledge is actively acquired while being engaged in the context of real work. According to Carroll (1990, 77f), "the key idea in the minimalist approach is to present the smallest possible obstacle to learners' efforts, to accommodate, even to exploit, the learning strategies that cause problems for learners using systematic instructional materials."

Minimalism can thus be interpreted as a use-centric approach to learning: it tries to support the user while he/she tries to accomplish a genuine task. As support is only necessary where the user fails to achieve a set goal with the available tools, minimalism consequentially tries to present help when break-downs become apparent. Instead of providing structured material that is designed optimally to convey the system designer's view of the application, minimalism tries to meet with the user in his work. This requires an under-standing of his previous knowledge and an adaptation of the knowledge to be conveyed to the user's viewpoint. Carroll (1998) notes that he conceived his notion of minimalism after reading Dewey, Piaget, and Bruner.

---

[3] PONG is the name of what is commonly referred to as the "first video game" and was produced by Atari (Winter, 1999). The mentioned inscription was the last of three lines serving as "the first minimal manual", the other two being "Deposit Quarter. Ball will serve automatically".

While minimalism is aptly named—Carroll undid the focus on structure inherent in classical manuals and replaced it with an on-demand approach, or, with reference to minimal art, an "objectness"—the declared focus of Carroll's minimalism is on computer documentation and learning. As the realms of software development and technical writing only seldom communicate, his minimalism touches only insofar upon system design as documentation is considered a part of the design. Also, Carroll's notion of minimalism is defined in relation to the comprehensiveness of technical manuals: the new, minimal manuals promise to take up only a fraction of the space of classical menus; thus, minimalism is not an extreme, but an ideal.

Carroll himself remarked in an interview with Dubinsky (1999): "It is funny to talk about the early minimalist work because it really is historical; it is like talking about the Renaissance. I mean it is not going to come again; we don't need to get it right because the problems are not going to come about it. Hopefully there is something you can extract, which is why you talk about the Renaissance. We'll never go back to that state again." As Meij (2003) documents, Carroll's Minimalism is still an actively pursued approach, and the focus of minimalism, namely extending on "people's prior knowledge, on their active construction of new knowledge and on their 'learning by doing'" (ibid.), has created a wide diversity of different results. One can, however, try to draw connections from Carroll's later work on design methodologies, and specifically on scenarios, to the foundations he laid out in minimalism.

Carroll's "Minimalism" will thus be not discussed in this book due to its focus on documentation. However, the principles defined therein will surface when a reduction of design scope on core tasks are discussed (Section 8.5). The idea underlying the documentation minimalism is similar to the iterative approach for development that is promoted by the notions of minimalism: design cannot systematically consider all alternatives, and sense is made only through use—and the resulting errors (comp. Carroll, 1992).

1.3.4 Minimalism—Folk Minimalism

> *Beauty is more than skin deep.*
>
> —Popular saying

Although, given its roots in art history and aesthetics, it is a paradox to state that minimalism is also not an aesthetic dimension, this statement is true for a "folk" understanding of aesthetics: if aesthetics, $\alpha\iota\sigma\theta\alpha\nu o\mu\alpha\iota$ (perception by means of the senses) (Baumgarten, 1983, 79), are understood solely in terms of superficial appearance. Although the application of certain minimalist principles often results in a distinct appearance that has consequently been identified with minimalism, in all disciplines, minimalism has denoted more a perspective than a "look". Minimalism is not simply monochromes in painting, it is not limited to atonality and absence of rhythm in music, nor is all minimalism in architecture connected to primary forms. Similarly, only a shallow transfer from typography would yield that minimalism is simply reduction of color and form. Minimalism is thus not just reduced design—doing away with too many colors, too many different typefaces, and too much screen clutter. And although simplicity is often a goal, minimalism cannot be equated with simplicity. Instead, as summarized in the final section of the first chapter, minimalism can be interpreted as different interpretations of "less is more", as a collection of principles that (while occasionally contradicting each other) go to extremes to create a focus of the recipient's—to increase "user" involvement, and as a way of looking at things—a minimal perspective.

Definitions for minimalism exist in abundance—a simple search of the Web delivers a wide range of definitions. Apart from those connected to art, music, and literature, a shared understanding of the term—and a view often taken by interface and Web designers—seems to be connected to an aesthetics owing partly to minimalist typography: sparing use of colors, excessive white space, the absence of animation and visually distracting content seem to suffice to classify a (web) design as minimalistic. According to Cooper and Reimann (2003, 487), "the Web's history, in which many commercial Web sites began as marketing vehicles" is responsible for this backlash, "fancy graphics are not only distracting, but users have been well trained to ignore [. . .] marketing ploy[s] on the Web" (ibid.). The (now offline) collection of "minimalist web sites" collected by the Minimalist Project[4] lists example Web sites that appeal to the need for simpler visual design. However, individual sites had little in common except for the generous use of white space and sans-serif fonts; the failure to capture similarities that go beyond the initial "look" of a site created a collection without creating a categorization; this could be one reason for the site's demise.

However, without conscious reference to the use of the term "minimalism" in other contexts, the informal, experience-based argument between different Web design blogs hints at the potential of minimalism as a concept: "dezwozhere" writes that "in short[,] a minimalist design may not always be what's needed[,] but a minimalist approach to design can be a powerful ally" (dezwozhere, 2003). And Olsen (2003) cautions his readers that "simplicity can be harmful", that a design aiming at visual simplicity can create structural complexities.

1.4 Finding a Minimalism for Interaction Design

Minimalism is almost everywhere, and it can take a number of different meanings. For most of these, however, it is difficult to either draw a straight relation to design or understand minimalism in a way that it goes beyond being a synonym of simplicity. Following this long list of negations, where can advice

---

[4] Site out of service. http://web.archive.org/web/20040930175437/textbased.com/minimalist/

be found for the design of interactive systems, where is guidance offered for creating the simple in the realm of complexity?

It would have been possible to look at specific difficulties encountered in interaction design that are caused by complexity, and then go to other disciplines and search for help on these fine-cut, specific problems. The approach chosen for this book is different: based on the unspecific disquiet created by increasing complexity in interactive systems, a general interpretation of minimalism is defined. This notion—or, as it was not possible to find a single meaning: these notions—of minimalism are then applied to interaction design.

In the following chapter, the term minimalism is followed back to its roots in art and music, where the term was originally coined. Art and music are ideal candidates for an examination of the meaning of minimalism as they tend to generate extreme positions anticipating social developments: a main criterion for quality in both domains is *novelty*. As an immediate result of this requirement, both art and music tend to be more experimental than other disciplines. It could be said that they are ahead of their time, they probe and experiment, and often anticipate changes that other parts of our culture will take years to experience. "Liberal" art and music are also, by definition, relatively free from external constraints—you can thus find some purity in the perspectives developed as they are often untainted by practical necessities. Novelty also introduces the constraint to be different—so expect extreme positions that shout rather than whisper their views. Novelty also generates the constraint of individuality—differences will be highlighted by individual artists even in a group of "minimalists" who work on the same topic.

Apart from that, this book will encounter some difficulties: the same criteria that make art and music an ideal object of study complicate the objective of producing design advice for digital products. A literal translation of the standpoint of individual artists is impossible. Instead, interpretations of minimalism are the basis for highlighting different perspectives on reduction that are then projected on design activities.

References

Baumgarten, A. (1983). Kollegium über die Ästhetik, Section 1. In HR Schweizer (Ed.), *Texte zur Grundlegung der Ästhetik*. 78–83. Hamburg: Felix Meiner.

Britannica (2003). *Encyclopedia Britannica: With 2004 Book of the Year (Britannica Books)*. Encyclopedia Britannica Corporation.

Calhoun, T. (2005). Bravo for the Duke iPod Experiment. *Campus Technology*, 21.06.2005 Available online: http://campustechnology.com/articles/2005/06/bravo-for-the-duke-ipod-experiment_633573772543619027.aspx.

Carroll, J. M. (1990). *The Nurnberg Funnel: Designing Minimalist Instruction for Practical Computer Skill (Technical Communication, Multimedia, and Information Systems)*. Cambridge, MA: The MIT Press.

Carroll, J. M. (1992). Making errors, making sense, making use. In C Floyd (Ed.), *Software Development and Reality Construction*. 155–167. Berlin Heidelberg, :New York: Springer.

Carroll, J. M. (1998). *Minimalism Beyond the Nurnberg Funnel (Technical Communication, Multimedia, and Information Systems)*. Cambridge, MA: The MIT Press.

Chageux, J-P., and Connes, A. (1995). *Conversations on Mind, Matter and Mathematics.* Princeton, N. J.: Princeton University Press.

Chomsky, N. (1968). *Language and Mind.* New York: Harcourt, Brace & World.

Chomsky, N. (1995). *The Minimalist Program.* Cambridge, Mass: The MIT Press.

Chomsky, N. (1997). Language and Mind: Current Thoughts on Ancient Problems (Part 1). *Pesquisa Lingüística*, 3(4).

Chomsky, N., Belletti, A., and Rizzi, L. (2002). *On Nature and Language.* Cambridge: Cambridge University Press.

Cooper, A., and Reimann, R. M. (2003). *About Face 2.0: The Essentials of Interaction Design.* New York, NY: Wiley.

Cornell, T. (1997). *Representational Minimalism.* Tübingen: SFB 340 Universität Tübingen.

Davis, P. J., Hersh, R., Marchisotto, E. A., and Rota, G-C. (1995). *The Mathematical Experience.* Birkhäuser Verlag.

dezwozhere. (2003). On a minimalist approach to design. http://www.dezwozhere.com/blog/archives/000003.html Accessed 10.10.

Dijkstra, E. W. (1982). How do we tell truths that might hurt? *SIGPLAN Not*, 17(5), 13–15.

Dubinsky, J. (1999). Fifteen ways of looking at minimalism. *SIGDOC Asterisk Journal of Computerised Documents*, 2(23), 34–47.

Gelernter, D. (1999). *Machine Beauty: Elegance and the Heart of Technology (Repr ed) (Masterminds)*. New York, NY: Basic Books.

Gibson, B. (2005). First on TMO – Apple Exec: Shuffle Grabs 58% of Flash Player Market; What Cell Phone Threat? http://www.macobserver.com/article/2005/05/04.4.shtml Accessed 2.10.2008

Greenaway, P., and Rauterberg, H. (2005, 29.12.). Rembrandt war kein Maler. *Die Zeit*, 41. Zeit Verlag.

Hardy, G. H. (1940). *A Mathematician's Apology.* Cambridge: Cambridge University Press.

Huntley, H. E. (1970). *The Divine Proportion: A Study in Mathematical Beauty.* New York: Dover Publications.

King, J. P. (1992). *The Art of Mathematics.* New York: Fawcett Columbine.

Lang, S. (1985). *The Beauty of Doing Mathematics.* Berlin, Heidelberg: Springer-Verlag.

Meij, Hvd. (2003). Minimalism revisited. *Document Design*, 4(3), 212–233.

Norman, D. A. (2002). Emotion & design: attractive things work better. *Interactions*, 9(4), 36–42.

Olsen, H. (2003). Balancing visual and structural complexity in interaction design: How visual simplicity can harm usability. http://www.guuui.com/issues/04_03.php Accessed 10.10.2008

Pressebox.com (2005). Drillisch AG startet mit SIMply durch. Available online at http://www.pressebox.com/pressemeldungen/simply-communication-gmbh/boxid-43428.html

Philips (2005). Philips shows innovations based on Simplicity-led design. Paris, France: Philips press information 21.9.2005. Available online at http://www.newscenter.philips.com/about/news/press/archive/2005/article-15108.page

Rothstein, E. (1995). *Emblems of Mind: The Inner Life of Music and Mathematics* (1st ed.). New York: Times Books/Random House.

Seuren, P. A. M. (2004). *Chomsky's Minimalism.* New York: Oxford University Press.

Stephens, M. (2005). The iPod Experiments. *LibraryJournal.com* http://www.libraryjournal.com/article/ CA515808.html

Williams, M. (2005). How Much Should an IPod Shuffle Cost? *PC World*.

Winter, D. (1999). PONG-Story. http://www.pong-story.com/ Accessed 10.10.2008

Part II
Defining Minimalism

Chapter 2
In Search of "Minimalism"— Roving in Art, Music and Elsewhere

This chapter provides you with an overview of some of the meanings that have been discussed under the label "Minimalism" to prepare the ground for a discussion of meanings that "minimalism" might assume for the design of interactive systems.

"Minimalism" is a term of many uses and diffuse boundaries. Time and protagonists of the exact coinage of the phrase differ according to perspective: The musician Steve Reich credited the critic Michael Nyman with the invention of the term and its application to music in the 1970s (Nyman, 1974); his colleague, Philip Glass, took Tom Johnson for the originator of the term. However, art critic, Barbara Rose, had already applied the term (along with her own conception, "ABC art") to the music of Young and the choreography of Judson's Dance Theater in fall 1965 (Rose, 1965a). She then credits Wollheim's January 1965 article in Arts Magazine (Wollheim, 1965) with the formal introduction of the term. Yet, this again is subject to debate, as—taking usual lead-time into account—two articles by Rose herself and sculptor Donald Judd published in February 1965 (Rose, 1965b; Judd, 1975, 35) might have been written before. Looking further back, Judd had used the term writing about Morris' work in March 1964 (ibid., 118), and, even in March 1960, described Paul Feeley's "confidence in the power of the minimal" (ibid., 17). Furthermore, David Burliuk described the painting of John Graham as "Minimalist" in 1929, noting "Minimalism ... is an important discovery that opens to painting unlimited possibilities" (cf. Strickland, 1991, 19).

One can safely assume only that the term "Minimalism" earned public attention during the 1960s and gradually replaced other, competing labels, such as the aforementioned "ABC art", and "reductive art" (Rose, 1965a), "literalist art" (Fried), "structurist" sculpture (Lippard, 1967), "object sculpture" (Rose, 1965a), "systemic painting" (Alloway, 1966), "specific objects" (Judd, 1975), "unitary forms" (title of Morris' 1970 San Francisco Museum of Art exhibition) or "unitary objects" (Sandler 1968)—to mention but a fraction of the terms used only within art criticism.

"Minimalism" denotes the minimal, often in relationship to contrasting practices, and according to context, the focus of the minimal changes. Until today, no single definition has been agreed upon and some authors even deny its

H. Obendorf, *Minimalism*, Human-Computer Interaction Series,
DOI 10.1007/978-1-84882-371-6_2, © Springer-Verlag London Limited 2009

possibility. To clarify the relative nature of the term, some recent examples are restated here:

> Minimalism – "an artistic tendency whose 'organizing principles' were 'the right angle, the square and the cube ... rendered with a minimum of incident or compositional maneuvering'" (Colpitt, 1990, 1).
>
> Minimalism – "a movement, primarily in postwar America, towards an art – visual, musical, literary, or otherwise – that makes its statement with limited, if not the fewest possible, resources" (Strickland, 2000, 7).
>
> Minimalism was "the last of the modernist styles" and thus "a transition between the modern and the postmodern" (Levin, 1979).
>
> "The only reason that I did any writing ... is really the fact that the critics had not understood things very well. They were writing about Minimal Art, but no one defined it ... People refer to me as a Minimal artist but no one has ever defined what it means or put any limits to where it begins or ends, what it is and isn't" (Sol LeWitt in Cummings, 1974).
>
> "This book ... views minimalism neither as a clearly defined style nor as a coherent movement that transpired across media during the postwar period. Rather, it presents minimalism as a debate ... that initially developed in response to the three-dimensional abstraction of, among others, Donald Judd, Carl Andre, Robert Morris, Dan Flavin, Anne Truitt, and [Sol] LeWitt during the period 1963–1968. ... Minimalism was a shifting signifier whose meanings altered depending on the moment or context of its use ... a field of contiguity and conflict, of proximity and difference ... a new kind of geometric abstraction" (Meyer, 2001, 1).

Definitions of minimalism range from the specific to the broad, from the temporal to the technical, from the impossible to the dialectic—depending on the motive of the author. Some of these definitions are more difficult to use as a basis for this work, as specificity complicates translation into a different field, temporality limits the meaning of minimalism to a single movement. The more technical definitions promise the viability of comparison with other "movements" and the dialectic analysis proposed by Meyer shows potential for understanding the dynamics of artists' self-definitions and their interactions with other practitioners, thus elaborating the essence of the term.

Yet, as the purpose of this overview is not to define minimalism within a particular context, but rather illustrate the broad range of meanings that was denoted by "minimalism" from the conception of the term sometime in the 1960s until the present day, a less strict approach is followed: For clarity's sake, the sequence of appearance is oriented on genre and temporal order; whenever deemed appropriate, a definition that was useful within a narrow context is mentioned and set in relation with contrasting positions. Although there are some exceptions, such as the concurrence of Young's and Glass's first musical experiments and the development of Minimal sculpture in the New York art scene, this approach works quite well, as minimalism was first used to describe painting, then sculpture and film, then music and eventually literature before the term was applied to subjects only marginally connected to art. The validity of applying the term "minimalism" to a range of styles that span different disciplines is certainly motivated by this work's aim of discerning meanings that might be transferred analogously to human-computer interaction, yet the connection of the different minimalisms, particularly of those in dance, music and art, is strengthened by the history of personal relationships of the artists that created their works with something that might be called a common spirit.

2.1 Minimalism in the Arts

Minimalism in the fine arts originated in painting, and was later continued in sculpture. Its different protagonists created very different artworks, and followed different conceptions of reduction. In reduction, they focused on topics such as color, material, and structure. An important consequence was the establishment of the object-character of artworks, and the use of readymade materials. While this was first developed in painting (e.g. in the works of Reinhardt), it later culminated in sculpture (and was made explicit by Judd). Consequently, the overall Gestalt of an artwork evolved into a central aspect of minimalist art, and relationships that extended beyond the object, and included the spectator, became relevant to minimalist artists.

2.1.1 Rauschenberg, Klein and Newman: Birth of Minimal Painting

Perhaps the first "Minimal" paintings were created by Robert Rauschenberg in 1951, six works composed of from one to seven panels of rolled white enamel paint, pioneering the use of housepaint on unprimed canvas and preceding the black paintings of Frank Stella by seven years. The simple whites were produced with a lack of painterliness that leaves little room for a more extreme reduction; in contrast to Robert Ryman's monochromes of the 1960s, Rauschenberg did not even concern himself with the calligraphy of the brushstroke (Fig. 2.1). He describes his paintings with great avidity, however: "They are large white (one white as God) canvases organized and selected with the

Fig. 2.1 Robert Rauschenberg: White Painting (1951). © VG Bild + Kunst, Bonn 2008

experience of time and presented with the innocence of a virgin. Dealing with the suspense, excitement, and body of an organic silence, the restriction and freedom of absence, the plastic fullness of nothing, the point a circle begins and ends. They are a natural response to the current pressures and the faithless and a promoter of institutional optimism. It is completely irrelevant that I am making them. Today is their creator" (quoted in Ashton, 1982, 71).

As Strickland (2000, 28) notes, "The paintings were not, however, as God- or nothing-like in practice as in theory"—they were instead viewer-interactive from the beginning: "I always thought of the white painting as being, not passive, but very—well, hypersensitive ... so that one could look at them and almost see how many people were in the room by the shadows cast, or what time of day it was" (Tomkins, 1981, 71). Besides the extreme reduction of means, we also find the inclusion of the viewer as one of the prime characteristics of these works; their reception differs with a different setting or a different frame of perception as they hold only a minimal amount of pre-defined information themselves. In contrast to the monochromatic works of Josef Albers (a retrospective can be found in Albers and Weber, 1988), Rauschenberg broke with the focus on the relationships within the painting, he shunned the use of hierarchical composition and figure/ground contrasts that Albers had concentrated upon (Albers, 1963): "I had been totally intimidated because Albers thought that one color was supposed to make the next color look better but my feeling was that each color was itself" (Rauschenberg in Rose, 1987, 37–38).

Yves Klein, a world-class provocateur and an art celebrity for the last five years of his life (1928–1962), also laid claim on the creation of the first monochromes, although his proofs are rather insufficient (Strickland, 2000, 33–34). He contributed the ultimately minimal exhibition to art history at the Iris Clert gallery in Paris in 1958—described in the invitation as "the lucid and positive advent of a certain realm of sensitivity ... the pictorial expression of an ecstatic and immediately communicable emotion" (quoted ibid., 35). The gallery in question was empty; Klein himself had painted the immediately communicable walls with white paint. Klein is best known for his monochromes painted in "International Klein Blue" (or a deep royal blue). He chose blue over other colors: "Blue has no dimensions, it is beyond dimensions, whereas other colors are not. They are prepsychological expanses, red, for example, presupposing a site radiating heat. All colors arouse specific associative ideas, psychologically material or tangible, while blue suggests at most the sea and the sky, and they, after all, are in actual visual nature what is most abstract" (Osborne, 1988, 295). In addition, Donald Judd stressed in 1965 the influence of absence of compositional space: "Almost all paintings are spatial one way or another. Yves Klein's blue paintings are the only ones that are unspatial, and there is little that is nearly unspatial, namely Stella's work" (Judd, 1975, 182).

Sometimes counted among the minimalists, Barnett Newman is usually considered one of the most influential predecessors to minimalism as his work determined the visual appearance of minimalist painting despite him maintaining contradicting theories (Strickland, 2000, 55): he tried to limit references to

Fig. 2.2 Barnett Newman:
Untitled (1969). © VG
Bild + Kunst, Bonn 2008

the work itself noting, "I hope my work is free of the environment" (Newman et al., 1990, 272), and rejected the void created by reduction in e.g. Klein's drawings (ibid., 249). Instead, his zip paintings (Fig. 2.2), the label stemming from the regularity of dividing the canvas into areas of different color, are not targeted at reduction, but rather try to create a unity of the whole artwork, "I feel that my zip does not divide my paintings ... it does the exact opposite: it unites the thing" (ibid., 306).

2.1.2 *Reinhardt: Art-as-Art*

Ad Reinhardt was perhaps the purest minimalist painter, Sol LeWitt called him "the most important artist of the time" and producer of "the most radical art" (Zelevansky, 1991, 19) and Rosenberg identified him as "the intellectual pivot" of the Minimalist movement (Rosenberg, 1964). He most vividly contrasted Klein and Rauschenberg in character: against their theatricality he set what was described as an "eremitic aesthetic and [...] near-obscurant technique" (Strickland, 2000, 40) and what Reinhardt summed up in 1962 as "The one thing to say about art is that it is one thing. Art is art-as-art and everything else is everything else. Art-as-art is but art. Art is not what is not art" (Reinhardt,

1975, 53). Art-as-art describes the total rejection of context and creator as meaningful aspects of the work—a piece of art is only what it is, no more, no less. It is directed against the mystification of "simple" art and the displacement of visual abundance by elaborate explanations and interpretations. He also vehemently refuted attempts to relate his work to the action painting of e.g. Pollock: "I suppose there is always an act or an action of some kind. But the attempt is to minimize it. There are no gymnastics or dancings over painting or spilling or flipping paint around" (ibid., 13).

Reinhardt tried to abolish all external references from his titles as from his paintings, most of which are simply signed "Untitled", "Abstract", or "Red/ Blue/Black Painting"—often on the back of the canvas, not always including the date. His aim was to create "the last paintings which anyone can make" (Lippard, 1981, 158); he tried to achieve maximum reduction. His "Twelve Technical Rules" read as follows: "No texture ... No brushwork or calligraphy ... No forms ... No design ... No colors ... No light ... No space ... No time ... No size or scale ... No movement ... No object, no subject, no matter. No symbols, images, or signs. Neither pleasure nor paint. No mindless working or mindless non-working. No chess-playing" (Reinhardt, 1975, 205f).

The reduction in Reinhardt's works did not come suddenly, it was a slow and steady development towards the minimal: "At many stages along the way, it seemed as if he had gone as far as he could go, but each year he reduced the elements in his art a little more" (Bourdon 1968). The premier example for his Minimalist works is the "black" paintings—he was far from being the first to explore black-on-black, as Rodchenko had executed a pure black in 1919, yet his approach is unique. The "black" paintings are not black at all; on close scrutiny, they are composed of deep blue, red and green pigments in various mixtures; he drew diagrams before executing his paintings that show that most of them consist of a nine-squares-within-a-square structure, with three different tones marked as "B", "R" and "G" occupying the corners, the middle row and the middle upper and lower square, respectively (Zelevansky, 1991, 21).

Reinhardt used hues of blue, red and green so dark that various critics have noted that the normal museum visitor does not and, literally, cannot see these paintings: the ocular adjustment necessary to perceive the shades of color takes time the casual viewer does not spend on the paintings; thus, they are often dismissed as a joke (Fig. 2.3). For the darkest, last paintings, only flashlight photography reveals the cruciform shape; Strickland notes, "from a phenomenological perspective, one might argue that they [the photographic reproductions] invent them" (Strickland, 2000, 49). Although the suggestion has been made frequently, the reason for the choice of color, or rather non-color is arguably not a religious one, as is the shape only superficially reminiscent of a cross: "The reason for the involvement with darkness and blackness is ... an aesthetic-intellectual one ... because of its non-color. Color is always trapped in some kind of physical activity or assertiveness of its own; and color has to do with life. In that sense it may be vulgarity or folk art or something like that"

Fig. 2.3 Ad Reinhardt:
Abstract Painting
(1960–66). © VG
Bild + Kunst, Bonn 2008

(Reinhardt, 1975, 87). He thus extends Klein's dismissal of all colors except blue to a complete dismissal of color for its relation to life and thus its potential "folk art" character; again, art is only art-as-art.

Beginning with the choice of the square as the simplest geometrical form as the basis of the structure of the painting and then further reducing the structure to the point of indiscernability by minimizing value contrasts, Reinhardt tried to achieve the greatest abstraction in painting. He even refrained from taping his canvases to avoid the "miniscule ridge which might define the border between squares and ... destroy the flatness of the surface" (Strickland, 2000, 49). His paintings tried not only to be non-relational in their inner composition, but also to be non-referential; he went so far as to drain the oil from his paints to reduce reflections: "There should be no shine in the finish. Gloss reflects and relates to the changing surroundings" (Reinhardt, 1975, 207). He did not view the individual canvas as an almost sacred source of inspiration, as the Abstract Expressionists did; although he employed painstaking brushwork to remove all traces of brushwork from his paintings, he has more in common with the Minimalist sculptors who "only" planned their works before they were industrially executed: When one of his works was damaged, and the museum asked him to repair it, he offered to substitute another version. "But you don't understand, Mr. Reinhardt," he was told. "Our Committee especially chose this one." "Listen," the painter answered, "I've got a painting here that's more like the one you've got than the one you've got" (Hess, 1963, 28).

2.1.3 Stella: To See What Is There

Between art critics, an argument developed in retrospect whether Reinhardt should really be considered minimal as he simply further reduced "pictorial asceticisms" from the past. Reinhardt was compared with Frank Stella who was more concerned with pure surface. Among others, Rosalind Krauss tried to differentiate them in her explicitly revisionist review: "it soon seemed obvious (in 1963) that what (Reinhardt's and Stella's 'black' paintings) had in common was, nothing" (Krauss, 1991, 123).

Without doubt, however, is Frank Stella, another of the central figures of Minimalist painting; he presented his first exhibition at the Museum of Modern Art an almost unbelievable two years after his college graduation, yet it took art critics until 1965 to agree that "the uncommon strength and integrity of Stella's young art already locate him among the handful of major artists working today" (Rosenblum, 1965). In contrast to the obscurity of Ad Reinhardt's near-black paintings, Frank Stella's monochrome works that he arrived at in 1958 after experimenting with alternating bands of color, speci-fically red and black, expose both the crude technique and the unmodified enamel housepaint used: "I knew a wise guy who used to make fun of my painting, but he didn't like the Abstract Expressionists either. He said they would be good painters if only they could keep the paint as good as it is in the can. And that's what I tried to do. I tried to keep the paint as good as it was in the can" (Glaser, 1966, 157). In contrast to the perfectly symmetrical and carefully executed paintings of Reinhardt, Stella's freehand technique resulted in an irregularity of the outlines of the bands and in an inexact placement (Fig. 2.4). The intent of Stella's works was to create truly non-relational paintings: "The black bands and interstitial canvas are not separated but joined by his initially smudged borders, which provide the unifying effect … Stella's smudging fuses the component lines on first glimpse, never allowing them an independence that would challenge the nonrelational, unitary effect he sought" (Strickland, 2000, 103).

The visual spareness and detachment but foremost the repetitive elements of his paintings might have been influenced by Samuel Beckett, as Stella pointed out in an interview, "pretty lean … also slightly repetitive … I don't know why it struck me that bands, repeated bands, would be somewhat more like a Beckett-like situation than, say, a big blank canvas" (Antonio, 1981, 141).

After the black paintings followed a series of "white" or "aluminum" or "notched" paintings; here again, although following Rauschenberg in color, the approach was radically different: rather that drawing patterns within the classic rectangular format, he cut out those parts of the canvas that did not conform to the pattern. This series is drawn only with verticals, the texture of the aluminum paint is smoother and the use of penciled guidelines creates an impersonal regularity in the pattern—often

seen as a precursor to the industrial streamlining of Minimalist sculpture.
Stella became the principal figure in the new attitude of American
"directness" and "anti-illusion"—he famously summed this up in an
interview with Glaser (1966, 158) as "What you see is what you see"—
only what can be seen is there. However, he was not alone in proposing
this new sense of wholeness, with both Newman and Pollock preceding
him; as Meyer (2001, 90) notes, "his painting-reliefs heightened an awareness of Rauschenberg and Johns ... The relationships were complex: the
impact of Stella's work ... elicited quite different readings."

The uncompromising two-dimensionality of Stella could be seen as the
end-product of an evolution of abstraction that had been started with the
Cubists who had freed themselves from the window of perspective: "In
Stella, the surface was neither a window into an illusionistic world nor a
skin for tattooing, but everything, all there was. It is more than a facile
oxymoron to note that the (anti-)spatial evolution of abstraction culminated in the concreteness of the object painting" (Strickland, 2000, 108).
An important characteristic of Minimal Art, namely the development of
the objecthood of art works, could be counted among Stella's achieve-
ments; although the term had been used before by e.g. Rauschenberg
(Colpitt, 1990, 109), Stella reversed the Duchampian notion of object-as-
artwork into the artwork-as-object.

2.1.4 Radical Minimalism and Post-Minimalist Painting

Later minimalist painters further radicalized reduction, a tendency that might have been aided by the need to distance themselves from their predecessors. A most notable example was Robert Mangold (Fig. 2.5): "He has excluded from his work all such concerns as illusion, image, space, composition, climax, hierarchy of interest, movement, emotional content, painterliness, interest in materials or processes, and any sort of association or reference to anything other than the physical painting itself . . . To have produced work of intellectual and visual power with such severity of means is impressive, and he [Mangold] is certainly among the most important of the 'Minimal' artists" (Spector, 1974).

Fig. 2.5 Robert Mangold:
Four Triangles Within a
Square (1974). © VG
Bild + Kunst, Bonn 2008

Robert Ryman, known primarily for his "achromatic" paintings, created in experiments dating from 1958 and executed since 1965, was one of the few painters able to follow Stella with a distinctive style. His "white" paintings are less rigidly white, the bands often interact with the different colors of his supports, normally are contiguous, and often expressively brushed, without an attempt of art concealing art. This painterliness—although the bands are still parallel to the frame, the furrows of the brushwork "suggest[s] fine gradients of linearity" (Strickland, 1991, 110)—is in stark contrast to the bluntness of Stella's works. Still, the explicit brushwork might be interpreted as a continuation of the reductivist aesthetic of economy and exposure of means, as Ryman stated, "There is never a question of what to paint, but only how to paint" (Art in Process at Finch College catalogue 1969, quoted ibid., 110).

Richard Tuttle, a less prominent Minimalist figure, might have been the painter who expressed the objecthood of the artwork in most radical terms. Like Stella, he was rather young when he had his first show at 24 in 1965 at the Betty Parsons Gallery. He is known for the modest nature of his work: in the 1970s, his works consisted of an inch of rope or a foot of polygonized wire nailed to the wall. Although these works count among the least flattering in art history, they were judged to be "not beautiful. But ... in some sense outrageously 'poetic'" (Perreault, 1968, 17).

A continuing refinement of minimalism can be observed in the later works of minimalist painters. As the most drastic or primitive interpretation of minimalism was already taken by Rauschenberg, more subtle forms of minimalism evolved. The question of defining a minimalist aesthetics emerged: What is a great work? How is art determined? The influential art critic, Clement Greenberg, defined artistic "quality" e.g. for the zip paintings of Newman that "look easy to copy, and maybe they really are. But they are far from easy to conceive" (Greenberg, 1962). Judd argued that a new kind of painting had been developed: "In earlier art the complexity was displayed and built the quality. In recent painting the complexity was in the format and the few main shapes ... A painting by Newman is finally no simpler than one by Cézanne" (Judd, 1975, 184). Judd used "interesting" as a criterion to determine works that are not "merely interesting" but "worth looking at". While "Greenberg is the critic of taste ...... behind every one of his decisions there is an aesthetic judgement", "in the philosophic tabula rasa of art, "if someone calls it art," as Don Judd has said, " it's art" (Kosuth, 1991, 17).

2.1.5 Judd, Andre, Flavin, and Morris: Minimal Objects

It looks like painting is finished

—Donald Judd

The role of sculpture in minimalist art is subject to scholarly debate. While for many artists and critics, sculpture provided new opportunities, after all possible reductions had been tried in painting, for others, the third dimension does not add significant new elements. Strickland notes: "The three-dimensional art is fundamentally an outgrowth of earlier work in its sister medium" (Strickland, 2000, 259).

Donald Judd, originally a painter, turned to sculpture as he disliked the "illusionistic quality of painting" and insisted on the necessity of working in 'real space'; the very development that minimal painting took, further and further reducing composition and painterliness made it difficult to continue further within the same medium. In sculpture as well as in painting, the question about how far reduction could go was soon raised as technical bravura and richness in composition or color lost their importance. By the end of 1964, Judd

Fig. 2.6 Donald Judd:
Untitled (1976), Flick
Collection Berlin

no longer created his sculptures by himself, but rather "sent out plans for works to factories, whose superior execution, he felt, would make his work perspicuous" (Meyer, 2001, 81; Fig. 2.6). As the new art approached the asymptotic limit of the readymade and the bare canvas, it became "concept art"; yet, at the same time, this opened the doors for criticism—Kramer suggested that this art was too easy to reproduce to be called art, "the work wasn't crafted enough . . . too simple to look at . . . boring" (ibid., 81).

In a discussion with Frank Stella, who was named as a principal influence on the object-sculptors, Donald Judd, one of the most prominent of minimalist sculptors, identified himself as seeking for wholeness in painting. This was the reason for symmetry in his work as he "wanted to get rid of any compositional effects, and the obvious way to do it was to be symmetrical" [1] (Glaser, 1966). Naming Newman as an example, he insisted that "You should have a definite *whole* and maybe no parts, or very few . . . The whole's it. The big problem is to maintain the sense of the whole thing" (ibid.). As Judd and Stella both knew nothing of similar tendencies in European art (Meyer, 2001, 88), they identified this objection to relational composition as a major feature of the typical American minimalism. An important aspect of minimal sculpture is thus the

---

[1] Judd later elaborated this position in "Symmetry" (1985, reprinted in Judd, 1975, 92-95).

wholeness of Gestalt; artists argued against the visual separation of parts in their specific objects. Retrospectively, wholeness became a key quality of both painting and sculpture (ibid., 134ff).

In the same interview, Judd places a strong verdict on previous approaches to minimalism; for him, "painting is finished" (Glaser, 1966). At the same time, he insists that in form, "the new work obviously resembles sculpture more than it does painting, but it is nearer painting" (Judd, 1975, 183), and coins the term *specific objects* for Morris' and his own work.

A prototypical work that was subjected to the accusation of trivial simplicity, and thus a lack of artfulness, was Andre's Lever (1966) consisting of 137 aligned firebricks (Fig. 2.7); a satire "exhibition" at Chapman College in Orange, California, organized by Harold Gregor, director of the college's Purcell gallery stated that anyone "could purchase a similar set of bricks and make an identical work", even "the subtraction or addition of a few dozen bricks" would "in no way change its form … [that was] boringly minimal in content" (quoted in Meyer, 2001, 82). However, this critique too simply dismissed the Lever's form as visually dull, and disregarded Andre's intention of demonstrating the nature of the building blocks in his art that was "installed by Andre himself, who prized each brick for its own material sake; and understood by the artist to be perfectly continuous with the modernist tradition of formal innovation rather than a dadaist legacy" (ibid., 82).

Fig. 2.7 Carl Andre: Lever (1966).© VG Bild + Kunst, Bonn 2008

The object character of minimal sculpture sharply contrasted even the most minimal painting. As one of the most radical protagonists of minimal sculpture, Dan Flavin used fluorescent light tubes for his works (Fig. 2.8)—while others like Judd developed his works out of industrial materials, he chose industrial objects as his medium, "My work becomes more and more an industrial object the way I accept fluorescent light for itself" (ibid., 92). Painting expert, Bob Rosenblum, noted that Flavin had thus "destroyed painting" for him (Judd, 1975, 189).

Fig. 2.8 Dan Flavin: The Nominal Three (to William of Ockham), 1963. Estate of Dan Flavin / © VG Bild + Kunst, Bonn 2008

Robert Morris introduced an art that—as architecture—related to human scale, "Architecture, the body, movement — these are the terms of Morris's early minimalism" (Meyer, 2001, 51). While his early artworks tried to interface with the context — as has been noted in different sources, a sculpture called "Column" was used as a prop in a performance at La Monte Young's Living Theater in New York in 1962 (Krauss, 1977)—he later removed himself from "such allusions" and argued for a purely abstract art (Morris, 1966) before returning to architecture as a source of inspiration in the 1970s. Yet, even in his abstract period, he produced an art that was quite different from Judd's plainly pictorial model. While Judd's "Specific Objects" were there to 'look at', Morris' works "were to be experienced by an ambient body that walked around, and through, the work itself" (Meyer, 2001, 51).

Returning to the question of wholeness, for Morris—who understood the term primarily in perceptual terms–only sculpture could be whole, a quality he referred to as Gestalt, as "wholeness seen". Judd, who started out as a painter rather than as a performer, admitted he did not want to "consider the viewer ...... I'm rather interested in what I want to think about, what I want to do"

(Glaser, 1966). While Judd carefully built and exhibited his works so that they could be seen, Morris consciously theorized the experience of his art by recourse to ultimate reduction, and proposed that "the most reduced shapes were the most desirable" (Meyer, 2001, 159). For his use of the pictorial relief, Morris even accused Judd of illusionism, "the autonomous and literal nature of sculpture demands that it have its own, equally literal space – not a surface shared with painting" (Morris, 1966), and claimed that "wholeness was an integral quality of sculpture alone, for wholeness could only be seen in three dimensions" (Meyer, 2001, 158; Fig. 2.9).

Fig. 2.9 Robert Morris: Corner piece (1964). © VG Bild + Kunst, Bonn 2008

In contrast with Judd's pictorial conception of artistic sculpture, the Specific Object that "presents a static, articulated shape to a viewer's gaze" (ibid., 51), Morris' involvement in performance art included the architecture, the human body, and movement in his understanding of sculpture. Judd was the leading advocate of the position Fried characterized as "literalist" (Fried, 1966, 22)— the compulsion to rid art of illusion, which, resulting in the production of objects, rendered painting obsolete (Fried, 1998, 12)" (Meyer, 2001, 230), while "Robert Morris conceives his own unmistakably literalist work as resuming the lapsed tradition of constructivist sculpture" (Fried, 1998, 12).

2.1.6 LeWitt: Minimal Structure in Minimalist Sculpture

Sol LeWitt, a graphic designer who worked for I.M. Pei in the mid-1950s, contributed his focus on structure to minimalism: "his major achievement in the 1960s as the assorted cubical structures whose skeletal nature was reinforced by their whiteness" (Strickland, 2000, 271). Echoing the five-foot square format of Reinhardt's paintings, he built his works based on five-feet-cubed cubes. By exposing the structure of his works, he created a "sense of dematerialization akin to the experience of both X-rays and architectural plans showing us the fragile framework ... which underlies the facade of daily existence" (ibid., 271).

Beginning with his second exhibition at the Dwan Gallery in New York in 1966, LeWitt experimented with white, modular open structures. He chose white as he considered it to be "the least expressive color" (quoted in Cummings, 1974)—white "enhanced the reading of his delicate geometries" (Meyer, 2001, 200). Feeling limited by the literalist tendencies of other minimalists and having the impression that "reductive Minimalism was self-defeating" (quoted ibid., 202), LeWitt used repetition to further expose not only the internal structure of an artwork but also the system behind the internal structure (Fig. 2.10). While the minimal object repressed its conceptual aspect, for LeWitt, geometry could become "a machine that makes the art" (LeWitt, 1978a). He chose the cube as it itself "is relatively uninteresting ... Therefore, it is the best form to use as a basic unit for any more elaborate function, the grammatical device from which the work may proceed" (LeWitt, 1978b).

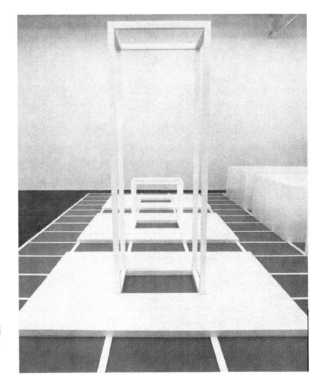

Fig. 2.10 Sol LeWitt: Serial Project #1, Set C (1966/85). © VG Bild + Kunst, Bonn 2008

2.1.7 Post-Minimalist Sculpture

Although minimalism itself is often seen as being limited to the 1960s (comp. Strickland, 2000, 6f), it formed an impression of art that was to last longer. Richard Serra, like Judd originally a painter, ranks among the most popular post-minimal artists. In his massive, stark works, optical qualities of minimalism are mirrored. However, most of his works "have an inherently more kinetic and menacing aura than the static and indifferent quality of earlier Minimal sculpture" (ibid., 290; Fig. 2.11). The monumental nature of most of Serra's later works tends to ignore the spectators, or at least make them feel insignificant; in his *Stacks*, massive sculptures "do not threaten to collapse on the spectator, enclose him in a vise, or even block his exit. They merely face each other and ignore him" (ibid., 291).

Fig. 2.11 Richard Serra: Strike (1970). © VG Bild + Kunst, Bonn 2008

Other artists took different and more inviting approaches to interacting with the audience. The non-communication of spectator and artwork was inspiration e.g. for Bruce Nauman's Sealed room (Fig. 2.12). In this sculpture, a room—four perfectly blank, white walls—is both presented to and hidden from the visitor. There is no way to determine what the sculpture looks like from the inside and, to add to this suspense, a humming voice is created by several large fans inside the sculpture. The artwork presents no image, and thus becomes a projection wall for the spectator's imagination.

Fig. 2.12 Bruce Nauman:
Sealed room—no access
(1970). © VG Bild + Kunst,
Bonn 2008

2.1.8 Minimal Art: Art as Art or Cooperative Sense-Building?

> *For the listener, who listens in the snow,*
> *And, nothing himself, beholds*
> *Nothing that is not there and the nothing that is.*
>
> —Wallace Stevens, The Snow Man

Although the first impression of a work of Minimal Art may be bewildering, it is also intriguing; it generates a need to explore, to solve the "puzzle", to fill in the details missing in the framework. This immediate interactivity that most strongly surfaces in the monochrome paintings, also of Reinhardt, is contrasted with his dictum of "art as art". Ultimate success in not only granting raw material its independence, but in insisting on conserving its modality—Stella trying to keep the paint "as good as it was in the can"—would create an art-object that simulated complete independence from the human will that created it. Stella objected to viewers "who ... retain the old values in painting ... If you pin them down, they always end up asserting that there is something there beside the paint on the canvas" (Battcock, 1968, 157 f.).

Consequently, some minimalists tried to eliminate the viewer from their art. If this degree of disconnection to anything human were reached, little value for the viewer could be found. Critic Naomi Spector enthusiastically hailed Mangold for excluding "from his work all such concerns as illusion, image, space, composition, climax, hierarchy of interest, movement, emotional content, painterliness, interest in material or processes, and any sort of association or reference to anything other than the physical painting itself" (Spector, 1974). This perspective was not widely shared and Strickland attributes her interpretation to "the Me Decade, an artistic analogue of Self magazine (I have no concern for the city, country, planet, or universe, but I'm looking good)" (Strickland, 2000, 114).

The creation of entirely self-sufficient objects without a relationship to a bigger whole would deny any possibility of interaction. Only few minimalists have tried to thus dominate the viewer; perhaps fortunately, Serra was unable to realize his statement about public places: "One has to consider the traffic flow, but not necessarily worry about the indigenous community, and get caught up in the politics of the site. There are a lot of ways one could complicate the problem for oneself. I'm not going to concern myself with what 'they' consider to be adequate, appropriate solutions" (Serra and Weyergraf-Serra, 1980, 63). After he had installed his metal Tilted Arc in 1981 (Fig. 2.13), the public

Fig. 2.13 Richard Serra: Tilted Arc (1981) on the Federal Plaza in New York. © VG Bild + Kunst, Bonn 2008

reaction was such that he was "perforce very much concerned with such issues ... he had blocked the view and escape of residents and employees on his sites. This time it backfired: the work was dismantled beginning March 15, 1989 after extensive and controversial public hearings" (Strickland, 2000, 290; comp. also Friedman, 1995; Senie, 2002).

Although some artists either ignored the audience or tried to exactly define the nature of perception for their art, most minimalist artists actively involved the context, and the viewer in the interpretation of their artworks. Elayne Varian (1967) introduced a minimalist show highlighting the relationship of viewer and object: "The purpose of this exhibition is to show the attitude of

contemporary sculptors to scale and enspheric space ... It is possible to have
positive (enclosure) and negative (exclusion) attitudes to define space, ...
equally important [is] their approach to the surrounding space, the negative
space". And critic Richard Wollheim (1965) notes that especially in the
reductionist artworks "the canvas, the bit of stone or bronze, some particular
sheet of paper scored like this or that" concentrates attention upon individual
bits of the world.

Minimalist artists focused on a constructive stance in the interaction of
viewer and art work; they were not interested in artfulness, and consequently they disliked artful analyses of their works. What was more
important was the immediate effect of a work: "One could stand in front
of any Abstract-Expressionist work for a long time, and walk back and
forth, and inspect ... all the painterly brushwork for hours. ... I wouldn't
ask anyone to do that in front of my paintings. To go further, I would like
to prohibit them from doing that ... If you have some feeling about either
color or direction or line or something, I think you can state it. You don't
have to knead the material and grind it up. That seems destructive to me;
it makes me very nervous. I want to find an attitude basically constructive
rather than destructive" (Glaser, 1966, 159).

2.2 Minimalism in Music

As the term minimalism was first used to describe painting, adoption is
part of the character of all subsequent uses. Bernard (1993) describes how
critics who argue that the term may hardly apply to music, who dispute
"the extreme reduction of the musical means is important enough to
function as a fundamental characteristic of this music" (Mertens, 1983,
11–12), oversee that the term minimal—as the last part tried to illustrate—
goes beyond mere reduction in meaning. It has also been quite successful,
as other labels, such as "phase-shifting", "repetitive", "systemic", or "process" music, are no longer used to refer to what is now known as *minimal
music*. Manifold connections of painters and musicians can be observed in
the New York art scene in the 1960s. The earliest performances of minimal
music took place in art galleries and individual figures collaborated over
extended periods of time: Philip Glass with Richard Serra, or La Monte
Young with Robert Morris, to name just a few. Bernard notes that "It is
interesting that no one seems to have thought to apply the term *minimal* to
this music, at least in print, before Michael Nyman did it sometime in the
early 1970s" (Bernard, 1993, 87).

In the following sections, the "minimalist" in minimal music is retraced to use
the many similarities with minimal art and some of the differences that emerged
as minimal music took a more independent path to add and differentiate the
previously detailed meanings of minimalism.

2.2.1 The Origins of Minimal Music

> *I have spent many pleasant hours in the woods conducting*
> *performances of my silent piece. . .for an audience of myself,*
> *since they were much longer than the popular length which I*
> *have published. At one performance. . .the second movement*
> *was extremely dramatic, beginning with the sounds of a buck*
> *and a doe leaping up to within ten feet of my rocky podium.*
>
> — John Cage, Silence: Lectures and Writings

After studying classical avant-garde with Arnold Schönberg in Los Angeles in 1934, John Cage became one of the main protagonists of "Concept Music", a style of music where the composition dominated the performance. He conceived of pieces where tossing coins determined musical events (*Music of Changes*, 1951), wrote for 12 radios (*Imaginary Landscape no.4*, 1951) and composed what was seen by some as "the prototype, the primordial piece of Minimalist conceptual art" (Rockwell, 1986), a piece called *4'33"* (1952) where the performer is directed to do nothing at all for that length of time. Strickland suggests that this piece was inspired by Rauschenberg's all-whites and represents the "conceptual ne plus ultra for radical reductivism" (2000, 30).

Concept music, with the Fluxus group being the most important source, is often considered as the predecessor of minimal music; Nyman describes that the Fluxus composers "reviewed multiplicity, found its deficiencies, and chose to reduce their focus of attention to singularity" (1972, 119). Yet, concept music often seems to border on arbitrariness—the limits composers set to chance are few (Bernard, 1993, 95), and it is difficult to decide whether only irony, or a serious intention (as is assumed in minimalist art) drives its principals. This question of control marks the differences between concept music (that widened the definition of what can be considered music) and early minimal music, which implemented "formal control" of chance elements (Gena, 1981).

Cage (1991) hints at nihilist Dada as a source of inspiration. This emphasis on the illogical and absurd, the creative techniques of accident and chance demonstrates the difference between Cage and some of the early pieces of La Monte Young and what later developed into minimalism. Bernard (1993,96) points out that—like Minimalist artists (e.g. Morris, Flavin, or LeWitt) deal with temporality using Serialism, or a gradual or systematic progress through a series of possibilities—Minimalist composers emphasize the passage of time by "*composing out*" the possibilities of their material *in a transparent manner*. Minimalism is thus marked by a conscious and transparent form of reduction that uses omission as an explicit element to target attention.

Perhaps even more important for the minimalist composers themselves, minimalism in music is both a counter-reaction and a derivation of the avant-garde style of Serialism (Potter, 2000, 20), and can also be understood in political, rather than aesthetic terms. Serialism had long been the predominant form of "new classical" music, dictating what defined good music, and even determining which techniques to employ when composing; it had become very difficult to think of a new form of music as the atonal revolution of "old" classical harmonics and structural principles had created new, equally restrictive rules. Minimalism established a radically different alternative both to the "old" and "new" classical music. For David Lang, minimalism "was a historic reaction to a sort of music which had a strangle hold on ... American musical institutions, and which none of us really liked. ... What most people really hated was the way that this other world had theorized that it was the only music possible ... I look at Minimalism ... as being just the battleground that was necessary to remove those forces from power: not to obliterate them or destroy them, but ... to loosen up the power structure in America. And I think that [one reason why] Glass's music and Reichs's music came out so severe, and so pared down, was that ... it was a polemical slap in the face ... That battle's been fought ... My job is to sift among the ashes and rebuild something" (Lang quoted ibid.).

The suggested lineage of minimalism includes also some more distant predecessors, yet in Richard Wagner's *Das Rheingold* (1854), the simplicity of long chords in the opening bars rather amounts to anticipation of the complex, virtuous tapestry that follows, Eric Satie's *Vexations* (1963) simply employs repetition without any development as an artistic means and the sometimes-mentioned *Bolero* by Maurice Ravel (1928) might be repetitious, yet the "Romanticism of the piece is the antithesis of austere Minimalism" (Strickland, 2000, 124) and its directionality in dynamics and rhythm is unidirectional.

Concentrating on the four musical figures most prominently identified as "Musical Minimalists", Terry Riley, La Monte Young and Philipp Glass are introduced in some detail in the following sections. For a more thorough and balanced account of their lives and works, I must refer the reader to Potter's excellent "Four musical minimalists" (Potter, 2000) and, for a different perspective, to Strickland's analysis of the origins of minimalism (Strickland, 2000). For a contemporary perspective, the collected articles of Tom Johnson are a worthwhile read (Johnson, 1991).

2.2.2 Terry Riley

Terry Riley was the minimalist composer with most connections to Cage's concept music, having practiced that style during his early career. Together with Young, however, he began to conceive a new style that would eventually turn into minimalism. A strong European influence, both from his studies and from living in France, links his works to Serialism. Strickland (2000, 133) highlights Riley's "two major contributions to early Minimalism: the reintroduction of tonality" and "the use of repeating musical modules". The former is first introduced in his 1960 *String Quartet*, where he returned to tonality, which had been absent from his earlier works, in long tone composition—fairly unusually long tones, for that matter. The latter became evident in his 1961

String Trio: "the unvaried repetition of tonal phrases marked a radical compositional simplification" (ibid., 143). Composing the Trio, his interest in Serialism remained visible–he had studied Stockhausen with Wendall Otey and Robert Erickson at San Francisco (ibid., 133), but tonal repetition became musically dominant, while chromaticism moved to the background; for Riley, "That was the transitional piece" (Strickland, 1991, 112).

Yet, his most important contribution to minimalism was *In C*, fifty-three "modules", supposedly written in one night (all patterns are shown in Fig. 2.14); *In C* is scored for "[a]ny number of any kind of instruments" (Potter, 2000, 112).

Fig. 2.14 Terry Riley: In C (1964), the first 10 of 55 patterns. With kind permission of Terry Riley

Its "ensemble can be aided" by a pulse that can be performed "on the high c's of the piano or on a small mallet instrument" (ibid.). Not all performers need to play all the modules; some are better suited to melodical instruments, such as wind instruments, while the faster patterns are fitting to be played by keyboard instruments. The piece starts with a pulse, synchronizing all performers; after that, each musician may start with module one in his/her own time, repeating as often as he/she wishes before moving on to the next module. Although in some performances, this has resulted in "a kind of glorious, hippie free-for-all" (ibid.) performances produced in cooperation with Riley "generally deployed a maximum of four modules at any time and thus encouraged the performers to work more closely together" (ibid.); in Riley's words, "no performer should draw attention to his own part at the expense of others, this would 'collapse the structure of the piece'" (ibid.).

By using repetition and relying on skillful improvisation, the score of *In C* fits onto a single page, and with written instructions is still shorter than three pages, although performances "normally average between 45 minutes and an hour and a half" (Riley, 1964). The resulting patterns are different in every performance, yet the overall impression is not completely different—one can recognize *In C*. This balance between freedom for the performers and careful composition for possibilities that are limited by cues rather than rules: Riley states "as the performance progresses, performers should stay within 2 or 3 patterns of each other. It is important not to race too far ahead or to lag too far behind" (ibid.). Also, a strict sense of rhythm is demanded for by Riley, to prevent an impression of disorder.

Repetition had been discovered long before by Riley: when he had worked at the San Francisco Tape Music center, he experimented with an echo effect to put a piece of Ramon Sender on a "sonic 'acid trip'" (Strickland, 2000, 148). Later, working in Paris, where he played jazz and ragtime in Pigalle, he composed *Mescalin Mix*, a piece elaborating this echo effect. After continuing playing lounge piano in officers' clubs and bars at American bases, he met a French engineer who "ended up hooking two tape-recorders together" (Strickland, 1991, 112). The tape ran along the record head of the first recorder and the play head of the second recorder, who thus played what had been recorded before, feeding the output back to the first recorder. Effectively, this resulted in a progressively complex structure as the recording was overlaid on itself. What might seem trivial today in an age of sampling was a revolution then, and for Riley a revelation that he was still enthusiastic about 25 years later (Strickland, 2000, 149).

2.2.3 La Monte Young

The music Terry Riley was using for his first tape experiments, *The Gift*, was the piece *So What* from *Kind of Blue*, one of the best-known jazz albums of all time, recorded in 1959 by Miles Davis, who pioneered modal jazz. The scarcity of melodic shifts—*So What* contained only two modes in thirty-two bars—allowed Riley to use repetition without immediately creating disharmonies. Jazz can be seen as one of the major influences on minimal music. Riley, La Monte Young and Steve Reich all played in jazz groups in their teens, and Coltrane, who continued to explore exotic modes "from Morocco to Afghanistan" (ibid., 150), made popular the soprano saxophone that Young adopted for his latest work period, where he turned to drone sounds.

In his early years, Young took up "the indeterminacy practiced by [John] Cage and his followers" (ibid., 144) in his "concept art" composition of April 1960, A*rabic numeral (any integer) to Henry Flint*: the Arabic number indicated the number of times a sound was to be repeated, with both the choice of number and sound left to the performer. Cage himself found the piece "relevatory" (Cage, 1961, 52). In an extended realization of repetition, Young composed *1698* in 1961, the title designating the number of times the same dissonant chord needed to be played on a piano—sometimes, Young was reportedly playing the piano until his fingers bled (Strickland, 2000, 145).

Young thus presented himself as uncompromisingly obsessed with repeating sounds—according to Potter (2000, 43,12), he was "wildly interested in repetition, because [he thinks] it demonstrates control". His *Composition 1961* with 29 identical instructions to draw a straight line and follow it represent another form of repetition. Young's repetition differed from the repetition used by Riley in his "still traditional, if highly experimental, score[s] primarily by means of notated and repeated musical phrases" (Strickland, 2000, 145) and has often been connected to a continuity derived from repeated repetitions: Smith (Smith, 1977, 4) notes that "witnessing a single activity extended in time, we begin to appreciate aspects and ideas that would otherwise remain hidden", and Mertens judges: "the term repetition, however, can hardly be used for La Monte Young's music since in this case the principle of continuity is decisive" (Mertens, 1983, 16).

What was later termed *additive processes* was—in a simple form—also pioneered by Young, who wrote *Death Chant* for the funeral of an acquaintance's child. To a minimal motive of two notes, a single note is added for every repetition; the resulting piece thus, although repetitive, demonstrates the slow progression of time (Fig. 2.15).

Fig. 2.15 La Monte Young: Death Chant (1961)

John Coltrane, who "used to construct modes or sets of fixed frequencies upon which he performed endlessly beautiful permutations" (Young and Zazeela, 1969), influenced Young to begin playing the saxophone, and partly by that instrument, a new composition phase was introduced: As in the 1964 *Sunday Morning Blues*, rapid five-second bursts of notes on Young's sopranino saxophone were contrasted with voice, guitar and viola drone sounds that were held continuously through the performance (Fig. 2.16).

Fig. 2.16 La Monte Young: Sunday Morning Blues (1964), excerpt

As Young himself notes (Young, 2001, Notes on Composition 1960 #7), the "use of sustenance became one of the basic principles of my work. When there are long sustained tones, it is possible to better isolate and listen to the harmonics." This principle has been perfected and applied in Young's best-known piece, the 1958 *Trio for Strings*, "which, while constructed as a serial piece, has pitches of longer duration and greater emphasis on harmony to the exclusion of almost any semblance of what had been generally known as melody" (Young, 2001, Notes on Composition 1960 #7). The Trio takes serial notions such as symmetrical row construction and static tonal surface to an extreme conclusion, and is comprised only of long sustained tones in varying alignments alternating with silences (Fig. 2.17).

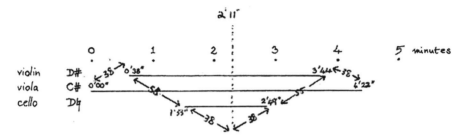

Fig. 2.17 La Monte Young: Trio for Strings (1958)

The use of long-held tones eventually led Young to the development of his "concept of the drone-state-of-mind" (Young, 2001, Notes on Composition 1960 #7); behind the use of sustained drone sounds stands the belief that "tuning is a function of time"(ibid.), and that "frequency environments" influence the nervous system, eventually "establishing periodic patterns" (Young, 2001, Notes on Composition 1960 #7). Young later became a disciple of the Pakistan (then-Indian) Raga singer, Pandit Pran Nath whom he admired for his ability to perfectly hit and sustain pitch (Strickland, 2000, 172f).

2.2.4 Philip Glass

Philipp Glass' interest in reduction developed under the influence of Samuel Beckett (Potter, 2000, 255): during his Paris studies, he created his first theater piece together with JoAnne Akalaitis. This play was later described by Glass as "a piece of music based on two lines, each played by a soprano saxophone, having only two notes so that each line represented an alternating, pulsing interval. When combined, these two intervals (they were written in two different repeating rhythms) formed a shifting pattern of sounds that stayed within the four pitches of the two intervals. The result was a very static piece that was still full of rhythmic variety" (quoted ibid., 256).

A second important source of inspiration was Indian classic music (ibid. 257ff), whose rhythmic qualities fascinated him: he felt that in contrast with the western "divisive" rhythm that divided a musical score in bars, and these again in beats, Indian (and other non-western) music created rhythms using additive methods (ibid., 270f). These influences lead him directly to his contribution to minimalist music, additive music became the "structural essence" (ibid., 284) of his musical work.

1 + 1 (1968), a piece for one player and amplified tabletop, is often taken as the initial milestone in Philip Glass' development. It is the earliest and most rigorous example of the composer's use of what he termed an "additive process". *1 + 1* is only concerned with rhythm: the player taps on a tabletop amplified via a contact microphone, two basic "rhythmic units" are offered and amended by suggestions how to use them as "building blocks" for a performance. The "additive process" is specified simply by instructing the player to combine the "two units in continuous, regular, arithmetic progressions"; the first of Glass' examples comes out as "1 + 2; 1 + 2 + 2; 1 + 2 + 2 + 2; 1 + 2 + 2; 1 + 2 etc.": the first unit is contained only once in each alteration while the second unit expands and contracts symmetrically.

This "additive process" served Glass as the main technique for structuring his compositions for some ten years from thereon. He remarked, "It's funny, it's such a simple idea, but believe it or not, I just hadn't thought of it then. Actually, it was the result of a year or two years' work: I looked back and thought of simplifying all the processes I had used into that one idea" (quoted in Potter and Smith, 1976).

Although Glass had previously applied similar techniques to sequences in his music, *1 + 1* is the first work that rigorously regimented the technique, applying systematic rules for expansion and contraction and thus making the unfolding structure clearly audible, transparent. As with Reich's works using phasing, "the compositional process and the sounding music become one" (Potter, 2000, 272).

Glass invented additive processes. They are no cyclic structures and they differ from the repetition that La Monte Young developed from working with tape interference: Glass additive processes follow strict rules, yet they describe a dynamic movement. The rules for creating structure are formalized, and can be perceived by the listener as such, yet the possibilities for combination allow the weaving of complex musical patterns. This also goes far beyond the inspiration that Glass found in Indian music: "The kind of additive processes which Glass made the basis of his own music are not, however, to be found in Indian practice; even the rigorous application of these is not a direct borrowing but an extrapolation of the composer's own from the Indian approach to rhythm." (ibid. 273).

Philip Glass continued to build more and more complex musical pieces on the principle of additive processes. He experimented with parallel movements in *Music in Fifths* (1969) and *Music in Similar Motion* (1969) and with tonal inversion in *Music in Contrary Motion* (1969) (ibid. 292–300). While the latter was written in "open form"–never ending, the piece just stops without reason, he later turned away from such playful experiments and sought to develop additive processes further. In what is considered his masterpiece, *Music in Twelve Parts* (1971–1974), construction rules guide not only rhythm, but also structure:

the composition was first played in 1971—and later turned into the first of twelve parts that followed a regular development (ibid., 312f).

2.2.5 Steve Reich

Steve Reich has become the most successful of the minimalist composers in commercial terms and as his later works are much more compatible with public taste, it has been forgotten that he was among the most rigorous minimalists. Brought up with "classical" music—his mother became best known as the Broadway singer June Carroll—his interest quickly turned to both older and more modern music: "It wasn't until the age of 15 that I heard the music that would end up motivating me to become a composer and informing what I did: that was jazz, bach and Strawinsky . . ." (quoted in Smith and Smith, 1994, 212). Reich majored in philosophy at Cornell University, and studied subsequently privately with Hall Overton in New York before attending Juillard School between 1958 and 1961—at which time he met fellow student Phillip Glass (Potter, 2000, 155). "Running away from home" (Reich quoted ibid., 156), he arrived in San Francisco where he composed *Music for String Orchestra* (1961), a twelve-note set that was to be repeated ad infinitum, and *Four Pieces* (1963), "twelve-tone jazz licks trying to become tonal" (Reich quoted ibid., 159).

Starting with *Four Pieces*, Reich felt "despite my limitations as a performer I had to play in all my compositions"—a decision whose practical consequences helped him towards a simpler, reductive style (ibid.). Meeting Terry Riley in 1964 and assisting the development of *In C* (ibid., 111–116), he was "pointed the way towards a more organized and consistent kind of pattern-making with highly reductive means" (ibid., 164). With *It's Gonna Rain* (1965; Fig. 2.18), Reich sought to reproduce the perfect synchronization of tape loops, using a Black American English sermon of Brother Walter; the first movement using only the words "it's gonna rain", the second drawing on a longer passage. However, technical imperfection of the Wollensak tape recorders he used let the two recordings fall out of synch, with one tape gradually falling ahead or behind the other due to minute differences in the machines and playback speed. Reich decided to exploit this *phase shifting* to explore all possible recursive harmonies.

When Reich returned to New York in 1965, he came into contact with minimal artists like Robert Rauschenberg, Sol Le Witt, and Richard Serra.

Fig. 2.18 Steve Reich: It's Gonna Rain (1965)—basic unit. (c) 1987 Hendon Music, Inc

Although he "was derisive about the term 'minimalist'" (Reich quoted ibid., 171), he acknowledged "there certainly was an attitude" (ibid.) he shared with the painters and sculptors; he was also financially supported by the already-established Le Witt and Serra as they purchased his original scores. He slowly built up an ensemble that became the center of his compositional activities. The life performance in "painstaking rehearsals" provided the basis for the development of compositions like *Drumming* (1970–71) as they allowed for "many small compositional changes while the work is in progress and at the same time [building] a kind of ensemble solidarity that makes playing together a joy" (ibid., 198). The composition was now only part of the musical product, and the performance and interpretation gained an important role.

This development culminated in *Music for Eighteen Musicians* (1976; Fig. 2.19): rehearsals for this piece were held over a period of two years and "structurally, the work is so complex that no attempt was made to notate repeats or achieve synchronisation in what was written down" (ibid., 199). The first complete score was published only in 1996, and consisted of a transcription of a 1973 recording. *Music for Eighteen Musicians* became Reich's most well-known piece and is valued for its "significant expressive extension of the composer's musical language" (ibid., 231). Reich still uses the development of patterns and rhythmical shifting as techniques, but combines them more subtly, for the first time exploring the technique of "underpinning a repeated melodic pattern by rhythmically shifting chord changes" (ibid., 233).

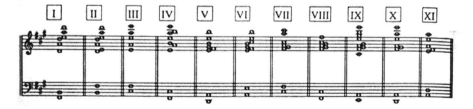

Fig. 2.19 Steve Reich: Music for 18 Musicians (1978)—cycle of chords. (c) 1978, 1998 Hendon Music, Inc. Printed with kind permission of Boosey & Hawkes Bote & Bock, Berlin

Reich gradually developed his interests "from 'structure' as such to a greater concern with sound" (ibid., 211). In *Drumming*, he introduced a rich variety of instruments—e.g. marimbas and glockenspiels, and combined them with voices (ibid., 212–225). This more symphonic style influenced his later works, although he sometimes returned to a more minimal instrumentation, e.g., in the 1972 *Clapping Music* that was written for the pairs of hands of two performers. Although the choice of ensemble was minimal, *Clapping Music* was still a highly complex piece, its basic unit throwing the 12/8 meter in doubt as notes follow on the 5th, 8th and 10th quaver. The resulting rhythm can be interpreted "in a number of ways; when performed in canon, the choice of downbeats is naturally increased" (ibid., 225). Listening to the piece, it can even be difficult to discern that both players clap the same pattern.

A significant portion of Steve Reich's reputation has been made in the world of pop music, where Brian Eno and Mike Oldfield popularized music influenced by Reich and other minimalists. Reich's influences in pop music can be retraced even in today's music. In 1999, *Reich: Remixed* was produced, with several leading "techno" artists, including Coldcut, Ken Ishii and DJ Spooky, reinterpreting the composer's music from 35 years.

2.2.6 Summarizing Minimalism in Music

Reviewing the contributions of the four musical minimalists to minimal music, similarities with minimal art are obvious: a reduction in means can be seen in the sparse orchestration of many pieces. Cageian influences lead also to some experiments with the reduction of meaning, yet as a whole, musical minimalism is less playful than its counterpart in art. The main focus of minimal music is on the reduction of structure and sound—often by employing repetition and through combination of simple patterns.

Distancing himself from Serialism, Riley reintroduced tonality to modern music and pioneered the use of repeating musical modules. La Monte Young started his composing career with tape experiments, slowly escaping the Cageian influence. His mature minimalist works experiment with repeating sounds, introduce rhythmic addition and make use of drone sounds to create powerful soundscapes. Philipp Glass was interested in structure and rhythm from his first works under the influence of Beckett, and later perfected structural transparency in his works by inventing additive processes that combine simple patterns using composed rules. This allows both the interpretation to *create* music based on the composition, and the listener to reconstruct the act of creation. Steve Reich also used reductive patterns and tape loops in his works, but later shifted his focus of attention from structural qualities of his work towards the creation of a sound. He built up an ensemble that was crucial in maturing his compositions—the interpretation was given an important role in the making of his music.

Another important aspect of minimal music is the involvement of the listener—as minimalist art focused on the necessity for the viewer to "complete the work", the same can be said for performances of minimal music. Brian Ferneyhough noted that "All music is many-layered ... Our ears impose on us, with any listening process, a number of possible strategies which we're constantly scanning and assessing and ... finding a new distance or new perspective in relation to what we're hearing at that particular moment. It's one of the few possible justifications for minimalist music, for instance: that the maximalisation comes through the individual, rather than through the object" (Brian Ferneyhough, in conversation with David Osmond-Smith during the interval

of a recording for BBC Radio Three, first broadcast on 18 July 1993, quoted
ibid., 14f).

The influence of minimalism extends to current pop music, as elements of
minimalism were introduced into pop, and even muzak by Brian Eno and Reich
himself; a generation of artists that are now creating electronic music have been
influenced by the minimalisms. Modern interpretations of minimalism, however,
are more easy to listen to and tend to view the original minimalist compositions
as refreshingly extreme, visible e.g., in the enthusiasm of Björk who celebrates
minimalism's ability to "shake off that armour of the brain" (Björk quoted
ibid., 46)

2.3 Minimalism Found Elsewhere

As this chapter aims to provide an overview of the broad range of historical
definitions of minimalism, it cannot be withheld from the reader that the term
"minimalism" has not been confined to art and music: it has since found wide
application in diverse areas, starting with typography, architecture and literature and reaching as far as food or politics.

However, while some of these uses enrich the definition of minimalism, other
applications of the term are motivated by rather superficial aesthetic similarities: using few and fresh ingredients for cooking (Katzen, 2006), or linking the
minimal amount of food in French Cuisine to minimalism helps little to further
explain the term. Even more serious uses of the term are often only using the
concepts transported by minimalism, and not adding to them, e.g. in the
minimalist conception of state (Nozick, 1974) that starts with the state-of-
nature of the individual and goes little beyond reducing the state to interfere
as little as possible (Böhr, 1985, 5 + 121f).

A focus on the original meaning motivated the following, necessarily small,
selection of "minimalisms": literature and architecture illustrate the meaning of
space, and typography adds the conflict between form and function that we will
return to when discussing minimal design (compare Section 4.1).

2.3.1 Literary Minimalism: Roots in Hemingway, Archetype
in Carver

> *The world is so complicated, tangled, and overloaded that*
> *to see into it with any clarity, you must prune and prune.*
>
> —Italo Calvino, If on a Winter's Night A Traveller

While "Minimalism" in the visual arts tried to avoid any implications beyond
the object itself, for literature, the opposite could be claimed: within a minimal
frame, the evocation of larger, unnamed issues is often effectuated by figurative
associations. Stella's "What you see is what you see" is contrasted with

Hemingway's "tip of the iceberg" aesthetic principle, by which he suggests that seven-eighths of the story lies beneath its surface. On the other hand, Minimal art in the post-modern tradition often requires the viewer for completion, and thus shares with Minimal literature an interactive character, the strong involvement of the viewer that John Perreault described as: "The term 'minimal' seems to imply that what is minimal in Minimal art is the art. This is far from the case. There is nothing minimal about the 'art' (craft, inspiration or aesthetic stimulation) in Minimal art. If anything, in the best works being done, it is maximal. What is minimal about Minimal art ... is the means, not the ends" (Perreault, 1967, 30).

As the art in Minimal art is rooted in the very difficulty of extreme reduction, the apparent simplicity of literary minimalism, with its stark prose and tacit narration, established a highly stylized language. Reflection and implication are used as means to express the unstated. This conscious, careful use of language was described by author Amy Hempel: "A lot of times what's not reported in your work is more important than what actually appears on the page". Minimalist short stories in particular often take working class reality (blue collar stories) as a subject; at first glance, only everyday activities are described—yet although the text resembles reality, the presentation suggests that there is more to the text than the narrated details. As Cynthia W. Hallett notes, "Minimalist writers ... employ an aesthetic of exclusion–a prudent reduction of complex equations, a factoring-out of the extraneous until the complicated is expressed in the simplest of terms. Generally in these texts, distraction and clutter are stripped from human commerce until the reader encounters the whole of society reflected in slivers of individual experience, the unstated present as a cogent force" (Hallett, 2000, 7).

Although scholars disagree about the value of covering different authors "in the same breath" for fear of watering the term (Trussler, 1994), literary minimalism has been traced back to the prose poem developed by Baudelaire and Russian poets such as Ivan Turgenev, Fedor Sologub and Daniil Kharms, who created an aesthetically stark language with symbolist, futurist and absurdist miniatures (Wanner, 2003). In American literature, minimalism owes much to the clean and spare literary style of Ernest Hemingway, but Edgar Allen Poe, Anton Chekhov and James Joyce are included as strong influences on the Minimalist style (Hallett, 2000, 12). Edgar Allen Poe's notions of "unity" and "singleness of effect" are both achieved through exclusion: "In the whole composition, there should be no word written, of which the tendency ... is not to the one pre-established design ... Undue length is ... to be avoided" (Poe, 1842). As selective inclusion is achieved primarily through conscious exclusion, secondly through omission of excess, an inner unity is achieved that delivers the "certain unique or single effect to be wrought out" (ibid., 950). Although he rejected rationality in the tradition of Romanticism, his calculated composition of emotions is a fine example for a rational, artificial process that "combines such events as may best aid ... in establishing this preconceived effect" (ibid., 950).

Chekhov continued the exploration of the singular effect using "a plotless design that focuses on a single experience ... [and] an objective presentation which so distances the narrative voice that the reader is drawn into closer association with the story" (Hallett, 2000, 31), the latter a typical treat of Minimalist fiction. Joyce—at least in his early works—established a minimal dependence on the traditional notion of plot, his use of seemingly static episodes and "slices of reality" is also part of the Minimalist style (ibid., 12). Samuel Beckett and his efforts "to present the ultimate distillation of his inimitable world-view ... to compress and edulcorate [purify] traditional genres" (Hutchings, 1986) have also influenced not only Minimalist writers (comp. Glass), yet the major contribution to the Minimalist style could be the "concept of language as an inadequate tool for communication, especially for conveying emotion, subjective concepts and intangible matters", later a "major element of the minimalist writer's sensibility" (Hallett, 2000, 35).

In the late 1960s and early 1970s, a new generation of authors including Ann Beattie, Frederick Barthelme, Raymond Carver, Amy Hempel, and Mary Robison rediscovered "simplicity and immediacy of fictional expression" (ibid., 10) for themselves and initiated a shift from "well-made" literature to a "growing concern with character and sensibility, with the inner dynamics of the landscape of individual psychology ... related to the historical shift from moral absolutism to moral relativism as the dominant sensibility in our culture" (Weaver quoted ibid., 126). The forms that minimalism takes in literature are as diverse as its authors: Barth notes that in Literature, minimalism can be of "unit, form and scale", of "style ... vocabulary", or of "material" (Barth, 1986).

The final meaning of a Minimalist story unfolds only within the personal context of the reader—as "simple" facts are interpreted, "metonymic matter is transformed into metaphoric signifiers" (Hallett, 2000, 11). Strong psychological, social and historical associations are generated by the indirection and understatement of the deceptively simple, figurative language of minimalist prose. What appears to be a single event or a depiction of "nothing happening" signifies human condition or capacity—a connection between the trivial and the significant is created. Also, what is omitted becomes prominent; often, the inner state of personas is communicated without speaking the exact words, but rather relying upon "ready phrases, expected responses ... or euphemism to say it any other way but outright" (ibid., 19). Just as one could claim that nothing exists unless it has a name, by alluding to the exact definition of inner feelings and motivations, they "keep their innocence", or with Sartre: "To speak is to act, and everything we name loses its innocence, becoming part of the world we live in" (Sartre, 1965).

Minimalist writers do not try to achieve closure within the narrative, but rather compose story elements for final assembly by the reader. [2] Thus, the

---

[2] If most of this sounded a bit heady for your taste, you could go to http://garfieldminusgarfield.net to experience some of the complexity created by reduction. And even if not, it is probably worth a look.

sentences, the ending as much as the first lines often seem disconnected, the works are "but shells of story, fragile containers of compressed meaning" (Hallett, 2000, 11). This results in an unusual open-endedness of most of the short stories and in a rejection of linear plots; even more, this illusion of a "storyless" story often goes along with a seemingly "authorless" story, as the reader seems to overhear a conversation, or eavesdrop on an event, rather than being told a story: the "suppression of the artist's personality can be virtually total . . . [the abnegation of individual style is so complete that . . . we cannot tell one writer's work from another's; yet the very suppression of style is a style – an aesthetic choice, an expression of emotion" (Gardner, 1991, 36).

The label minimalism also implied some negative meaning in literature, some critics drew a curtain between prose poetry as an art and short fiction as a mere craft that did not allow them to appreciate the carefully crafted language of Minimal fiction. Jerome Klinkowitz was convinced that minimalist writers did not dare to judge human behavior and lost the "artfulness" of storytelling in their oversimplified descriptions, that Minimalist fiction "suspends all aesthetic innovation in favor of parsing out the most mundane concerns of superficial life (for fear of intruding with a humanly judgmental use of imagination)" (Klinkowitz, 1993, 364). Sven Birkerts was dissatisfied with the lack of resolution and asked for fiction "to venture something greater than a passive reflection of fragmentation and unease" (Birkerts, 1986, 33).

Barthelme gave the following advice to those "convicted" of minimalism, again highlighting the importance of the reader, and the virtue of being open for interpretation: "Tell them that you prefer to think you're leaving room for the readers, at least for the ones who like to use their imaginations; that you hope those readers hear the whispers, catch the feints and shadows, gather the traces, sense the pressures, and that meanwhile the prose tricks them into the drama, and the drama breaks their hearts" (Barthelme, 1988, 27).

2.3.2   Minimalism in Architecture

Minimalism has also been used to describe the architecture of human dwellings. In this discipline, a fairly clear line can be drawn between those who favor a "minimalist look" because of its clear lines and impressive shapes, and those who focus on a minimal visibility of architecture for its users. As perhaps the most prominent representative of the former approach, Ludwig Mies van der Rohe adopted the motto "less is more"; for him, this meant flattening and emphasizing the building's frame, eliminating interior walls and adopting an open plan (cf. Schulze, 1986). Thus, he aimed to reduce the structure to a strong, transparent, elegant skin—he termed this "skin and bones" architecture.

The clear forms of minimalism in architecture were interpreted as a reaction to the attention-calling visual excess of the supermarket culture. Minimalism is still a label that is broadly used for current industrial and civil architecture. The use of the label itself is seldom discussed, and in contrast to other disciplines, definitions are given using a multitude of examples rather than a formal explanation (Cuito, 2002a, b; Petterson, 2003, 2004; Castillo, 2004). Minimalism is also used as a term to describe the outer surroundings of buildings, gardens (Levy, 1996; Bradley-Hole, 1999) and public spaces (Cuito, 2001), and interior design (O'Bryan, 2002; Rossell, 2005).

Architecture tends to shy away from standardization almost as much as art. Combining the clear lines of minimalism with great visual variation, maximalism evolved in turn as a reaction to minimalism in architecture (compare Fig. 2.20). This counter-reaction was based on a rejection of the total reduction of forms and colors that threatened to create a sterile environment. In *Learning from Las Vegas*, Venturi et al., (1972) argued that within the visual chaos of Las Vegas, signs are not any longer only decoration but acquire a central function in architecture. He criticizes minimalism succinctly: "Less is not more. Less is a bore." (ibid.).

Fig. 2.20 Will Alsop: Peckham Library (1999), a maximalist design, private photograph

Although these new decorative elements have strongly influenced modern architecture, minimal architecture has not gone out of fashion. Yet, as architects Pawson and de Moura argue, it has gone beyond the simple geometrical forms and moves "towards concrete attempts, albeit thinly scattered over time and space and in modest quantities, to introduce a life more imbued with spirituality, clarity and harmony" (quoted in Bertoni, 2002, 149ff). This tendency towards integration of existing spaces is often marked by the integration of existing architecture.

As architect John Pawson notes, in minimal architecture, "Emptiness allows us to see space as it is, to see architecture as it is, preventing it from being corrupted, or hidden, by the incidental debris of paraphernalia of everyday life" (quoted ibid., 134ff). Architect Michael Gabellini adds: "Many people think that Minimalist art or architecture is something cold, abstract and sterile. Instead, minimalism is not only art or architecture, actually it is an idea that does not elude existence. It is analogous to the editing of a film, where there is an inherent concentration of form and experience. More than a subtraction, Minimalism is an inherent concentration of experience and pleasure" (quoted ibid., 183ff). Franco Bertoni highlights the contribution of minimalism to the discipline, namely a heightened awareness for space: "Leaving aside present-day misuse and the inflation of the term, Minimalist architecture represents one of the most significant contributions to a review of a discipline, and an attempt to endow it with new foundations, and a way of life" (ibid., front flap).

As in other disciplines, minimalism connotes a collection of works of architects from profoundly different origins and cultural backgrounds; common to most approaches is primarily the rediscovery of the value of empty space, and extreme simplicity. Bertoni further lists "a reduction in expressive media, and a radical elimination of everything that does not coincide with a programme" as characteristics for minimalist architecture, often resulting in "minimalistic design overtones, ... and formal cleanliness" (ibid., front flap).

2.3.3 Minimalism in Typography

Although the use of the notion of minimalism is not agreed upon within typography and terms such as modernist and functionalist typography are often used interchangeably, again, an immediate and a more reflective understanding of minimalism can be observed. The direct translation of "minimal" is exemplified by designer Ron Reason's claim that minimalism results in better typography: "minimalism in typography translates immediately into cleanliness, orderliness, ease of navigation, and consistency" (Reason, 2001). Here, minimalism is understood as the reduction of means—the use of less typefaces.

In contrast, the more reflective understanding results in the use of less, and less ornamental typefaces and the accented use of whitespace to structure content; its foundations are rooted in the conceptual shift of typography as functional design—following the development in the liberal arts. According to Ferebee (1994, 107), "Two extensions of Cubism—de Stijl and Constructivism—were the primary influence on Functionalist typography and poster design". The work of de Stijl and Bauhaus typographers was consolidated in Tschichold's (1928) *The New Typography* (1994, 110).

Jan Tschichold summarizes the intention of his typography in three sentences: "1. The new typography is purposeful. 2. The purpose of all typography is communication. 3. Communication must be made in the shortest, simplest, most definite way" (quoted in Good and Good, 1995). This striving for functionality has been understood as a reaction to on the one hand the possibilities opened by mass production—much as the minimalist artists auseinandersetzten with artificiality and new materials—and on the other hand the increased scale of the consumer market for printed articles. Seeking solutions to communication problems, typographers around Tschichold tried to enhance effective communication. This interpretation is exemplified by Katherine McKoy, historian of graphic design: "Modernism, especially at the Bauhaus, was a response to the economies of scale and standardization in the new mass societies. This functionalist design philosophy of 'form follows function' is based on standardized processes, modular systems, industrial materials and a machine aesthetic of minimalist form. Universal design solutions were sought to solve universal needs across cultures" (McCoy, 1995).

Tschichold understood himself as a typographic designer, a profession that did not exist before and that aimed to create graphic designs using typefaces. Previously, typesetters followed the rules of their trade and understood typesetting as a craft that tried to create products that excelled merely in their usability. *The New Typography* has been understood as technical-symbolical formalism, providing rules and examples for creating typographic designs. It is not. As Tschichold notes, "Merely to copy its external shapes would be to create a new formalism as bad as the old. ... It will come only from a complete reorientation of the role of typography and a realization of its spiritual relationship with other activities" (Tschichold, 1928, 7). And further, "Despite its many illustrations, this is not a copybook. It is intended to stimulate the printer and make him aware of himself and the true nature of his work" (ibid.). Tschichold

Fig. 2.21 Typographic design by Jan Tschichold (1924), Poster for Philobiblon Press, Warszaw

emphasized the conceptual frame that is the basis for his designs; his minimalism is of more than superficial nature.

A number of influential minimal designs were created by Tschichold in the 1920s and 1930s, and the minimalist font *Grotesk* became popular (Fig. 2.21), yet Tschichold himself returned to the use of ornamentals in his later work period, and also started using serif fonts, creating the Sabon face, a Garamond variant, in 1964. After having to emigrate to Switzerland, he slowly acknowledged the *function of ornamentals* in typography and the benefits of creating a pleasant and less harsh layout (Aynsley, 2001, 68). One could also argue that he never became "playful" (in a negative sense) and always kept true to his sense of functionalism as "serving a communication purpose" (Tschichold, 1928). His work with Penguin Books, for whom he overhauled the typography of their paperback series, is visible to the day.

2.4 Homing in on Minimalism: Summarizing the Art perspective

> *If the doors of perception were cleansed,*
> *everything would appear to man as it is, — infinite.*
>
> — William Blake, The Marriage of Heaven and Hell

Although this chapter started out contesting the feasibility of a universal definition for minimalism, it attempts to close with a short synopsis of the characteristics that have been subsumed under this label. Although almost every use of the meaning of the term minimalism refers to a unique meaning, some common motives can be identified that appear in several contexts. Among these repeating motives in minimalism are a *minimality of means*, and a *minimality of meaning*, a *minimality of structure*, the repeated *use of patterns* and the focus on *involvement of the recipient*. The following chapter refers to these motives as it redefines minimalism within the context of designing of interactive systems.

Before this chapter concludes with a description of the identified motives, however, a short note on methodology must be allowed. Computer science has a tradition of unscrupulously borrowing from other sciences. In its beginnings, this need arose from the novelty of the subject, and many methods that seemed to prove useful but originated in other disciplines were quickly adopted to form the new core of computer science. This book does not try to integrate or assimilate yet another discipline, instead a more modest aim is followed: minimalism as a concept from the liberal arts is borrowed to illustrate existing practice within computer science. Although computer science tends to prefer simplifications if they generate working models suitable for implementation, this terminological transfer cannot yield engineering rules but rather promises to deliver a critical perspective that helps to find and judge design decisions.

Even if a definition of minimalism existed, the transfer into computer science would require both interpretation and speculation. However, within the liberal arts, there is a rich literature that describes an even richer microcosm of definitions for minimalism, and subtle differences are considered valuable. The notion of minimalism in art is descriptive—it cannot be used to create art. This is partly owing to the definition of an artist—artworks cannot be constructed using blueprints (and where they can, e.g. in concept art, the blueprints assume the role of the artwork), and artists don't follow rules, they follow their inner musings. And it is partly caused by the wealth of different styles that are subsumed under the term minimalism.

2.4.1 Minimality of Means

A recurring issue in minimal art and music is the choice of *minimal means*: painting with enamel paint, choosing monochromes as a medium, tap-playing a desk, or a single-string instrument. Whether this minimalism can be interpreted as a reaction to pop art's excessive use of symbols in the monochromatic paintings of Klein, Reinhardt, Rauschenberg and others, or the static harmony, steady beat and static and sparse instrumentation in Glass' and Young's early compositions, minimal materials are consciously chosen as the basis for artworks. Minimalist plastic art was constructed with the most simple shapes, cubes or cuboids. This motive is perhaps the least controversial, and often Young is quoted to have defined minimalism as "that which is made with a *minimum of means*" (quoted in Schwartz, 1996, 7).

2.4.2 Minimality of Meaning

Before minimalism, painting was dominated by Abstract Expressionism that is related to Surrealism in its focus on emotions. Minimalism was considered much more impersonal, and took abstractness to the next level—some paintings had neither title nor intended meaning, and great care was taken to avoid visible traces of the artist and his intentions. "What you see is what you see" summarizes this approach to both painting and sculpture—there is no more to art than can be seen. The usual "function" of art, the expression or embodiment of values, visions, or emotions, was reduced to the maximum. In music, the interpretation of *minimality of meaning* was different; music was used to create hypnotic stances, or a singularity of mood, e.g. by Young in his drone period. Here, the "function" of music was to create a singular feeling, or, expressed negatively, monotony—often with the intention of sharpening the listener's awareness. In other fields, a similarly strong focusing effect can be observed, e.g. in architecture or literature, where open spaces and ellipses work to concentrate the attention of the observer.

2.4.3 Minimality of Structure

Not only the materials of minimalism are often minimal, it is also their combination in the artwork that is minimal in *structure*. Both in art and in music, the exposition of the inner structure is purposefully executed, whether in Young's additive rhythms or Judd's square-based sculptures. Simple rules and repetition are used to make the structure transparent for the recipient.

A different approach is taken in minimal literature: here, structure is limited by the formal choice of the short story as a medium, minimizing the textural complexity found in other literary works—without ado, the reader is plunged deep into the story. The structure of minimalist literature is often thoughtfully composed, yet readers are encouraged to simply follow the author's lead without reflecting about a text's structure. Instead, they are immediately confronted by topic and message. Similarly, minimal typography aims to reduce decoration and distraction, thus reducing cues for the visible structure of the layout. And even in painting, structure is not only minimized to make its underlying principles transparent to the recipient. Often, the minimization of structure follows the objective of finding a balance of inner structure and the artwork's other qualities. Judd described this as, "Take a simple form—say a box—and it does have an order, but it's not so ordered that that's the dominant quality. The more parts a thing has, the more important order becomes, and finally order becomes more important than anything else" (Glaser, 1966, 156).

2.4.4 Use of Patterns

Repeating elements have been found in both art and music long before minimalism. The excessive use of patterns, however, introduced a new quality and differentiates minimal music from other "contemporary classical" music. This use of patterns is closely linked to the question of control: On the one hand, control is lost as not pieces but only patterns are composed and combined with rules for correct combination or progress. On the other hand, some minimalist composers expose a tendency to completely control not only the performance but also the form of reception. Between these extremes, composers give performers a before-unknown freedom of interpretation within a strict rule system. Through additive processes and phase shifting, the patterns—even if simple in themselves—can be used to create very complex sound textures. In minimal art, serial paintings use small variations to create an overall impression; again, the combination of individual pieces is more complex than the individual works. When recipients learn to identify these patterns, they learn a new perspective that focuses on the combinatory possibilities hidden in the work of art.

2.4.5 Involvement of the recipient

"Serious art" is usually "displayed" in art museums, special places built specifically for the enjoyment of art. The division of roles is clear: a piece of art is shaped and given a meaning by the artist, the consumer, or "art connoisseur", can observe and make his interpretation, but he is clearly separated from the artwork. By stripping painting from everything that is usually connected with meaning, by presenting pure white surfaces, minimalist artists forced the artwork to take on meaning through observation. Minimalist art is different from concept art, where a blank sheet would not reflect the onlooker's thoughts but would be based on the artist's (possibly most complex) conception. Minimal art cannot stand for itself, it is not depictive yet it also does not require explanation. This consciously unartistic method of producing art creates a new freedom of meaning for the spectator, who in turn becomes part of the artwork.

2.4.6 The Minimalist Perspective and Criticism

Many artists that were associated with the label of minimalism did not agree. Partly, this is because artists never like labels, they tend to understand their work as unique, and consequently resist categorization. And partly, it is because minimalism is understood as a negative term. It denotes the minimal—that which is so reduced that there is nothing that could be less.

Minimalism is thus often linked with the obscure and simplistic. This critique, however, does not extend deep enough. Minimal art seems simplistic only if the effect is examined without observing the cause—minimalism is as much a set of mind as it is a set of practices. A canvas painted with pure white enamel paint, without traces of the artist remaining, is meaningless without the conception of the artist behind it. For the artists, as for this book, this theoretical conception behind minimal works is crucial.

However, this highlights an important quality of the minimalist perspective: it draws attention to the extreme. A key "feature" of the notion of minimalism is its ability to draw critique. As modern electronic musicians, designers must decide how far towards the minimal they dare go.

References

Albers, J. (1963). *Interaction of Color*. New Haven and London: Yale University Press.

Albers, J., and Weber, N. F. (1988). *Josef Albers: A Retrospective*. New York: Solomon R. Guggenheim Foundation.

Alloway, L. (1966). Systemic Painting. Introductory essay from the exhibition catalogue systemic painting, Solomon R. Guggenheim foundation, New York. In G Battcock (Ed.), *Minimal Art: A Critical Anthology. 1995.* 37–60. Berkeley, Los Angeles and London: University of California Press.

Antonio, Ed. (1981). Interview between Emile de Antonio and Frank Stella. *GEO Magazine.* Special New York. Hamburg: Gruner + Jahr.

Ashton, D. (1982). *American Art Since 1945.* Oxford: Oxford University Press, USA.

Aynsley, J. (2001). *A Century of Graphic Design.* Hauppauge, N.Y: Barron's Educational Series.

Barth, J. (1986, 28 December). A few words about minimalism. *The New York Times Book Review,* 36(2), 25.

Barthelme, F. (1988, 3 April). On being wrong: Convicted minimalist spills bean [sic]. *New York Times Book Review,* 25–27.

Battcock, G. (1968). *Minimal Art: A Critical Anthology* (1st ed.). New York: E. P. Dutton.

Bernard, J. W. (1993). The minimalist aesthetic in the plastic arts and in music. *Perspectives of New Music,* 31(1), 86–132.

Bertoni, F. (2002). *Minimalist Architecture.* Birlhauser (Princeton Architectural Press).

Birkerts, S. (1986). The school of Lish. *The New Republic,* 28–33.

Bourdon, D. (1968). The razed sites of Carl Andro. In G Battcock (Ed.), *Minimal art: A critical anthology.* (pp. 103–108). New York, NY: EP Dutton & Co.

Böhr, C. (1985). *Liberalismus und Minimalismus.* Decker R. Von.

Bradley-Hole, C. (1999). *The Minimalist Garden.* Monacelli.

Cage, J. (1961). *John Cage: Silence. Lectures and Writings by J.C.* Middletown, Conn.: Wesleyan University Press.

Cage, J. (1991). An autobiographical statement. *Southwest Review,* 76(1), 59.

Castillo, E. (2004). *Minimalism DesignSource (DesignSource).* Collins Design.

Colpitt, F. (1990). *Minimal Art: The Critical Perspective.* Ann Arbor: UMI Research Press.

Cuito, A. (2002a). *Minimalist Lofts.* Loft & Hbi.

Cuito, A. (2001). *Minimalist Spaces: Housing/Commercial Spaces/Offices and Public Buildings.* HBI.

Cuito, A. (2002b). *From Minimalism to Maximalism.* Loft Publications S.L. and Hbi.

Cummings, P. (1974). Interview with Sol LeWitt.

Ferebee, A. (1994). *A History of Design from the Victorian Era to the Present: A Survey of the Modern Style in Architecture, Interior Design, Industrial Design, Graphic Design, and Photography.* Van Nostrand Reinhold/co Wiley.

Fried, M. (1998). *Art and Objecthood: Essays and Reviews.* Chicago: University of Chicago Press.

Fried, M. (1966). Shape as form: Frank Stella's new paintings. *Artforum,* 5(3), 18–27.

Friedman, D. S. (1995). Public things in the modern city: Belated notes on "Tilted Arc" and the Vietnam Veterans memorial. *Journal of Architectural Education,* 49(2), 62–78.

Gardner, J. (1991). *The Art of Fiction: Notes on Craft for Young Writers (Vintage).* Vintage.

Gena, P. (1981). Freedom in Experimental Music: The New York Revolution. *Tri-Quarterly,* 52, 223–243.

Glaser, B. (1966). Questions to Stella and Judd. Art News, Reprinted in: Battcock, Gregory (ed.): *Minimal Art: A Critical Anthology.* University of California Press, Berkeley, Los Angeles and London, 148–164, 1995.

Good, J. V., and Good, P. (1995). Is functionalism functional? The relationship between function and purity. *Communication Arts,* 37(1), 27.

Greenberg, C. (1962). After abstract expressionism. *Art International,* VI(8), 30–32.

Hallett, C. W. (2000). *Minimalism and the Short Story–Raymond Carver, Amy Hempel, and Mary Robison (Studies in Comparative Literature).* Edwin Mellen Press.

Hess, T. B. (1963). The phony crisis in American art. *Art News, Summer,* 24–28.

Hutchings, W. (1986). Abated drama: Samuel Beckett's unbated 'breath'. *Ariel,* 17, 85–94.

Johnson, T. (1991). *The Voice of New Music.*

Judd, D. (1975). *Complete Writings 1959–1975.* New York: New York University Press.

Katzen, M. (2006). Delicious minimalism. *Harvard Magazine,*31–32.

Klinkowitz, J. (1993). The new fiction. In M Cunliffe (Ed.), *The Penguin History of Literature: American Literature since 1900.* 353–367.

Kosuth, J. (1991). *Art After Philosophy and After: Collected Writings, 1966–1990.* Cambridge, Mass: MIT Press.

Krauss, R. E. (1977). *Passages in Modern Sculpture.*

Krauss, R. E. (1991). Overcoming the limits of matter: On revising minimalism. In J. Elderfield (Ed.), *American Art of the 1960s.* New York: Museum of Modern Art.

Levin, K. (1979). Farewell to modernism. *Arts Magazine*, 54(2), 90–91.

Levy, L. (1996). *Peter Walker Minimalist Gardens.* Whitney Library of Design.

LeWitt, S. (1978a). Paragraphs on conceptual art. In A Legg (Ed.), *Sol LeWitt.* New York: The Museum of Modern Art.

LeWitt, S. (1978b). The cube. In A Legg (Ed.), *Sol LeWitt.* New York: The Museum of Modern Art.

Lippard, L. (1967). Sol LeWitt: Non-visual structures. *Artforum, April 1967*, 42–46.

Lippard, L. (1981). *Ad Reinhardt.* New York: Abrams.

McCoy, K. (1995). Graphic design in a multicultural world. *HOW: The Bottomline Design Magazine*, X (2), 146–147.

Mertens, W. (1983). *American Minimal Music.* London: Kahn & Averill.

Meyer, J. S. (2001). *Minimalism: Art and Polemics in the Sixties.* New Haven: Yale University Press.

Morris, R. (1966). Notes on Sculpture, part 2. *Artforum,* Reprinted in: Battcock, Gregory (ed.): *Minimal Art: A Critical Anthology.* University of California Press, Berkeley, Los Angeles and London, 228–235, 1995.

Newman, B., O'Neill, J. P., and McNickle, M. (1990). *Barnett Newman: Selected Writings and Interviews*(1st ed ed.). New York: Knopf : Distributed by Random House.

Nozick, R. (1974). *Anarchy, State, and Utopia.* New York: Basic Books.

Nyman, M. (1972). S R-mysteries of the phase. *Music and Musicians, June 1972*, 20–21.

Nyman, M. (1974). *Experimental Music: Cage and Beyond.* New York: Schirmer.

O'Bryan, L. (2002). *Minimalist Interiors.* Atrium Publishers Group.

Osborne, H. (1988). *The Oxford Companion to Twentieth-Century Art.* Oxford [Oxfordshire]; New York: Oxford University Press.

Perreault, J. (1968). Simple, not simple-minded. *Village Voice,*16–17.

Perreault, J. (1967). The term minimal. *Arts,* Reprinted in: Battcock, Gregory (ed.): *Minimal Art: A Critical Anthology.* University of California Press, Berkeley, Los Angeles and London, 260–261, 1995.

Petterson, E. (2004). *New Minimalist Architecture.* Collins Design.

Petterson, E. (2003). *Minimalist Architecture.* Atrium Publishers Group.

Poe, E. A. (1842, April). Twice-told tales. Graham's Magazine, Reprinted in *Edgar Allan Poe: Essays and Reviews,* The Library of America, 1984, 568–569.

Potter, K. (2000). *Four Musical Minimalists: La Monte Young, Terry Riley, Steve Reich, Philip Glass (Music in the Twentieth Century S.).* Cambridge University Press.

Potter, K., and Smith, D. (1976). Interview with Philip Glass. *Contact*, 13, 25.

Reason, R. (2001). Typography: Less Is More. http://www.poynter.org/dg.lts/id.33/aid.3308/column.htm Accessed 12.10.2008

Reinhardt, A. (1975). *Art-as-Art: Selected Writings of Ad Reinhardt.* New York: Viking.

Riley, T. (1964). In C.

Rockwell, J. (1986, December 21). The death and life of minimalism. *New York Times*, p. 29.

Rose, B. (1987). Interview with Robert Rauschenberg. *Rauschenberg.* New York: Vintage.

Rose, B. (1965a). Looking at American sculpture. *Artforum,* 29–36.

Rose, B. (1965b). ABC Art. *Art in America,* 57–69.

Rosenberg, H. (1964). *The Anxious Object.* Chicago: University of Chicago Press.

Rosenblum, R. (1965). Frank Stella. *Artforum,* III(6), 20–25.

Rossell, Q. (2005). *Minimalist Interiors.* Collins Design.

Sandler, I. (1968). Gesture and non-gesture in recent sculpture. In G Battcock (Ed.), *Minimal art.* (pp. 308–316). New York, NY: EP Dutton & Co.

Sartre, J-P. (1965). *What is Literature?* New York, NY: Harper.

Schulze, F. (1986). *Mies Van Der Rohe.* Germany: Ernst,Wilhelm & Sohn,Verlag fur Architektur und Technische Wissenschaften Gmbh.

Schwartz, K. R. (1996). *Minimalists (20th-century Composers S.).* Phaidon Press.

Senie, H. (2002). *The Tilted Arc Controversy: Dangerous Precedent?* Minnesota: University of Minnesota Press.

Serra, R., and Weyergraf-Serra, C. (1980). *Richard Serra, Interviews, etc., 1970–1980.* Yonkers, N.Y. (Trevor Park-on-Hudson) [S.l.]: Hudson River Museum Distributed by Art Catalogues.

Smith, D. (1977). Following a straight line: La Monte young. *Contact*, 18, 4–9.

Smith, G., and Smith, N. W. (1994). *American Originals: Interviews with 25 Contemporary Composers.* London ; Boston: Faber and Faber.

Spector, N. (1974). Essential painting. *Robert Mangold.* La Jolla: La Jolla Museum of Contemporary Art.

Strickland, E. (1991). *American Composers: Dialogues on Contemporary Music.* Bloomington: Indiana University Press.

Strickland, E. (2000). *Minimalism: Origins* (2nd edition ed.). Bloomington: Indiana University Press.

Tomkins, C. (1981). *Off the Wall: Robert Rauschenberg and the Art World of Our Time.* New York: Penguin Books.

Trussler, M. (1994). The narrowed voice: Minimalism and Raymond Carver. *Studies in Short Fiction, 31.*

Tschichold, J. (1928). *Die neue Typographie : ein Handbuch für zeitgemäss Schaffende*(1. bis 5. Tsd ed.). Berlin: Verl. des Bildungsverb. der Dt. Buchdrucker.

Varian, E. (1967). Schemata 7 catalogue.

Venturi, R., Scott, B., Denise, and Izenour, S. (1972). *Learning from Las Vegas.* Cambridge, Mass: MIT Press.

Wanner, A. (2003). *Russian Minimalism: From the Prose Poem to the Anti-Story* (Studies in Russian literature and theory). Evanston, Ill: Northwestern University Press.

Wollheim, R. I. (1965). Minimal art. *Arts Magazine, January 1965*, 26–32.

Young, L. M., and Zazeela, M. (1969). *Selected Writings.* Munich: Heiner Friefrich.

Zelevansky, L. (1991). Ad Reinhardt and the younger artists of the 1960s. In J. Elderfield (Ed.), *American Art of the 1960s.* New York: Museum of Modern Art.

Chapter 3
Minimalism for Interaction Design: a Proposal

This chapter lies at the heart of this book: it puts forward four notions of minimalism as tools for the analysis and design of interactive systems. The notions of minimalism presented here can be used to describe *motivations* underlying use-centered design; they focus on a particular set of goals for human-computer interaction shared by experts who would otherwise hesitate to agree with each other. While this role could also be fulfilled by the related notion of "simplicity"—an often-used value in human-computer interaction, the latter is, as an exclusively positive term, difficult to criticize, and thus less useful for analysis and reflection. The four notions of minimalism presented here promise a more accurate understanding of the what and where of reduction and suggest themselves for a more detailed analysis of design.

Before introducing the perspective that is created through the transfer of minimalism to design, human-computer interaction (HCI) is defined as the target domain of the transfer (Section 3.1), and differences of the new terminology and both simplicity (Section 3.2.1) and existing concepts of minimalism (Sections 3.2.2, 3.2.3, 3.2.4, and 3.2.5) are examined to minimize the risk of misunderstandings. Consequently, functional, structural, architectural and compositional minimalism are defined as four notions of minimalism (Sections 3.3.1, 3.3.2, 3.3.3, and 3.3.4), and their interrelationships are discussed to form a minimalist terminology.

3.1 Meanings of Minimalism in HCI—A Transfer from the Arts

Although the design of interactive systems is sometimes called an "art" (Laurel, 1990; Bickford, 1997; Cameron and Limited, 2004), this is done more in mockery than in admiration. Design is often seen as a craft (Wroblewski, 1991)—and for commercial applications, designers of interactive systems often have a training that is unlike the instruction of artists, or even designers: a team of "interface designers" can consist exclusively of technically trained (software) engineers. Engineering typically seeks to provide optimal solutions for well-specified problems: the Encyclopedia Britannica defines engineering as the "professional art of applying science to the optimum conversion of the resources

H. Obendorf, *Minimalism*, Human-Computer Interaction Series,
DOI 10.1007/978-1-84882-371-6_3, © Springer-Verlag London Limited 2009

of nature to the uses of humankind" (Britannica, 2003). The specification of requirements for complex interactive systems represents a new dimension of complexity (Pohl, 1997; Nuseibeh and Easterbrook, 2000). As it is difficult to perfect systems for a constantly evolving and inherently imperfect context, this has lead to approaches that separate the computational from the contextual: Dijkstra (1989; 1981) used the metaphor of a firewall that would separate all imperfection from the programmer's view. However, this only relocates the responsibility of dealing with real-world applications, and in practice, ignorance of the context is not helpful (Coy, 1997)—a "design" approach is required that considers the activities and needs of end users (comp. Oberquelle, 2005; Winograd and Flores, 1987). Floyd (1993) introduced a process perspective to software engineering that is based on the assumption that design is not limited to the product, but that the process of design must also be subject to active development during software construction (comp. also Floyd, 1994).

This balance between the technical engineering side and the artistic designer's view is a difficult one (comp. Mackay and Fayard, 1997; Wolf et al., 2006), and requires this text to follow both a more formal approach, and the abstract perspective on design. To satisfy the former, the object of study must first be defined more clearly. This starts with the context in which the notion of minimalism is to be used: the design of interactive systems. While the definition for interactive systems is rather undisputed (Definition 3.1), the engineer's perspective manifests itself already in the terms "user" and "user interface" (Definition 3.2).

Definition 3.1 Interactive systems *Interactive systems* are a class of information processing systems where control is exerted *by users* in an *interactive* manner.

Definition 3.2 User Interface The interaction between a user and an interactive system is mediated by a *user interface*, which comprises *all parts*—both hardware and software—of the interactive system *with which the user is able to interact*. (comp. Moran, 1981) The term user interface is elsewhere sometimes used in a broader sense that includes the aesthetic appearance of the device and the content that is presented to the user within the context of the user interface (e.g. Preece, 1994).

Definition 3.3 Human-Computer Interaction *Human-Computer Interaction (HCI)* is the process of *information exchange between a user and an interactive system*. The quality of HCI is usually measured based on the effectiveness and efficiency in accomplishing pre-defined goals for (work) tasks and the satisfaction of the user. (ISO 9241, 1998)

Grudin raises the point of distinguishing between "'the user interface' to a computer and 'the computer interface' to a user or users" (Grudin, 1990a, 1): the normal, "technology-centered" use of the term, which is also adopted in this book—the *user* interface is seen as part of the *system*—shows that the engineer's focus on the system is prone to mask requirements of the user (Grudin, 1990b); the problem is even more severe for groups of users and their requirements (Grudin, 1990a).

A more complete view on user interfaces has been advocated by numerous disciplines, making HCI (Definition 3.3) an intensively interdisciplinary field (comp. Myers et al., 1996; Rozanski and Haake, 2003): to provide some examples, psychologists have increased awareness of "human factors", cognitive scientists stressed the relevance of information processing and learned to value (Winograd and Flores, 1987), perusing anthropology, ethnomethodological observation techniques were introduced to study the behavior of users in their natural habitats (Suchman et al., 1987; Button and Dourish, 1996; Martin and Sommerville, 2004), following activity theory lead Bødker to stress that "users interface through computers with their work" (Bødker, 1990), and distributed cognition theory was used to explain the role of environments (Hutchins, 1996; Hollan et al., 2000).

In this study, the term *use-centered design* (comp. Vredenburg et al., 2002) will be used as it integrates the two before-mentioned notions of interface and the examination of user needs as well as the analysis of technological possibilities in a single term (Definition 3.3). Use-centered design is also not only interested in the user and his/her well-being, it assumes a holistic socio-technical perspective that includes other tools, and work practices to contextualize the user's needs, his/her perception, intentions and goals. Minimalism, here, is used as a term to analyze aspects that touch both the users' goals, needs and tasks and the material structure and technological architecture of design artifacts— following the tradition of industrial design, the user interface and the machine interface, the task structure and the system structure are taken to be interdependent.

> **Definition 3.4 Use-centered design** *Use-centered design* focuses on the goals and tasks associated with the use of technology. As user-centered design, it tries to structure the functioning of a user interface around how people can, want or need to work, rather than the opposite way around. The focus is, however, not on the user alone, but also on the tool and the task. (cf. Flach and Dominguez, 1995)

3.2 Defining Four Notions of the Minimal for Interaction Design

As minimalism is proposed as a tool to further the understanding of designing interactive systems, a first step is determining what aspects of the notion of minimalism in the fine arts are applicable to human-computer interaction, and what aspects cannot be transferred easily. It might be useful at this point to revisit the initial motivation to propose minimalism as a desirable alternative. This motivation starts with interactive systems that become too complex to be usable—McGrenere et al. (2002) introduced the term *feature creep* for a frequent cause: the tendency of software products to accumulate more and more features, thus becoming more and more, and eventually too powerful. This in turn leads to *feature fatigue* (Thompson et al., 2005) on behalf of the users: the goal is the design of simpler systems. As the inner complexity of interactive systems is, however, often caused by the complexity of the environment, designers cannot reduce inner complexity as they wish. While artists can reduce the statement of their work, and can fall back on enamel paint or the bare canvas to minimalize their art, designers must take into account the application context. Also, "industrial production" does not present an exception as it does in art, where the stroke of the painter was long taken as a measurement for quality—instead, "industrially" produced interactive systems must cope with a wide variety of situations.

This illustrates that a literal transfer of minimalism is of little use. What can be transferred is the mindset that stands behind employing minimal means, creating minimal structures, using minimal pattern, and including the recipient's interpretation in the initial design. For this book, these concepts define the minimalist standpoint[1] that is for HCI here defined in the following four notions of minimalism:

Definition 3.5 Four notions of minimalism *Functional minimalism* denotes the reduction of the functionality of an interface. Ideally, only necessary core functionality is left in a functionally minimal design.

Structural minimalism refers to an access structure for an interface's functionality that is perceived to be minimal. In an ideal structurally minimal system, immediate support is lent by appropriate functionality.

Architectural minimalism focuses on reducing the complexity of an interface by transparently distributing its functionality across minimal parts. As an ideal result, the overall complexity is reduced without compromising the power of an architecturally minimal design.

Compositional minimalism stresses the importance of the appropriation process for an interface. Paradoxically, compositionally minimal design must allow use patterns to develop after the design activity is over.

After an extended but necessary discussion of different interpretations of minimalism not covered in this book, defining what minimalism denotes here takes but a few words. The four notions that are presented above as a brief, informal characterization of the underlying ideas are in the following paragraphs, individually deduced from characteristics of minimalism in the liberal arts and music, and set in relation to existing uses of the defining adjuncts before

---

[1] The term *standpoint* was chosen here to distinguish the individual minimalist perspective that relates to one of the four notions of minimalism from the stance that all four perspectives share. Although minimalism lacks the social orientation that is customarily associated with a standpoint (comp. SEP, 2003), it shares the claim of epistemic privilege over what construes reduction, and simplicity.

a more formal definition is given. What follows is a discussion of the possible interaction between the different notions of minimalism—based on their roots in the other disciplines.

3.2.1 Minimal Functionality for User Interfaces

As mentioned in the previous chapter, painting in minimalism tried to further reduce modern painting. This was achieved in two distinct ways, that of reducing the means, and that of reducing the meaning. While the reduction of means focused on the artist, his actions, and on the concept of artistry, the reduction of meaning used similar techniques, but focused on the *function* of painting. Once the depiction of reality was devalued by photography, abstract painting focused on depicting the unreal—and carried it to an extreme: painting was considered to be nothing but what is visible; color and form stood only for themselves. Thus, painting became devoid of function; in Reinhardt's words, it became "art-as-art" (Reinhardt, 1975, 53).

Although some interaction designers go to similar extremes and design objects that are without a function, more often, the extreme minimum of functionality is a singular function. The idea underlying this *functional minimalism* is grounded in a common observation: a good tool can often *only* do one thing, yet do this one thing very well. The concentration on a single purpose allows it to be adapted very well to the task, trading off flexibility. The focus on the whole is translated as a focused competency of the tool: as the tool's functionality is clearly defined, all energies can be concentrated on perfecting its performance. The construction of such tools is common in many traditional crafts; an example for classes of such tools would be the variety of hammers and drills a woodworker chooses according to the task.

Between interactive systems and manual tools, however, there is a difference in complexity: while the construction process of an analog tool, such as a hammer or drill, may be based on complex testing and accumulated experience, and the production process can be very elaborate (e.g. for damascene steel), the resulting tool itself is often not complex. Interactive systems, however, are almost never internally simple, as even the operating systems needed as a basis are the most complex construct. Thus, the focus of *functional minimalism* is not on building simple tools in a simple way, it is about perceiving tools as functionallyminimal— i.e. as useful for only a single purpose. As perceived functionality is not a reliable measure, the stricter notion of *accessible functionality* takes its place. A functionally minimal tool (e.g. a mobile phone) can have complex functionality (e.g. accessing radio cells, choosing a provider, keeping track of battery life) that— as long as it is never visible to the user—does not decrease its functional minimality.

Definition 3.6 Functional Minimalism *Functional Minimalism* refers to a reduction in *accessible functionality*. An interactive system is increasingly *minimal$_F$* as it presents fewer features to the user. A *minimal$_F$* system is identified by its focused competency.

3.2.2 Minimal Structure for User Interfaces

It is very tempting to take functional minimalism as the most important quality that minimal products can possibly have. If the purpose of a device is both singular and clearly defined, the ideal consequence is that the device simply functions—without navigational overhead. However, examples that come close are either replacing technology with intelligence, e.g. in the beginning of the phone era, where operators did all the work, or devices that must operate in emergency situations, where operational mistakes can be fatal or high stress is expected (e.g. elevator intercoms tend to have few buttons). Few technical designs are that simple in terms of functionality.

Instead, complexity could almost be said to be a hallmark of digital designs. As computers are understood as universal machines, there is obviously little that they can't do, and less that products don't promise to do. Striving for functional simplicity directly conflicts with the users' call for power that is amplified by marketing (feature comparison) and echoed in research and development (feature addition). Thus, an often- sought solution is to create not a product that is actually minimal in features, but to change its *perception* towards the minimal.

One aspect of minimalist painting is that it tried to reduce the function of the artwork; consequently, the inner structure was minimized. While this compares to functional minimalism, structural minimalism is more similar to another perspective inherent in minimalism: other minimalist art only tried to seem simple—either through making its structure transparent, or by cleverly hiding complexity (Section 2.4.3). The latter approach is mirrored in digital designs—here, complexity is commonly hidden through layered *access* to features—functionality that is generally used more often, or in specific, system-determinable situations, is made directly accessible; if necessary, this involves a trade-off where less immediately necessary functionality is made more difficult to access. Structural minimalism describes this reduction of structure in designs—and focuses the meaning of structure to the *structural access to functionality*. By contrast, computer science usually uses structure in a broader sense, and includes the invisible inner structure; within the context of this book, inner structure that remains invisible is of no interest, and inner structure that defines the interface is covered by the notion of architectural minimalism below.

> **Definition 3.7 Structural Minimalism.** *Structural Minimalism* refers to a reduction in *perceived access structure*— in some cases, this is equivalent to a reduction in *visible functionality*. An interactive system is increasingly *minimal$_S$* as it confronts the user with less navigational structure. A *minimal$_S$* system is discerned by its optimal fit of provided and necessary functionality—at any point in time.

3.2.3 Minimal Architecture for User Interfaces

Taking seriously the idea that interaction design reaches beyond designing pretty (useful) interfaces, architectural minimalism takes a more technical perspective to the adaptation of functionality to use situations, and focuses on the activity of *building*, or on the resulting *construction* of the interactive system. The etymology of architecture leaves wide room for interpretations of the term: the Greek "master builder" (a compound of αρχι, "chief", and τεκτων, "builder, carpenter") has, in modern architecture, developed into a designer, engineer, and facilitator (comp. Kostof, 1977, 324; Straus and Doyle, 1978). Architecture is interpreted as "the art of the articulation of spaces" (Zevi, 1957), and although architecture lacks the self-referential and self-modifying power of language (Johnson, 1994, 423), it shares with language the quality of communication; "the public can respond to the explicit metaphors and messages of the sculptors" (Jencks, 1977, 6).

This wide spectrum of meanings is echoed in the current use of the term architecture in computer science, where it is mainly referred to in software engineering: Architecture is used to describe both the (social) process (comp. e.g. Coplien, 1999) and the product of conscious structuring activities aiming to improve the legibility, maintainability, and reusability of source code (e.g. Bass et al., 1998). As software engineering focuses on the engineering process used to manufacture complex software systems, architecture defines in this scope the internal qualities of a software, and need not be visible to the end user at all (Floyd and Oberquelle, 2003).

Within the context of this book, the use of architecture is not limited to the domain of implementation; instead, based on the focus on user interface design, *minimal architecture* refers to qualities of building and construction that are still visible in the design and can be experienced by the end user. This use of architecture is more closely related to another use of the term in computer science: the notion of information architecture, which is used to describe the practice of structuring information (for the World Wide Web). Its definitions tend to extreme generality; Wurman and Bradford (1996) defined information architecture as "the merging of three fields: technology, graphic design, and writing/journalism"; due to these different perspectives, collaborative definitions of information architecture add little detail, e.g. "Information Architecture is inherent, practical or theoretical knowledge having to do with the presentation of written, spoken, graphical or other information." (IAwiki, 2006). By contrast, architectural minimalism puts emphasis only on the reductive qualities of "architectural practice" in design.

Based on the characteristics of minimalism identified in the previous chapter, the architectural perspective on the interfaces of interactive systems focuses on how necessary complexity can be achieved with simple elements that are combined transparently for the end user—as elements of a music piece or of a piece of artwork can be simple in themselves, yet complex in combination (Section 2.4.4). An architecturally minimal system groups functionality according to its use; unlike the perspective defined by structural minimalism, architectural minimalism starts beneath the superficial understanding of interface: minimal building blocks are combined as simple, identifiable tools—just like the reduced form of the square used by minimalist artists—to form a more complex system. Acknowledging the fact that few information processing tasks can be solved by appliances, finding small, comprehensible or at least recognizable parts within the system helps the user to understand system reactions and correctly predict system behavior.

Definition 3.8 Architectural Minimalism. *Architectural Minimalism* refers to a reduction of perceived complexity by *externally visible distribution of responsibility* (in the sense of partitioning of functionality). An interactive system is increasingly *minimal$_A$* as it provides combinable blocks of coherent functionality to the user. A *minimal$_A$* system is typically not adapted to a specific task. Through combined use of its parts, necessary functionality can be combined as necessary.

3.2.4 Minimal Composition for User Interfaces

The design of interactive systems is often based on predictions about their use— and taking them for truth, will often determine exactly how they are to be used and consequently, how tasks have to flow, how work is to be performed. Although a functional specification, and thus implementation, is aided by clear and well-defined sequences of activities, from the perspective of human-computer interaction, the trade-off in flexibility can overshadow the technical benefits.

In art, many artists are very decided on what their works describe, and what they mean. Some minimalist artists took a different stance: the spectator was included in the work as the meaning unfolded only with the viewing, and the personal experience was valued above the artist's private conception. In minimal music, the "formal specification" of music was often considered less valuable than the experience created by performing a piece with other musicians (Section 2.4.5).

Compositional minimalism stresses that the performance is more important than the composition—it proposes that composition should be minimal in order to allow a maximum of interpretation. As minimalist painters stressed that the value of their pictures lies within the spectator, the value of an interactive system does not exist without its users. For a tool to be optimally useful, it must do the user's bidding, not the other way around. However, even when a tool is designed with minimal functionality, and more so when it is designed for a single task, unnecessary constraints might be introduced. Like the minimalist composers, designers should carefully consider where one should refrain from assuming use contexts and well-defined sequences of actions to be static. If it is possible to limit the design to minimal use patterns that can be appropriated in use, the result is a more flexible design. This does not mean that tools should not be conceived for a very specific purpose—examples for successful adoption for other tasks will be given. Instead, the modularity of a system should not only be considered on an infrastructure level, but also on a task level: systems should be designed in a way that their building blocks can be combined in new ways to master new use situations.

Definition 3.9 Compositional Minimalism. *Compositional Minimalism* refers to a reduction of aspects decreasing the tool's usefulness for other tasks through *specificity for planned tasks*. An interactive system is increasingly *minimal$_C$* as it makes fewer assumptions about its use and places less restrictions upon its users. A *minimal$_C$* system encourages its use in contexts and tasks not considered during design.

3.2.5 A Minimalist Terminology for the Design of Interactive Systems

In the previous sections, differences between the four notions of minimalism put forward here have been marked out. All four notions of minimalism describe aspects in which the design of a *user interface* for an interactive system can be considered minimal, and although they are each based on a different understanding on what should be minimized, some overlap, or at least strong interactions between the different notions can be observed. To illustrate this, the four notions of minimalism have been laid out as four sectors (Table 3.1): Functional minimalism and structural minimalism both affect the system's *user interface* directly, while architectural and compositional minimalism work at different levels, namely the inner construction of the system and the

Table 3.1 Arrangement of the four notions of minimalism in four fields

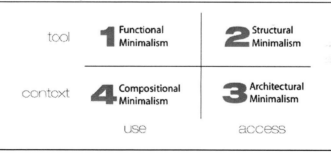

users' "interface" to the system, or the integration with other tools. Structural and architectural minimalism both focus on adapting the tool to the task, modifying the structure by which functionality is accessed, while functional and compositional minimalism stress the use of the tool and the context of use.

Each of the four notions of minimalism defines a different perspective on an interaction design; although different designs will exhibit properties that match these notions to different degrees, it will be difficult to impossible to find practical examples demonstrating to a single notion of minimalism. How much conceptual overlap exists is best demonstrated in the practical application of the notions of minimalism for analysis (Chapter 6). Here, some of the manifold interactions between the different notions of minimalism are anticipated:

(1–2) Functional and structural minimalism: Minimal functionality can be easily provided using a minimal structure—fewer functions are less difficult to structure. At first glance, a differentiation between functional and structural minimalism might, thus, not seem useful. However, although a truly minimal functionality (a single function) can map naturally to a minimal access structure (a single button), the reverse is not necessarily given. As the example of the Morse key (Section 3.2.1) demonstrated, the two notions of minimalism are almost perpendicular: a minimal access structure can be created for complex functionality. And even for a minimal functionality, a complex access structure can be constructed by introducing many options that concern the status of the tool instead of the task. The minimality of an access structure—its "optimal fit of provided and necessary functionality" (Definition 3.6)—becomes effective only if a prioritization of functionality is possible. Alan Kay coined the proverb "Simple things should be simple. Complex things should be possible" on this subject (Smith et al., 1982).

(2–3) Structural and architectural minimalism: Both structural and architectural minimalism affect the perceived access structure to functionality. The difference given in the definitions is that structural minimalism concerns primarily the superficial structure that is overlaid on functionality to make it accessible, while architectural minimalism also denotes the internal construction of an interactive system; it suggests distributing functionality over building blocks that transparently form the overall design. A challenge for the latter part of this book is thus to test whether this discrimination yields practical value analyzing and constructing interactive systems. Often in HCI, the difference between superficial decoration, access structure (information design) and system construction is blurred; however, the tendency to prefer early intervention by usability methods is clear and partly stems from the desire to reorganize work rather than screen layout (def. interaction design, CD, etc.). Architectural minimalism as defined here minimizes the access structure of a design, as a clear division of work between individual tools (i) allows the user to choose his tools, and (ii) makes the individual tools functionally simpler.

(3–4) Architectural and compositional minimalism: As the summary of the use of building blocks in minimalism suggests (Section 2.4.4), an architecturally minimal system will enable interpretation by the user, and thus further the system's qualities that are referred to by compositional minimalism. Common to both architectural and compositional minimalism is a design perspective that includes aspects going beyond the single product. Architectural minimalism tries to partition functionality within a single application or environment into interoperable modules. Compositional minimalism tries to extend the usefulness of a design beyond a single application or environment; much of the still-emerging field of ubiquitous computing that interacts with stationary computing systems applies a mixture of both minimalisms. Another, more technical, area where architectural and compositional minimalism overlap is the development of open standards for data interoperability (e.g. in the World Wide Web). The minimalisms differ in perspective; while architectural minimalism explicitly considers the

whole functionality of a design, compositional minimalism focuses on the use of often only partial functionality within a larger context.

(4–1) Compositional and functional minimalism: To demonstrate differences between compositional and functional minimalism, the analogy of the simple craftsmen's tools that make a skillful orchestration of different tools necessary must be extended as, in this example, compositional and functional minimalism seem to fall together. While functional minimalism often creates the need for more tools and thus the basis for an orchestrated activity, compositional minimalism is possible using very complex tools (e.g. a combination of spreadsheet, statistics, drawing, and text-processing software is often used to generate scientific illustrations, engaging only a tiny subset of functionality of the complex systems involved in the process). Compositional minimalism is thus about interoperability and about enabling the user to orchestrate use of component working together to achieve the set goal—different tools within a software, different applications within a system, or even different systems within a network are used to implement his/her instructions.

The relationship of notions of minimalism that are arranged in adjacent fields in Table 3.1 is comparatively close and some conceptual overlap exists. Looking at the more remotely connected notions of minimalism, the differences become clearer:

(1–3) Functional and architectural minimalism: Both functional and architectural minimalism reduce functionality; the scope of reduction in functional minimalism is the total design; in architectural functionality, functionality is reduced by defining modules that encapsulate functionality that is similar with regard to the task. The resulting partition of functionality remains visible in the user interface—their appearance can range from "sub-applications" to "inspector tools". A functionally minimal system is, by definition, difficult to split into several parts, and architecturally minimal systems are designed to allow complex interactions of their building blocks—thus, they are often not functionally minimal. Functional and architectural minimalism can thus be considered *alternative approaches* to reduction.

(2–4) Structural and compositional minimalism: Making the life of users easier is the purpose of both structural and compositional minimalism; both try to give the user more freedom, structural minimalism by freeing her from unnecessary navigation, compositional minimalism by removing unnecessary workflows that might contradict her action plans. However, following a paradigm of structural minimalism can effect a more restrictive composition; as the access structure is increasingly tailored for one task, it assumes a standard workflow that will help those following it, but make "creative misuse", or appropriation (cf. Pipek, 2005) more difficult.

3.3 Summary

This chapter defined four notions of minimalism that apply to the design of interactive systems. The four notions draw on aspects of minimalism that were identified in the last chapter as being shared by art, music and other disciplines

(Section 2.4). Each notion identifies an individual perspective on design, and suggests a certain form of reduction.

The four fields for reduction are the *functionality*, the *structure*, the *architecture*, and the *composition* of a design. Together, these four different interpretations of minimalism form a minimalist standpoint that goes beyond simplicity[2] (Section 3.2.1) and differs from existing concepts that are used by computer science (Sections 3.2.2, 3.2.3, 3.2.4, and 3.2.5).

The definition of four different notions of minimalism (Sections 3.3.1, 3.3.2, 3.3.3, and 3.3.4) does not imply that a designer can assume one of the presented perspectives, and reduce without influencing other aspects of her design. Instead, some conceptual overlap, and interactions between the different notions of minimalism are made explicit (Section 3.3.5).

References

Bass, L., Clements, P., and Kazman, R. (1998). *Software Architecture in Practice*. Reading, Mass: Addison-Wesley.

Bickford, P. (1997). *Interface Design: The Art of Developing Easy-to-Use Software*. San Francisco: Morgan Kaufmann Pub.

Bødker, S. (1990). *Through the Interface – A Human Activity Approach to User Interface Design*. Hillsdale, NJ: Lawrence Erlbaum Associates.

Britannica. (2003). *Encyclopedia Britannica: With 2004 Book of the Year (Britannica Books)*. Encyclopedia Britannica Corporation.

Button, G., and Dourish, P. (1996). *Technomethodology: Paradoxes and Possibilities*. CHI '96: Proceedings of the SIGCHI conference on Human factors in computing systems, New York, NY, USA, 19–26.

Cameron, A., and Limited, S. D. (2004). *IdN Special 04 – The Art of Experimental Interaction Design*. Berkeley, CA: Gingko Press.

Coplien, J. O. (1999). Re-evaluating the architectural metaphor: Towards piecemeal growth. Guest editor introduction to IEEE Software Special Issue. *IEEE Software Special Issue on Architecture Design*, 16(5), 40–44.

Coy, W. (1997). Defining discipline. In C Freksa, M Jantzen, and R Valk (Eds.), *Foundations of Computer Science*. Berlin-Heidelberg-New York: Springer.

Dijkstra, E. W. (1981). The Psychology of the User. http://www.cs.utexas.edu/users/EWD/transcriptions/EWD07xx/ EWD791.html Accessed 13.10.2008

Dijkstra, E. W. (1989). On the cruelty of really teaching of computing science., V32 1398–1408. *Communications of the ACM*, 32(12), 1398–1108.

Flach, J., and Dominguez, C. (1995). Use-centered design: Integrating the user, instrument, and goal. *Ergonomics in Design*, 3(3), 19–24.

Floyd, C. (1993). STEPS – A methodical approach to PD. *Communications on ACM*, 36(6), 83.

---

[2] Minimalism is introduced in this book as a conceptual tool to distinguish different types of simplicity. Reduction is used as a means to achieve simplicity. Different approaches to reduction can be differentiated using the notion of simplicity, e.g. returning to the wire telegraphs, the dial telegraph is structurally minimal, while the lever telegraph is functionally minimal, making it a more universal tool that can be easily misused, or linked to other tools (e.g. the structurally minimal Morse code, or machines that are much faster at creating the binary signal transmitted)—it is more minimal in both composition and architecture.

Floyd, C. (1994). Software-engineering – und dann? *Informatik Spektrum*, *17*(1), 21–28.

Floyd, C., and Oberquelle, H. (2003). Softwaretechnik und –ergonomie. Skript zur Vorlesung.

Grudin, J. (1990a). *Interface*. CSCW '90: Proceedings of the 1990 ACM conference on Computer-supported cooperative work, New York, NY, USA, 269–278.

Grudin, J. (1990b). *The Computer Reaches Out: The Historical Continuity of Interface Design*. CHI '90: Proceedings of the SIGCHI conference on Human factors in computing systems, New York, NY, USA, 261–268.

Hollan, J., Hutchins, E., and Kirsh, D. (2000). Distributed cognition: toward a new foundation for human-computer interaction research. *ACM Transactions an Computing Human Interactions*, 7(2), 174–196.

Hutchins, E. (1996). *Cognition in the Wild*. The MIT Press.

IAwiki (2006). Defining the Damn Thing. http://www.iawiki.net/DefiningTheDamnThing Accessed 3.10.2008

ISO9241 (1998). *ISO 9241: Ergonomic Requirements for Office Work with Visual Display Terminals* (VDTs).

Jencks, C. (1977). *The Language of Post-modern Architecture* (An Architectural design monograph). London: Academy Editions.

Johnson, P-A. (1994). *The Theory of Architecture: Concepts, Themes & Practices (Architecture)*. Van Nostrand Reinhold.

Kostof, S. (1977). *The Architect: Chapters in the History of the Profession*. Oxford University Press, USA.

Laurel, B. (1990). *The Art of Human-Computer Interface Design*. Addison-Wesley Professional.

Mackay, W. E., and Fayard, A-L. (1997). *HCI, Natural Science and Design: A Framework for Triangulation Across Disciplines*. DIS '97: Proceedings of the conference on Designing interactive systems, New York, NY, USA, 223–234.

Martin, D., and Sommerville, I. (2004). Patterns of cooperative interaction: Linking ethnomethodology and design. *ACM Transactions an Computing Human Interactions*, 11(1), 59–89.

McGrenere, J., Baecker, R. M., and Booth, K. S. (2002). *An Evaluation of a Multiple Interface Design Solution for Bloated Software*. CHI '02: Proceedings of the SIGCHI conference on Human factors in computing systems, New York, NY, USA, 164–170.

Moran, T. P. (1981). The command language grammar: A representation for the user interface of interactive computer systems. *International Journal of Man-Machine Studies*, 5(1), 3–50.

Myers, B., Hollan, J., Cruz, I., Bryson, S., Bulterman, D., Catarci, T., et al. (1996). Strategic directions in human-computer interaction. *ACM Computing Surkeys*, 28(4), 794–809.

Nuseibeh, B., and Easterbrook, S. (2000). *Requirements Engineering: A Roadmap*. ICSE '00: Proceedings of the conference on the future of software engineering, New York, NY, USA, s35–46.

Oberquelle, H. (2005). *Gestaltung von Benutzungsschnittstellen: Geht es ohne Design-Kompetenz?* INFORMATIK 2005 – Informatik LIVE! Band 1, Beiträge der 35. Jahrestagung der Gesellschaft für Informatik e.V. (GI), Bonn, 19. bis 22. September 2005, 232–237.

Pipek, V. (2005). *From Tailoring to Appropriation Support: Negotiating Groupware Usage*. University of Oulu, Oulu, Finland. Available online at http://herkules.oulu.fi/isbn9514276302/

Pohl, K. (1997). Requirements engineering: An overview. In A Kent and J Williams (Eds.), *Encyclopedia of Computer Science and Technology*. Volume 36, Supplement 21. New York: Marcel Dekker, Inc.

Preece, J. (1994). *Human Computer Interaction (ICS S.)*. Addison Wesley.

Reinhardt, A. (1975). *Art-as-Art: Selected Writings of Ad Reinhardt*. New York: Viking.

Rozanski, E. P., and Haake, A. R. (2003). *The Many Facets of HCI*. CITC4 '03: Proceedings of the 4th conference on Information technology curriculum, New York, NY, USA, 180–185.

SEP. (2003). Feminist epistemology and philosophy of science: Feminist standpoint theory. *Stanford Encyclopedia of Psychology* http://plato.stanford.edu/entries/feminism-epistemology/#standpoint Accessed 13.10.2008

Smith, D. C., Irby, C., Kimball, R., and Verplank, B. (1982). Designing the star user interface. *Byte*, 4, 242–282.

Straus, D., and Doyle, M. (1978). The architect as facilitator: A new role. *Journal of Architectural Education (JAE)*, 31(4), 13–15.

Suchman, L. A., Pea, R., Brown, J. S., and Heath, C. (1987). *Plans and Situated Actions : The Problem of Human-Machine Communication (Learning in Doing: Social, Cognitive & Computational Perspectives)*. Cambridge: Cambridge University Press.

Thompson, D. V., Hamilton, R. W., and Rust, R. T. (2005). Feature Fatigue: When Product Capabilities Become Too Much of a Good Thing. *Journal of Marketing Research*, 42, 431–442.

Vredenburg, K., Mao, J-Y., Smith, P. W., and Carey, T. (2002). *A Survey of User-Centered Design Practice*. CHI '02: Proceedings of the SIGCHI conference on human factors in computing systems, New York, NY, USA, 471–478.

Winograd, T., and Flores, F. (1987). *Understanding Computers and Cognition : A New Foundation for Design*. Addison-Wesley Professional.

Wolf, T. V., Rode, J. A., Sussman, J., and Kellogg, W. A. (2006). *Dispelling "design" as the black art of CHI*. CHI '06: Proceedings of the SIGCHI conference on human factors in computing systems, New York, NY, USA, 521–530.

Wroblewski, D. A. (1991). The construction of human-computer interfaces considered as a craft. In J. Karat (Ed.), *Taking Software Design Seriously*. 1–19. New York: Academic Press Professional, Inc. San Diego, CA, USA.

Wurman, R. S., and Bradford, P. (1996). *Information Architects*. Graphis Inc.

Zevi, B. (1957). *Architecture As Space*. Horizon Press.

Part III
Rethinking Minimalism

Chapter 4
Minimalism, Industrial Design and HCI

This book tries to establish minimalism as a novel perspective for the analysis of design for interactive systems. The merit of the different notions of minimalism lies in their focusing function: *functional, structural, architectural,* and *compositional minimalism* highlight different *reductive tendencies* of a design. In Chapters 6 and 7, their function is to identify simple aspects of existing designs and how new and existing design techniques can be used to create simplicity. The purpose of this chapter is to examine how the minimal standpoint differs from established points of view.

To this end, this chapter begins with a historical look at industrial design as the forerunner of HCI as a discipline—designing interaction even before there were computers. The relationship of minimalism and design principles represented by international standards for usability calls for a focus shift from individual functionality to the larger context of use. Minimalism as a perspective for existing HCI lore is examined using popular guidelines as an example. Advice resulting from longtime individual experiences of renowned HCI experts illustrates the importance of reduction in design.

4.1 Following the Roots in Industrial Design

It must be borne in mind that the object being worked on is going to be ridden in, sat upon, looked at, talked into, activated, operated, or in some way used by people individually or en masse. If the point of contact between the product and people becomes a point of friction, then the designer has failed. If, on the other hand, people are made safer, more comfortable, more desirous of purchase, more efficient—or just plain happier—by contact with the product, then the designer has succeeded.

—Henry Dreyfuss, Harvard Business Review, November 1950

While computer scientists often consider themselves as part of an engineering-tradition (e.g. Jehn et al., 1978), the part of human-computer interaction that tries to gather contextual knowledge and transfer that into the design of an interactive system is heavily influenced by industrial design (Sloan, 1975; McCrickard et al., 2004; Wolf et al., 2006). Not only do product designers contribute to the field of human-computer interaction—visible in conferences,

H. Obendorf, *Minimalism*, Human-Computer Interaction Series,
DOI 10.1007/978-1-84882-371-6_4, © Springer-Verlag London Limited 2009

series such as *ACM Designing Interactive Systems* and special tracks of most HCI conferences—but industrial design can be considered an important predecessor to the design of interactive systems.

Today, when we design a computer artifact, when we build an operating system, develop a service or design an application, we are directly changing the organization of work and thus impacting the lives of people. Industrial design became conscious of this responsibility before the widespread use of computing technology, and can in many aspects be called a precursor to the discipline of human-centered design. In early industrial design, experiences from designing for audiences, e.g. from designing theater stages, were transferred to the design of mass produced technology.

Industrial designers had to mediate between stake-holders—much as usability experts today, they had to find compromises that would make CEOs, engineering and marketing departments equally happy—and find useful designs for the prospective users. As the role of the designer has not changed as much as one might believe, it is not surprising that many of the tools applied in interaction design were already in the hands of industrial designers: Mock-ups were widely used, focus groups were common, and even a form of personas was employed to communicate target groups to the design team—although more in the form of generalized measurement for ergonomic designs (Dreyfuss, 1955, 69f).

Industrial design is a profession formed during the 1950s when the shift from manufacture to mass production allowed a before unheard-of abstraction in the design of everyday products (Bürdek, 1991, 2005) where one successful design could reach millions of households—instead of only a few customers of the traditional craftsman. The new form of production led to a different approach to thinking about design; since many different users would be targeted by the design, the functional aspect was stressed (Dreyfuss, 1955). This replaced the focus on decoration that before had identified the individual craftsman who created a product.

Henry Dreyfuss gives an example for this new type of design, created when "the manufacturers of the Mason jars sought a change. Here was a temptation to prettify a familiar object. Happily, we resisted it. We made the jar square with tapered sides, thereby ... saving storage space, providing a jar that wouldn't roll off the table, and handing the manufacturer a thumping sales advantage. It was another lesson in the basic simplicity of good design" (ibid., 78). While some of his contemporary designers enjoyed the ubiquitous streamlining that started with vehicles, and did not spare the breakfast table (Fig. 4.1), he noted "call it cleanlining instead of streamlining, and you have an ideal that the designer today still tries to achieve" (ibid., 77).

Industrial design tried to find an aesthetic form that was both pleasing and functional, sometimes sacrificing originality for functionality: "If something is to be lifted or operated by a handle, we try to integrate the lifting device into the design, but never to conceal it. At the expense of forfeiting originality, and it is a great temptation to hide locks and access panels, we try to make things obvious

Fig. 4.1 American Airstream caravan (1964), streamlined to an idealized "teardrop shape"

to operate" (Dreyfuss 1955, 71). This did not lead designers to ignore other qualities—as Dreyfuss recalls, "One time, I arranged to get behind the counter of a drugstore to catch reactions to a new ... clock we had designed. My first customer was a woman, and I showed her our model and a competitive clock of the same price. I watched her weigh a clock in each hand. I was confident in her choice, for we and our client's engineers had labored long and hard to make out clock light, believing lightness was an expression of its excellence. I had a sinking feeling as she bought the heavier clock. But it brought home the lesson, that to some people, weight can be a sign of quality; also, that the designer must appreciate that some things demand weight and some lightness, and he/she must determine when each is a virtue." (ibid., 68). This point is taken up by Don Norman (2004), who criticizes pure functionalism: "If something is to be lifted or operated by a handle, we try to integrate the lifting device into the design, but never to conceal it ... At the expense of originality ... we try to make things obvious to operate."

In the same collection of ideas, Norman argues that rich and complex objects can hold our attention longer, giving the example of the ever-new experience of listening to richly-textured classical music (ibid., 109f). When design becomes purely emotional, however, it ceases to create tools. An example Norman (ibid., 112ff) gives is the lemon press designed by Philippe Starck that looks great, but poorly performs[1] when one tries to actually use it.

---

[1] Norman, by the way, "admits" to owning a gold-plated version that, naturally, should never come in contact with acids.

The emphasis on beauty as an end in itself is also contradicted by Christopher Alexander's Zen View, who advises that the transient is more attractive: "If there is a beautiful view, don't spoil it by building huge windows that gape incessantly at it. Instead, put the windows which look onto the view at places of transition—along paths, in hallways, in entry ways, on stairs, between rooms" (Alexander, 1977, pattern #134).

Among designers, preferences are not distributed evenly. While there is a long tradition of functionalism and industrial design anticipated many of the practices of interaction design, designers can also simply be interested in beauty for itself. Following Gelernter's (1999) perception of "machine beauty", this book limits itself to discuss those aspects of design aiming at the creation of powerful tools. Vice versa, one can conclude that the reflective notion of minimalism is useful only for some designs, as it inherently focuses on the tool-qualities of a design.

4.2 Standards in Interaction Design and Minimalism

For those in doubt about the meaning of usability and about the goals interaction design strives to achieve, there is an international answer: formal standards of the International Standards Organization (ISO) represent an agreement between international experts; for the sake of clarity, these standardstend to define desirable values for software (Bevan, 2001).

Minimalism is proposed here as a perspective on the proposed values that focuses on a distinctive set of similarities and thus promises to highlight some implicit connections between the values, and between the values and the methods discussed later. Even in this informal format, this is a useful complement to a direct match of evaluation methods and values: HCI tends to place less weight on the design aspect, which, in turn, makes evaluation a dull tool—the evaluated designs do not specifically aim for the tested qualities, and constructive rather than comparative criticism becomes difficult. As will be illustrated briefly, quantitative evaluation is also incapable of capturing the more complex connotations created between the values by the minimalist perspective. Minimalism is put forward here to explain why the values described here—and later, why existing guidelines and methods—can lead to better design results. The reflection on the values set by HCI standards is thus a first test whether minimalism can be used successfully to assess the design of interactive systems; as a further benefit, already this first application adds to the specification of what is understood here by minimalism.

While a multitude of different standards exist that formalize requirements for hardware or software interfaces, or the development process (comp. Bevan, 1995), only a single, standard, international standard exists that aims to define general measures and values of usable systems: *ISO 9241*, now retitled "Ergonomics of Human System Interaction", defines usability as a measurable quality of a product based on effectiveness, efficiency and user satisfaction in part 11 (see Definition 4.1).

Definition 4.1 Measurements for the use quality of software according to ISO 9241/110

Usability

The *effectiveness, efficiency* and *satisfaction* with which specified users achieve specified goals in particular environments.

Effectiveness

The *accuracy* and *completeness* with which specified users can achieve specified goals in particular environments.

Efficiency

The *resources expended* in relation to the accuracy and completeness of goals achieved.

Satisfaction

The *comfort* and *acceptability* of the work system to its users and other people affected by its use.

ISO 9241-110 thus defines usability as effectiveness, efficiency and satisfaction. All three can be measured quantitatively using pre-defined tasks, time measurements and questionnaires for user satisfaction. The measures do not, however, attempt to explain why a software is more usable or even more effective, efficient or satisfactory. To this end, ISO 9241 further defines a number of qualities for usable software. While software is usually examined for compliance with 'inner qualities' (Floyd and Oberquelle, 2003)—software should be correct, easily understood and changed—in ISO 9241-110, the 'outer quality', or use quality of software is defined in the following terms:

Definition 4.2 Use qualities of software according to ISO 9241/110

Suitability for the task

A dialog is suitable for the task if the dialog helps the user to complete his task in an effective and efficient manner.

Conformity with user expectations

A dialog is conforming with user expectations if it is consistent and complies with the characteristics of the human user, that is his knowledge of the task, his education and expertise and generally accepted conventions).

Self descriptiveness

A dialog is self descriptive if every single dialog step can immediately be understood by the user based on the information displayed by the system or if there is a mechanism to obtain any additional explanatory information on request of the user.

Controllability

A dialog is controllable if the user can start the dialog and influence the direction and speed of the dialog at any point in time until the task has been completed.

Error tolerance

A dialog is fault tolerant if a task can be completed with erroneous inputs with minimal overhead for corrections by the human user.

Suitability for learning

A dialog is suitable for learning if it helps and guides the novice user to learn about other perhaps more efficient or effective ways to use an application.

Suitability for individualization

A dialog is suitable for individualization if the system allows to adapt the interaction style to a particular task and the specific capabilities and preferences of the user.

These use qualities universally define how usable designs should behave. The relationship between the seven qualities mentioned in ISO 9241/110 and the four notions of minimalism can be subsumed as follows:

Functional minimalism has two immediate consequences for the use qualities of a design: fewer functions mean that there is less to learn—which will often result in encouraging the user to better apply a minimal tool, and that control of the the less complex functionality is supposedly easier—complexity often causes the users' mental models to fail predicting system responses. There is also a shift in the meaning of suitability for the task: this is often interpreted as effectiveness, meaning "will do anything that the task requires". Instead, for functionally minimal designs, the question of *toolness*, or "will do something that the task requires" becomes more central. Functional minimalism could contribute to self-descriptiveness, but it might harm error tolerance in the sense that understanding errors can become more difficult when they are not produced by a single tool, but through the interaction of different tools.

Structural Minimalism means fitting the access structure of the system to the tasks that will be executed. Generally speaking, often-used functionality should be readily available, at the cost of less-often-used functionality which may be accessible, but more difficult to invoke. This can be understood as a fit created either by explicit design, or by customization—customization of interactive systems often begins with users changing access structures such as menus or toolbars to improve the accessibility of often-used functionality. Two different approaches to structuring functionality can be distinguished: If the design of a structurally minimal system groups functionality not only according to frequency, but also into meaningful units, discovery of functionality and, thus, learning is supported. This can involve a trade-off as consistency with other applications is reduced, and initial learning hindered. The definition of structural minimalism is based on the "minimal perceived structure"—which is partly congruent with conformity with user expectations: when user expectations regarding which functionality should be invoked are met, navigation in e.g. menus is reduced. A structurally minimal system can be easier to control—but if it is structured only based on frequency, users might have problems getting an overview, and actions the designers did not plan for can decrease the users' sense of control.

The partitioning of functionality that characterizes *Architectural Minimalism* results in a transparent distribution of responsibility for task activities across the tools a system is composed of. This contributes to the suitability for learning as tools can be discovered and mastered individually. As users can simply choose which tools—and thus which part of functionality—to use, it shifts the meaning of suitability for individualization from interface customization to appropriation; the interface is not changed, but instead used with a different focus. Conformity with user expectations is supported by the grouping of functionality into visible tools; if users share the designer's understanding about the utilization of these tools, conformity is established on the tool level and the location of individual functionality becomes more predictable.

Finally, *Compositional Minimalism* continues the change of focus introduced by the preceding notions of minimalism: the interactive system and its design become less important than its actual use. Qualities that ISO 9241 considers to be attributes of the software become both requirement for and result of a design. For example, the conformity with user expectations on the tool level is necessary to enable appropriation. Appropriation then results in conformity on the system level that was not determined by the initial design. Individualization partly corresponds to compositional minimalism—a compositionally minimal system tries to allow different individual uses. Yet, these uses do not always result in a changed tool. Similarly, the focus in learning shifts from discovering new functionality to discovering new uses of known functionality.

The perspectives created by the four different notions of minimalism demonstrate an understanding of usability that relates to the standard, yet changes the viewpoint of analysis in fundamental ways (Fig. 4.2):

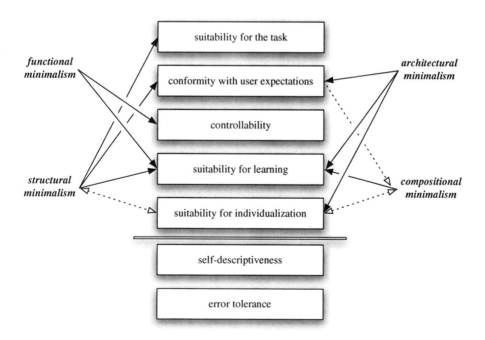

Fig. 4.2 Notions of minimalism and the use qualities of ISO 9241/110

(1) *Functional, structural, architectural* and *compositional* minimalism focus on *qualities of a design* that further its use qualities. The relationship cannot be mapped directly as several aspects of minimality influence, e.g., the use of learning. Minimalism, however, provides a more constructive than reflective perspective, allowing prediction of use qualities.

(2) The scope of *use* and *learning* is extended beyond the single system. An interactive system becomes a tool among other tools. Instead of *use qualities* of an interactive system, the interaction with work processes, other tools and other users becomes central.

Carroll (1990, 322) notes that "an important body of work in current HCI stresses that designed artifacts cannot be understood apart from the situations in which they are used." Minimalism further implies that not only the situation, but also other designs used situatively need to be included in design considerations. The all-present opportunities for interactions with other designs are stressed by the important theme of ubiquitous computing (Weiser, 1991) in HCI.

As a consequence of this broadened perspective, evaluation becomes inherently more difficult. While usability metrics have been developed (comp. Dix et al., 1997) to measure the standard use qualities of software, these are either determined by what can be measured quantitatively, or necessarily indirect and relative as they measure the interpretation of users (cmp. Table 4.1).

Table 4.1 Methods for measuring usability according to ISO 9241/110. Excerpt from Dix et al. 1997

Usability Objective	Effectiveness Measures	Efficiency Measures	Satisfaction Measures
Suitability for the Task	Percentage of goals achieved	Time to complete a task	Rating scale for satisfaction
Appropriate for trained users	Number of "power features" used	Relative efficiency compared with an expert user	Rating scale for satisfaction with "power features"
Learnability	Percentage of functions learned	Time to learn criterion	Rating scale for "ease of learning"
Error Tolerance	Percentage of errors corrected successfully	Time spent on correcting errors	Rating scale for error handling

The definition of these usability metrics demonstrates that evaluation is often focused on features, not on tasks. Functions of the design are no longer tools to accomplish tasks, but their number is used as a benchmark for software quality itself, e.g. when learnability is measured as learned features set in relation to total features. Measuring the minimality of a design simply by asking users promises limited success as it is difficult to separate the aesthetic and the functional perspective in user surveys (Section 5.5.1). Users may also not care about minimality as they do about learnability or suitability for the task (Section 5.1.3).

The minimal perspective, however, demonstrates limitations of the usability metrics: Comparing a functionally minimal design with a design providing more functions highlights the importance of task design for measured user satisfaction—often, task design is oriented on collected requirements, and thus on a tool's functionality, rather than on real user needs. Satisfaction is an inexact measure as it is the result of complex interactions and cannot be linked unambiguously to a single-use quality. Usability metrics focus on the designed system alone, e.g. by observing the use of its "power features". By contrast, the notion of compositional minimalism indicates that, instead of examining the system in isolation, intelligent appropriation of tools within actual work is more relevant for the usability; it cannot, however, easily be measured in laboratory environments.

From the standpoint of minimalism, the use qualities defined by ISO 9241 seem limited in their usefulness to guide and evaluate usability. Karat and Karat (2003) agree: "The importance of these two documents lies not as much in the specifics of the guidelines included in the various parts as it does in the acknowledgment that usability is complex and context-dependent. Designing for usability should be seen as involving both attendance to high-level principles (such as those in Part 10) and selection of particular approaches that are determined by a context of use that is broader than we have generally attended to."

4.3 HCI Lore and Minimalism

After international standards, the most important guides for usability are collections of heuristics that describe "good practices", or qualities of software in more concrete terms than ISO standards. In the next two sections, "Golden" and "Silver" rules for design are linked to minimalism, as are interface guidelines that exist for most operating systems.

4.3.1 Rules of Noble Metal and Minimalism

The standards provide an authoritative source of reference, but designers without usability experience have great difficulty applying these types of guidelines (Souza and Bevan, 1990). The services of renowned usability experts are thus in high demand—yet these are not always available. Experience gathered over the course of many design projects is what usually distinguishes an expert. Often, the resulting how-to knowledge is communicated to less experienced designers by means of "rules". These guidelines are often used in practice, as they are concise, often catchy, and the nature of their source—respected members of the community—gives them great authority.

Following the realization that graphical user interfaces are not automatically "easy to use" (Zanino et al., 1994), rules were contrived to guide design and evaluation. The first set of rules that became well known are the *Eight Golden Rules* that were coined in 1987 by Ben Shneiderman (Shneiderman, 1987). Yet, in his latest recollection of these rules, Shneiderman and Plaisant (2004, 63) acknowledge previous work that they built upon. An example is Smith and Mosier's (1986) data display guidelines; they present five high-level goals for data display and data entry each (Table 4.2).

Table 4.2 High-level goals for data display and data entry (Smith and Mosier, 1986)

1. Consistency of data display	1. Consistency of data entry transactions
2. Efficient information assimilation by the user	2. Minimal input actions by user
	3. Minimal memory load on users
3. Minimal memory load on the user	4. Compatibility of data entry with data display
4. Compatibility of data display with data entry	
5. Flexibility for user control of data display	5. Flexibility for user control of data display

The second and third goal immediately link to structural minimalism: Smith and Mosier require the access structure to information and functionality to be as minimal as possible. They also stress, as a final goal, the flexibility of use. While their scope is only a single dialog, compositional minimalism builds upon this flexibility. Both the first and fourth goals concern questions of internal consistency—this important aspect is discussed below (Section 4.6).

Shneiderman's *Eight Golden Rules of Interface Design* (Shneiderman, 1987; Shneiderman and Plaisant, 2004), reproduced in Table 4.3, present a different focus. These rules, much as those formulated by Molich and Nielsen (Molich and Nielsen, 1990), result from testing the usability of different designs— Molich and Nielsen note that "This checklist reflects our personal experience". Molich and Nielsen's *Silver Rules* were coined to guide heuristic evaluation, Shneiderman gives advice to designers. Both sets of rules, however, try to improve a design by preventing common usability mistakes. Thus, they focus less on qualities of a design, but rather present advice in the form of principles.

The rules of both Shneiderman and Molich and Nielsen can be traced back to a cognitive science background—models of human memory (comp. e.g. Anderson, 1994) and theories for categorizing human error (older theories include e.g. Norman, 1981; Reason, 1982; Rasmussen, 1986) provide an informative basis for possible design errors. In practice, these rules are often known to designers, but difficult to interpret in terms of a specific design context due to their high level of abstraction (Tetzlaff and Schwartz, 1991). From these rules, only the last directly relates to reduction; it is, however, formulated in such an abstract manner that no direct guidelines for design can be deduced—functional, structural, and architectural minimalism would all be candidates to reach the goal of reducing short-term memory load.

Table 4.3 Excerpts from Shneiderman's eight golden rules of interface design

1. *Strive for consistency.*
   ... consistent sequences of actions should be required in similar situations; identical terminology should be used ... consistent color, layout ... should be employed throughout. Exceptions ... should be comprehensible and limited in number.
2. *Cater to universal usability.*
   ... design for *plasticity*, facilitating transformation of content. Novice-expert differences, age ranges, disabilities, and technology diversity each enrich the spectrum of requirements that guide design. ...
3. *Offer informative feedback.*
   For every user action, there should be system feedback. ...
4. *Design dialogs to yield closure.*
   Sequences of actions should be organized into groups with a beginning, middle, and end. Informative feedback at the completion of a group give operators the satisfaction of accomplishment, a sense of relief, the signal to drop contingency plans from their minds, and a signal to prepare for the next group of actions. ...
5. *Prevent errors.*
   ... design the system such that users cannot make serious errors ... If a user makes an error, the interface should detect the error and offer simple, constructive, and specific instructions for recovery. ...
6. *Permit easy reversal of actions.*
   ... actions should be reversible. This ... relieves anxiety ...
7. *Support internal locus of control.*
   Experienced operators strongly desire the sense that they are in charge of their interface and that the interface responds to their actions. ...
8. *Reduce short-term memory load.*
   ... displays [should] be kept simple, multiple-page displays be consolidated, window-motion frequency be reduced ...

4.3.2 Interface Guidelines and Minimalism

Interface designers refer more often to more concrete guidelinesthat provide reference and guidance in their daily work (comp. Souza and Bevan, 1990). These exist in platform-independent form (e.g. Smith and Mosier, 1986; Brown, 1988), but were more successful as platform-specific style guides (Computer, 1987; Microsoft, 1995; Nextstep, 1992). Although similar standards exist for other products e.g. the KDE environment (KDE, 2005) or the Qt library that the Gnome desktop is based upon (Benson et al., 2004), the guidelines that are developed by Apple and Microsoft for their windowing systems MacOS and Windows have the longest history and the largest user base in the industry (Apple, 1992, 2006; Microsoft, 1999, 2006).

In the *Apple Macintosh Interface Guidelines* from 1987, in addition to concrete advice about window design, interaction techniques and even menu item placement, general design principles are provided in the first section of the book. "User control: The user, not the computer, initiates and controls all actions" is one of the first principles; its interpretation—asking whether the user really wants to invoke a function using alert boxes, however, is not as far-reaching as compositional minimalism would imply. The list of principles closes with "Simplicity" and "Clarity". Both are interpreted in terms of visual layout, e.g. for dialog boxes fewer choices should be presented, information should be made visible by both icons and text, etc. This interpretation is still current—the draft *User Experience Guidelines* for Windows Vista (ibid.) includes "Clean up the user interface: Remove clutter. . ." as one of the top 12 rules.

The call for visual clarityis clearly connected with reduction; it remains, however, on a superficial level of the interface—the guidelines do not mention application functionality. Interface design here is still ascribed a decorative role. Ample evidence, however, suggests that even the question of visual clutter is strongly connected to deeper design decisions. In Apple's most recent guidelines, the 80/20 rule (for a more thorough discussion, see Koch, 1999) is used to illustrate that trying to serve power users will often result in suboptimal interfaces. As the guidelines tell us, by trying to reach the other 80% of users, design "typically favors simpler, more elegant approaches to problems" (Apple, 2006, 29). Later, they even note, "The best approach to developing easy-to-use software is to keep the design as simple as possible" (ibid., 47). Simplicity is interpreted as reduction of visible features, and supplemented by "Availability: a corollary of simplicity" (ibid., 41).

4.3.3 Discussion

From a minimalist standpoint, neither the heuristics developed by usability experts nor the guidelines describing concrete system use help define reduction. Usability heuristics focus on cognitive limitations of the user and intend to make designers aware of these. They, thus, limit their focus to individual aspects of the design, and although they suggest that mental effort on behalf of the user should be kept minimal, they fail to provide concrete advice how to do so. Guidelines, on the other hand, provide a wealth of examples and advice. Simplicity is here, however, understood in mostly visual terms, aiming at a "clean" interface. Although the importance of functional simplicity is also recognized by the Apple Guidelines, the notions of structural, architectural and compositional minimalism as alternative perspectives for creating simplicity even for functionally-complex designs are not covered.

4.4 Summary

This chapter touched some of the existing perspectives on design that have long taught and practiced reduction. The discussion of industrial design (Section 4.1) pointed out that the practice of interaction design draws many of its methods and concepts from the practice of industrial design, and that the differentiation of function and decoration was always difficult. Although the discussion in this book does not explicitly focus on aesthetics and joy of use, these are influenced by functional design, and vice versa. Some of this relationship is later discussed in Chapter 9.

International standards were cited to illustrate the difference of the minimalist perspective. To enable constructive design, there is a need for explaining the objective measures defined for the ease of use in standards. While use qualities define aspects that are desirable in designs, the minimalist standpoint introduces a shift in focus to a more constructive stance that examines not only aspects of a single system, but a broader use context (Section 4.2). An examination of the often-cited "Golden" and "Silver" rules of Ben Shneiderman and Ralf Molich, and a look at interface guidelines for different platforms suggests a limitation of their focus on functional and structural aspects of a design, and the interpretation of simplicity in purely visual terms (Section 4.3).

Neither standards nor rules nor guidelinesseem to thus be able to provide guidance in designing "simple" products—at least, if simplicity is meant to refer to more than visual impression. In the next chapter, this connection between superficial clutter and deeper design questions is further examined, and consistency, prominently featured as a guiding value in every set of interface guidelines, is set in relation to minimalism to clarify its use as a principle guiding design.

References

Alexander, C. (1977). *A Pattern Language: Towns, Buildings, Construction (Center for Environmental Structure Series)*. Oxford: Oxford University Press.

Anderson, J. R. (1994). *Learning and Memory: An Integrated Approach*. San Francisco, CA: John Wiley and Sons (WIE).

Apple. (2006). *Apple Human Interface Guidelines*. http://developer.apple.com/documentation/UserExperience/Conceptual/OSXHIGuidelines/OSXHIGuidelines.pdf Accessed 2.8.

Apple. (1992). *Macintosh Human Interface Guidelines (Apple Technical Library)*. New York: Addison-Wesley Professional.

Benson, C., Elman, A., Nickell, S., and Robertson, C. Z. (2004). *GNOME Human Interface Guidelines 2.0*.

Bevan, N. (1995). Human-computer interaction standards. *Proceedings of HCI International 95; Vol. 2. Advances in Human Factors/Ergonomics*. Vol. 20B, 885–890. Amsterdam, The Netherlands: Elsevier.

Bevan, N. (2001). International standards for HCI and usability. *International Journal of Human-Computer Studies*, 55(4), 533–552.

Brown, C. M. (1988). *Human-Computer Interface Design Guidelines* (Human/Computer Interaction, No 5). Norwood, NJ: Ablex Pub.

Bürdek, B. E. (1991). *Design. Geschichte, theorie und Praxis der Produktgestaltung*. Ostfildern: DuMont Reiseverlag.

Bürdek, B. E. (2005). *Design. Geschichte, theorie und Praxis der Produktgestaltung*. Switzerland: Birkhäuser.

Carroll, J. M. (1990). *The Nurnberg Funnel: Designing Minimalist Instruction for Practical Computer Skill (Technical Communication, Multimedia, and Information Systems)*. Cambridge, MA: The MIT Press.

Computer, I. A. (1987). *Apple Human Interface Guidelines: The Apple Desktop Interface*. New York: Addison-Wesley (C).

Dix, A., Finlay, J., and Abowd, G. D. (1997). *Human-Computer Interaction*. New Jersey: Prentice Hall.

Dreyfuss, H. (1955). *Designing for People* (Reprinted in Allworth Press, 2003 ed.). New York: Simon & Schuster.

Floyd, C., and Oberquelle, H. (2003). *Softwaretechnik und –ergonomie.* Skript zur Vorlesung.

Gelernter, D. (1999). *Machine Beauty: Elegance and the Heart of Technology* (Reprinted ed.) (Masterminds). New York, NY: Basic Books.

Inc NC. (1992). *Nextstep User Interface Guidelines: Release 3 (Nextstep Developer's Library).* New York: Addison Wesley Publishing Company.

Jehn, L. A., Rine, D. C., and Sondak, N. (1978). Computer science and engineering education: Current trends, new dimensions and related professional programs. *SIGCSE Bulletin,* 10(3), 162–178.

Karat, J., and Karat, C. M. (2003). The evolution of user-centered focus in the human-computer interaction field. *IBM Systems Journal,* 42(4), 532–541.

KDE. (2005). *KDE 3 Styleguide.* http://developer.kde.org/documentation/standards/kde/style/styleguide.pdf Accessed 20.7.2008

Koch, R. (1999). *The 80/20 Principle: The Secret to Success by Achieving More with Less.* New York: Currency.

McCrickard, D. S., Chewar, C. M., and Somervell, J. (2004). Design, science, and engineering topics? Teaching HCI with a unified method. *SIGCSE '04: Proceedings of the 35th SIGCSE Technical Symposium on Computer Science Education* 31–35. New York, NY USA: ACM Press.

Microsoft. (2006). *Windows Vista User Experience Guidelines.* http://msdn.microsoft.com/library/?url = /library/en-us/UxGuide/UXGuide/Home.asp Accessed 2.8.2008

Microsoft. (1995). *The Windows Interface Guidelines for Software Design: An Application Design guide.* Redmond, Washington: Microsoft Press.

Microsoft. (1999). *Microsoft Windows User Experience (Microsoft Professional Editions).* Redmond, Washington: Microsoft Press.

Molich, R., and Nielsen, J. (1990). Improving a human-computer dialogue. *Communications of the ACM,* 3, 338–348.

Norman, D. A. (1981). Categorisation of action slips. *Psychological Review,* 88(1), 1–15.

Norman, D. A. (2004). *Emotional Design: Why We Love (or Hate) Everyday Things.* New York, NY: Basic Books.

Rasmussen, J. (1986). *Information Processing and Human-Machine Interaction: An Approach to Cognitive Engineering.* Amsterdam, The Netherlands: North-Holland.

Reason J. T., and Mycielska, K. (1982). *Absent Minded? The Psychology of Mental Lapses, Little Slips, and Everyday Errors.* Englewood Cliffs, N.J: Prentice Hall.

Shneiderman, B. (1987). *Designing the User Interface: Strategies for Effective Human-Computer Interaction.* Reading, MA: Addison-Wesley.

Shneiderman, B., and Plaisant, C. (2004). *Designing the User Interface: Strategies for Effective Human-Computer Interaction* (4th ed.). Reading, MA: Addison Wesley.

Sloan, M. E. (1975). A design-oriented computer engineering program. *ISCA '75: Proceedings of the 2nd annual symposium on Computer architecture,* New York, NY, USA, 220–224.

Smith, S. L., and Mosier, J. N. (1986). *Guidelines for Designing User Interface Software* (Report ESD-TR-86-278). Bedford, MA: MITRE Corporation. Available online: http://www.dfki.de/~jameson/hcida/papers/smith-mosier.pdf.

Souza, F., and Bevan, N. (1990). The use of guidelines in menu interface design: Evaluation of a draft standard. *INTERACT '90: Proceedings of the IFIP TC13 Third Interational Conference on Human-Computer Interaction* 435–440. Amsterdam: North-Holland.

Tetzlaff, L., and Schwartz, D. R. (1991). The use of guidelines in interface design. *CHI '91: Proceedings of the SIGCHI Conference on Human Factors in Computing Systems,* New York, NY, USA, 329–333.

Weiser, M. (1991). The computer for the twenty-first century. *Scientific American,* 265(3), 94–104.

Wolf, T. V., Rode, J. A., Sussman, J., and Kellogg, W. A. (2006). Dispelling "design" as the black art of CHI. *CHI '06: Proceedings of the SIGCHI Conference on Human Factors in Computing Systems*, New York, NY, USA, 521–530.

Zanino, M. C., Agarwal, R., and Prasad, J. (1994). Graphical user interfaces and ease of use: some myths examined. *SIGCPR '94: Proceedings of the 1994 Computer Personnel Research Conference on Reinventing IS: Managing Information Technology in Changing Organizations*, New York, NY, USA, 142–154.

Chapter 5
Minimalism, Simplicity and Rules of Design

This chapter examines rules for interaction design—the results of many years' experience from distinguished practitioners—and discusses them in terms of minimalism. The objective of this discussion is to find out whether "simplicity is not enough", whether minimalism is helpful in understanding design rules and differentiating between different forms of simplicity that are confounded in the literature.

The visual simplicity of interfaces is often directly connected to their ease of use—it is assumed that by simplifying the impression of the interface, the usability would increase. Bruce Tognazzini (1992) drastically illustrates the need for simplicity: "Designers learn in 6 months, users have to learn the same in 6 minutes." He proposes visual simplicity as a means of helping the user: "In the Macintosh, we try to be as sparing of words and extra visual clutter whenever possible" (ibid.). However, "create visual simplicity" could not be called exact instructions, "sometimes we all overdo it. (Our original control panel . . . had no words explaining what the icons stood for, and everyone was confused. . . .)" (ibid.).

Jakob Nielsen interpreted "less is more" in *Usability Engineering* in feature terms, "every single element in a user interface places some additional burden on the user in terms of having to consider whether to use that element. Having fewer options will often mean better usability"(Nielsen, 1993, 15). According to Nielsen and Mack (1994), "Aesthetic and minimalist design" means: "Dialogues should not contain information which is irrelevant or rarely needed. Every extra unit of information in a dialogue competes with the relevant units of information and diminishes their relative visibility".

Simplicity, minimalist design and aesthetics are not only used interchangeably, they are also commonly positively annotated and associated with "good design" and "high usability". This makes it often difficult to find out what exactly is simpler—simpler is most certainly what is better. That, in turn, prevents the simpler to present a choice, or the designer to choose one kind of simplicity over another. The following sections bring together some evidence that interface design must be more than decoration, that access to functionality is determined by the visibility of interface elements, and that structure for access to information and functionality is often linked to simplicity. Consistency and

H. Obendorf, *Minimalism*, Human-Computer Interaction Series,
DOI 10.1007/978-1-84882-371-6_5, © Springer-Verlag London Limited 2009

conceptions of design are touched before discussing differences of simplicity and minimalism.

5.1 Deep Design: Causes of Clutter and Excise

> *Both the internal design and the user interface can have
> simplicity, but the interaction between the user and the
> program is what concerns us here, and frequently we have to
> sacrifice the simplicity of internal design to make the user interface simple*
>
> —Paul Heckel (1984)

In 1983, Donald Norman proposed a separation of interface design and "other programming tasks. Make the interface a separate data module ... then the interface designer could modify the interface independently of the rest of the system. Similarly, many system changes would not require modification of the interface." (Norman, 1983, 2) Nowadays, we often have a division of labor, with some designers creating the interface and software programmers devising the application logic. The positive result of this separation is the inclusion of designer skills—previously, design was considered an additional task for programmers. However, the fact that the underlying architecture influences the visible interface limits the effectiveness of a clear separation. Often, a design should influence the application logic, yet in real projects, the influence is often from the programmers and engineers who can determine design decisions.

Alan Cooper started his career as a programmer (Cooper, 1996), but turned into a critic of his old trade as he became interested in design. In *The Inmates Are Running The Asylum* (Cooper, 1999), he describes how an *implementation-centric* perspective contributes to unusable software through uninformed analysis of tasks and system-centered development processes: those who engineer applications should not be trusted; they tend to regard their own conceptual model as the only possible perspective. In *About Face 2.0* (Cooper and Reimann, 2003), a practitioner's handbook for designing software applications, Cooper recollects his design experiences and presents a variety of design guidelines, iterating on goal-directed design (ibid., 12) and Personas but also on his perspective of how software can be tailored to not impede on users' work.

The topic of reduction is addressed in a chapter called *Orchestration and Flow* (ibid., 123): for Cooper, the most important characteristic of "well orchestrated user interfaces" (ibid.) is that they enable the users' flow, a state of total concentration on an activity, losing awareness of peripheral problems and distractions (comp. Csikszentmihalyi, 1991). To achieve this flow, Cooper asks for less visible interfaces: "No matter how cool your interface is, less of it would be better" (Cooper and Reimann, 2003, 119). In the tradition of Bødker (1990), he positions transparency as the prime value for interface design: "the interface must not call attention to itself ..., but must instead, at every turn, be at the service of the user" (Cooper and Reimann, 2003, 120). Consequently, he criticizes the existing transparency that exposes inflexible qualities of a system on the interface: "they show us, without any hint of shame, precisely how they are built. There is one button per function, one dialog per module of code, and the commands and processes precisely echo the internal data structures and algorithms." (ibid., 248) Thus, instead of being able to work on their goals, users "*must* learn how the program works in order to successfully use the interface" (ibid.).

Cooper lists four guidelines that help reduce the visibility of the interface (ibid., 120ff), all working towards the provision of functionality without controlling work flow:

> **Definition 5.1** Cooper's guidelines for reducing the visibility of the user interface
>
> - *Follow mental models* involves the adaption of often-used functionality (e.g. menus) to the user groups' conceptual model; different users may have different perspectives on the same tasks and the same data.
> - *Keep tools close at hand* complements this by pointing out that most applications are too complex to allow one mode of direct manipulation control all their features; Cooper advises to provide tool palettes and inspectors to allow direct access to functionality without the need for modes, and without forcing users to tidy up tools after use.
> - In a similar vein, *modeless feedback* is asked for; status should be reported without interrupting the users' task flows.
> - *Direct, don't discuss* finally stands for respecting the user's control; Cooper notes that while developers tend to view human-computer interaction as a two-way conversation, most users don't care to be interrogated by a program.

These guidelines are closely connected to what has been introduced in this book as structural minimalism. Cooper's key concern is "distinguishing possibility from probability" to prevent cluttered interfaces that make tasks more complex than they need to be. This touches upon the structure of interfaces—according to Cooper, not every possible function needs to be given equally accessible screen real estate, and hiding some functionality increases the accessibility of what is left (ibid., 124f). Examples he gives to illustrate the difference of possibility and probability include the "delete cells" dialog in Excel that always asks whether to delete all, formats, formulas or just notes—more than a minor disturbance (ibid., 124), or the Windows print dialog that does not separate printing from print setup, mixing configuration and invocation (ibid., 130).

Navigation is, for Cooper, something that should be avoided if possible. He goes as far as to suggest removing hierarchies in file systems (ibid., 156), and instead of folder inside folder, use grouping, search and attribute-based access (ibid., 204). Where structure cannot be avoided, it should be optimized: he demands designers should "inflect your interface" (ibid., 154). Under this label, he demands to minimize *typical* navigation. Yet, his ideal system is not structurally minimal, "users make commensurate effort" for "fancy features" (ibid., 155)—on the other hand "users will be willing to tolerate . . . complexity only if the rewards are worth it" (ibid., 155). Cooper identifies three attributes that should govern the accessibility of features:

Definition 5.2 Attributes influencing the necessary accessibility of features

  – *Frequency of use*: Frequent items and tools should be no more than a click away.
  – *Degree of dislocation:* Amount of sudden change caused by invocation of a command.
  – *Degree of exposure:* Irreversible or dangerous functions need to be protected.

Cooper's first attribute alone follows the ideal of structurally minimal access to functionality, while his other attributes introduce his understanding of protecting the user: both focus on minimizing possibly harmful or disorientating effects. While this is probably a good heuristic for a pleasant and safe interface, it might not be useful to overprotect powerful commands that create a large amount of sudden change.

According to Cooper, excise is harmful as it "stop[s] the flow" (ibid., 139ff). He gives the advice "avoid unnecessary reporting" and "don't use dialogs to report normalcy" (ibid., 129)—if the system repeatedly asks the obvious, automatization will prevent users from identifying critical situations, such as deleting the wrong file (ibid., 129). Cooper metaphorically calls this "the dialog that cried, 'wolf!'" (ibid., 447f). All of these hints aim to reduce unnecessary access structure imposed upon the user by the programmer who unnecessarily requires entering information. Cooper finds the same words that describe minimalism to summarize his guidelines: "adding finesse: less is more" (ibid., 124). For him, all "navigation is excise" (ibid., 143), which includes windows, panes and menus mapping; scrolling should be minimized (ibid., 146), but also for different screens in applications should be reduced: "reduce the number of places to go" (ibid., 148). Cooper lists different types of excise: apart from the interruptions caused by the systems and navigation enforced on the user, he criticizes "training wheels" for "power users" (ibid., 137), "pure excise" (ibid., 137), e.g., hardware-management tasks that users should not have to deal with, and "visual excise" (ibid., 167) that he mostly finds in the Web in form of too many visual metaphors.

Cooper also gives some advice how to improve designs: Interruptions by dialog boxes could be minimized if "they" would "know where you are needed" and "Know if you are needed" (ibid., 412f)—dialogs that remember their last position and state and do not appear if not necessary—unlike e.g., the "save changes" dialog in Microsoft Word that is raised by pagination after printing, not a user action, but a change by the program. Confirmations should only be used where a negative answer is expected. For all other cases, user actions must be reversible, and system exceptions should be handled by default procedures (e.g. when directory does not exist, or file is not writeable), although in some cases (e.g. overwriting a file), deep changes can be required to allow report and undo functionality (e.g. versioning file systems[1]) (Cooper and Reimann, 2003, 449). Navigation could be reduced—although this would violate the "number of places" rule above—by breaking up functionality into smaller dialogs, not forcing the use of stacked tabs: "everybody hates it when the tabs move underneath the cursor" (ibid., 418f). Persistent navigation items like the tabs on the Amazon web site, and overviews such as the Adobe Photoshop navigator palette could further aid navigation. Users should be treated as "intelligent but with very little time" (ibid., 36) to avoid patronizing, and the problem of novice/expert interfaces is evaded as designers should "optimize for intermediates" (ibid., 35).

5.2 Visibility of Interface Elements

Leibniz sought to make the form of a symbol reflect its content. "In signs," he wrote, "one sees an advantage for discovery that is greatest when they express the exact nature of a thing briefly and, as it were, picture it then, indeed, the labor of thought is wonderfully diminished."

Frederick Kreiling, "Leibniz", Scientific American, May 1968

User interface design is more than decoration. Yet, observation of the visual attributes of an interface yields important clues about its functionality—the visibility of elements of the user interface determines the access to functionality. A balance has to be found between immediacy and richness of interaction. As Don Norman put it in his influential *Psychology of Everyday Things*,[2] "[j]ust the right things have to be visible to indicate what parts operate and how, to indicate how the user is to interact with the device. Visibility indicates the mapping between intended actions and actual operations." (Norman, 1989) He made popular the suggestion that design must anticipate possible actions and incorporate elements that make obvious both the functionality and correct use of a device.

The notion of "perceived" affordances, adapted from James J. Gibson (1979), lies at the heart of his turn towards design. In the tradition of cognitive science, trying to explain thought using symbolic processes, Norman suggests that attributes inherent in objects around us guide our interaction with them.

---

[1] These are not to be confused with journaling file systems that keep a journal of I/O operations that can be executed after a delay or system failure, thus ensuring atomicity of operations and a consistent state. Versioning file systems were first introduced in the TENEX operating system (Bobrow et al., 1972) to allow concurrent processes continue using old files; today, some experimental implementations exist (Cornell et al., 2004; Peterson and Burns, 2005)—and Apple announced TimeMachine, a journaling system, as part of MacOS X 10.5 (Apple, 2006).

[2] This book, in a second edition more appropriately named *Design of Everyday Things*, has become part of the standard curriculum for interaction designers.

Originally, Norman did not differentiate between Gibson's notion of affordance as an action possibility and the way that this possibility is conveyed—later, he termed the notion "real affordance" for the former and "perceived affordance" for the latter. Although there have been suggestions to extend this typology further to include the sensory apparatus and differentiate between physical and functional possibilities for action, the differentiation between functionality and perception—as proposed by Gaver—seems to have had the most practical impact.

The perceived affordance of an object (or interface element) is affected by factors including its context in an environment or process, culture, or the influence of societal "norms" on the individual's understanding and use of an object, and the user's mental model, her understanding of and expectations for interaction with the object. Perceived affordances point out an important concept for designers—although not necessarily a revolutionary, as designers know that sometimes "form follows function" should be applied (compare Section 4.1). Still, it is very useful as it relates a tool's functionality to properties communicating this functionality.

An example for conflicting affordances is illustrated in Fig. 5.1. To switch off a stereo receiver, a switch has to be slid downwards (outer left); this is only obvious after both reading the text *and* interpreting the meaning of the arrows.

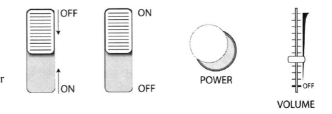

Fig. 5.1 Power switches for stereos: mapping and affordance

A better mapping is created when the labels are switched, eliminating the need for arrows (left). A push switch (right) eliminates the need for label as its position communicates the state by convention. A volume slider that integrates power control completely eliminates the need for a power switch—lowering the volume eventually switches the device off (outer right).

Affordances point out where design must focus, they can be used to simplify the mapping of functionality and interface elements. Reduction plays an important role in designing for perceived affordances: In the given example, although the match with the user's mental model is probably quite fine, the arrows indicating the proper action are superfluous. Instead, the final states should rather be labeled, as the nature of the switch already communicates the possible actions. The last solution is only best if the volume is changed often, it does not support switching the radio off and on to continue listening at the same volume. This is an example for a forcing function (Norman, 2002, 133f). Physically combining two functions to force an activity can be problematic; Norman gives the example of cars that would not start without seat-belts fastened: they mistook a parcel for a passenger, and most users disliked them so intensely that they had their mechanics remove them (ibid., 133f).

5.3 Access Structure

> *A user expects that his programs be no more complicated*
> *to understand than the task they are doing for him*
> —Paul Heckel (1984)

Functionality is not only exposed, or combined for forced access. On the contrary, it is often hidden in layers. These *access structures* become necessary when no direct mapping is possible, and interface elements must serve different functions that depend on the system's state. Different terms have been invented for designing access structure, ranging from the general interaction design to the more fashionable experience design. *Information architecture*[3] is a related discipline that aims to improve the users' access to information. An important aspect of all structuring approaches is the criteria they develop to differentiate between signal and noise, between the information or functionality a user needs, and what obscures relevant information or blocks access to functionality.

In *Designing Web Usability: The Practice of Simplicity* (Nielsen, 2000), Jakob Nielsen gathers advice on how to design Web pages, with special attention to screen real estate and transmission times. He summarizes his guidelines as "Simplicity should be the goal of page design. Users are rarely on a site to enjoy the design; instead, they prefer to focus on the content". (ibid., 97) According to Nielsen, visual design is thus an important element of information design. He propagates the "less is more" rule also for information content of individual screens (Nielsen, 1993, 121)—Web site content should, according to Nielsen, be "succinct", scannable and partitioned into multiple pages[4] (Nielsen, 1997; 2000, 101).

According to Nielsen, partitioning information is a good way to enforce this reduction. His guideline that text on Web pages should be split in smaller units connected by hyperlinks (ibid., 112ff) derives partly from his previous work on hypermedia (e.g. Nielsen, 1995), and partly from his emphasis on the visible part of Web pages in browser windows (see e.g. Nielsen, 1995; ibid., 18ff). He has continued to emphasize this guideline (Nielsen, 1999; Nielsen and Tahir,

---

[3] The term might originate from Xerox PARC, which was founded in 1970 with the mission to create an "architecture of information" and has become popular with the rise of the World Wide Web when the structure of information became a problem for every Web designer (Wurman and Bradford, 1996; Rosenfeld and Morville, 1998).

[4] Nielsen presumably based much of his advice on "writing for the Web" on a SunSoft usability study (Morkes and Nielsen, 1998) where fictitious travel content was rewritten in different styles and judged by sample users.

2002), and expanded it to also refer to forms that should be converted into "applications"—by which he seems to understand not the increased use of dynamic techniques on the Web but a series on traditional non-interactive screens (Nielsen, 2005). The assumption that users do not scroll—that he bases his argumentation upon—could, however, not be reproduced in empirical studies; rather, it was shown that users do scroll if something interests them (Byrne et al., 1999). And although a recent study found that clicks on links concentrate on the upper region of Web pages, an interdependence with the positioning of navigation elements is probable (Weinreich et al., 2006b). Yet, Nielsen's advice contains another aspect. If information is split "into coherent chunks that each focus on a certain topic" (Nielsen, 2000, 112), the user is enabled to "select those topics they care about and only download those pages." (ibid.) Thus, Nielsen's guideline can be understood as a call to adapt the information structure to the user's needs—minimizing the structure that permits users to access information, or functionality.

The ideal of structural minimalism as defined in this book marks out a specific approach to structure that does not necessarily yield a simpler system. However, what is—to the user—more important than the actual simplicity of the system is a perceived simplicity. Tognazzini noted "In my mind, perception is stronger than reality" (Tognazzini, 1992). When he was designing a small text editor, horizontal scrolling was perceived to be slow, and users complained. When the screen refresh algorithm was changed to first copy the visible parts and then display the new text—actually making display slower—an immense speed increase was perceived.

A structurally minimal system is thus not necessarily simpler, yet it may appear simpler to the user. John Maeda's *First Law of Simplicity* (2005c) illustrates an obvious mechanism: "A complex system of many functions can be simplified by carefully grouping related functions." Taken literally, Maeda's rule focuses on relations between functions, while structural minimalism suggests a focus on similarity between the *use* of functions. This difference can also be found looking at structuring techniques for menu systems (for an overview see Norman, 1991), e.g. top-down or bottom-up clustering techniques (ibid., Chapter 11.3; McDonald et al., 1982; Chin, 1987), and the commonly used novice/expert differentiation for application design that is essentially a primitive distinction between use situations. Information architecture draws on both users' static conceptions of categories—e.g. in the popular card-sorting technique (e.g. Fuccella 1997; Hudson, 2005; Rosenfeld and Morville, 1998, 202)—and the analysis of use situations, providing comprehensive support for navigation and offering search as an alternative, structureless access method (Rosenfeld and Morville, 2002).

This match between an interface and users' expectations has been described using the term "directness" (Hutchins et al., 1986). *Semantical directness* denotes the match of objects and operations between user and system on a conceptual level. *Articulatory directness* builds upon this and denotes the translation of user goals into interface commands. A further level of directness is described using the notion of *transparency* by Bødker (1990), who suggests that digital tools should let users work directly on their tasks, the interface becoming invisible.

Often, for different users, different solutions are sought—as supposedly, their requirements differ. The common practice of designing two interfaces for interactive systems—one for beginners and one for expert users—is, however, not without criticism. Raskin (2000a) writes: "Designers speak in terms of 'the tradeoffs between ease of learning and speed of execution in a system'"(Card, 1983, 419). This may be true of particular interface designs, but I have seen no demonstration that it is necessarily a property of all interface designs ... Present desktop GUIs are a compound of at least two distinct interfaces, a relatively visible and learnable but time-consuming, menu-based system and an incomplete keyboard-based collection of hard-to-learn and unmemorable shortcuts. Two wrongs do not make a right." Raskin makes the point that users of complex systems cannot easily be rated on a scale between "beginner" and "expert", but rather focus on a part of the functionality, even to the degree of becoming an expert: "people may seek your advice on using it. Yet you may not know how to use or even know about the existence of certain other commands or even whole categories of commands in that same package. For example, a user of a photo-processing application who produces only online images may never need, or even learn of, that same application's facility for doing color separations, a feature needed primarily by commercial printers." (Raskin, 2000a) This analysis of system use clearly calls for a modularization of functionality that is transparent to the user—architectural minimalism.

Instead of the two-interface approach, Raskin proposes to create systems that are both *monotonous* and *modeless*. Monotonous systems have only one way to accomplish a task. In modeless interfaces, the mapping of commands and system reaction is static, a given user command has one and only one result. Raskin argues that "An interface that is completely modeless and monotonous has a one-to-one correspondence between cause (commands) and effect (actions). The more monotony an interface has for a given task space, the easier it is for the user to develop automaticity, which, after all, is fostered by not having to make decisions about what method to use" (ibid.). Modeless interfaces are an often-sought feature. Alan Cooper remarks that errors can be prevented by using "rich modeless visual feedback" (Cooper and Reimann, 2003, 451ff), giving the example of printing in word processors; instead of raising a dialog box "some clipping will occur", the printable region could be highlighted within the document, immediately opening a path for user responses.

In practice, however, modeless interfaces are the exception—there are simply too many functions in most applications, not necessarily to the benefit of the user: although more functionality is often equalled with more power, a reduction of vocabulary can increase the power available to users. When David Curbow demonstrated the Xerox Star at ACM CHI 1998, he introduced the machine with "Kudos to who was responsible for this—how many times have you seen a version 2 have fewer commands than version one?" (Curbow, 1998a), and praised it later at Xerox PARC as "from a user interface perspective, this interface [the Star] has still not been surpassed [...] in the *very few* commands that you need to do complicated things[5]" (Curbow, 1998b).

Direct manipulation (comp. Shneiderman, 1997; Hutchins et al., 1986) had two different effects: (1) The number of commands was reduced, increasing their individual visibility. (2) commands could be combined to allow sophisticated operations. GUIs can be understood as—on the level of interaction—architecturally minimal, and thus structurally minimal. They were superior to the command line because they "required a restriction on the range of vocabulary by which the user interacted with the system" (Cooper and Reimann, 2003, 255).

5.4 Minimalism and Consistency

One of the strengths of the digital medium, its versatility, presents a major difficulty for designers. While physical tools need to honor physical rules, and the design activity in the physical domain is an intense interaction with limitations, digital designs enjoy far more freedom. David Gelernter rephrased this as "If you make a dam the wrong shape, it will crumble. If you shape a telephone like a Volkswagen or a tomato, it can still work, divining the shape that seems inevitable, creating the 'inevitability illusion'—the impression that you are looking at the pure visual embodiment of science of engineering—is an art, pure and simple" (Gelernter, 1999). As Gelernter proclaims, "When the illusion succeeds, the outcome is technology that works beautifully and is beautiful" (ibid.). Without physical limitations, the design is bound by expectations—and consistency becomes an important aspect of design.

Consistency is probably the most commonly cited principle for the design of interactive systems. Almost every guideline lists consistency as an explicit value, and encourages consistency with "interface standards" using a multitude of suggestions, rules and examples. Almost every usability expert will agree that consistency is important, and heuristics for evaluating interfaces are bound to demand consistency. All the more, it is surprising that consistency is not well defined. As Kellogg (1989) points out, "Consistency has no meaning on its own; it is inherently a relational concept. Therefore, to merely say that an interface is consistent or that consistency is a goal of user interface design is also meaningless". Even a committee of international usability experts was unable to agree on a definition after two intensive days of discussion (Nielsen, 1989). Grudin (1989) makes a case against consistency, arguing that without a reliable

---

[5] The Xerox Star differentiated data icons and function icons, a function like copy could thus both mail and print documents, depending on the context.

definition, the concept becomes only a secondary guideline. He argues that many successful interfaces are inconsistent and demonstrates that, in some cases, consistency may even be harmful in interface design. His examples include keyboard mapping that demonstrates ease of use can conflict with ease of learning, menu behavior patterns that vary with different tasks (e.g. after copying text, paste should be selected, after italicizing a text, the italic attribute should be selected by default), and the form of consistency that exposes system architecture (e.g. the file system) to the user (cf. Bernard et al., 1981; Grudin, 1988). Grudin previously pointed out that simplicity can be harmful if systems are simpler than the real world: "If the system does not preserve a distinction that users actually make, there will be no way for the Interface dialogue to match the user's expectations." (Grudin, 1986)

Despite his critical stance, Grudin tries to redefine consistency and differentiates between three types of consistency: *Internal consistency* within an application, *external consistency* with other applications, and *consistency with familiar features* from the real world (Grudin, 1989). An ambitious formal approach of defining consistency was taken by Wiecha et al. (1989), Reisner (1990) or Rieman et al. (1994), starting a heated debate (comp. Grudin, 1992; Wiecha, 1992); yet, as Chimera and Shneiderman (Chimera and Shneiderman, 1993) note, the formal approaches "get more elusive as they are scrutinized".

In practice, informal factors were shown to have great influence. Tognazzini reported that the immediate availability of key applications, MacWrite and MacPaint in the case of the Apple Macintosh, was vital for achieving interface consistency (Tognazzini, 1989). In *Tog on Interface* (Tognazzini, 1992), he advises a selective approach to consistency: "(1) If it ain't broke real bad, don't fix it. (2) Reflect the illusion of the interface, not the realities of the hardware. (3) Build on existing visual/behavioral language. (4) Use big concepts. (5) Depend on precedent. (6) Invent new objects, with new appearances, for new user behaviors".

Consistency is often connected with the use of metaphors, which is held to be an important factor for the initial appeal and learnability of a system. The desktop metaphor of the Xerox Star is a famous example: "Even on first contact, the machine will appear to be as familiar, friendly and easy to cope with as well as the top of the desk" (Xerox, 1983, 3:43). Consistency with metaphors, however, often does introduce unnecessary restrictions. An example is a calendar "month view" that prevents users from inspecting entries that cross the border of two months (Cooper and Reimann, 2003, 30). Nielsen joins those who are critical of employing one, over-arching metaphor in design (Nielsen, 2000, 180): "The greatest weakness of metaphors is that they ... push the site in directions that seem fun and appropriate within the metaphor but leave users' real goals behind." Most successful metaphors (e.g. the shopping cart for e-commerce sites) are, according to Nielsen (ibid., 188), successful not because of their inherited meaning, but due to the standardization that creates a consistent interface to shared functionality over different sites.

Cooper suggests replace metaphors with idioms (Cooper and Reimann, 2003, 248–250): "Metaphors are hard to find and they constrict our thinking" (ibid., 252) Nelson called this "the design of principles" (Nelson, 1990)— learning idioms is compared by Cooper to learning the meaning of figures of speech. Cooper points out that often, we do not use interface elements because we immediately understand their meaning through the embedding metaphor, but because we learn how to use them by observing others: "Windows, title bars, close boxes, ... hyperlinks ... are things we learn idiomatically rather than intuit metaphorically" (Cooper and Reimann, 2003, 250). Examples include interaction techniques, e.g. the computer mouse: "We don't know how mice work, and yet even small children can operate them just fine" (ibid., 251). He illustrates the extensibility of idioms with mouse clicking: a single click means placement, a single click combined with dragging characterwise selection. This functionality is intuitively extended by double clicking that selects a word, and double clicking and dragging that activates wordwise selection. Triple clicking, finally, invokes selection for paragraphs.

Tognazzini reported that on the Macintosh, a switch of metaphor from Finder to Switcher and back to MultiFinder (known as simply 'Finder' again under System 7) was made. Switcher introduced a metaphor that "existing users had to form new and somewhat confusing mental models to be able to understand" (Tognazzini, 1992). In retrospect, the original metaphor was restored with Multi-Finder: "It was far more powerful than Switcher, and yet, as a model, didn't require the user to learn anything new." For Tognazzini, this demonstrates "the importance of really considering the impact that features added to the second or third release of a product will have on the metaphor" (ibid.). Here, the *stability* of the work environment is the cause for consistency. This is further illustrated by Dennis Austin, the creator of Powerpoint, originally an application for the Macintosh: "The Apple Desktop Interface ... defines a number of consistent graphic elements (menu bar, window border, and so on) to maintain the illusion of stability. ..." Hiding the menu bar resulted in severe disorientation: "I have seen, during user testing, the very real fear etched on the face of users when the menu bar disappears. I have watched them literally panic as they are trapped in a strange world" (quoted ibid., Weinreich et al., 34).

Consistency can serve as a replacement for simplicity. If most of a new design is already known, or consistent with a known design, only new additions have to be learned and mastered. Thus, the impression of even extremely complex systems can be simple—if they adhere to standards set by legacy systems. The disadvantage of consistency here is clear: it inhibits change, and better solutions have a hard time to become accepted—or are never adopted because it seems more complex to relearn conventions. One well-known example is the Dvorak keyboard, which is often considered to be superior to current QWERTY-type keyboards, but never even had the slightest chance of commercial success (Diamond, 1997; Liebowitz and Margolis, 1990; Brooks, 1999).

On the World Wide Web, consistency has been an important argument for the increasing use of Web-based applications. To some degree, Web browsers unify the use experience for these applications. However, their interface is still based on the Hypertext document metaphor and lacks support for the requirements of interactive applications (Weinreich et al., 2006b, 2008). This illustrates that consistency alone is not always sufficient, but that consistency with conventions limiting necessary interaction can be very harmful for usability.

To summarize, consistency remains, for the design of interactive systems, an important concept of relative nature. According to common agreement, "Users' tasks and application domain are a major focus for providing consistency" (Chimera and Shneiderman, 1993). This very generic claim can be specified in the light of architectural minimalism by demanding that individual tools need to form a consistent whole. For individual tools and in some cases—as the concept of structural minimalism indicates—other factors, such as immediacy, can become more important for a useable design than consistency. Although metaphors can be helpful, they are also a dangerous tool for design as their analogical function places restrictions on digital design that can limit usability. The stability of an interface is an important motivation for consistency, and thus finding initial metaphors becomes a crucial part of design; this is even more critical for systems with minimal functionality—if later functionality is to be expected, the chosen application model needs to allow for an expansion.

5.5 Minimalism and Conceptions of Design

The design of interactive systems is a multidisciplinary field. Consequently, manifold conceptions of the design activity accompany those who try to achieve usability: the field of Requirements Engineering follows an engineering approach, Human Factors tried to optimize the "human variable" in the organizational system, and user-centered design uses the technology-centered term "user" (Grudin, 1990b) to identify basic priorities. The latter perspective is illustrated by Bruce Tognazzini: "I was overprotecting my users. I kept them from straying from the safe, sure path I had plotted through my application. ... In general, I drove the users stark, raving mad. Every time they tried to make a move, I was one step ahead of them, protecting them from any possible hurt. ... Consider how you'd feel if every day when you came into work, Mom was there to make sure your nails were clean and your seat wasn't too high and you didn't have too much coffee. Mea culpa. This is what I did to my users." (Tognazzini, 1992)

Design has been described as an industry—as a form of mass production, a single application can be replicated and used by millions. It has also been described as a craft (Wroblewski, 1991, 7–12); according to Wroblewski, when software cannot easily be specified in formal terms "only craft-like efforts have succeeded" (ibid., 10). This does not imply that informed design decisions are inferior, only that "building human-computer interfaces involves applying the relevant knowledge in a complex problem solving context to tasks and artifacts too complex to be completely understood[6]" (ibid., 12).

Yet, not only are many design efforts of immense complexity, but as design involves context, designers cannot even influence all parts relevant to a design. This is documented even by Jakob Nielsen—who is, judged by the number of generic recommendations and his acknowledgment of a preference for standardized guidelines ruling Web design (Nielsen, 2000, 217), unsuspicious of giving control away too freely: he observes a shift in the control over navigation that is created by the hypertextual origin of the Web (ibid., 214); designers cannot plan for, or control all aspects of navigation. Instead, users can enter a site via search engines on other pages than the home page, and bookmarks and backtracking may also allow them to navigate pages in a sequence that the designer never planned for.

Tognazzini changed his initial attitude to software design: "In my new designs, my users are truly in control. I assume they have an IQ that lies above room-temperature. ... I assume they can make their own decisions on how they want to work" (Tognazzini, 1992). The computer assumes the role of a communications partner and control is shifted to the user—commands are centered around the users' needs, instead of walking users through a "maze of commands" (ibid.).

The discussion of minimalism in art (Chapter 2) identified a similar struggle for control, eventually leaving the artwork in control of context and user. Similarly, the role of designers changes to enablers of actions. This shift is echoed in e.g. the stage metaphor that Brenda Laurel (1993) introduced into HCI: A story offers a context; within the context, it offers activities and plots played by characters. In her transfer from her dramaturgical background to the design of interactive software, Laurel continues: "The users of such a system are like audience members who can march up onto the stage and become various characters, altering the action by what they say and do in their roles." (ibid., 16). The designers role is to set the stage, provide meaningful characters, and a draft plot. The storyline—what is happening on stage—lies within the control of users; control is not immediate, and not complete.

Also in 1993, Tognazzini (1993) drew a comparison of stage magic and usability: "Showmanship is the gentle seduction of the users, leading them to accept, believe in, and feel in control of the illusory world we have built for them." While Laurel concentrates on the interaction itself, Tognazzini also mentions the preceding step: a product must appeal to the user, or he/she will not buy it. The affective power of designing (perceived) freedom is also reflected

---

[6] T-shirts with the text "It depends", fashionable in the HCI community, and probably first introduced by Jared Spool's User Interface Engineering company, represent a less scientific version of this statement.

in Don Norman's parallel between Boorstein's (1992) description of designing movies in *The Hollywood Eye: What Makes Movies Work* and his own three levels of design (Norman, 2004, 112).

5.6 Minimalism and Simplicity

> *Good design, like good writing, is simple and economical. Simple design makes the product easier to maintain and use. No magic formula will enable us to create simple designs; they are the result of creativity, false starts, and hard work. But when we can achieve most of our design objectives while making something simple, our results are likely to be good.*
>
> —Paul Heckel (1984)

As the previous take at simplicity (Section 3.2.1) demonstrated, the notion of simplicity is used by different authors to describe different qualities of interactive systems. Sometimes, it refers to visual qualities, although it is difficult to differentiate the superficial from the more fundamental design. Sometimes, it is used to describe the perceived affordances of nonphysical interaction widgets, yet these seamlessly blend into access structures provided by the interface. A distinctly different take on minimalism is offered by Donald Norman in his book *The Invisible Computer*: "Simplicity design axiom: The complexity of the information appliance is that of the task, not the tool. The technology is invisible." (Norman, 1999) An invisible interface certainly solves all problems of mapping and structure—or does an interface only become invisible after they have been solved? Bill Buxton adds: "My view is that very strong, specific devices are how you make computers disappear, and how you change the computer from something that gets in the way into a prosbook that helps empower us and actually makes the world simpler" (Anderson, 2000).

The question of appropriate functionality is deeply rooted in the design of interactive systems. Although not so long ago, computing was mainly thought of as computation, culminating in the famous prophecy ascribed to Thomas Watson, chairman of IBM, in 1943, "I think there is a world market for maybe five computers", the PC revolution brought a powerful general-purpose computer to every workplace and home. The generality of the PC was heavily criticized as it required trade-offs impeding the usability for specific applications. Instead of general-purpose tools, computing machines were devised for specific tasks. Some attribute their invention to Vannevar Bush's concept of a *Memex device* that was conceived to access information, and build information paths (Bush, 1946; Müller-Prove, 2002). Jef Raskin, founder of Information Appliance Incorporation, is said to have developed the concept of *information appliance*(Raskin, 1982; Voelcker, 1986). The notion of information appliances was explained in more detail in *The Invisible Computer* by Don Norman (1999), and has since entered HCI vocabulary. While the term was initially meant to describe a functionally-specialized appliance that tried to perform a single function well, it is often used to denote more universal appliances—an example is the *universal information appliance* coined by IBM's TSpaces project (Eustice et al., 1999).

5.6.1 Limits of the Notion of Simplicity

> *When you actually sit down and analyze*
> *what you need to get the job done, it's not simplicity.*

—Don Norman (quoted in Park, 2008)

Simplicity is often an aspired value in the design of human-computer interaction.[7] The positive nature of simplicity is obvious: "simplifying" the user experience—removing hassles and unnecessary tasks, making the task at hand and life generally easier—will improve usability. However, to make simplicity more than a symbolic value, it would have to satisfy the same criteria that are here put forward towards minimalism—it must make a useful tool for analysis and, possibly, for construction of interactive software.

This, however, remains unproven with as undefined a term as simplicity: often, circular reasoning suggests something is usable if it is simple, and it is simple if it is usable—or a definition is omitted completely as in Nielsen's *The Practice of Simplicity* (2000). As a purely positive measure, simplicity is difficult to criticize; this prevents the discussion of the negative traits of simplicity as, clearly, others might find that the sophisticated is preferable to the simple. Questions of direction and degree, "What shall be simplified?", and "When should one choose the complex over the simple?", cannot be easily answered—and simplicity is also suspiciously subjective in its focus. Furthermore, interactive systems are complex in themselves. Considering their context further increases complexity, and simplicity in design can only be procured for certain, well-defined aspects. Simply stated, while simplicity can be a useful value to pursue, it is not a helpful guide in pursuit. Minimalism, however, is—rather than a value—a means of describing different ways of reaching simplicity.

As an example, consider a fundamental task of today's information society: instantaneous information transmission over large distances. When first implemented in the form of electric telegraphs, different technologies were competing that built on the electromagnet demonstrated by William Sturgeon in 1825. The European version of the telegraph was patented in 1837 by William Cooke and Charles Wheatstone in Great Britain. It featured what is arguably the most simple interface to transmit English letters over a wire: a dial to choose a character, and a button to transmit a sign indicating that the chosen character is to be

---

[7] This yearning for clarity can be found in numerous reactions to computer dialog. Perhaps one of the most prominent examples is Ted Nelson's: "featuritis and clutter... [which] is taking on new forms. In the popular iconic world, it becomes a new style of screen clutter. You face a screen littered with cryptic junk: the frying pan, the yo-yo, the bird's nest, the high-button shoe. Or whatever. You must learn the nonobvious aspects of a lot of poorly designed screen furniture and the visual toys: what they actually do, rather than what they suggest. You must explore the details of each until you understand what it 'really' means." (Nelson, 1990, 236).

received and added to the transmitted text. Although Wheatstone's first telegraphs needed up to five wires for transmission, an improved version was designed and consequently marketed by Werner von Siemens in 1847, needing only a single transmission wire (Fig. 5.2). Unknown to the user, small electric impulses were transmitted as the dial was turned, thus enabling the receiver's dial to copy the motion of the sender's dial.

This "simple" interface was competing during the second half of the 19th century with an interface that was simple in different ways: the Morse telegraph. The Morse telegraph uses but a single key to encode characters in sequences of dots and dashes—or short and long electric impulses sent over the wire. A predecessor of the groundbreaking Morse code was demonstrated in 1838 by Alfred Vail (Pope, 1888; Calvert, 2004), but it was his partner, Samuel Morse, who became famous as he built the device used in the first continental demonstration of delivering a telegraph message from Baltimore to Washington in 1844 (Fig. 5.3). While the efficient use of Morse telegraphs is a learned skill, the Morse alphabet was designed

Fig. 5.2 "Zeigertelegraph" designed 1846 by Werner von Siemens, built by Johann Georg Halske, private photograph

Fig. 5.3 The original "lever correspondent" used in the 1844 Baltimore-Washington demo; historical photograph

so effectively to match the task of transmitting English texts that not only the reliability of transmission but also the speed of transmission exceeded those of the dial telegraphs (the speed of professional Morse telegraphs exceeds 20 words per minute).

The dial telegraph offered a direct mapping of interface and functionality and was easy to use. Yet, it was slow and in contrast to the Morse telegraph, it could not transmit other characters than those conceived of during construction. The Morse telegraph is constructed in the most simple way imaginable, its mode of operation is immediately transparent, it is simple to extend the alphabet, and easy to adapt to other uses (even music Tulga and Tulga, 2005). Which of these interfaces is simpler?

To clarify this point, Japanese text input serves as an illustrative example: equivalent to the dial telegraph are approaches that try to build a Japanese "keyboard" (see Fig. 5.4). In order to construct typewriters able to print *kanji*, the smaller, yet still numerous subset of Chinese characters used in Japanese language, 2,400 characters were chosen as a result of analyzing their frequency of use in public documents. The characters were arranged by classification on a character carriage, and the chosen character was raised by a type bar and typed against a cylindrical paper supporter. This typewriter was patented by Kyota Sugimoto in 1929 and consequently used for the production of office documents. As a consequence, typists rushing out to the next

Fig. 5.4 First Japanese typewriter designed by Kyota Sugimoto (1929)

typewriter store, trying to purchase new letters not included in the standard set (often used in names) were a common sight in the 1930s (Jun'ichiro, 2001). However, typing was still slow, skilled typists could manage to type up to 2 characters per second, about twice the speed of handwriting. Efforts to produce a keyboard for Chinese characters did also fail to gain wide adoption—direct access to all letters becomes more difficult as the number of letters increases (Fig. 5.5), and Chinese newspapers require knowledge of around 4,000 characters while dictionaries can contain up to 50,000 characters (Zhou, 2003, see Fig. 5.6).

Fig. 5.5 Chinese keyboard prototype, National Chiao Tung University, Taiwan

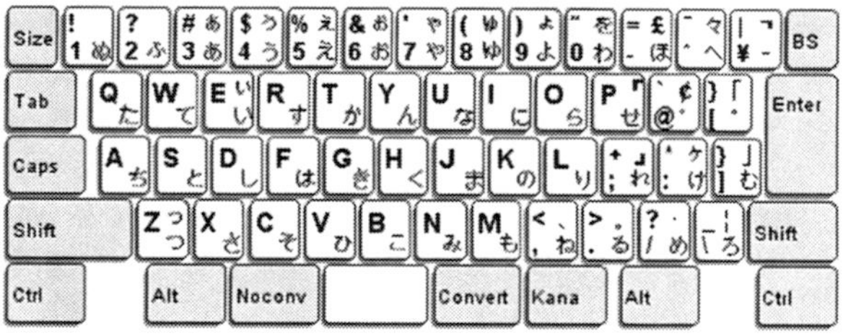

Fig. 5.6 Kanji Keyboard layout for Microsoft Windows Operating Systems

Japanese and Chinese text input nowadays is a compromise between the number of buttons and the complexity of combining different keystrokes. The keyboards used for Japanese and Traditional Chinese are based on the standard 106-key keyboard, adding two letter keys (from within the backspace and right shift keys) and function keys along the space bar. These extra function keys are used to control the character composition (e.g. with the Microsoft Input Method Editor, Rolfe, 2003, Fig. 5.6).

John Maeda of MIT, an advocate for simplicity in HCI design, summarizes the problem of defining what is simple with a clever redefinition of simplicity: "Simplicity is not about living at the poles of simple versus complex. It is not about being zero or none. Instead, it is about some." However, with this redefinition in his "tenth law of simplicity", Maeda (2005a) makes finding flawed uses of simplicity impossible. Furthermore, simplicity is used as a value that is ascribed to objects after it has been proven that they work; the term, thus, has neither an explanatory function nor does it spend advice on design extending beyond the examples.[8]

Don Norman (2007) and Spolsky (2006) reiterate on another difficulty of the term simplicity—its purely positive connotation can make it difficult to correctly judge its role in marketing: complex interfaces can be preferred by customers when deciding what device to buy as visual complexity is linked with potency (as opposed to power). So, although it is difficult to say:[9] a design can be too simple.

5.7 Revisiting the Four Notions of Minimalism

Persuading through Simplifying—Using computing technology to reduce complex behavior to simple tasks increases the benefit/cost ratio of the behavior and influences users to perform the behavior.

— B.J. Fogg (2002)

The discussion of aspects of the heterogeneous literature on HCI that touch upon reduction indicated that minimalism describes aspects of simplicity, which exist in the literature, but are understood in inconsistent terms: *orchestrated flow*, *affordances*, and *information appliances* are all shows to relate to different notions of simplicity (Section 5.1). To anchor the minimal standpoint in the existing literature, different conceptions of design are discussed, arguing for understanding design as a *craft* (Section 5.5), and the notion of *consistency* was discussed as a possible replacement for simplicity: while it reduces the amount of work needed to learn the use of a new tool, possibly

---

[8] Instead, as a designer, Maeda uses Gestalt laws to explain phenomena found e.g. in the iPod design.

[9] The positive value ascribed to simplicity is so strong that Don Norman had to add the following disclaimer to his column: "Comment: This is one of the most misunderstood of all my columns. So after you finish, read the 'Addendum' before you Slashdot or otherwise flame me. ... So, of course I am in favor of good design and attractive products. Easy to use products. But when it comes time to purchase, people tend to go for the more powerful products, and they judge the power by the apparent complexity of the controls."

harmful effects of consistency are illustrated as it inhibits the evolution of design (Section 5.4).

The conflict of complexity and simplicity is identified as a recurring theme, experts agree that a reduction is often necessary, yet the degree and direction remain debatable. The four notions of minimalism put forward in this book help to identify areas of reduction. Revisiting them individually, it becomes clear that *functional minimalism* is often sought for, and closely linked with *information appliances*, a concept of simple tools that perform only a single function.[10] *Structural minimalism* is one of the most popular interpretations of simplicity—transparency and directness are positive values for design. These values, just as "suitability for the task" defined in ISO 9241, however, give no constructive advice and can only be evaluated indirectly through the user—if it fits, it fits. *Architectural minimalism* and *compositional minimalism* present novel concepts—although the necessity is illustrated by the discussion on access structures and modelessness, and the values defined in international standards.

Simplicity and reduction are often mentioned in guidelines and heuristics and expert advice often relates to options for reducing complexity. This illustrates the need for an understanding of reduction and reductive methods; there is, however, no systematic examination of reduction in the literature: only specific aspects, such as the visibility of interface elements, the problem of modes,[11] or the mapping of interface elements and functionality have been formalized in terminology and descriptive theory. The terminology of the simple is overloaded with different meanings—simplicity is not enough to explain or understand reduction. If it is used as a synonym for "good", and complexity for "bad", no differentiation of function, design and use is possible (comp. Szafranski and Maeda, 2008; Norman, 2007). Minimalism tries to fills this void as it sets out to differentiate different notions of simplicity and presents an alternative to the exclusive use of techniques building on consistency and metaphor.

Taken together, the different notions of minimalism form a standpoint for design. This standpoint is marked by a shift towards a both holistic and fragmenting[12] perspective—designs need to reduce their individual complexity to allow designing complexity on a second level. The scope of HCI analysis widened as the object of research includes not only a single application and its users and context, but networks of interoperable tools. A second shift induced

---

[10] It is, however, doubtful that pure information appliances do really exist.

[11] Modality can be considered a method for attaining structural minimalism as it decreases the number of options for the user. It does, however, also increase the amount of composition as the designer plans in advance what actions users are allowed to perform—this is a central aspect of critique for modal systems.

[12] Design structure is to my knowledge not an explicitly discussed topic—in software development, the study of software structure surfaced as programs became too large to manage as a single block; architectural minimalism suggests that a similar approach to design simplifies the life of both users and designers.

by the minimalist perspectives leads away from interface design, and towards system design. This demands a conception of interface design as a deep-reaching discipline—away from decoration towards functional analysis.

References

Anderson, R. I. (2000). Conversations with Clement Mok and Jakob Nielsen, and with Bill Buxton and Clifford Nass. *Interactions*, 7(1), 46–80.

Apple. (2006). Time Machine. A giant leap forward for backup. http://www.apple.com/macosx/leopard/timemachine.html Accessed 7.8.2008

Bernard, P., Hammond, N., Morton, J., Long, J., and Clark, I. (1981). Consistency and compatibility in human-computer Dialogue. *International Journal of Man-Machine Studies*, 15(1), 87–134.

Bobrow, D. G., Burchfield, J. D., Murphy, D. L., and Tomlinson, R. S. (1972). TENEX, a paged time sharing system for the PDP-10. *Communications of the ACM*, 15, 135–143.

Boorstein, J. (1992). *The Hollywood Eye: What Makes Movies Work*. New York, NY: Perennial.

Bødker, S. (1990). *Through the Interface – A Human Activity Approach to User Interface Design*. Hillsdale, NJ: Lawrence Erlbaum Associates.

Brooks, M. (1999). *Introducing the Dvorak Keyboard – Dissenting Opinions*. http://www.mwbrooks.com/dvorak/dissent.html

Bush, V. (1946). As we may think. Reprinted in 1996. *Interactions*, 32, 35–46.

Byrne, M. D., John, B. E., Wehrle, N. S., and Crow, D. C. (1999). *The Tangled Web we Wove: a Taskonomy of WWW Use*. CHI '99: Proceedings of the SIGCHI conference on Human factors in computing systems, New York, NY, USA, 544–551.

Calvert, J. B. (2004). The Electromagnetic Telegraph. http://www.du.edu/~jcalvert/tel/morse/morse.htm Accessed 2.3.2008

Card, S. K. (1983). *The Psychology of Human-Computer Interaction*. Philadelphia, PA: Lawrence Erlbaum Associates.

Chimera, R., and Shneiderman, B. (1993). User Interface Consistency: An Evaluation of Original and Revised Interfaces for a Videodisk Library. In B Shneiderman (Ed.), *Sparks of Innovation in Human-Computer Interaction*. 259–273. Norwood, NJ: Ablex Publishers.

Chin, J. P. (1987). *Top-Down and Bottom-up Menu Design*. Proceedings of the second international conference on human/computer interaction, Honululu, HI, 144–147.

Cooper, A. (1999). *The Inmates Are Running the Asylum : Why High Tech Products Drive Us Crazy and How To Restore The Sanity*. Indianapolis, IN: Sams.

Cooper, A. (1996). Why I am called "the Father of Visual Basic". http://www.cooper.com/alan/father_of_vb.html Accessed 20.4.2007

Cooper, A., and Reimann, R. M. (2003). *About Face 2.0: The Essentials of Interaction Design*. Hoboken, NJ: Wiley.

Cornell, B., Dinda, P. A., and Bustamante, F. E. (2004). *Wayback: A User-level Versioning File System for Linux*. The 2004 USENIX annual technical conference, FREENIX track.

Csikszentmihalyi, M. (1991). *Flow: The Psychology of Optimal Experience*. New York, NY: Harper Perennial.

Curbow, D. (1998a). CHI'98 Xerox Star demo.

Curbow, D, (1998b). Final Xerox Star demo Palo Alto, CA.

Diamond, J. (1997). The Curse of QWERTY O typewriter! Quit your torture!. *DISCOVER*, 18(4).

Eustice, K. F., Lehman, T. J., Morales, A., Munson, M. C., Edlund, S., and Guillen, M. (1999). A universal information appliance. *IBM Systems Journal*, 38(4), 575–601.

Fogg, B. J. (2002). *Persuasive Technology: Using Computers to Change What We Think and Do (The Morgan Kaufmann Series in Interactive Technologies)*. San Fransisco, CA: Morgan Kaufmann.

Fuccella, J. (1997). Using user centered design methods to create and design usable Web sites. SIGDOC '97: *Proceedings of the 15th annual international conference on computer documentation*, New York, NY, USA, 69–77.

Gelernter, D. (1999). *Machine Beauty: Elegance and the Heart of Technology (Repr. ed) (Masterminds)*. New York, NY: Basic Books.

Gibson, J. J. (1979). *Ecological Approach to Visual Perception*. Boston: Houghton Mifflin.

Grudin, J. (1986). *Designing in the dark: logics that compete with the user*. CHI '86: Proceedings of the SIGCHI conference on human factors in computing systems, New York, NY, USA, 281–284.

Grudin, J, (1988). *Why CSCW Applications Fail: Problems in the Design and Evaluation of Organization of Organizational Interfaces*. CSCW '88: Proceedings of the 1988 ACM conference on Computer-supported cooperative work, New York, NY, USA, 85–93.

Grudin, J. (1989). The case against user interface consistency. *Communications of the ACM*, 32(10), 1164–1173.

Grudin, J. (1990b). *The Computer Reaches Out: the Historical Continuity of Interface Design*. CHI '90: Proceedings of the SIGCHI conference on Human factors in computing systems, New York, NY, USA, 261–268.

Grudin, J. (1992). Consistency, standards, and formal approaches to interface development and evaluation: a note on Wiecha, Bennett, Boies, Gould, and Greene. *ACM Transactions on Information Systems*, 10(1), 103–111.

Heckel, P. (1984). *The Elements of Friendly Software Design*. Clayton VIC: Warner Books.

Hudson, W. (2005). Playing your cards right: getting the most from card sorting for navigation design. *Interactions*, 12(5), 56–58.

Hutchins, E., Hollan, J. D., and Norman, D. A. (1986). Direct Manipulation Interfaces. In D. Norman and S. Draper (Eds.), *User Centered System Design: New Perspectives on Human-Computer Interaction*. 87–124. Philadelphia, PA: Lawrence Erlbaum Associates.

Jun'ichiro, K. (2001). Wapro: the interface between the Japanese language and the computer. *The Book and the Computer. Online journal. Special Series: Japanese in the age of Technology*, 5(1).

Kellogg, W. (1989). The Dimensions of Consistency. In J Nielsen (Ed.), *Coordinating User Interfaces for Consistency*. 9–20. Boston, MA: Academic Press.

Laurel, B. (1993). *Computers as Theatre*. Addison-Wesley Professional.

Liebowitz, S. J., and Margolis, S. E. (1990). The Fable of the Keys. *Journal of Law & Economics, 33*, 1–25.

Maeda, J. (2005a). Less is Greater Than Zero. Thoughts on Simplicity http://weblogs.media.mit.edu/SIMPLICITY/archives/000230.html#law Accessed 28.7.2008

Maeda, J. (2005c). First Law of Simplicity. Thoughts on Simplicity Maeda http://weblogs.media.mit.edu/SIMPLICITY/archives/000113.html#firstlaw Accessed 28.7.2008

McDonald, J. E., Stone, J. D., Liebelt, L. S., and Karat, J. (1982). *Evaluating a Method for Structuring the User-System Interface*. Proceedings the 26th annual meeting of the human factors society.

Morkes, J., and Nielsen, J. (1998). Applying Writing Guidelines to Web Pages. http://www.useit.com/papers/webwriting/rewriting.html Accessed 22.4.2008

Müller-Prove, M. (2002). *Vision and Reality of Hypertext and Graphical User Interfaces*. Universität Hamburg, Bericht FBI-HH-B-237/02, Hamburg, Germany. Available online at http://www.mprove.de/diplom/

Nelson, T. H. (1990). The right way to think about software design. In B. Laurel and D. Mills (Eds.), *The Art of Human-Computer Interface Design*. Ontario: Addison-Wesley Publishing Company Inc.

Nielsen, J. (1989). Coordinating user interfaces for consistency. *SICCHI Bulletin, 20*, 63–65.

Nielsen, J. (1993). *Usability Engineering*. Boston: Academic Press.

Nielsen, J. (1995). *Multimedia and Hypertext*: the Internet and beyond. Boston: AP Professional.

Nielsen, J. (2000). *Designing Web Usability*. Indianapolis, IN: New Riders.

Nielsen, J. (1997). Be Succinct! (Writing for the Web). *Alertbox* http://www.useit.com/alert box/9703b.html Accessed 20.4.2008

Nielsen, J. (1999). Ten Good Deeds in Web Design. *Alertbox* http://www.useit.com/alertbox/ 991003.html Accessed 21.4.2008

Nielsen, J. (2005). Forms vs. Applications. *Alertbox* http://www.useit.com/alertbox/forms. html Accessed 21.4.2008

Nielsen, J., and Mack, R. L. (1994). *Usability Inspection Methods*. New York, NY: Wiley.

Nielsen, J., and Tahir, M. (2002). *Homepage Usability : 50 Websites Deconstructed*. Indianapolis, IN: New Riders.

Norman, D. A. (2007). Simplicity Is Highly Overrated. *Interactions,* 14(2), 40–41.

Norman, D. A. (1983). *Design Principles for Human-Computer Interfaces*. CHI '83: Proceedings of the SIGCHI conference on human factors in computing systems, New York, NY, USA, 1–10.

Norman, D. A. (1999). *The Invisible Computer: Why Good Products Can Fail, the Personal Computer Is So Complex, and Information Appliances Are the Solution*. Cambridge, MA: The MIT Press.

Norman, D. A. (2002). Emotion & design: attractive things work better. *Interactions,* 9(4), 36–42.

Norman, D. A. (1989). *The Psychology of Everyday Things*. New York, NY: Basic Books.

Norman, D. A. (2004). *Emotional Design: Why We Love (Or Hate) Everyday Things*. New York, NY: Basic Books.

Norman, K. L. (1991). *The Psychology of Menu Selection: Designing Cognitive Control at the Human/Computer Interface (Human/Computer Interaction)*. New York, NY: Ablex Publishing Corporation.

Park, A. (2008). The Brash Boys at 37signals Will Tell You: Keep it Simple, Stupid. http:// www.wired.com/techbiz/media/magazine/16-03/mf_signals?currentPage = all

Peterson, Z., and Burns, R. (2005). Ext3cow: A time-shifting file system for regulatory compliance. *Transactions Storage,* 1(2), 190–212.

Pope, F. (1888, April). The American inventors of the telegraph, with special references to the services of Alfred Vail. *The Century: Illustrated Monthly Magazine*.

Raskin, J. (1982). Computers by the millions. *SIGPC Newsletter,* 5(2). Available online: http://www.digibarn.com/friends/jef-raskin/writings/millions.html.

Raskin, J. (2000a). The humane interface (book excerpt). *Ubiquity,* 1(14), 3.

Reisner, P. (1990). *What is Inconsistency?* INTERACT '90: Proceedings of the IFIP TC13 third interational conference on human-computer interaction, 175–181.

Rieman, J., Lewis, C., Young, R. M., and Polson, P. G. (1994). *Why is a Raven Like a Writing Desk?: Lessons in Interface Consistency and Analogical Reasoning from Two Cognitive Architectures*. CHI '94: Proceedings of the SIGCHI conference on human factors in computing systems, New York, NY, USA, 438–444.

Rolfe, R. (2003). What is an IME (Input Method Editor) and how do I use it? http://www. microsoft.com/globaldev/handson/user/IME_Paper.mspx Accessed 20.7.2008

Rosenfeld, L., and Morville, P. (2002). *Information Architecture for the World Wide Web*. Sebastopol, CA: O'Reilly.

Rosenfeld, L., and Morville, P. (1998). *Information Architecture for the World Wide Web*(1st ed.). Cambridge ; Sebastopol, CA: O'Reilly.

Shneiderman, B. (1997). *Direct Manipulation for Comprehensible, Predictable and Controllable User Interfaces*. IUI '97: Proceedings of the 2nd international conference on Intelligent user interfaces, New York, NY, USA, 33–39.

Spolsky, J. (2006). Simplicity. http://www.joelonsoftware.com/items/2006/12/09.html

Szafranski, R., and Maeda, J. (2008). Information Overload. *Economist Debates.* http://www. economist.com/debate/overview/125.

Tognazzini, B. (1989). Achieving consistency for the Macintosh. In J Nielsen (Ed.), *Coordinating User Interfaces for Consistency.* 57–73. San Diego, CA: Academic Press Professional, Inc.

Tognazzini, B. (1993). *Principles, Techniques, and Ethics of Stage Magic and Their Application to Human Interface Design.* CHI '93: Proceedings of the SIGCHI conference on human factors in computing systems, New York, NY, USA, 355–362.

Tognazzini, B. (1992). *Tog on Interface.* Addison-Wesley Professional.

Tulga, P., and Tulga, D. (2005). Morse Code Music – Connecting Rhythm and Language with Morse Code. http://www.philtulga.com/morse.html Accessed 3.8.2008

Voelcker, J. (1986). The Information Appliance. *IEEE Spectrum, 23*(5), 65.

Weinreich, H., Obendorf, H., Herder, E., and Mayer, M. (2006b). *Off the Beaten Tracks: Exploring Three Aspects of Web Navigation.* WWW '06: Proceedings of the 15th international conference on World Wide Web, New York, NY, USA, 133–142.

Weinreich, H., Obendorf, H., Herder, E., and Mayer, M. (2008). Not quite the average: An empirical study of web use. *ACM Transactions on the Web, 2*(1).

Wiecha, C. (1992). ITS and user interface consistency: a response to Grudin. *ACM Transactions on Information systems, 10*(1), 112–114.

Wiecha, C., Bennett, W., Boies, S., and Gould, J. (1989). Tools for Generating Consistent User Interfaces. In J Nielsen (Ed.), *Coordinating User Interfaces for Consistency.* 107–130. Boston, MA: Academic Press.

Wroblewski, D. A. (1991). The construction of human-computer interfaces considered as a craft. In J. Karat (Ed.), *Taking Software Design Seriously.* 1–19. New York: Academic Press Professional, Inc. San Diego, CA, USA.

Wurman, R. S., and Bradford, P. (1996). *Information Architects.* New York, NY: Graphis Inc.

Xerox (1983). Xerox Star and the Professional : Promotional Video for the Xerox Star.

Zhou, Y. (2003). *The Historical Evolution of Chinese Languages and Scripts [Zhongguo yu wen de shi dai yan jin]* (Pathways to advanced skills ; vol. 8). Columbus, Ohio: National East Asian Languages Resource Center, Ohio State University.

Part IV
Applying Minimalism

Chapter 6
Detecting the Minimal

Designing products for the mass market is inherently difficult. Some designs work better than others and while public apprehension of design is certainly subject to fashion, mode, style and vogue, *minimalist* design has regularly been blessed with some success; in recent history, it even seems to have become fashionable: Philips advertises "simple is beautiful", mobile communications companies introduce no-frills tariffs using the "less is more" motto and, last but not least, the profits Apple Computer wrings out of the "stylishly minimal" iPod music player series seem to have no end.

Different designs claim simplicity for themselves, while the number of interpretations of the term approaches the number of design examples. In this chapter, a selection of existing designs is made to illustrate that minimalism delivers a terminology that helps to analyze designs and to further clarify the meaning of the individual notions of minimalism. The selected examples come from a wide range of designs that were attributed with the label "simple" by the public; they were chosen as they exemplify at least one aspect of minimalism and while there are aspects of all notions of minimalism in almost all designs, this discussion tries to highlight the most prominent aspects of a design.

The discussion in each section starts with an "artificial example" that was selected to illustrate the direction of reduction. Following it, several examples are discussed whose main design tendency is identified as belonging to the notion of minimalism in discussion; in these examples, other notions of minimalism are often discussed as well. Each design discussion is assessed in minimal terms—without intending to rate design quality. Instead, minimal qualities are exposed and minimal terminology is sharpened. The closing example is always chosen from the domain of word-processors to demonstrate the applicability of all minimalist perspectives to a single application domain.

6.1 Functional Minimalism

As functional minimalism is perhaps the best documented form of minimalism, it will be used to start discussion in this chapter. But, before the practice of Apple Computers to acquire owners of complex software suite and release

H. Obendorf, *Minimalism*, Human-Computer Interaction Series,
DOI 10.1007/978-1-84882-371-6_6, © Springer-Verlag London Limited 2009

functionally reduced versions, the CommSy CSCW system and a first aspect of
word processing are discussed, the idea of functional minimalism shall be
reassessed by looking at analog tools: the knives of the traveler and of the cook.

6.1.1 Cutting Edges

The archetype of the multi-functional tool is a knife that was never used in the
manner it is named for: the Swiss officers' knife, or more aptly, the Swiss army
knife—the Swiss army uses a much simpler and sturdier metal-plated version
with only four functions; officers never received a dedicated knife (Jackson,
1999). The knife's design approach appears to be to integrate every possible
functionality into the pocket knife—which will always be with you, anyway.
Swiss army knives (Fig. 6.1) are able to open cans, turn different types of screws,
uncork wine bottles, saw wooden logs, do needlework, cut and file fingernails—
the list is almost endless, as specific knives were produced for many target
groups, and the most powerful knife integrates 33 different functions (the
XAVT special model even boasts 80 functions). After September 11, 2001,
and the consequential intensification of airport security protocols, sales
dropped sharply as sharp knives were banned from hand luggage. The company's solution was consequently following previous policy: a USB drive
pocket knife was produced that no longer had an edge.

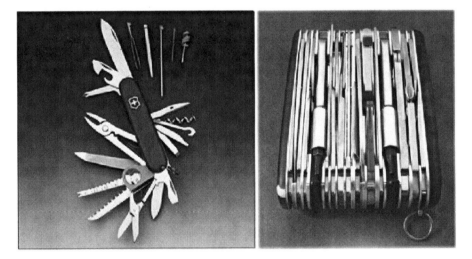

Fig. 6.1 Swiss army knives: the most powerful serial model and the special XAVT model

On the other side of the spectrum, one finds the multitude of knives a
professional cook will use. As an example, some knives commonly used to
prepare sushi are depicted in Fig. 6.2: while there is an "almighty", all-purpose
knife (third from right, *Kurouchi Santoku*), special knives are built for very

specific tasks: from left to right, the Sashimi knife is for slicing raw fish, the *Nakkiri* knife for cutting vegetables, the *Kurouchi Mioroshi Deba* for cutting fish with bone, the *Korouchi Santoku* for cutting everything else, the *Mukimono* for paring vegetable and fruit, and the *Kaiwari* for extracting meat from shellfish. Blades vary in form, length, thickness, and steel and are built to specifically cater to the needs their appointed task requires.

Fig. 6.2 Assortment of Sushi knives

These knives are all specifically built for a single purpose; their focus on very few tasks allows to specify exact requirements and construction can be tailored to meet these specific needs. Although each knife only fulfills a single function, it will do so much better—and to greater satisfaction of the user—than a multi-purpose knife.[1]

---

[1] The reason for the recent appearance of many interaction designs that focus on a specific functionality is related to the popularity of the term information appliance—although in its absoluteness, the term never fits; most devices tend to accumulate functionality—a PDA acquires telephone qualities, mobile phones are used to access shared calendars. In the literature, this tendency is described as *convergence*.

6.1.1.1 Discussion

Functional minimalism first and foremost means a reduction of functionality—not necessarily a common goal of information science. Tools for professionals—many from the physical world—the woodworker's shop, the many instruments of a percussionist, or the utilities of a system administrator, and here specifically the knife example demonstrate that *functional minimalism* can be translated in terms of a quality trade-off: a reduction of the number of functions allows an *increase in the quality* with which functions are performed. Reversely, adding additional functions to a tool will *compromise* existing functionality. The example also demonstrates the close relationship of functional minimalism and architectural minimalism—if functionality is distributed among tools, a reduction of the functionality of individual tools is the logical result; and reciprocally, reducing the functionality of tools creates the need for a concerted ensemble of complementing tools.

6.1.2 Apple GarageBand (i-Series 1)

> *[Innovation] comes from saying no to 1,000 things to make sure we don't get on the wrong track or try to do too much.*
>
> —Steve Jobs (2004)

Apple is often entitled not a software company but a design company. Traditionally, it provided both hardware and operating systems but the design of productive software was—but for some notable exceptions, such as Hypercard—left to third parties (e.g., Microsoft for the Office suite). However, with the introduction of MacOS X, Apple began packaging software with the operating system: first, small appliance-like tools such as an e-mail client, an address book, and a Web browser were included free of charge. Subsequently, bundles of multimedia (iLife) and office (iWork) software were being sold by Apple. Some of these products were created from scratch by small development teams—e.g., iMovie 1.0 was finished with a team of three programmers (Sellers, 2005)—but most were not built in-house at Apple but resulted from buy-ins of smaller companies; e.g., technology for iTunes—in a product called Soundjam—was acquired from Casady and Greene in 2000 (Smith, 2005) and GarageBand was developed on the basis of Emagic technology (Orlowski, 2004; Boddie, 2005)—before the acquisition by Apple, Emagic was the second largest player in the market of electronic music composing software (Apple, 2002).

6.1.2.1 Description

GarageBand demonstrates both the marketing and the design approach taken by Apple. As Apple previously used a three-segment approach to the video market, installing iMovie/iDVD as consumer applications, Final Cut Pro that was acquired from Macromedia as mid-range products, leaving competitors such as Adobe only the high-end market, the music market is now also served by an entry-level product, GarageBand, an intermediate Logic Express, and the professional Logic Pro (Leishman, 2004).

What is most interesting in terms of design is the use Apple made of the sophisticated music recording technology that was acquired from Emagic. Instead of continuing along the lines set by competitors, e.g., with Cubase SL3 that was advertised with "50 new features" (Steinberg, 2006a), and providing what is essentially a crippled version of the professional product able to record fewer tracks, use less voices and exclude certain high-end features (Steinberg, 2006b), Apple chose to follow a much more rigid path. The entire application was redesigned to match other i-Series products in look and feel, and the features included in GarageBand were reduced to include only the absolutely necessary— in this context, a quote attributed to Apple CEO Steve Jobs relating to iTunes might explain the direction of design, "...we don't want a thousand features. That would be ugly. Innovation is not about saying yes to everything. It's about saying NO to all but the most crucial features" (Steve Jobs quoted in Sievers, 2004). Features dropped for GarageBand included a score editor, MIDI import and output, most sophisticated MIDI manipulation functions, tempo or key change within a song, and strictly limited plugin support (Macjams.com, 2004b, see also Pogue 2004). What was left was an audio sequencer that could be used in combination with almost unprocessed MIDI tracks.

Apple made every effort to conceal that more powerful features could exist while it was very much in the interest of its competitors, e.g., Steinberg, to illustrate that there existed a better, albeit more expensive version of their software that users could upgrade to. As a consequence, the "breaks" in the design are not visible and the software was designed as a self-sufficient "whole". The interface of GarageBand (Fig. 6.3) is relatively simple—at least if compared with other music recording software (comp. Fig. 6.4): there are fewer overlapping controls and the number of different screens is significantly reduced; most of the work in GarageBand is done directly in the main window. Integrated instruments offer less options for tweaking the sound but rely on presets useful for most home recording needs. All in all, most of the complexity that burdens other recording software was stripped off, leaving only those features that are most necessary for GarageBands key functionality, that of quickly arranging lead and arrangement tracks.

At the same time, the concept of audio loops, segments of recorded audio that could be combined to form patterns, with a huge library of pre-produced patterns designed to form an accompaniment to self-conceived melodies, was introduced. Thus, even without all the features dropped, hobby musicians were able to quickly generate professional-sounding tracks, and community Web sites blossomed to facilitate the exchange of music (Macminute.com, 2004).[2]

---

[2] Among the most active GarageBand communities are iCompositions (http://www.icompositions.com/) and MacIdol (http://www.macidol.com).

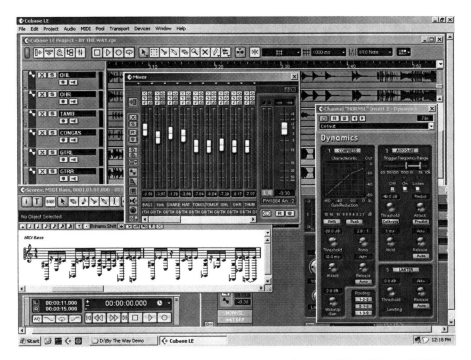

Fig. 6.3 Apple Garageband 1.0 screenshot. Courtesy of Apple

Fig. 6.4 A long-time standard music software in its introductory edition: Cubase LE 3.0

With the loop concept, Apple introduced direct-manipulation into the field of music production as patterns can easily be moved (arranged), resized (time-stretched or looped), dragged from the repository, or copied from other projects.

The result for the user is a minimal amount of distraction, enthusiastic reviews of GarageBand demonstrate that even professional musicians use GarageBand for sketching new song concepts "with a minimum of hassle" (Macjams.com, 2004a; see also Pogue, 2004; Preve, 2004; Schumacher-Rasmussen, 2004). Referring to Csikszentmihalyi's (1991) notion of flow, musician Spencer Critchley states, "Why not just start in Logic, since Logic can do everything Garageband does, plus about a universe-full of other things? Because in flow, every second counts" (Critchley, 2005).

Due to its simple functionality and the conscious limitation of features, GarageBand seems to be an attractive tool for sketching musical concepts. And, as some things, such as adding many layers of self-recorded sounds upon one another, become very simple through the focus of the software, users report "it also inspires me to do more. To experiment with layering. To arrange new songs. To create things that I wouldn't otherwise have the resources to create"—GarageBand is perceived as "so easy to use and, in several important ways, powerful as well" (Nagel, 2005). This combination of simplicity and power, Gelernter's *machine beauty*, allows both novices and experts to very successfully use GarageBand as a tool—always within its narrowly defined scope of competence (Boddie, 2005).

On the other hand, GarageBand uses the same technology internally that Logic uses, making it seem natural for ambitious musicians to continue work within the same product family; thus, providing a low-cost alternative with minimal functionality might be generating more profit for Apple as two products are bought by customers and used in different stages of production.

6.1.2.2 Discussion

The Apple i-Series moves the focus on the speculative and the temporal nature of minimality, two important aspects of the notion of minimal functionality: the minimal set of functionality not only is difficult to determine and cannot simply be found by reduction alone, but is also subject to changing demands and requirements of the users.

The GarageBand case highlights the question of how minimal functionality can be defined; as opposed to the Steinberg line of music sequencers, minimal functionality will not be reached by placing artificial restrictions on the underlying engine while keeping the same interface (comp. Fig. 6.4). Instead, Apple succeeded with GarageBand because it designed a new application—that builds upon a common engine but exposes only selected features. The success of this strategy depends upon the ability of the designers to predict which selection of features forms a "core" that is complete in its simplicity.

Yet, GarageBand also highlights that later product versions tend to accumulate more features even for a functionally minimal application: In Garage-Band 2.0, new features were introduced. Some of these follow from the paradigm shift that GarageBand introduced with its emphasis on loops: New loops can be created and the categorization of existing loops can be altered by the user; this makes the new paradigm more useful and although it adds some interface complexity, it provides a simple opportunity for users to tailor the existing interface and adopt its structure to their tasks. Some features are useful without complicating the interface, e.g., recording up to eight audio channels simultaneously with appropriate hardware. Other features, however, undo simplifications of the interface: e.g., GarageBand 2.0 (re-)introduced a score editor, thus restoring a feature common to competitive products (Fig. 6.5). The duplication of functionality in the piano roll and score editors makes Garage-Band more complex—yet, it was often remarked that without it, it would be no real match for musicians (e.g. Morgan, 2005)—although other applications exist that provide exclusive functionality for arranging and printing scores, something even the newest GarageBand does not do very well.

Fig. 6.5 Score editor added to GarageBand 2.0. Screenshot courtesy of Apple

Other i-Applications demonstrate a similar procedure, e.g., iPhoto 2.0 boasts a "host of new features" (Pogue and Story, 2006), and Keynote 3.0 introduced 3D-charts, new transitions, additional views, and many more (Tessler, 2006). This *2.0 syndrome*— the differentiation by additional features—can become dangerous for an application suite that tries to deliver the essential functionality with a clean and simple interface.

Apart from the risk of "adding more of the same", another risk lies within the changing focus of a tool. While a craftsman's tool is reserved for a single, unchanging purpose, digital tools are often required to also support the latest fashion. GarageBand 3.0 again added functionality but, this time, with a new focus: as *podcasts,* audio files distributed using RSS or Atom feeds and stored on computers or mobile players, such as the iPod, were becoming increasingly popular, Apple chose to add some features to GarageBand that would ease the production and publication of podcasts (Breen, 2006).

Table 6.1 Minimal Aspects highlighted in Apple's Garageband

Functional	Structural	Architectural	Compositional
Minimalism	Minimalism	Minimalism	Minimalism

6.1.2.3 A Minimal Assessment

- *Functional Minimalism*: Relative to its competitors, GarageBand provides a drastically reduced functionality. Its development history demonstrates that shrinking the feature list of a product can create a tool that is both successful in the mass market and also used for specific purposes by professional experts.
- *Structural Minimalism*: The interface of GarageBand is very similar to that of other digital music recording software—e.g., it also simulates the physicality of real studio equipment. Its simpler structure is mainly effected by the reduction in functionality. GarageBand also provides fewer "views" on the data, the missing score editor demonstrates the difficulty of differentiating between structure and functionality.
- *Architectural Minimalism*: In the professional use of GarageBand as a specialized tool for musical prototyping, GarageBand can be seen as part of the Apple music suite. It does not, however, provide a clearly distinct functionality from the more sophisticated applications, as innovations in Garage-Band were later incorporated into the more expensive members of the series. The differentiation between tools is here created by GarageBand's focus on speed and semi-automatic accompaniment, with the Loops concept introducing a rapid technique of composing music to mass market sequencers.
- *Compositional Minimalism*: GarageBand's field of competency is clearly defined as music production, and users generally use it only for this purpose. GarageBand 3.0, however, enabled many amateurs to produce podcasts—streamed recordings of voice and music—and contributed to their steeply rising number; podcasts are used as a generic type of media to record university courses, create autobiographical histories, blog on audio, or distribute personal music compilations, much like the mix tapes of years ago.

6.1.3 The CommSy Community System

CommSy is a web-based groupware designed to support communication and coordination in working and learning groups with a focus on the exchange of documents and the sharing of important notes and appointments between

users. Comparable systems include, e.g., BSCW (Bentley et al., 1997), phpBB
(phpBB, 2006), and Moodle (Hilgenstock and Jirmann, 2006); yet, in contrast
to other CSCW systems, simplicity was defined early in the development
process as a primary goal. As a consequence, the CommSy development process
explicitly aims to question the usefulness of new features (see Section 6.3) and
although the first version was presented in May 1999 and CommSy can be
considered a mature software product, it lacks many features other systems
provide: there is, e.g., no sophisticated access control mechanism and ownership rules are very simple (Jackewitz et al., 2004; Obendorf, 2003); closed groups
are supported through "rooms" with restricted access; within a room, an
information entry is either writable exclusively by its creator or writable for
all while everything is readable for all. CommSy also refrains from imitating
hierarchical folders common in "desktop" interfaces; due to technical
restrictions—drag and drop does not work as expected, exchange with the
desktop computer is cumbersome—a folder metaphor can currently not be
fully implemented by a Web application. Furthermore, folders define a single
fixed information structure that may present problems to different users.

6.1.3.1 Description

CommSy is trying hard to minimize functionality following the ideal of *functional minimalism*. Its primary function was storing documents for closed
groups and offering equal access to these. Quickly, other types of information
items were integrated: appointments, news announcements, persons, and
groups. Although it is now used outside university courses and other contexts
have created new requirements—the increased use, e.g., in secondary schools,
led to changes in wording and users from virtual networks and commercial
companies demanded the integration of more advanced functionality, such as
graphical calendars and active assignment of users to tasks—the initial concept,
storing information items in time-ordered lists, has scaled surprisingly well for
new users from other contexts.

Feature requests reaching the development team were often discussed by the
team as a whole and when no majority could be found in favor of the request, it
was put off until either the requesting stakeholders found a way of appropriating CommSy to their needs or enough (financial) resources were found that the
specific feature would be implemented. Features were even removed from the
system when too few members of the development team found them useful or
too little use was observed; they were either integrated with other, existing
functionality or made optional. An example for the former was the ability of
creating structured documents; initially, this was introduced as an additional
category, but when little use was observed and the team found users did not
understand the concept, the functionality was integrated with the existing
document type of information items. An example for the latter is the already-
mentioned calendar: because it was vehemently required by some users who
were willing to pay for development, it was implemented and integrated with the

CommSy system. But as it seemed to make little use for most contexts, it is hidden by default. Other parts of CommSy functionality can be configured by users: e.g., the extent of displaying news items can be configured to show individual news titles, just the news category, or nothing. Configuration, however, is limited to the core functionality of CommSy as even the typical room coordinators have little or no background in computer science and little tolerance for unnecessary complexity.

Structural minimalism in CommSy is only visible on second glance. It is, however, one of the main strengths of the system and has grown through yearlong refinement of individual categories. Screens for different categories display slightly different selections of information, and the placement of information is optimized to allow easy reading and intuitive understanding. This became apparent when the system, which was initially programmed in PHP5, was migrated to Java-based technology (Jeenicke, 2005). Within a single semester, the functionality for a single category was implemented almost fully and an integration with the PHP-based system was possible (ibid.). It was, however, far more difficult than anticipated to "get the design right" (Finck, personal communication): the automated test suites that were used to guarantee correctness of the re-implementation failed to detect subtle details of placement and differences between categories. This made it necessary to return to manual testing and also contributed to an unexpected prolongation of the migration process.

It is a matter of perspective whether to attest architectural minimalism to CommSy: the underlying PHP code is structured in a manner that every requested view is catered for by a dedicated "page" module; these "pages" combine views on information item to form the designed layout and these, in turn, refer to "data" classes that model the underlying structures. Thus, CommSy makes no attempt to introduce a global partitioning of functionality, and additional functionality is not integrated using a plug-in mechanism, but by insertion of control structures in the affected "page" modules.

On the other hand, the "pages" served by CommSy are structured into categories that are presented to the user (Fig. 6.6). There is some evidence that different categories are recognized by the users as different tools for different uses. Typical questions to the user support include the question of what the different categories should be used for and how to best combine their use; this information was also made available in an introductory guide (CommSy, 2005). 6.6 This argument is further supported by anecdotal evidence: the introduction of a "document" category that allowed users to add sections to existing documents failed as its functionality was not considered to be different enough from the existing "material" category; the new "tool" was never accepted, and consequently merged with the existing category.

The use of categories alone does also not qualify CommSy for minimalist structure. Rather, the aforementioned year-long process of incremental refinements has stringently created an access structure that is now adopted so well to the users' tasks that it qualifies for structural minimalism. Individual "pages" optimize placing and filtering of available information—a good example is the

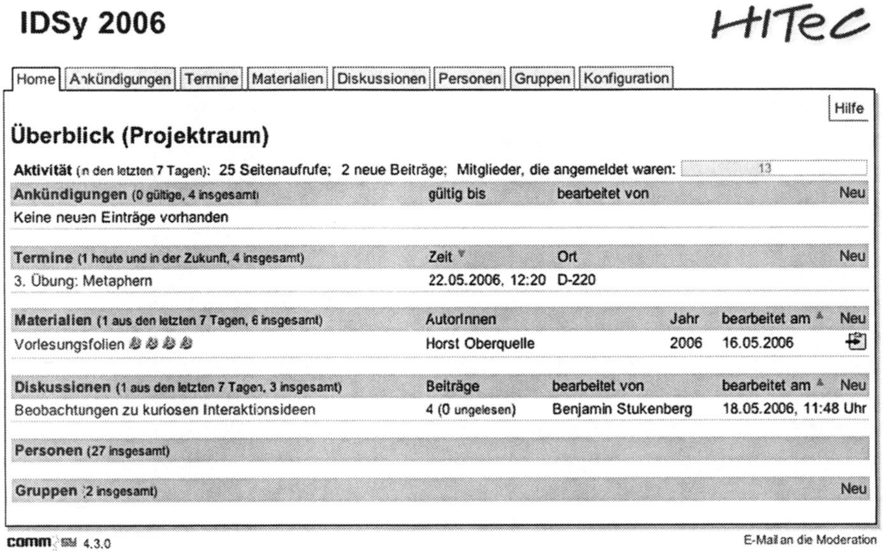

IDSy 2006   *HITeC*

| Home | Ankündigungen | Termine | Materialien | Diskussionen | Personen | Gruppen | Konfiguration |

Hilfe

Überblick (Projektraum)

Aktivität (in den letzten 7 Tagen): 25 Seitenaufrufe; 2 neue Beiträge; Mitglieder, die angemeldet waren: 13

Ankündigungen (0 gültige, 4 insgesamt)	gültig bis	bearbeitet von	Neu
Keine neuen Einträge vorhanden			

Termine (1 heute und in der Zukunft, 4 insgesamt)	Zeit	Ort	Neu
3. Übung: Metaphern	22.05.2006, 12:20	D-220	

Materialien (1 aus den letzten 7 Tagen, 6 insgesamt)	AutorInnen	Jahr	bearbeitet am	Neu
Vorlesungsfolien 🖹🖹🖹🖹	Horst Oberquelle	2006	16.05.2006	📧

Diskussionen (1 aus den letzten 7 Tagen, 3 insgesamt)	Beiträge	bearbeitet von	bearbeitet am	Neu
Beobachtungen zu kuriosen Interaktionsideen	4 (0 ungelesen)	Benjamin Stukenberg	18.05.2006, 11:48 Uhr	

Personen (27 insgesamt)

Gruppen (2 insgesamt)	Neu

comm 🖳 4.3.0   E-Mail an die Moderation

Fig. 6.6 CommSy main page with access to categories via both links and tabs

"network navigation" introduced with version 3.0 in 2004 (Janneck et al., 2006; Fig. 6.7): while previously, access to information items was only possible via lists of items, the "network navigation" introduced direct associations between different items; however, as developers and users felt that only some associations were useful, the selection and order of association types differs with the type of information item displayed (Obendorf et al., in prep; Janneck et al., 2006). This optimization aims at minimizing interaction complexity; as unnecessary choices are eliminated, functionality is reduced to a "core". CommSy is an interesting example for the structural similarity of dealing with similar information items in different contexts as new users quickly identify this grown ease-of-use as one of the software's key qualities, and have only a few problems arising from differences in workflows—often, their critique focuses on functionality that they feel is necessary but that is unavailable within the software.

Part of this extended functionality, according to an initial assumption of CommSy development (use within a media mix, see e.g. Pape et al., 2002), would be provided by other tools. Its developers regarded CommSy as only one tool in the portfolio of university teachers and students; depending on the type of course, other tools would supplement or even replace the functionality of CommSy. One example for this is the limited e-mail functionality within CommSy. As users already employ a dedicated application for sending and receiving e-mail, replicating part of this functionality within the web-based system would create problems of redundancy and ambiguity: it can no longer easily be determined where an e-mail was sent or where one was received. While there is some evidence that some users move important data from their e-mail to

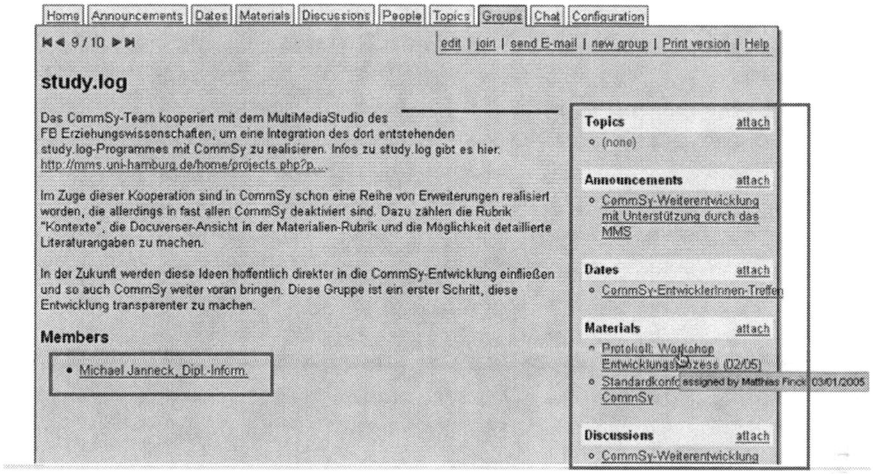

Fig. 6.7 CommSy group detail page with highlighted "network navigation"

dedicated places such as a calendar (Gwizdka, 2004), there is a general consensus that e-mail is a unifying application (Whittaker et al., 2006; Bergman et al., 2003; Boardman and Sasse, 2004). Consequently, introducing an additional application to manage e-mail seemed unprofitable; making the single existing application responsible was preferred to avoid making organization of received and sent e-mail more difficult for users.

In contrast to other systems, syndication was also opposed on the same terms—a motivating effect for users to keep themselves updated was assumed: for competitors, such as BSCW, extensions have been developed that notify users when new information becomes available (BSCW); technically, this is often realized using generated e-mails or RSS feeds (Hammersley, 2005; Board, 2006).

6.1.3.2 Discussion

CommSy represents a product in change—developed for a single purpose, simplicity became an important quality of the software. For mostly economical reasons, the use of CommSy has spread to other contexts and while simplicity remains an important value for the developers, its meaning for the product has changed: it was necessary to add new functionality—new use contexts come with new requirements, and when there is a commercial interest, a feature will be added. As in the discussion of the Apple i-Series, new versions tend to attract new features—even though CommSy is not sold as a product but rather as a service. The need for new functionality is thus not simply caused by a need to create "more of the same", but rather by changing tasks and new users from different contexts.

Functional minimalism is slowly being replaced as an approach by structural and compositional minimalism, and simplicity takes on the meaning of "ease of use" rather than "simple functionality"; interviews with members of the development team indicate that "simplicity" still remains a key value, and that it is used in discussions as an argument both for and against the introduction of new features—a result of the gradual shift described here (see the discussion of the CommSy development process in Section 6.2).

For CommSy, as one of two analyzed systems that were developed locally, the theoretical analysis was supplemented by an empirical evaluation of how the notions of minimalism qualify as analytic criteria. To this end, a survey with 69 students was conducted. Two groups of 53 undergraduate students and 16 graduate students differed by experience level and rated CommSy's overall ease of use, as well as specific aspects such as sufficient and superfluous functionality, simplicity of access structure, the visibility of different tools in CommSy, and the support CommSy lent to their specific tasks or the variability they saw in CommSy. The survey questions were deduced from the different notions of minimalism to find out whether the design would be uniformly rated on the resulting scales and to examine the effects of rating on the different scales on overall ease of use.

The survey results show a large variance of answers, users specifically disagreed about whether CommSy consisted of tools that were termed "areas" in the questionnaire to accommodate the navigation metaphor. CommSy was not unanimously rated simple, by contrast, 36% indicated that it had too many unnecessary features (rating "too many features" as true with 4–7 on a 7-item scale). CommSy was rated significantly easier to use by the group of students with less experience (scoring 5.6 vs 4.5, $p<0.05$). This result is possibly confounded with their use of the tool, which was mainly employed to distribute assignments and material needed to complete these, to a lesser degree to communicate important dates and continue discussions off-line.

In comparison with earlier analyses (comp. Janneck, 2006; Strauss et al., 2003), CommSy was consistently judged to be easy to use, the verdict, however, was less unequivocal. Looking for the reasons, a multivariate analysis revealed only two factors with a significant influence on overall ease of use: CommSy use was judged to be significantly less easy to use when the users believed it did have too many functions for their needs ($p<0.01$); the mean rating for ease of use fell from 5.8 to 5.2 and 4.5 on a scale from 1 to 7 as users were either indifferent about the number of features or felt them to be too much. Another important influence on ease of use had the users' perception that CommSy did not hinder their individual work flow ($p<0.05$); here, users that felt constricted by CommSy only rated the ease of use at 3.9 in average compared to a mean of 5.8 for all others. All other factors were, at best, weakly correlated with usability, one cause being the high variation in the individual scales, and the relatively low number of students in the graduate course.

A highly significant correlation was thus found between those users who considered CommSy to support different ways of working and believed it to be easy to use, and those users who believed CommSy had too many functions and found it more difficult to use. While the sample size is too small to draw further conclusions, the evaluation indicates that it might be indeed possible that there exists a direct link between functional, respectively, compositional minimalism and usability.

Table 6.2 Minimal Aspects highlighted in CommSy

Functional	Structural	Architectural	Compositional
Minimalism	Minimalism	Minimalism	Minimalism

6.1.3.3 A Minimal Assessment

- *Functional Minimalism*: Again, relative to its competitors, CommSy limits the amount of accessible functionality, thus creating a comparably simple interface. Primarily during the foundation of the project but also in current development, "Simplicity" is used as a value to guide design, highlighting the trade-off involved with the introduction of new features, often resulting in a careful and hesitant extension of functionality (some empirical evidence is provided in Section 6.3, along with an example technique using values as guides).

- *Structural Minimalism*: While other systems chose to follow consistency to desktop GUIs over structural simplicity, CommSy's unusual approach to storing documents in flat lists, enhanced by meta-data, displayed a high learnability, especially for non computer-savvy users. A compromise was made to create a high internal consistency—the structure to access functionality seems very similar between the different categories; yet, although the differences only appear at second glance, the network navigation differs with every information type and the display of associations is carefully prioritized according to their usefulness.

- *Architectural Minimalism*: CommSy is quite very visibly divided into different categories. The user can choose whether he/she wants to use a category, and the administrator can also hide categories not used. Categories could thus be considered "tools" that can be combined to adapt the CommSy system to a certain use context, partly by adoption, and partly by configuration. CommSy's categories work best when they provide clearly divided functionality. The category system, however, turned out to be not generic enough or, at least, not applicable to all contexts, and categories were partially renamed for specific use contexts (e.g., schools).

- *Compositional Minimalism*: Although CommSy's use domain was initially very specific and included only a single type of University courses, its use has spread to other course types, universities, and, most recently, also to schools, companies, and virtual networks. In all these contexts, it is—often successfully—used to support communication. Apart from the dynamics created by value-based development (see Section 6.3.2), the functional minimalism and the generality of the task of "exchanging documents" that CommSy fulfills are both responsible for the simple appropriation of the application. In some places, explicit abdication of functionality, e.g., access rights, has resulted in the replacement of an inadequate technical solution with an adequate social convention—and enabled the use of CommSy in contexts that it does not "support" per se. New use contexts create requirements for new features, threatening to undo functional minimalism as a quality (compare Section 6.2).

6.1.4 Word Processing

In this chapter, word processing will consistently be used as the closing example as this is one area where for all four notions of minimalism can be related to specific mechanisms that were employed in real-world products. For functional minimalism, two projects are discussed here in more detail—both try to reduce the functionality that Microsoft Word or its competitor StarOffice offer by providing several interfaces that limit the available functionality.

6.1.4.1 StarOffice 4 Kids

The first project, *StarOffice 4 Kids* (Baumert, 2004), was initiated by Kippdata and the Heinz-Nixdorf Institute in Paderborn and is an example that shows both the potential and some of the main problems with functional minimalism: within the scope of the *Lernstatt Paderborn*, computer labs were installed at primary schools in town (Keil-Slawik and Baumert, 2004; Baumert and Meiners, 2003b). To provide the pupils, most of whom had little or no previous contact with word processing, with a tool that could be used to support learning (instead of replacing the object of learning), a simple alternative to normal word processors was developed. Using the software base of the open source project *OpenOffice.org*,[3] a prototype was developed and deployed for a pilot study. Although the project also included a teacher interface (a slightly modified, full version of StarOffice), the student's interface is more interesting in this context. Underlying the development was the proposition that fewer functions would allow children to quickly learn the basics of word processing; as new function-ality was necessary for the tasks the teacher set, the interface would change and acquire access to new functionality with the addition of new buttons to the toolbar (Fig. 6.8).

StarOffice 4 Kids emphasizes the use of an open format, both as a distin-guishing feature to Microsoft Word and as a basis for allowing different ver-sions of the software to access the same data. Although Keil-Slawik and Baumert (2004) claim that different tools thus use the same file format, in this context, the more important consequence is that the same document can be

---

[3] OpenOffice.org is an office suite that was released in 2000 into the open source after StarDivision, a small German software company, had been acquired by Sun Microsystems in 1999. Since then, it has been developed both by volunteers and by employees of Sun and became a well-known competitor to Microsoft Office.

Fig. 6.8 StarOffice 4 Kids prototype screens

edited with differently limited interfaces. Used in conjunction with pre-defined tasks for teachers and students, this promises to provide some degree of seamless degradation of features.

In the evaluation report, Baumert and Meiners (2003a) mention that children had difficulties learning the meaning of the icons—a possible explanation is that they were not adapted to the school context from the original software but used unchanged in the changed interface. As the teachers reported, the prototype was "too simple"—this was repeatedly mentioned in the interviews. It does not become clear whether the students were also convinced they needed "more" as interviews were only held with teachers.

The StarOffice 4 Kids example demonstrates how the direct implementation of the "less is more" idea can lead to mixed results. Implementing fewer functions in the initial interface lead to reports of a better learnability—although problems with icon recognizability persisted. Among the teachers, the acceptance of the new software was affected by their knowledge of the full functionality of a word processing application. They were missing features implemented in the existing de-facto standard, Microsoft Word. Although it is not clear whether they would actually have used these features, providing users with an interface that creates the feeling of being actively limited is not a promising approach. Another problem that was not mentioned in the report is that each new successive addition to the interface violated the internal consistency of the interface; it is very probable that this kind of extension will not scale up to the full functionality. The problems with icons might be partially rooted in the constant changes in their arrangement as their unstable placement prevented the effective use of spatial memory.

6.1.4.2 Evaluating Multiple Interfaces

As part of her PhD work, Joanna McGrenere examined the implications of providing different interfaces for word processing. To this end, Microsoft Word was altered using the internal Visual Basic for Applications scripting language, and a menu was added that could be used to switch between a minimal, a personalized, and the default interface (compare Fig. 6.9). Both the minimal and the personalized interface were created by omitting menu items and toolbar icons.

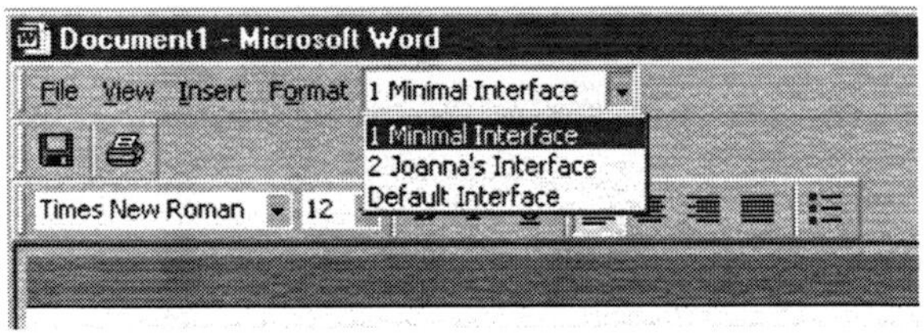

Fig. 6.9 Multiple Interfaces: Menu to switch between the different levels. (McGrenere, 2002)

The second project was targeted not at children, but at "normal" professional workers: participants in the pilot studies included not only computer scientists but also office staff. In contrast to the child users of the first project, these users did not have to learn the basics of word processing, they were adept users of the standard interface. As "expert" users, they were first asked how much functionality they really used. Only about 15% of all functions were used regularly in average and only 12 of 265 functions were used often by more than three-quarters of the users while 91 functions were used by not a single user within the sample of 53 participants (McGrenere and Moore, 2000). This indicates that typically, dramatically less functionality is used than provided.

McGrenere concludes that the overlap of functionality between users is small enough to motivate the development of a personalizable interface. In a study with four participants trying out the three interface types, McGrenere found her personalized interface prototypes to be preferred to both the standard Word interface and the minimal interface (McGrenere et al., 2002; compare Figs. 6.10 – 6.12).

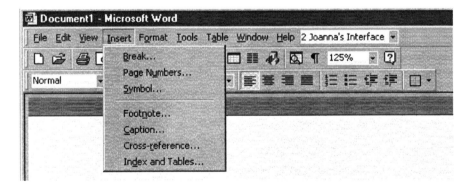

Fig. 6.10 Multiple Interfaces: Insert Menu of the most complex personalized interface in the study (McGrenere, 2002)

What is most interesting in this context is that the minimal interface used in her first pilot study was preferred by one of two office users and one of two researchers, and continued to be used by one user after the study—as this interface provided less functionality than even Wordpad (comp. Fig. 6.10). The minimal interface featured only nine functions in toolbars and had but a single entry in all menus but the File menu, where in addition to opening, saving, printing and quitting, the last four documents were listed (McGrenere, 2002, 248).

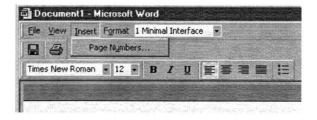

Fig. 6.11 Multiple Interfaces: Insert Menu of the Minimal Interface (McGrenere, 2002)

The preferred use of this Spartan interface indicates that Word might often be the wrong tool. This is only more surprising as McGrenere's use of minimal— "the 10% of the functions from the DI [default interface] that are most frequently used" (ibid., 77)—demonstrates that, for her, minimality does not require the remaining core to be whole; functionality is not balanced using real-world tasks. As functionality that is used infrequently can still be considered vital (e.g., printing), it is doubtful that the core functionality identified by a frequency-based method matches the core functionality for real world tasks. It is thus not surprising that participants expressed their preference for a less-crippled interface—rather, it is surprising that the minimal interface was used at all.

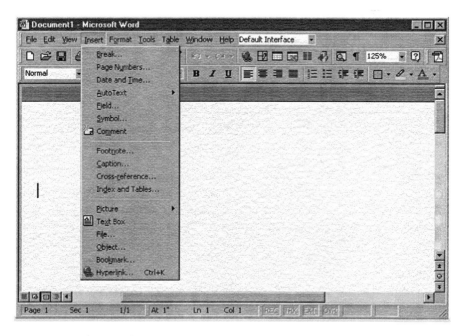

Fig. 6.12 Multiple Interfaces: Insert Menu of the standard Microsoft Word 2000 interface (McGrenere, 2002)

The second word processing case demonstrates that standard office software, and Microsoft Word in particular, is commonly perceived as being overladen with features. Generally, participants expressed their liking of having less functionality, and for feature-shy users, McGrenere found an increase in the sense of control. The studies also suggest that it might be necessary to redefine the meaning of "functionally minimal" in personal terms—a simple dualism of novice and expert users is insufficient to describe differences between users: individual users use different functionality. A mandatory solution is not provided; what is missing is an extension on McGrenere's research—that focused on finding mechanisms for personalization—to a comparison with other methods of providing the best fit of functionality, e.g., a task-centric approach that tried to define a common, shared subset of functionality.

6.1.4.3 Discussion

The StarOffice 4 Kids case demonstrates that simply omitting functionality to make a product simpler will not necessarily yield a good design. As the required functionality grows with increasing mastery of the software, the use of new, more powerful interfaces becomes necessary—which introduces new inconsistencies. This highlights that functionally minimal designs create a need for tailoring, which can compensate the initial advantage gained by a deliberately primitive interface.

Tailoring functionality to individual users is the approach put forward by McGrenere. Although this might mark an ideal solution—everyone would be using a tool that would be completely customized to fit the individual needs—there are some problems with this approach: It is not always a cost-effective solution to have experts tailor interfaces to individual users; as with other tools, this still might be a viable solution for a few high-performers. Studies have observed that specific employees in larger organization adopt this role as "tinkerer" (MacLean et al., 1990), or "local developer" (Gantt and Nardi, 1992). Yet, customization is not possible for all target groups and will not always be efficient—there are trade-offs involved (Mackay, 1990; Mackay, 1991). Specifically, for cooperation between several users, customization effectively prevents cooperative reflection about the tool; users are hindered to help other users, use practices cannot spread easily (Grudin, 1994).

Both examples can be seen as examples for *layered interfaces* (comp. Shneiderman, 2003). Layered interfaces hide the full complexity of an application and expose partial functionality in layers. Each layer builds upon another and exposes more functionality. While StarOffice 4 Kids closely follows the layer concept, adding functionality sequentially as the learner progresses, McGrenere's layers in her multi-interface are partly caused by the study design that aims to test the concept of a personalized interface. The benefits for expert users are unclear as better learnability is not a vital factor for them. If reduced interfaces are useful even for expert users as they perform less demanding tasks, this points towards severe deficiencies of the original interface that harm the user's performance.

The concept of layered interfaces is not undisputed—although it is put forward as a strategy to further universal usability (ibid.) and simplify the initial learning curve (Kang et al., 2003), it has not turned into a movement extending beyond Shneiderman's HCI laboratory and the "graceful evolution" of interfaces (Shneiderman, 2003) can be problematic. Earlier research indicated that non-layered software might provide a better basis for seamlessly learning advanced features of an application. Nardi stated in 1990 (Nardi and Miller, 1990a) that Microsoft Excel allows for a multitude of different uses at different levels of proficiency. This can be generalized to other spreadsheets—the table model has been identified as a conceptual basis for the discipline of end-user programming (Nardi and Miller, 1990b; Nardi, 1993; Myers et al., 2006; Myers et al., 2006).

While support for end-user-programming is from a user's perspective to be welcomed,[4] it is not a good design solution per se. Rather, it could be named an indicator of defeat—as the designer does not know what features are going to be used in which conjunction, he settles for providing a toolkit that the user then has to pick the useful tools from. This represents an antagonistic position to a functionally minimal design. Mass market design is generally unable to depend on users to tailor the design to their individual needs and tries to find a common core of functionality—which steadily grows as new users are examined, a certain factor driving the feature frenzy.

6.1.5 Refining the Notion of Functional Minimalism

Judging from its definition, *functional minimalism* is the most trivial form of minimalism and can be immediately measured: the less functions a design has, the more minimal it is. However, the discussion of actual products has shown that (1) minimal functionality is closely connected to other forms of minimalism, (2) defining what is minimal is far from trivial, (3) definitions of what is minimal are subject to change as tasks change and new design revisions are based on previous designs, or (4) new groups of users are targeted, exemplified by the CommSy system. As the analysis of word processing applications demonstrated, a form of functional minimalism can be achieved by (5) layering the functionality in several interfaces that the user can progress as he/she learns to use the program or choose according to task.

Both the Commsy developers and Apple designers tried to achieve a reduction in functionality through a shift in responsibility. Their designs do not try to provide all necessary functionality, but rather limit themselves to a basic set of functions. As both designs target users who are more concerned about the ease of use of their tools than about their comparative power, or have other, more

---

[4] Other perspectives, e.g., that of the "professional programmer", tend to fear user programmers for their well-adapted but poorly engineered code which may create severe security problems (Harrison, 2004).

sophisticated tools in their toolkits, the design choice is met with approval. Even here, however, the consequences of the *2.0 syndrome* become obvious— subsequent versions of the software tend to accumulate functionality, blurring the difference between the new tools designed to be clean and simple and their more complex competitors.

Word processing applications face a more direct dilemma. As their producers fear to alienate potential users, the functionality considered as belonging to word processing has grown to an enormous amount of different features. The question of how much functionality is really necessary gives room to a dynamic that requires new functionality in each new release. An empirical indication that new functionality can actually harm performance was delivered in a study by Franzke and Rieman (1993) with 12 users who had an average of two years' computer experience. Two different versions of a graphing package were used to create a default graph. The task was performed significantly faster ($p<0.05$) using the earlier version of the package than the later version,[5] demonstrating the possibility of a negative performance impact of new features.

Limiting the functionality of an application to support use on different levels is not a new concept in itself. In the 1980s, John Carroll and his team created the *Training Wheels Interface* for a commercial word processor, an interface that blocked some functionality, displaying a message when a blocked function was accessed. Two studies with 12 novice users each compared the training wheels system to the complete system. Results of the first study indicated that users could complete a simple word processing task about 20% faster with the blocked interface. More importantly, they spent significantly less time recovering from errors.[6] Comprehension of word processor basics was significantly better for users of the blocked interface, as was their score in a questionnaire designed to reveal users' attitude towards their work. Results of the second study were almost identical, lacking only significant differences in the tests on comprehension and work attitude. While blocking of functionality is still used and has been promoted as a *layered approach* by Shneiderman (2003), who suggests that novice users should start with a minimal subset of functionality to protect them from making errors and progressively learn more and more advanced features of the software, its usefulness for expert users—and all users are bound to lose their novice state—is not clear. It is also not trivial how to design a layered interface and whether there should be more than one path of progressing through layers. Shneiderman doesn't suggest specific design guidelines to accomplish this design strategy.

---

[5] Task design plays a role here; if the experimental task had required the use of features available only in the newer version, then using the newer version might have been faster, or a comparison might have been impossible.

[6] The experiment defined error as deviation from the ideal action path, and recovery as steps in the subsequent return to that path.

6.2 Structural Minimalism

Distrahit animum librorum multitudo.
A multitude of books distracts the mind.
— Seneca, epistulae morales ad Lucilium

When functionality is more than minimal and a tool serves more than a single purpose, a selection of functions by the user must be possible. The *access* to the functionality of a device is structured by the designer—he/she chooses which knobs, buttons or menus to provide, in short: he/she designs the *interaction structure*. Using the notion of minimalism, an access structure can be considered more minimal as it is perceived to a lesser degree by the user. That is, while the size of the structure (and the number of menu choices or buttons) can be fairly large, the required functionality must always be "at hand", and no "navigational excise" (Cooper and Reimann, 2003, 135) be required from the user

6.2.1 Remote Controls

As a real-world example for dealing with access structures that is known and feared even by those who are hesitant to use a computer, home entertainment systems may be a good example for the difficulty of using technology: as is widely propagated, few people and even fewer computer scientists are able to program their home video recorder (e.g., Norman, 2002b). Looking at the remote controls

Fig. 6.13 Selection of some remote controls for contemporary DVD players (studio photo)

that ship with a current DVD player (Fig. 6.3), an intimidating display of functionality threatens to allow the effective use of the device—few people will need all the functionality that the multitude of buttons can set in motion.

Apple designed a minimal remote control that concentrates on the key functionality required for a home theatre, namely play and pause, skip and search (Fig. 6.14). While this remote could also be classified as functionally minimal at first sight, the menu button in conjunction with the (then) direction buttons allows the execution of more advanced functionality by navigating a menu system.

Fig. 6.14 Apple Front Row remote (Photo Courtesy of Apple Computer Inc.)

Bang and Olufsen, a Danish company producing high-end Hi-fi technology, tried a similar concept in the late 1990s with their remote control *Beo 1*, launched as an alternative to the *Beo 4* (Beocentral, 2005) (see Fig. 6.15). Both superseded the *Beo 5000* that isolated infrequently used functionality on the back of the remote; while the *Beo 4* was a conventional universal remote control—its modes (that relate to the devices in the stereo set) determine key mapping, the *Beo 1* was an attempt to minimize the number of visible buttons. As their designers state in a press release: "None of its buttons are numeric or source related, instead the operation focusses upon an intuitive interaction with on-screen display. It takes product control to a new transparent level where operation becomes a part of the total experience." (Bang and Olusen, cited after Kiljander, 2004, 160). This concept proved to be unsuccessful, as the navigation was only displaced to a screen interface. This required the television to be switched on continuously and also provided only a poor alternative to directly mapped keys; timeouts were applied by the interface so that "key press sequences felt even longer to the users" (ibid., 160). Fortunately for B&O, the *Beo 4* used compatible IR signals and the experimental *Beo 1* was dropped silently.

Fig. 6.15 Bang and Olufsen remotes: Beo 5000, Beo 1, and Beo 4 (Photos Courtesy of Bang and Olufsen)

Another possibility for interpreting minimal structure is represented by the harmony remote control that was reviewed by Don Norman (2004b): as B&O's Beo 4, it is a remote control that tries to replace several other remote controls. But it is not simply reprogrammed to make available all functionality that the individual remotes offer to the user; it rather groups them according to activity—a single keypress can switch on the television set, DVD player, and stereo, and reroute all input signals so as to enable the activity of "viewing a DVD". This instance of 'activity-based design', so Norman claims, greatly simplifies the task of coping with expensive electronics in the home and makes for satisfied users (Fig. 6.16). However, the approach has limitations as problems arise quickly if the system's prioritization is not similar to the users (for a less satisfied customer, see DeBoer, 2004). The activity-centered design illustrated here adds a new layer of understanding to structural minimalism: not only can atomic functionality be ordered according to task demands but new atomic operations—that may even span several information systems—can be composed; if they closely match the user's actual activities, an increased sense of simplicity is created.

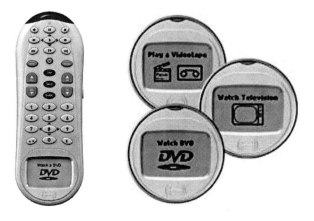

Fig. 6.16. Harmony remote control (Photos Courtesy of Harmony Inc.)

6.2.1.1 Discussion

Structural minimalism was defined as the access structure to functionality that presented the minimal perceived structure. This does not equal the minimal amount of structure, but rather forces the designer to think about how his layout of functionality will be perceived. The remote control example shows that mindsets are very different when it comes to structuring complex functionality. There are those who believe that every function should have its physical counterpart—and are bound to fail as the number of functions grows faster than the space on remote controls. There are those who reduce the physical interaction to a minimum, trading off increased complexity in menu systems; whether users accept this shift seems to depend on the application domain. A possible solution for some applications might be the combination of individual functions into larger scripts and the contextualization of commands. However, this approach will only work where function sequences are often similar and contexts can be clearly identified.

6.2.2 The Palm Handheld

There have been few commercially successful revolutions in the design of interactive systems since the Graphical User Interface "desktop" metaphor has been widely accepted. One notable exception is the introduction of the Palm Pilot (Fig. 6.17) in 1996, an extremely useful information appliance that had very limited functionality but happened to work in practical environments. In contrast to its more elegant and powerful but less useful predecessors, like the Apple Newton, it won the market and created a new way of computing.

Palm Computing started off very quickly, selling almost half a million units in the first seven months and quickly gaining dominance in the handheld computing market. Currently, for 2004, the market volume for handheld computers is estimated to be around 11.3 million units. This immense market did not exist prior to the introduction of the Palm Pilot, the first palm-sized organizer. But the market has diversified, today the Palm series has to compete against the Windows CE handhelds, generally equipped with better displays, faster processors, and better networking capabilities. Despite these unfavorable engineering figures, the Palm series sells very well. It still draws on the qualities that enabled its success and fights with difficulties because changes to the original concept always carry the danger of losing its outstanding position. But what exactly are the qualities of the Palm handheld? Although economic factors such as the acquisition of Palm Computing by US Robotics made the Pilot's success possible in the first place, the reason why exactly the Palm succeeded not only over its competitors but also in forming a new market segment is to be sought in its superior usability and practicality.

Fig. 6.17 Palm Pilot 5000
(1996), an early model
(Photo Courtesy of US
Robotics)

6.2.2.1 Description

A number of things in Palm carry the notion that reduction was the key to success. In an unusually open interview, Rob Haitani, a former Sony employee in charge of the Palm UI development, claims "every pixel counted", that giving up three-dimensional button emulation and the reduction of font size were important to the success of the product. (Bødker, 1990) Jeff Hawkins, the founder of Palm, was said to walk around with a block of carved wood in his pocket, a prototype smaller than the PDAs at that time, to demonstrate that size and features had to be reduced to achieve greater portability.

However, as the perspective of time shows now, these were solutions to immediate limitations that the Palm faced during its conception phase: They made it possible to construct the device in its time, allowed useful information content to be displayed and processed—an example of brilliant engineering—but, today, they don't give the Palm series a principle advantage anymore as processor speeds, screen resolution and color depth keep increasing. Instead, the advantage turned into a disadvantage when, during the introduction of high-res Sony handhelds, no accepted standard was available; even the newest Palm OS draws little benefit from the increased pixel count for the sake of compatibility.

Previous attempts to create a handheld computer were commercially unsuccessful. The most prominent example was the Apple Newton: it had a very sophisticated interface, yet one of the primary functions, the handwriting recognition software, was severely lacking functionality when the Newton was first released. In contrast to other companies, Palm did not believe that "the first-generation handhelds failed because they did not provide enough functionality" (Bergman and Haitani, 2000). The Palm was less ambitious and tried to concentrate on the essential functionality that an ultra-portable computer needed. The design goal was to create a small, fast and inexpensive device.

As the traditional crafts differentiate between numerous types of tools for different tasks (e.g., hammers for hitting nails, paving stones or knees) and multi-function-tools are more often sold in do-it-yourself stores than success-fully employed at work, it is attractive to transfer the concept of single-purpose tools to interactive systems. Don Norman's (1989) notion of *Information Appliance* is commonly applied to the Palm—and even to the functionally more sophisticated Blackberry (Shedroff, 2001). While this seems fitting at first, Palm Pilots not being general purpose computers, it is misleading: the Palm could always do more than one thing. It was designed to replace the business traveler's organizer, an analog physical tool with many functions. Precisely this combination of functions promises an added value of the electronic version, as cross-references need not be maintained by hand and copies for backup or communication are faster and cheaper.

In the Palm Pilot, we find a high degree of structural minimalism, as a number of metaphors common to the desktop world have been replaced by a simpler internal structure that is transparently conveyed to the user. Design penetrates the system: Palm did not just design a user interface; the whole architecture is designed to fit the requirements. The initial versions of Palm OS allowed only one application to run at a time, introducing a simple mapping between what the device was doing and what it would display on the screen: what you see corresponds directly to the internal state. Likewise, the direct access to applications provided by four buttons on the lower front of the Palm case represents again a direct mapping, this time from input to state.

Because of this ease of switching between applications, the necessity of preserving changes arose. In contrast to almost all the known computing world, the Palm Pilot rejected the notion of files. There is no save; there is no file system (but for an invisible flat database store), so there is only the current state that will be automatically preserved. This simplified model of dealing with data has been present in Apple's Lisa, but since then, operating systems forced users to differentiate between memory and disks, volatile and permanent information.

It is interesting to note that the design concepts for the Palm were not developed up-front, as Haitani says, "It was more an end result of our prag-matic design approach, starting with the fact that we could only fit four buttons on the screen" (Bergman and Haitani, 2000). By rigorous user testing, the most often used commands were optimized for performance. Haitani even developed something his fellow workers called religion—"minimal click counting" (Butter and Pogue, 2002): the ultimate goal for designing a given functionality was to reduce the number of stylus movements for the user. The result was an uncon-ventionally structured, yet rapidly usable interface.

The Palm device was specifically designed as a business tool—in contrast to today's often Windows-based PDA, it had a different look-and-feel, and none of the applications common on desktop computers were available on the Palm, e.g., there was no functionality to view or edit office documents. The number of existing applications was extremely limited: a calendar, an address book, and a notepad. Each of these applications was designed with only minimal functionality as "most people only use a small percentage of the features in an app" (Bergman and Haitani, 2000). Still, the combined use of these applications can create a powerful tool supporting complex tasks. Specifically, the integration with the "Palm Desktop" on the desktop computer allowed a synchronization of events and notes and thus enabled a division of labor: the Palm was used "on the go", as a tool in meetings and for phone calls, while the desktop computer handled e-mail and document management with its larger display and faster input channels. The Palm was a supplement that could do things the PC could not. Strictly speaking, this disqualifies the Palm as an information appliance— its integration and ability for cooperation with a PC was one of the key features for its success.

This *architectural minimalism* created, however, difficulties when Palm was later forced to compete against Microsoft-powered PDAs. These PDAs offered more functionality to the broadening user base. As a reaction, key people at Palm left the company to form HandSpring and take the initial idea to the next level: The "SpringBoard" was to extend the essential functionality of the Palm where needed, a byproduct of Palm's strategy of supporting only the minimal set of functions and also the beginning of competition with other devices. This venture, however, proved to be more difficult than expected. Apart from reasons such as the difficulty of transforming a software company into a hardware supplier or the limited financial resources, the development of a proprietary slot for seamless plug and play made the hardware expensive, expansions often matching the original device in price. While the initial PalmPilot provided basic functionality for everyone, HandSpring would provide specialized features for those who sought them—too few in the end. Finally, the company was bought again by Palm and hope for Palm's future still relies on their latest development, the integration of mobile phones and the Palm device.

6.2.2.2 Discussion

The Palm is a straightforward example for the rigorous application of usability methods to attain a minimal access structure. For the sake of structural minimalism, even internal consistency was sacrificed—menu items that would traditionally have been grouped together are presented in different layers and as the Palm is for minimal clicks, every application behaves slightly differently. Although the criterion of consistency was violated so rigorously, the Palm felt very easy to use; so much was stated in all initial reviews. Instead, a key component of the Palm's success was its compatibility: because the exchange of data between standard PC applications and the Palm was so easy, the inconsistencies did not matter. After the initial niche was occupied and more functionality was sought, Palm lost its advantage—as other PDAs directly mimic PC applications, the mapping of extended functionality is much easier. And while the ease of handling may decrease, consistency with known applications became more important than optimal adaptation to the task—the lack of external consistency became an important negative factor for Palm sales.

Structural minimalism as defined here can be pursued with common HCI techniques. The development of the Palm Pilot was largely carried out using prototyping.[7] Using real or simulated tasks, the interface was adapted to small tasks, trying to optimize those tasks that were carried out the most often. This resulted in a smooth and intuitive handling. By contrast, PDAs are now developed and sold by the number of features, technology such as WLAN and G3 mobile communication connectivity, integrated cameras or voice recorders has become more important than the basic functionality. With competition from mobile phone companies and major desktop software vendors, the direction that development will take is still not decided (Shim, 2001; Gartner, 2004).

Again, a *2.0 syndrome* limits the success of a minimal design. The picture is even more dramatic; by introducing a new computing paradigm with a minimalist device the demand was immediately created to expand the initial, minimal functionality. This is why the Palm series is losing ground today—even though most people still need only basic functionality. Extending a minimal device is a challenge and whether selective addition of key features can outweigh the marketing power of missing features is yet to be decided. The convergence or diversification in the mobile computing domain remains an interesting subject of study.

Table 6.3 Minimal Aspects highlighted in the Palm handheld

Functional	Structural	Architectural	Compositional
Minimalism	Minimalism	Minimalism	Minimalism

6.2.2.3 A Minimal Assessment

- *Functional Minimalism*: Although the Palm is the most prominently used example for an *information appliance*, it is not functionally minimal in the sense of focus on a single function. Rather, its field of competence is clearly defined by excluding those areas of use a PC is better suited for, thus limiting the duplication of functionality. The orientation on this use setting created a minimal, yet whole set of necessary functions.

- *Structural Minimalism*: The "counting clicks"-technique in association with iterative prototyping has made the Palm the most convincing example for the interpretation of *structural minimalism* that tries to reduce the

---

[7] This begins with the anecdotal wooden prototype that the Palm founder, Jeff Hawkins, carried around to show the form factor of the future device and is most visible in the many iterations that were used to optimize the click (or rather tap) interaction with the Palm applications.

visibility of access structures by optimizing the structure to fit to the probability with which a function is needed. This is not limited to menus, it also extends to information layout or automatic modes that are chosen, e.g., when the notepad is opened, or the calendar selected—functionality is contextualized, trading off immediacy for (internal) consistency. The combination with the relatively minimal functionality and the focused area of competency allow this approach to create a very simple seeming, intuitive device. Problems became visible as the functionality needed to be expanded.

- *Architectural Minimalism*: "The Palm" is actually more than the hardware device. Only the close integration the free Palm Desktop builds with PC applications generates the value in using a Palm: all changes—whether on the PC or the Palm—become immediately synchronized with a single button press, and data is automatically forwarded to third-party applications, most notably Microsoft Outlook. The close integration frees users from having to remember where they stored notes or appointments and creates the illusion of using two tools within a single system.

- *Compositional Minimalism*: The access structure of the Palm was optimized for very specific tasks and the functionality tailored to the exact needs of a business user. Some functionality was missing, however, as users despite the form factor wanted to use the Palm to, e.g., edit office documents. The Palm could be programmed to adopt it to other tasks and some applications were developed for other contexts, but the unique design that proved so beneficial for its initial fit to the task made it inferior to Windows CE handhelds, where applications could build upon the consistency with existing PC applications.

6.2.3 Minimal Access Structures for Mobile Communication

Mark Weiser is often referred to as originator of the label of *ubiquitous computing* (Weiser, 1991, 1993; Weiser and Brown, 1997). This label describes research directed at the interface of computers becoming invisible and includes a vision of a tight integration of technology with everyday life. Regarding information appliances (Norman, 1999a)—integrated computers that exist in, e.g., washing machines or electric drills, mobile phones have perhaps had the most fundamental impact on daily life.[8] In contrast to other visions, e.g., designing for smart homes, domestic use and smart environments, in mobile phones, computers have actually managed to "vanish into the background" (Weiser, 1991) to some degree.

---

[8] Continental Research conducted a study for Vodafone UK in 2002 indicating that half of British business travelers state that their mobile phone is their most important possession on a business trip—more important than clean underwear, a razor, or toothpaste.
During another study by Codacons Italy in 2001, 300 volunteers were parted with their mobile phones. 15 days later, 70% reported problems including loss of appetite, sexual problems, depression, and a general blow to their confidence. http://www.wired.com/news/business/0,1367,48008,00.html

6.2.3.1 Description

An approach adhering to structural minimalism for mobile phones mobile phones must tackle the difficulty of providing an access structure that seems to be simple, yet allow access to the manifold functions of today's mobile phones. Traditional phones used to feature a number wheel (Fig. 6.18) or a numerical keypad. Additional functionality, such as repeated calls, listing received calls or quick dialing of stored numbers, was typically mapped to new keys that were added to the phone's interface. For mobile phones, the problem became much more complex, as new functionalities like SMS exchange were integrated with the phone and the internal status—settings for ringtones, vibration alarm, provider selection, address book management to name but a few—created new tasks in itself.

Fig. 6.18 Analog phone dial
(Historical Photograph)

Facing the difficulty of providing simple access to this complex functionality, Nokia used an approach very similar to the click-counting of the Palm developers in the commercially very successful 3100-, 3200- and 3300-series of mobile phones (Kiljander, 2004, 80); these phones were targeted directly at the mass consumer (comp. Karjalainen, 2003) and little tolerance for complexity was assumed during design. In addition to a standard numerical keypad, they featured a *Navi-Key*, a "softkey" whose semantics changed according to the user's actions—or rather, whose functional mapping changed according to the system's state (comp. Kiljander, 2004, 109ff). The function that a key press initiates is determined based on the frequency of functions chosen from the current system state. Although other functions can be reached using the scrolling keys, this is often not necessary. Thus, the interface (compare Fig. 6.19) was reduced to include only the Navi-Key, scrolling keys, and a clear (undo) key

(Lindholm and Keinonen, 2003, 24); the intended message was "Anybody can
master this phone as it is operated with only one key" (ibid., 25).

Fig. 6.19 Nokia 3310 phone
with the Navi-key right
below the display (Photo
Courtesy of Nokia)

   In usability tests, a preference was noted for phones with the Navi-Key as
perceived usability (comp. ibid., 25) was higher than both for the older 2110 series
and current mobile phones (ibid., 85). Ziefle (2002) compared the Nokia 3210
interface with a Siemens C35i and a Motorola P7389, and test users showed
higher performance with the Nokia phone. Bay and Ziefle (2003) furthermore
compared the menu structures of the C35i and the 3210 and found that, for the
Siemens phone, menu structure was significantly more complex and use of
control keys was significantly more difficult than Nokia's—users took twice the
time to complete tasks and made thrice as many detours in the menu.[9] Finally,
Kiljander (2004, 191) found that Nokia Navi-Key users rated the new interface of
the Nokia 6650 as "less easy to use" compared with their old phones. Interestingly, the Nokia designers themselves differentiate *actual* "ease of use" and
perceived "ease of use": for the actual usability, the total number of keystrokes
necessary to select a function is authoritative. Thus, by their definition, a reduction of keys decreases the actual "ease of use", while the perceived usability is
increased (comp. Lindholm and Keinonen, 2003, 25).

---

[9] It should be noted that the result of the cited usability test cannot be traced to a single UI
element, i.e. the Navi-Key might contribute to, but is not solely responsible for the better
performance of the Nokia phone.

Yet with all its merits, the Navi-Key approach has some drawbacks: Mapping the Navi-Key to the most often used function in a certain situation will not work for all users—Nokia nonetheless chose not to implement a learning algorithm in their phones. Access structures were slightly reordered in the development from the 3210 to the 3310 phone, but no adaptation mechanism created an individual structure that would optimize access for an individual user. Adapting menu structures is known to cause problems due to a lack of consistency (Mitchell and Shneiderman, 1989; Tsandilas and Schraefel, 2005). In an interface where a single function is mapped to an element, system reactions are very predictable (see Section 4.4.3). As the phone menu interface does not provide a history of menu selections, error recovery caused by assumed consistency becomes very difficult. Furthermore, the menu system and, with it, the conceptual model for phone usage, are still technically oriented, e.g., regarding dual memory (Klockar et al., 2003): messages or numbers are treated differently according to their storage location (SIM-card or internal memory).

The culmination of minimal structure was implemented in a different market segment: luxury phones, such as the Vertu concierge line[10] are bought in combination with a service contract. This "concierge" service is contacted with a designated button—a human answers the call and any further function, ranging from looking up a number to booking a hotel room or ordering tickets, is then executed by this human agent (Nokia, 2002). If nothing else, this non-technical solution points towards limits of our interaction with technology.

6.2.3.2 Discussion

Again, the Nokia 3110 phone follows the ideal of a *minimal access structure*, and again, the result is reviewed favorably. The design of the Navi-Key is the result of a simple design technique, the selection of functionality based on use frequency. The single-key concept performs surprisingly well, but does not scale to newer Nokia models that feature more functions: here, the single Navi-Key has been replaced by two reprogrammable keys.

As new phones acquire new functionality, their technical innards become more visible for the user—the introduction of technobabble like WAP, GPRS, MP3, Bluetooth, etc., that is little understood by end users (Metafacts, 2003) into phone ads may suffice as proof—and the computer within the phone surfaces again. Although terms such as "Simplicity" or "Ease of Use" are featured prominently when mobile phones are advertised (RPO, 2005), usability studies indicate that phones are increasingly difficult to use (Dahm et al., 2005; eco, 2005), and that consumers are overwhelmed by technical features (de.internet.com, 2004); especially for older adults, the use of "advanced" technology becomes problematic. Mobile phones are still primarily used for tasks the Nokia 3310 can handle, voice and SMS messaging—the need for sophistication of mobile phones is thus not obvious. However, the *2.0 syndrome* here is driven by the telecommunication

---

[10] http://www.vertu.com

Fig. 6.20 Vertu concierge
phone (Photo Courtesy of
Vertu)

companies trying to find the next killer application that will help pay for their
high-speed networks.

The Vertu concierge line (Fig. 6.20) underlines that even "user-friendly"
interfaces are inferior to the speech-based interface of person-to-person communication. HCI has not been able to come up with an alternative to this really
intelligent interface yet. Just as the reduced number of buttons on remote
controls, the single button on the Vertu phone is no technical solution, it only
shifts the users' problems to another, more friendly modality.

Table 6.4 Minimal Aspects highlighted in Nokia's 3310 series

Functional	Structural	Architectural	Compositional
Minimalism	Minimalism	Minimalism	Minimalism

6.2.3.3 A Minimal Assessment

- *Functional Minimalism*: At first glance, the Nokia 3310 line of mobile phones
  limits itself to the core functionality associated with phones: voice and
  messaging. This is, however, partly confounded with the age of the phone:
  contemporary low-cost phones targeting the mass market have a similar
  range of functionality. As the phone's deep menu structure proves, much
  of the functionality, e.g., for programming ring tones or configuring network
  services, is accessible, alas well hidden.

- *Structural Minimalism*: This seemingly simplistic design of the Navi-Key is a prime example of a probabilistic context-based access structure. As in many situations, a single function is chosen with extreme preference (e.g., ending a call while talking, or reading a message after receiving a notification), the "one-key" solution is often able to suggest the "right" action. As the minimal remote controls, the Navi-Key also has a communicative function: it suggests visually that this phone is simple to use. As an important aspect of *structural minimalism* is that the design is in itself not truly simple, nor offers only minimal functionality, this could be interpreted as deceitful and the simplifying effect could be reversed if the deception becomes obvious. Later variations of the Navi-Key concept that use two or more "smart keys" demonstrate—although the concept can be extended by adding more probabilistic buttons preventing the more sophisticated functionality to become hidden by the mundane, often-used features—that the clear mapping between feature and physical interface is lost through the addition of functionality.
- *Architectural Minimalism*: As the 3310 series was primarily designed as a stand-alone device, its design does not imply its use as a "tool"—only the infrared connection that allows synchronization of event reminders might be considered as a link to a Microsoft Outlook calendar application.
- *Compositional Minimalism*: Nokia's concentration on voice and short messaging services have created a simpler device, but there is no evidence suggesting that this increased the use of the 3310 series in unconventional domains. On the contrary, specific types of phones are designed, e.g., with four buttons as an emergency phone for the elderly, or with parental budget control for children. The Vertu concierge series has implemented a Wizard-of-Oz-like variant of the ideal of an intelligent phone, relaying the intelligence into the human operator; although this creates a universal tool, it does not generate design advice—except that it may sometimes be adequate to accept limitations of technology and find a social rather than a technical solution.

6.2.4 HyperScout: Enhancing Link Preview in the World Wide Web

> *Wherever you go, there you are.*
> Buckaroo Banzai. rock star, neurosurgeon, inventor, movie character

Links are the most prominent medium for interaction with the World Wide Web, and thus should be listed among the most important interface elements of today. However, the interface of links—their graphical representation and the actions afforded—has not been a field of intensive research. Rather, the design of hyperlinks has been inherited from the first accidental renderings in early browsers (Weinreich et al., 2001) and the fact that small changes in the appearance of link markers can dramatically change reading behavior (Obendorf and Weinreich, 2003) has been largely ignored.

As disorientation has repeatedly been stated as one of the major problems of navigation in the Web—for Hypertext systems, Conklin took note of this problem even in 1987 (Conklin, 1987)—the *enhancement of the link interface to better support navigation* is an important but underestimated problem. The HyperScout project (Weinreich et al., 2004) is an effort to ease navigation in the World Wide Web by providing link preview information.

Technically, it is based on IBM's *intermediary* concept (Paul and Rob, 2000) and the Scone framework (Weinreich ct al., 2003): Web pages requested by the user are filtered by the intermediary, allowing the addition, subtraction, or modification of all data. HyperScout adds information to links in Web pages— information about the target of the link; this information is collected invisibly in the background while the page is being rendered and displayed in tooltips when the user moves the cursor above a link marker (compare Fig. 6.21).

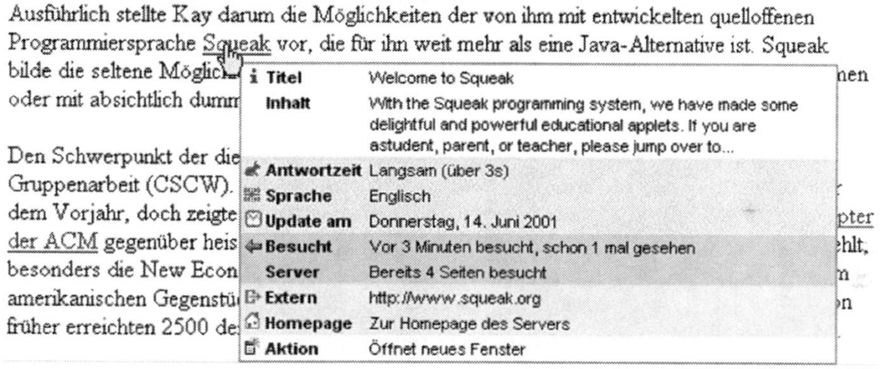

Ausführlich stellte Kay darum die Möglichkeiten der von ihm mit entwickelten quelloffenen Programmiersprache Squeak vor, die für ihn weit mehr als eine Java-Alternative ist. Squeak bilde die seltene Möglich...

i Titel	Welcome to Squeak	
Inhalt	With the Squeak programming system, we have made some delightful and powerful educational applets. If you are astudent, parent, or teacher, please jump over to...	
✦ **Antwortzeit**	Langsam (über 3s)	
▦ **Sprache**	Englisch	
▣ **Update am**	Donnerstag, 14. Juni 2001	
⬅ **Besucht**	Vor 3 Minuten besucht, schon 1 mal gesehen	
Server	Bereits 4 Seiten besucht	
▷ **Extern**	http://www.squeak.org	
▣ **Homepage**	Zur Homepage des Servers	
▢ **Aktion**	Öffnet neues Fenster	

Fig. 6.21 HyperScout popup window displaying meta-information about the link target (Screenshot Courtesy of Harald Weinreich)

An important aspect of the design of the HyperScout system is the selection and granularity of preview information. To actually support navigation, it is vital not only that all the displayed information is useful, but also that the displayed information is sufficient—it must be minimal but also complete. If the information satisfies these needs, the user is freed from "navigation excise" (Cooper and Reimann, 2003, 135ff) as he/she is empowered by the additional information to better judge which link is leading to the desired information.

6.2.4.1 Description

In terms of minimalism, HyperScout is untypical as it explicitly adds information to Web pages. This is necessary as, although the Web itself is abundant with information, users are provided insufficient means to cope with the information overload that has become a hallmark of the information society (Wurman, 1990; Berghel, 1997a; Farhoomand and Drury, 2002). HyperScout follows the proposition that additional information about hyperlinks will help users assess the importance of the linked information, thus enabling a fair judgement whether it is necessary to follow a link. The expected benefit for the individual user is a reduction in visited pages as detours are reduced, combined with a lower cognitive load as link meta-information is provided by the system and does not need to be kept track of by the user.

Often, type information for links is referenced as the most important information source as it would, in principle, allow a detailed analysis of link usefulness (comp. Weinreich et al., 2001). It is, however, rarely provided in the Web, dramatically limiting its usefulness. Often, the technically trivial thumbnails are used as preview information in research prototypes. Although they look impressive, they are unfortunately of little practical use as the content is rendered illegible and many sites use a corporate design that prevents the identification of individual sites in thumbnails.[11] Web design conventions that unify, e.g., navigation menus across sites do not help distinguish their visual appearance.

There are different types of implicit meta-information: Weinreich et al. (2004) list contents of the target document, link topology, use history, media type, browser action, target status, and expected reaction time as information that is implicitly available in the Web. Using this existing information that only has to be harvested in advance, a detailed picture of the target document can be created without having to navigate there. To actually effect a lowering of the cognitive load, a vital part of the HyperScout system is knowing which information is useful in what situation.

The amount and type of useful information depends on the status of the linked page. For example, the necessary information for a non-existing page is very different—HyperScout indicates the link as broken (compare Fig. 6.22)—than the information for an existing page. For certain types of pages that are updated often (e.g., news sites), the number of changes is more interesting than the last update; the number of visits to a page is especially important for long-term revisits—a large number of heuristics can be identified that will lead to a choice and ranking specific to a certain use case.

An important aspect of the link interface is the visualization of link markers within the currently read document. From the many existing possibilities (comp. Noirhomme-Fraiture and Serpe, 1998), underlining is the de-facto standard—not the result of a conscious design process, but a historical heritage—and other alternatives (comp., e.g., Weinreich et al., 2001) have not been successful. Only in the recent past, a trend towards simplification—omitting the

---

[11] Some approaches use thumbnails for link preview (e.g., Kopetzky & Mühlhäuser, 1999; Nanno et al., 2002); this was also implemented using the Scone framework (Wollenweber, 2004) but was found to be not very useful in user tests.

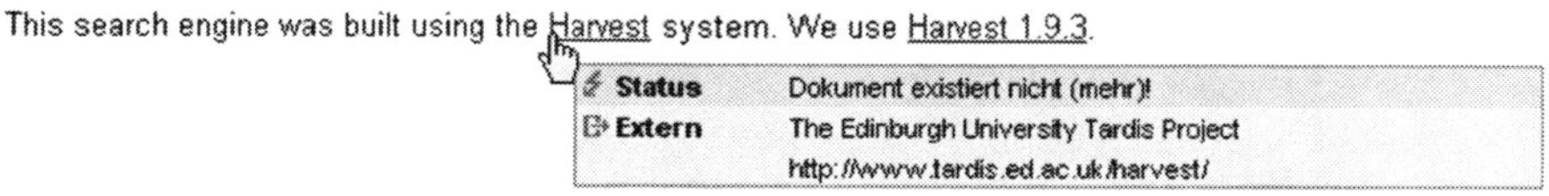

This search engine was built using the Harvest system. We use Harvest 1.9.3.

✓ **Status**	Dokument existiert nicht (mehr)!
⊡ **Extern**	The Edinburgh University Tardis Project
	http://www.tardis.ed.ac.uk/harvest/

Fig. 6.22 HyperScout pop-up showing information about a dead link

underlines, leaving only color to mark links—can be observed in the Web; a trend that increases the readability of Web pages (Obendorf and Weinreich, 2003).

A challenge for the HyperScout system was thus to make additional information available to the user without increasing the complexity of the layout. While icons are often proposed to add preview information[12] (comp., e.g., Hightower et al., 1998; Campbell and Maglio, 1999), informal tests with the HyperScout system showed that the textual form of meta-information was often superior in ease of understanding. As the textual information could not directly be added to the Web page, pop-up information windows were chosen to display link meta-information—just as context menus allow access to functionality useful to manipulate the current selection (Koved and Scneiderman, 1986), these pop-ups display contextualized information providing useful information about the link under the cursor. This follows the perspective of *structural minimalism*: link pop-ups are a compromise of providing functionality only on demand and providing it as soon as possible.

The standard interaction technique used could be improved by increasing sensitivity towards context. The information structure delivered by HyperScout must trade off consistency in placement, allowing spatial memory to support the digestion of the presented information, and conciseness, suppressing information that is not useful within the context. For some applications (e.g., search engine results), the presentation of information within tabular lists has advantages over pop-up information.

Using pop-ups or tool tips for the display of meta-information has also the handicap that different links cannot be compared; HyperScout was extended to use "thumbtacks" to this end (Witt and Tyerman, 2002). However, this places further demands on the user, and the question remains whether it would not be easier to compare the target pages directly. For search engine results, the information for different links will often need to be compared. Annotations

---

[12] In previous versions, Sun's Web design guidelines (Levine, 1996) and Yale University's Web Style Guide (Lynch, & Horton, 1999) included hints to decorate external links with icons. Parts of the Microsoft web site also follow this practice (e.g., Windows Hardware Developer Central at http://www.microsoft.com/whdc/Legend.mspx), and plug-ins for CMS systems allow the automatic decoration on the server side, e.g. for Wordpress at http://sw-guide.de/wordpress/link-indication-plugin/.

using pop-ups (used, e.g., in Sharon et al., 2003) do not allow the side-by-side comparison. Direct changes of the link marker visualization, e.g., coloring links according to implicit types (Obendorf and Weinreich, 2003), can be useful for providing information without creating the need for a user to use pop-ups (Weinreich et al., 2004).

6.2.4.2 Discussion

The HyperScout case demonstrates that not only the structure of information but also its visualization can affect the resulting access structure. HyperScout provides a minimal interface as it does not add visible information to Web pages at first. Information about target pages is provided only on demand. The structural minimalism in this is that the original interface—a Web page filled with text, graphics and hyperlinks—remains virtually unchanged. Only when it becomes necessary for the user to decide whether to follow a link or not, decision support is provided.

This marks both a strength and a weakness of the concept. The user can freely decide whether he wants to trade off speed and conciseness for completeness and certainty. If response and rendering times continue to drop significantly, the temporal cost difference between displaying the result page and information about the result page is reduced. As meta-information can be incomplete and erroneous, this will shift the balance to the disadvantage of HyperScout. A further problem is that although the look of the interface is unchanged using HyperScout, the feel changes: informal observations indicated that, usually, users don't hover over links before they click on them. If users liked HyperScout, their behavior changed and an additional navigation step (read–hover–click) was introduced.

As users tend to rapidly navigate on the Web—in a recent study, we found that most pages are visited only briefly, with 25% of all documents displayed for less than 4 seconds and 52% of all visits being shorter than 10 seconds (Weinreich et al., 2006b; Weinreich et al., 2006a)—this additional step could slow down navigation behavior. Yet, while we previously found that small changes, such as the marking method for links could have large effects on reading behavior (Obendorf and Weinreich, 2003), quantitative data is difficult to interpret as many different activities are overlaid in the data (Obendorf et al., 2007; Herder et al., 2006; Weinreich et al., 2006b). Also, if the information was really helpful for the user, those navigational steps that only deal with retracing detours would become obsolete.

Following a user study that tried to study what information would be most useful for the users, version 2 of HyperScout was developed. Here, interviews examined which information would be useful for each link type (comp. Weinreich et al., 2004). The resulting version displayed much less information, concentrating on the most useful items in the pop-ups. Further options were added that marked out, e.g., external links on demand.

Table 6.5 Minimal Aspects highlighted in HyperScout

Functional Minimalism	Structural Minimalism	Architectural Minimalism	Compositional Minimalism

6.2.4.3 A Minimal Assessment

- *Functional Minimalism*: While the HyperScout system is technically complex, with filter, crawl and proxy mechanisms working together, backed up by a database, the functionality is simple: displaying additional information as the user moves the mouse over a link. In the second version, first experiments were made what other uses the existing information could have.
- *Structural Minimalism*: As HyperScout competes with Web download times and rapid navigation events, the most important requirement that users named during the test runs were the immediate accessibility of information "at one glance". A categorization of different link types and of automatically generated meta-information allowed the prioritization of pertinent information that is displayed for different types of links. HyperScout thus does not base its minimal structure on frequency of use, but on the related measure of "perceived usefulness" for link types.
- *Architectural Minimalism*: HyperScout is a tool adding functionality to Web browsers. Although it is technically realized as a Web intermediary, this is only due to its prototypical status; a final release would rather be integrated into the browser. It would still add features almost without complicating the interface as its functionality remains invisible unless explicitly invoked by mouse-overs or modifier keys.
- *Compositional Minimalism*: Due to its specificity not only in the information provided but also in the structure of information and the mode of interaction, appropriation of HyperScout is unlikely and has not been observed.

6.2.5 Word Processing

Word processing applications have acquired functionality that extends far beyond the task of processing words alone, they are able to manage bibliographies, print serial letters, and produce sophisticated layouts. The number of features in Microsoft Word has risen steadily. This is not only a common perception, Microsoft itself has documented the feature increase in an official blog on the usability of Office 2007 (Fig. 6.23, Harris, 2005).

The accumulated features have created the need for an increasingly complex interface. Judging by the number of tool bars and task panes alone, the rise in interface complexity is even more dramatic than the accumulated functionality (Fig. 6.24, ibid.).

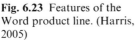

Fig. 6.23 Features of the Word product line. (Harris, 2005)

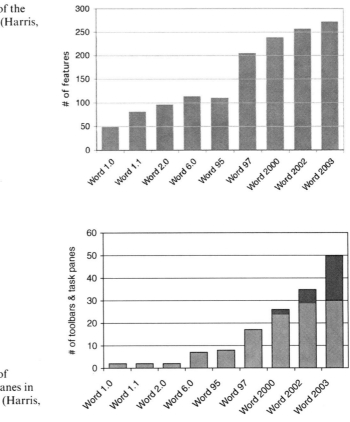

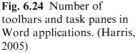

Fig. 6.24 Number of toolbars and task panes in Word applications. (Harris, 2005)

While word processors have become very complex applications, the complexity of work tasks is unlikely to have increased proportionally. This means that many users use only a few functions. The use of functionality follows a Zipf distribution: a few functions are used very often, while others are used much more infrequently. However, most functions are used by someone, the resulting distribution of used events is a long-tailed distribution (Harris, 2006f). The five most-often-used commands for Word 2003 were paste, save, copy, undo and bold. Paste actions alone account for more than 11% of all commands and, together, these five actions are performed in 32% of all cases (ibid.). As the designers of Office believe that all functions are used by someone, removing functions was not an option—the intended goal was rather to make users use more features (Harris, 2006a). The question was thus how to adapt the access structure in a manner that would provide easy access to often-used functionality.

Adapting structure to fit the users' needs has long been a focus of research and there exist many techniques to design menu systems according to users' expectations and needs (Norman, 1991; Obendorf, 2003). It is also not a new idea that systems should "behave intelligently" by adapting their access structure automatically to better meet the individual user's needs. Various approaches for adaptive menus have been discussed in the literature (e.g., Mitchell and Shneiderman, 1989; Sears and Shneiderman, 1994), and although some experiments showed that techniques like split menus can decrease task time, other experiments showed that simple ordering by frequency did not improve efficiency of users—while it might generally be assumed that the mild disorientation caused by changing menu layouts could harm user satisfaction. A recent controlled study found that users both prefer adaptable menus to adaptive menus and work more efficiently with the former (Findlater and McGrenere, 2004).

Nonetheless, for its *Office 2000*, Microsoft chose to implement adaptive menus (Fig. 6.25): "Word 2000's new adaptive menus display only the most commonly used commands at first, and then expand to show all of their commands" (Rubin, 1999, 163). Infrequently used menu entries were first

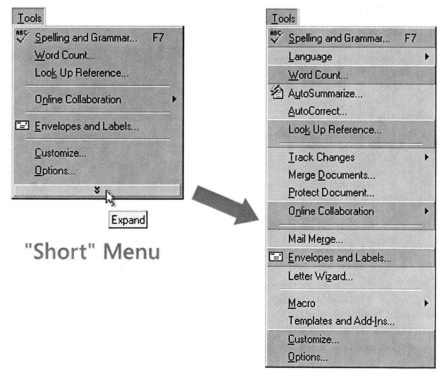

Fig. 6.25 Adaptive menus in Microsoft Word 2000: only after clicking on expand, the full menu is shown (Screenshots taken from MS Word 2000)

hidden, then grayed out when the full menu was requested. However, in contrast
with the menu system of, e.g., the Palm, Microsoft's solution had two drawbacks:
the absolute position of menu items would change as other items were included or
excluded automatically, and a menu item that was important but would be used
infrequently could disappear. This behavior of the menu system irritated many
users as they could not understand why adaptation was taking place; even if they
understood the underlying mechanism, it was working against them and forced
them to wait for the expanded menus to select their target item. As menu recall is
aided by spatial memory (Norman, 1991, Chapter 13), the adaptive menus were
prone to hurt not only the users' feelings but also the measured task performance.

Microsoft also implemented adaptivity for toolbars. The so-called "rafted"
toolbars (Fig. 6.26) were displayed when not all icons would fit on the screen.
Some icons were moved to a drop-down dialog that would appear upon clicking
on an expand arrow. The selection of icons in these rafted toolbars also
depended on the frequency of their use: often-used icons were moved from
the dialog to the bar, where infrequently used icons had to make room. Thus,
Word 2000 was trying to provide an exact fit to the user's use frequency, trading
off consistency of placement.

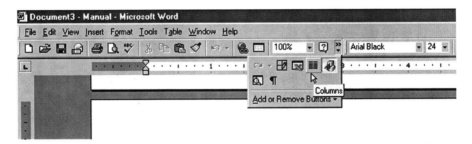

Fig. 6.26 A "rafted toolbar" in Microsoft Word 2000

6.2.5.1 Description

While adaptive menus create a minimal access structure if one takes frequency
of use as the primary measure, the question remains whether the resulting
menus form a whole—no vital options are left out—and whether frequency of
use is a good indicator for personal importance. Problems with adaptivity have
been listed in a review of the current state of research by Christina Höök (2000)
as adaptive systems may create a *lack of control* for the user—mechanisms for
adaptation are often complex or cannot be controlled at all. They can also cause
unpredictable results, decrease *transparency*, intrude on the user's *privacy*, and
reduce the user's *trust* in the system.

Some of these problems also surface in practice: users seem to generally
dislike adaptive menus in Microsoft Word 2000 and, among a list of the "top
12 tips for MS word" users by the author of *Word 2000 in a Nutshell* (Glenn,

2000b), number 1 reads "Turn Off Adaptive Menus" (Glenn, 2000a). Personal preference of users was found by Findlater and McGrenere to tend towards manually adaptable menus in a controlled study (Findlater and McGrenere, 2004); and in an experiment with different interfaces for Microsoft Word, McGrenere also found a preference for individual tailoring (McGrenere et al., 2002). After Office 2003, Microsoft seems to intend to switch off adaptive menus by default (Harris, 2006b).

With the newest version of its Office suite, Microsoft is going to introduce a number of dramatic changes to the interface. "The user-interface is startlingly different—and better," according to Darren Strange, Product Manager for Office in the UK (Hales, 2006): "In the first Word for Windows there were 100 features . . . while in Office 2003 there were 1500, all buried in the program in places many users dare not go . . . users found it difficult to remember where everything is . . . [so now] everything will be contextualised."

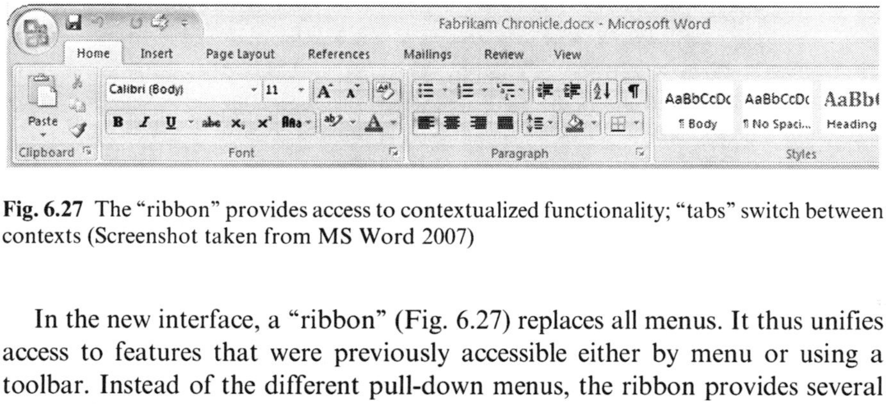

Fig. 6.27 The "ribbon" provides access to contextualized functionality; "tabs" switch between contexts (Screenshot taken from MS Word 2007)

In the new interface, a "ribbon" (Fig. 6.27) replaces all menus. It thus unifies access to features that were previously accessible either by menu or using a toolbar. Instead of the different pull-down menus, the ribbon provides several "tabs" that group functionality. While the menus, however, grouped functionality according to consistency with other applications and according to objects and attributes that could be manipulated (format, table), and had little success finding a better label for those features hidden in the tools and edit menu, the ribbon groups Word's increasing number of features in tabs that relate to steps in the work process.

Microsoft's switch from using adaptive menus and toolbars to creating a static interface that can be used in different ways according to the user's activity is much more in line with minimal structure; it is able to deliver a completeness of the interface that adaptive techniques cannot. As quantitative input is used to group functionality into activities, the design is based on actual user behavior. Still, the designer can include vital functionality that is necessary but not often used—automatic quantitative evaluation of how often a function is used does not necessarily account for its importance to the user.

On the other hand, an increasing adaption to certain tasks bears the risk of too narrowly defining the user's course of action and limiting his/her freedom to

Fig. 6.28 The "Microsoft Office Button" provides access to most often used functions (Screenshot of MS Word 2007)

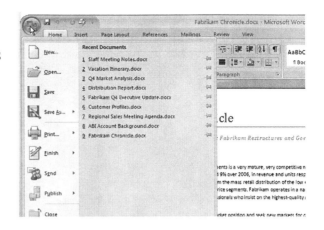

choose the right path of action. This aspect is further investigated below (see *compositional minimalism*) but has also been addressed by Microsoft: with the introduction of a generally accessible menu containing the most important options (called "Microsoft Office Button" (Fig. 6.28) in the public beta version), and with the ability to quickly change contexts using tabs, the user can both access basic functionality at any time and choose between access structures tailored to a certain context.

While it was possible in previous versions of Office to show, e.g., image manipulation toolbars only when an image was selected, this has now become the default behavior. The number of active toolbars is thus massively decreased—at the cost of having an interface that changes according to the current selection: as the user selects, e.g., a picture, an additional tab becomes available (Fig. 6.29).

6.2.5.2 Discussion

The underlying principle of Microsoft's approach in Office 2007 is contextualization; the complex functionality of Word is broken down according to use contexts—Word still appears as a single, powerful tool, albeit with contextualized menus. This approach has been used very successfully in context menus (comp. Koved and Scneiderman, 1986) appearing on a right mouse click. The difference here is that the new "ribbon" interface makes the contextualization immediately visible; in this respect, it bears some resemblance to inspector windows that appear only for certain types of selections—this approach has long been used, e.g., in PowerPoint for processing images. Comparable functionality existed in previous versions of Word as Toolbars would only be displayed as necessary. The difference, however, is that the ribbon adds an additional, optional *mode* without adding to the interface complexity whereas appearing toolbars immediately complicated

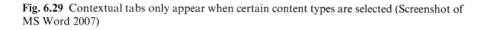

instruments and equipment sold to professionals who insist on the highest-quality sound. Most of our customers are concert musicians.

Now is not the time to consolidate our market position and seek new markets for our products. The market for musical instruments divides easily into several segments. Several market segments are relevant, and for this discussion we define the segments in which Fabrikam operates:

Customers

Customers. Customers range from children learning how to play to professional musicians in concert settings. However, Fabrikam sells almost exclusively to professional musicians.

Instruments

Instrument or type of instrument. Fabrikam manufactures and distributes both acoustic and electric guitars, electric keyboards, speakers, electronic music equipment, and related accessories.

Type-of-music

Fig. 6.29 Contextual tabs only appear when certain content types are selected (Screenshot of MS Word 2007)

the interface. As an alternative approach, *architectural minimalism* is discussed in the next section; in contrast to the contextualized interface presented here, it focuses on presenting several distinct tools that can be used together to provide the designed functionality.

6.2.6 *Refining the Notion of Structural Minimalism*

Structural minimalism was introduced as the question how to order functionality in a manner that minimizes the perceived structure for the user. Remote controls as examples (1) introduced the mapping problem and demonstrated the shift to other modalities. The design of the Palm and the Navi-Key demonstrated (2) how usability tests can generate an optimal fit of the access structure to sub-tasks and (3) how frequency-based selection of functionality can generate the impression of simplicity. HyperScout posed the question when to (4) actively hide functionality, and the redesign of Word 2007 suggests to (5) adapt the access structure to activities rather than to the use frequency of functions.

It is unclear when reducing the number of physical controls increases the usability of a design. Contradicting the conclusions from the remote control example, Norman (Norman, 1989) favors his car's interface over his telephone's: Automotive engineers and designers have traditionally mapped new functionality to new controls, increasing the number of controls. With minor exceptions, there is one control for each function and each control can be labeled naturally. By contrast, in Norman's reference phone, 24 functions map to only 15 controls, none of which are labeled for specific actions. According to Norman, the visible car controls remind the user from the available possibilities, unlike the phone with unlabeled controls telling nothing about the device functionality. The good relationship between the car controls and what they do also makes it easier for the user to master the car's function—especially for fast-moving vehicles, it can be dangerous to reduce the number of controls and shift the access structure into menu systems.

This benefit was lost when BMW introduced its iDrive system. The habitual mapping between controls and their functionality was lost as the iDrive introduced a turnable knob controlling a complex menu system—a single control for all of the car's advanced functionality. Jef Raskin attributes this to the introduction of modes: "Turning the iDrive knob shouldn't mean different things in different modes. You shouldn't need to stop and ask, 'What mode is this thing in right now?'" (Wilkinson, 2002); however, there seems to be a limit to direct mapping—the 112 controls in Don Norman's Mercedes Benz fail to compare to the 2002 BMW 700 series with its controversial iDrive interface: One of its designers noted, "The people who designed the interface, we didn't need 700 functions. We always discussed whether we need this function or that function, because it would have made it for us much easier to build a simpler system. But OK, if our marketing department says we need it, we design it in" (quoted in Kiljander, 2004, 159).

The design of the Nokia 3300 series highlights that it can be useful to differentiate between the *actual* and the *perceived ease of use*. Although the Nokia designers do not give a definition for measuring the actual ease of use, and problems such as whether a more sophisticated interface can be used more efficiently after training or whether a direct mapping between interface and functionality is desirable remain, making this distinction allows to extend design beyond the measurable usability and towards the users' experience: reducing an interface visually has an important effect on users, adding to their perception of simplicity.

However, if the overall complexity cannot be reduced, the trade-off introduced by making a system structurally minimal can result in less usable systems. John Maeda introduced the *Goldilocks* metaphor for hiding the right amount of supportive information in the forest of consumable information: navigation in a beautiful forest motivates the provision of not-too-large signposts—they would defer attention from what is really interesting (Maeda, 2005b).

The question whether functionality should be actively kept hidden is not only crucial for research projects, Google as one of the major Web companies faces similar problems: its home page is commonly rated as very simple and as very easy to use. It features most prominently a search form and a submit button. If one compares this to Yahoo, Web.de, or other large portals, the Google home page indeed seems to be much simpler—although it has become somewhat more complex over time (compare Fig. 6.30). However, its simplicity is owed largely to obscurity: many of the additional services that Google offers (Google Maps, Google Mail, Google Earth, etc.) are never mentioned on its home page. This has led Don Norman to comment: "Is Google simple? No it is deceptive!" (Norman, 2004c). More importantly, Google realized it hurt itself with its strategy when they launched Google Video and movie sales were hurt by the fact it was not mentioned on their home page (Post-Intelligencer, 2006).

The Nokia example raises another issue for structural minimalism: is "intelligent" (read automatic) adaptation minimal? By definition, minimal structures are those that are not visible to the user. If a design adopts its structure to the task—as, e.g., Microsoft Word 2000 does with its toolbars and adaptive menus—it risks disappointing the user by failing to meet his/her expectations. It seems that this problem is fairly common, as many adaptive systems are only designed with an incrementally optimal fit to task in mind and disregard effects of the observable changes in access structure. While this is not sufficient evidence to deduce that adaptive systems cannot be structurally minimal, the examples for minimal structures found here are static: they focus on *reduction by design* rather than *designed reduction*.

The application of *structural minimalism* to the Palm design, but even more to word processing software, demonstrated a central difference of structural and architectural minimalism: in the case of structural minimalism, the complex functionality of a single tool is organized according to tasks. While the new Office 2007 will probably introduce a few hundred new features, it tries to group access to this abundance of functionality in accordance with the users' needs. Where information is given preference to function, this process is also known as *information architecture* (comp. Wurman and Bradford, 1996; Rosenfeld and Morville, 2002). While this introduces a terminological overlap with *architectural minimalism*, the meanings of these terms differ decisively: information architecture is often used as an umbrella term for the graphical and structural design of Web sites (ibid.), or takes on an even broader meaning, including questions of emotion or empowerment (Dillon in Carliner et al., 2001). Both structural and architectural minimalism can thus be seen as focused perspectives on information architecture, only that their design scope extends beyond Web pages.

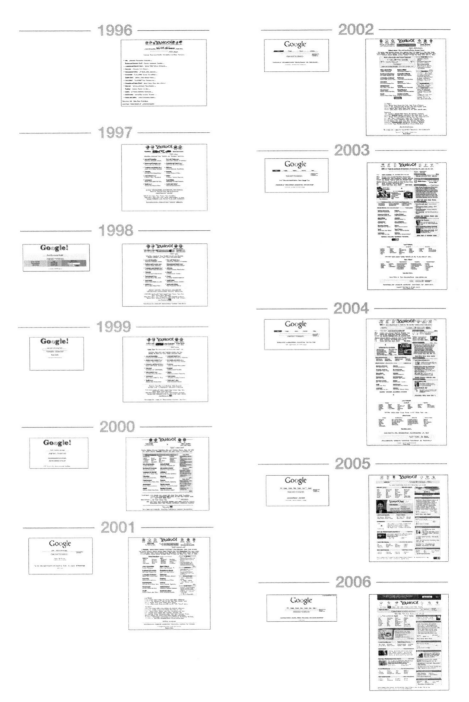

Fig. 6.30 Yahoo and Google home pages from 1996 to 2006 (Screenshots taken using Firefox 3.0 and www.archive.org)

6.3 Architectural Minimalism

The whole is simpler than the sum of its parts.

—Josiah Willard Gibbs[13]

The notions of *functional minimalism* and *structural minimalism* concentrate on properties of the interface—what functions are provided and how access to functionality is adapted to a task. *Architectural minimalism* denotes a minimality in the constituents of an interface and assumes that the interface itself can be modularized. The "interface" is thus expected to consist of several visibly distinct tools, interaction is split into distinct dimensions. As examples for architectural minimalism are described here based on observations of interfaces, but the notion is defined as resulting from the underlying architecture, this analysis serves as an indicator whether the distinction of functional, structural and architectural minimalism is useful in practice.

6.3.1 Building Blocks

The 1958 Lego brick is an example for the possible complexity that can be created by combinations of very simple building blocks. Lego bricks have been used to model lifelike scenes or recreate hallmarks of civilization. There are two lessons for architecture built into the bricks: First and most in the spirit of the minimal, identical blocks can be combined to form most complex shapes (Fig. 6.31). Many Lego builders make exclusive use of the "original" Lego brick[14] (Fig. 6.32); the architecture of their models is based on the primitive cuboid.

Although the backwards compatibility of Lego bricks is unequalled in computer science—bricks fresh from the store mix nicely with those inherited from the previous generation—some changes have occurred. The second lesson of the Lego brick is that although new forms are continuously introduced (more than 2500 different LEGO elements have been designed[15]), the binding principle remained simple and thus, the "original" brick still interfaces with all new elements (see Fig. 6.32).

---

[13] Gibbs, a physicist and mathematician, lived from 1839 until 1903 and worked as a professor in Yale. The citation cannot be reproduced here without alluding to its original context, thermodynamics (cf. Jaynes, 1992).

[14] The first bricks were copycats of a British invention, the Kiddicraft Self-Locking Building Brick from 1940 and were introduced in 1949 under the label Automatic Binding Bricks. They lacked the Stud-and-Tube Coupling System that holds together today's bricks; the tubes on the underside increase the stability of the bricks, and, most importantly, the grip on other bricks. Only thus, complex constructions were made possible and the product became a huge commercial success. (Lithgow, 1987; Hughes, 2005)

[15] http://www.lego.com/eng/create/designschool/lesson.asp?id = 1_a

Fig. 6.31 The original Lego brick, and an animal made of some of its brethren. Lego elephant (Product Photograph, Lego and picture taken in Legoland, DK)

Fig. 6.32 New Lego elements (Product Photograph, Lego)

The artful composition of standard, mass-production tiles can create an infinite wealth of different forms. Using only the rectangular basic Lego brick, sophisticated models have been formed by Lego enthusiasts all over the world, and the Lego amusement parks rebuild real landscapes, buildings, or life forms by individually combining bricks to form new shapes. Sometimes, special pieces are used that have been designed by Lego for that purpose, but most model builders base their designs on the original 4 x 2 brick.

While the standard Lego sets still form the main business, Lego had some success introducing the Lego Technic series where simple mechanics can be rebuilt using special tiles. An important success factor was the compatibility to standard tiles, enabling model builder to integrate mechanics into their designs. Lego also built the Mindstorm robots, whose first version did not create a universal commercial success—the robot series became immensely popular for teaching and research purposes (Klassner, 2002; Hood and Hood, 2005), but many end users felt the included software placed unnecessary restrictions on the possible designs, and few customers were able to custom-build their own driver or operating system for the robots.[16] Lego manager Lund believed that "Mindstorms' main flaw . . . was its complexity; many kids lost interest before completing their first robot . . . Lund wanted novices to be able to construct and program a robot in 20 minutes. The biggest barrier to making that happen was the Mindstorms programming language, known as RCX-code. Though simple by computer science standards, it was too frustrating for many programming neophytes" (Koerner, 2006). For its new robot series, Lego partnered with Microsoft (Microsoft, 2006c) to provide both a novice and an expert program-ming environment. Although Lego discontinued packaging the classic tiles in the new NXT Mindstorms series as they want to change to a more modern look, the studless Technic tiles are still compatible (Koerner, 2006).

6.3.1.1 Discussion

The example of Lego bricks highlights a necessary differentiation to understand "architectural" minimalism correctly. The notion of *architectural minimalism* refers to the architecture of the interface, providing different tools that can be recombined by the user to adapt the designed system to his/her needs. In the context of information systems, architecture is often understood as an internal aspect of a design that is not necessarily visible to the user.

The building blocks of Lego could be set in relation to the plug-in concept that can be found, e.g., in the Eclipse development environment. However, this assumes that the user is the spectator, not the builder: functionality can be configured by adding or removing plug-ins, yet these do not necessarily show up in the interface and if they do, they are often not recognizable as individual tools, but instead aim for a close integration with the existing interface, *only adding* buttons, menu items and automated behaviors. If plug-ins were designed so that end users could adapt them, they would rather follow an *architecturally minimal* approach to interaction design, differentiation and combination would be valued over integration—the additional functionality would only become

---

[16] Examples for user-supplied drivers can be found at http://www.crynwr.com/lego-robotics/ and the operating system BrickOS is available at http://sourceforge.net/projects/brickos/.

active as the user adapted the tool for his/her needs. Although Eclipse is often presented as an example for exemplary user-interface design, and although it certainly introduced many excellent ideas that were adopted by other integrated development environments, it should be kept in mind that the prototypical Eclipse user is a programmer, and thus both in the role of configurator and user—an important difference to typical end users. By contrast, the visibility of the building blocks played a decisive role for the Mindstorm robots: the lack of transparency that users perceived in the first version of the Lego robots could partly derive from the failure to provide tools for individually programming the individually visible physical parts.

The power of user-controlled adaptation is clearly demonstrated by the Lego bricks: as users build models, they "interpret" the simple rules provided by the Lego system and their interpretation becomes more important than the design of the individual brick. The Lego brick demonstrates the strong force of internal consistency and interoperability of tools: complex designs can be created with simple building blocks as they interlock and build upon another. The design of more and more specialized bricks on the one hand gives these creative builders more expressive power, yet on the other hand, it generates additional sales and broadens the user base to also include those who are satisfied with recreating pre-designed models.

6.3.2 Apple Automator (i-Series 2)

When Apple designed the i-Series applications, their main intent was to provide the *core functionality* that most users would want to use. One answer to the consequently rising expectations in terms of functionality—as users learned to use the first, simple version of a tool, they discovered new requirements—was the gentle introduction of new features, with a careful eye on the wholeness of the design (compare Section 5.1.2).

6.3.2.1 Description

Another approach that targets "power users" who wish to use new functionality that will only be needed by specific groups of users is exemplified by Apple Automator: Almost every Apple application designed for consumers (Mail, iCal, Address Book, iPhoto, iWeb, GarageBand, etc.) exposes an application programming interface (API) that can be used to script the application using the AppleScript programming language. Part of this functionality can also be used by the Automator application. Automator allows users to graphically design custom workflows. Users can, e.g., process files in specific directories, create image filters, auto-mail processed content to specific addresses, download and store news papers, or convert text to PDF files—repeated tasks that would normally be taken care of by script programming. Automator promises to enable end users to create such scripts, or "workflows" in its own terminology.

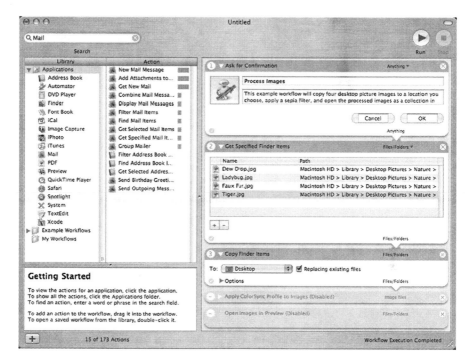

Fig. 6.33 The interface of Automator 1.0 with a script on the right, and actions on the left (Screenshot of Apple Automator 1.0)

Automator features a graphical interface instead of a textual command language, and guides the creation of a workflow by allowing only correct types of information to flow into the next action. Individual actions are first chosen by selecting the application and the desired functionality and dragging it to the workflow area on the right. Options for actions can be modified by parameters changing the result of the action, e.g., providing storage locations, or selecting a compression quality. Apple has also consciously chosen not to implement control structures—there are no conditionals or loops available (comp. Rosenthal, 2006).

The combination of several applications is often capable of delivering the functionality that would require a single application to be much more complex. Apple follows this line of thought and exposes the functionality of its entry level applications to the Automator application, which tries to enable end users to create their own customized features. Users, however, cannot generate new tools. Rather, actions within tools that are already used in conjunction by a user manually are automatically combined, and a new single-purpose function is created. For the Apple i-Series, the Automator concept eliminates the need to cater to all use cases; responsibility for programming is redistributed to the user who can build a specific work environment for himself/herself.

Table 6.6 Minimal Aspects highlighted in the Apple i-Series (Automator)

Functional Minimalism	Structural Minimalism	Architectural Minimalism	Compositional Minimalism

6.3.2.2 A Minimal Assessment

- *Functional Minimalism*: The Automator tool has only a specific function: drawing together the functionality of other applications that form a part of the bundles that come either as part of the operating software, or in the form of inexpensive suites for multimedia (iLife) or office work (iWork). Each of these applications has only a very specific use in itself. This creates both the need for additional functionality and the possibility to create part of this functionality through new "automated" combinations between tools.
- *Structural Minimalism*: While the Automator builds upon the simplicity of access to the tools' services, the resulting access structure is the creation of the end-user programmer. As the designer has no part of it and no technique is employed to ensure structural minimalism, it is of no importance to the discussion beyond the access structure of the Automator tool itself; some reduction of the high complexity of end-user programming is created by dispensing with control structures and through typing of the information piped through the tools' services.
- *Architectural Minimalism*: The division of responsibility for work tasks between different applications *forms the basis* for Automator—without this architecturally minimal system design, scripting would only be possible within single, monolithic application. The standardized API exposed by the installed applications allows Automator to use the applications as *interoperable tools*. As users are already accustomed to switch between tools and use several different tools on a single work task, the aptly named Automator only *automates* their tool use, thereby creating a new, specialized workflow. The new workflow tool draws on services the individual tools provide but is specific to a given task; strictly speaking, it does thus not provide additional functionality but rather a shortcut to access existing functionality.
- *Compositional Minimalism*: End-user programming is *one* approach that allows the user to determine the use of a tool—instead of offering choice between processes, individual services are provided that the user, or a supporting expert, can tailor to suit a specific use situation. While the existing applications in Apple's i-Series provide ready-made bundles of these services, using Automator users can create new sequential bundles of functionality and distribute these as scripts to other users who either make direct use of them or base their specific customizations on them. From the perspective

of *compositional minimalism*, however, this corresponds more closely to a second-level *composition* than to an *interpretation-in-use*. This composition of effective and efficient workflows complements the freedom of use when users employ another tool through the many pre-defined links already implemented in applications (e.g., use mail for sending e-mail, iCal to store appointments, Address Book for contact information).

6.3.3 SketchUp

Sketchpad by Ivan Sutherland revolutionized both computer graphics and human-computer interaction in the early 1960s (Sutherland, 1963); it was the first interactive, object-oriented, direct-manipulation drawing application—in a time where an average computer took the space of a whole room for itself and input was still mostly done by punched cards, it featured an interactive graphical display with a light pen.

Since computer-aided design (CAD) arose as a discipline in the 1980s, most software required the user to draw polyhedral surfaces in wire-frame (Lipson and Shpitalni, 1996), or input exact data using numerical dialogs. 2D input for 3D construction has always been cumbersome and more complicated than simple drawing, so simpler approaches were sought. Researchers have tried to target unintuitive input by using drawing techniques that allow unambiguous interpretation in three dimensions (Eggli et al., 1995). Systems like SKETCH and Teddy demonstrated that gesture-based interfaces are a powerful and intuitive base for 3D model design (Zeleznik et al., 1996; Igarashi et al., 1999). However, these approaches need to trade their simplicity against limitations on the appearance or on the topology of the generated models. SketchUp[17] is a commercial product targeted at the early phase of designing interior and exterior architecture and builds upon some of the techniques listed; in contrast to the research prototypes that experiment with gestures, SketchUp's qualities lie in the excellent facilities for combining different tools.

6.3.3.1 Description

SketchUp presents the user with a conventional 2½-D projection window. The interesting part of SketchUp is the minimal number of tools available to the user and the ability to combine them. As the name indicates, SketchUp is largely based on sketching techniques; the main tool for object creation is a pencil. As a 2½-D projection would normally present many ambiguities for positioning the

---

[17] Sketchup was an example for minimalism since 2003 for me; apparently, Google has also found the application noteworthy and bought it in 2006 (SketchUp, 2006)—now, there's a limited free version called Google Sketchup, http://sketchup.google.com.

pencil cursor in 3-D space, the pencil tool and many other tools feature automatic alignment, e.g., to planes, or existing surfaces or edges. This makes it extremely easy to sketch 2-D surfaces in the perspective view. Alignment can be controlled as existing vertices, edges or faces can be selected as cursor guides; e.g., a line can easily be made the same length or orientation as another visible line or an existing face can be used to find its midpoint and use that as a guide.[18] Closure is automatically detected by the program, creating faces from closed shapes.

The creation of three-dimensional bodies is also consequently controlled by tools in SketchUp—there is no need to use extrusion commands as is common in other construction packages. Instead of these number-based dialog interactions, a push/pull-tool can be used to extend a selected face into three-dimensional space. While, at first, this allows only perpendicular surfaces to be generated, edges can easily be moved afterwards to generate more complex forms (Fig. 6.34).

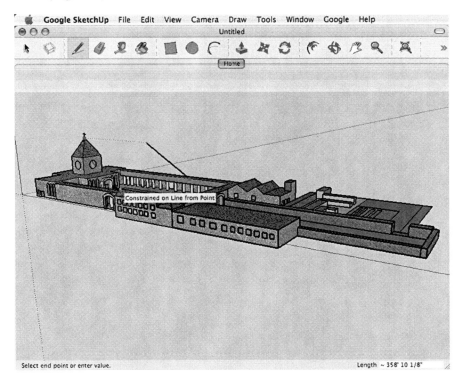

Fig. 6.34 Google SketchUp (Screenshot of initial release for Mac OS X)

---

[18] It is inherently difficult to write about dynamic interaction. The 1:08 hour-long demonstration video provided by SketchUp (http://download.sketchup.com/downloads/markets/SketchUp_Live_demo.wmv) does a much better job of illustrating the rich interaction made possible.

With only these two tools and the alignment features that remind of Sketch-pad, complex three-dimensional bodies can be constructed. A review stated, "SketchUp has a minimalist easy-to-learn interface … SketchUp's simplicity does not come merely from a stripped-out set of 3-D modeling features but from the development of some very innovative ideas of how 3-D modeling can be made easier and more intuitive. The application actually incorporates some very complex inference algorithms that constantly look for alignments, snapping, and directions based on the mouse movements, minimizing the input that is needed from the user to perform modeling operations" (Khemlani, 2004).

Other tools can be used as necessary; there is a tool for curves, for circles, for rectangles, and for freehand drawing. Furthermore, there are tools to manipulate the geometric models created with the drawing tools, such as tools for color or texture manipulation. Since the application has been bought by Google, tools for obtaining and sharing models and for integration with Google Earth have been added.

6.3.3.2 Discussion

Although SketchUp's application domain, the construction of three-dimensional models, is one of the most sophisticated uses for computers, SketchUp succeeded in providing an unusually easy-to use interface: "The simplicity of … SketchUp makes three-dimensional drawing possible even for those who lack knowledge of design or perspective" (Glinert, 2006). SketchUp does not aspire to replace modelers targeting photorealistic rendering, but it is widely used as a sketching tool for architecture and also for interior design (Lok, 2004).

There are several aspects of SketchUp which can be considered minimal. It is not functionally minimal, although it lacks some of the sophisticated and complicated drawing functions of other software. It provides a multitude of functions distributed over dedicated tools that work intensely hand-in-hand. This alone might qualify SketchUp as an example for architectural minimalism—but it does not distinguish the application from other object-oriented drawing applications.

What is really unique about the way sketches are created with SketchUp is the complex functionality hidden within the automatic alignment function and the interaction of drawing tools and the push/pull tool that manipulates a different dimension. The latter is more easily illustrated without hands-on experience: Sketching in SketchUp is often first done in a planar fashion. This 2-D sketch is then used as a basis for creating a 3-D model; e.g., starting from an architectural outline to model buildings of different height, two-dimensional faces are "pulled out" or "pushed in" to interactively create a three-dimensional body. While this limits the modeling of the third dimension at first to perpendicular movements, faces can later be moved to create skewed bodies. While the traditional extrusion mechanism used in modeling applications allows a very precise specification of dimensions, it does not create the immediate effect of Sketch-Ups push/pull tool.

The inaccuracy of the direct-manipulation modeling is countered by alignment interaction techniques: all elements of the existing sketch can function as guides. While automatic perpendicular guide-lines are created from all surfaces and edges that are aligned with the currently pushed/pulled face—and within reasonable proximity and from their midpoints—specific guides can be used by depressing a modifier key whilst over a certain vertex or face. This allows very complex comparisons and operations in the third dimension can create dimensions consistent with already existing elements of the sketch.

The responsibilities for manipulating points and edges on the one hand and faces on the other hand is distributed between the move and rotate tools and the push/pull tool. Limiting the manipulation of the third dimension to perpendicular movements allows this complex functionality to be handled with surprising ease. Cooper and Reimann (2003, 314) noted in their discussion of interaction techniques that "because the application is focused on architectural sketching, not general purpose 3-D modeling ... the designers were able to pull off a spare, powerful and simple interface that is both easy to learn and use."

Google integration created a further layer of tool architecture: apart from providing a web-accessible library with pre-defined and user-contributed objects, the combination with Google Earth positions SketchUp as an application that provides three-dimensional models as content for Google Earth that uses the model data to overlay renderings of architectural landmarks on satellite imagery.

Table 6.7 Minimal Aspects highlighted in SketchUp

Functional	Structural	Architectural	Compositional
Minimalism	Minimalism	Minimalism	Minimalism

6.3.3.3 A Minimal Assessment

- *Functional Minimalism*: Compared to other modeling packages, SketchUp is functionally reduced—mainly due to its focus on simple and quick model sketching. Consequently, rendering functionality is less sophisticated than in competitive products, e.g., 3D Studio or Maja.
- *Structural Minimalism*: The number of tools in SketchUp is minimal and only their combined use allows the user to initiate complex manipulations of models. SketchUp is not optimized for a specific use case, its comparably simple access structure is created by its architecturally minimal design.
- *Architectural Minimalism*: The ease-of-use that defines SketchUp's initial impression—especially for novel users—is created by a clear distribution of responsibility between tools whose individual effects are easy to understand and predict. The almost seamless introduction of the third dimension that builds upon conventional 2-D drawing tools becomes possible through SketchUp's introduction of the push/pull tool.

- *Compositional Minimalism*: On the one hand, SketchUp's use is clearly defined by its functional limitations and by its special area of competence: it is often used by model builders to quickly draft ideas, or by architects who are less interested in perfect modeling than in modeling speed and variability. On the other hand, it can be integrated in different ways in production processes leading to more refined models: its ability to import pictures makes it a powerful tool for converting floor plans to three-dimensional models and its ability to export models can place it at the beginning of a production line. The integration with Google Earth as a viewing tool adds a different layer of use as SketchUp can create content that is integrated into Google Earth's satellite and aerial imagery rendering, thus much improving the realism factor.

6.3.4 Apple iPod

After the initial success of the Apple II and later the Apple Macintosh, Apple computers had to weather a number of crises, as computers were priced too high for the average consumer (comp. Carlton and Kawasaki, 1997, 103) and market shares were steadily declining (Burrows, 1997). CEO Steve Jobs had left and later rejoined Apple, having founded NeXT and Pixar in between, and design again became an important aspect of Apple computers—most visible in the colored iMacs that heralded a new design fashion (Deutschman, 2001). When he introduced the iPod in 2001 (Jobs, 2001), the company's change from a software and hardware producer into a purveyor of fine media began. Today, Apple sales and revenue depend on the iPod series more than on its computers (BBC, 2004; Martell, 2006).

6.3.4.1 Description

While the initial iPod was already comparably simple, the introduction of the scroll wheel as an interaction device made navigation through its menu system much more pleasant: users could rotate first a plastic disc, then only their fingers on the iPod surface, and were thus able to rapidly browse their music library (Buskirk, 2004). With the clickable scroll introduced in 4th generation iPods and the iPod mini, separate buttons for playing and skipping could be removed, further simplifying the interface (Fig. 6.35).

The basis of the iPod's simplicity is the organization of the music (and later photo) library that is done *before* the music is downloaded to the music player. Without this organization by artist, album, and, most importantly, by playlist,[19] the wheel interface would still have a difficult time making scrolling through thousands of songs a pleasant experience. Instead of letting users organize their music on the iPod, Apple introduced the iTunes software for these tasks (Fig. 6.36, Siracusa, 2001; Apple, 2001; Levy, 2006a).

---

[19] Users can customize the main menu of their iPod to adapt the menu structure to their preferred organization system (Kiljander, 2004, 153).

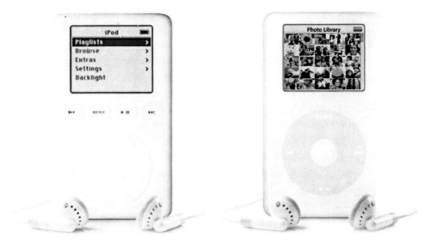

Fig. 6.35 The Apple iPod (3rd and 5th generation). Courtesy of Apple

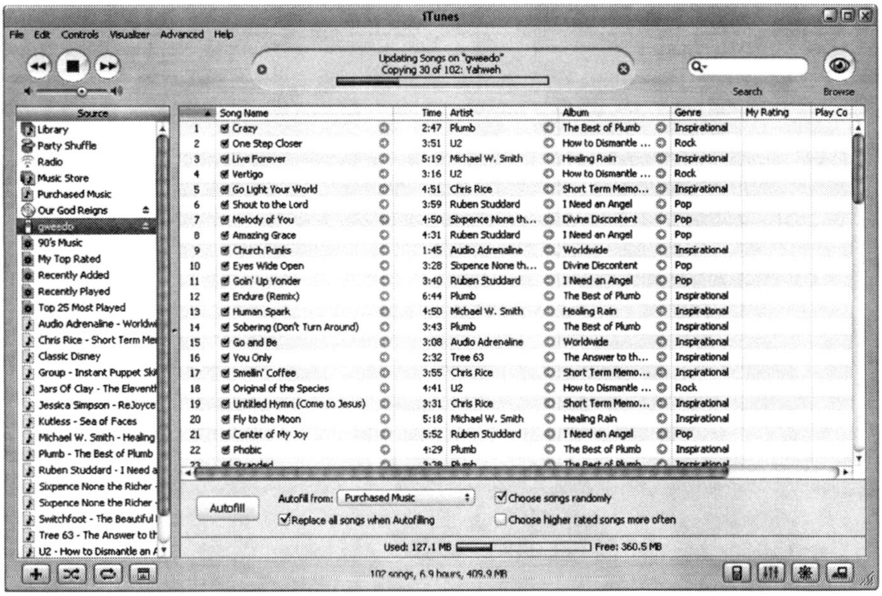

Fig. 6.36 Apple iTunes is used to generate playlists and fill the iPod with music. Courtesy of Apple

iTunes can import music from CD, it automatically tries to retrieve the artists' names, album and song titles, genre, and even cover artwork from an Internet database. It can also be used to buy music from Apple's online music store. Individual songs can be rated by the user. Playlists can be generated by hand or using automatically updated filters such as "was played recently", or "was rated highly". This makes iTunes a very versatile application that can provide quick access to even very large music libraries (Norman, 2005) and has made iTunes the basis of new social practices for music sharing (Voida et al., 2005).

However, Apple did not stop there—parallel to introducing more sophisticated iPods that could also play small video clips (Levy, 2006b), in January 2005 they introduced the iPod Shuffle (Apple, 2005; Fig. 6.37). The iPod Shuffle was stripped of most of the features of its solid state MP3 competitors: it has no display and no means of navigating through playlists. It can only sequentially skip through an existing playlist using a "next" and a "previous" button or it can randomly skip through the playlist (ibid.). This reduction intended to shift the task of composing a playlist from a device that is not good at doing it—the flash memory player—to a device that has far better physical conditions—the computer running iTunes (Jobs, 2005).

Fig. 6.37 The 2006 2nd Generation Apple iPod Shuffle. Courtesy of Apple

This division of labor between a device that is only used for playing and a device that is used to compose the playlist for the next hour(s) of listening, is reducing the requirements for the iPod Shuffle to an extreme minimum. Apple's designers were thus able to design an MP3 player that is "smaller and lighter than a pack of gum" (Apple, 2005). Although Apple openly communicated that the iPod Shuffle actually had less features than its competitors, the product was an immediate success, sparking reports of "mass hysteria" (Terdiman, 2005), and capturing a 58% share among flash music players in less than six months (Gibson, 2005). The second generation of this product built upon the qualities of its predecessor. It added no features to the player itself—which became only slimmer and more elegant in 2006. Instead, software features were added to iTunes that, e.g., helped to increase the variation of songs synchronized with the iPod shuffle.

6.3.4.2 Discussion

The minimal perspective leads directly to the evolution towards the iPod Shuffle. However, other trends accompany this reduction and specification of the playing device. The iPod video demonstrates an important lesson for integration: choose the right time and the right modality and do only what you can do well.

Apple's range of iPod models, particularly the iPod Shuffle, demonstrates the effectiveness of distributing a fairly complex task across two devices. This suggests that designs fitting Norman's notion of appliances (Norman, 1999a) denoting *functionally minimal* devices devoted to a single purpose are possible if they are integrated within a context that shares functionality with the appliance. *Architectural minimalism* is thus a necessary prerequisite for *functional minimalism* and only the focus on the "intelligent" context or the "single-purpose" device determines the relevant notion.

Table 6.8 Minimal Aspects highlighted in the Apple iPod series

Functional Minimalism	Structural Minimalism	Architectural Minimalism	Compositional Minimalism

6.3.4.3 A Minimal Assessment

- *Functional Minimalism*: With the exception of the iPod Shuffle, Apple's iPod series did not publicly aspire to reduce functionality—although, e.g., video features were only introduced after a satisfying user experience could be assured, both by technical means and regarding the availability of appropriate media. The iPod's selling point was thus never that it could do more than competitive players, but that it would deliver a better use experience. Apple positioned the iPod successfully to provide a "natural" way of listening to music, etc., while special needs, e.g., recording functions, were left to third-party suppliers—even when the technical possibility was already implemented in the manufactured device.
- *Structural Minimalism*: The patented click wheel technology that evolved from the turning wheel of the first-generation iPod provides fairly adequate means of accessing items in long, ordered lists, which are frequently accessed in the large music libraries that are commonly stored on iPods. Still, the menu structures in the iPod are deep and not easily navigated.
- *Architectural Minimalism*: All iPod players were designed keeping in mind that their screen space would be relatively limited and that a personal computer would still offer better means to structure a personal music library. The iTunes software thus takes an important position for the iPod players as it functions as a second tool that creates the use experience together with the portable player. The iPod Shuffle is the extreme example for this strategy—a device strictly devoted to playing or shuffling pre-compiled playlists. Apple also developed a business model based on this differentiation, using iTunes

not only to load new Podcasts but also to access its music store, which in turn became the most successful venture in digital music so far.

- *Compositional Minimalism*: Although the iPod is first and foremost a portable music player, some degree of *compositional minimalism* was important for it to become such a huge success. Factors that contribute to the many different uses that people find for iPods, apart from carrying and listening, are its many different models that cater to specific needs, from the music collector to the casual listener and the modular architecture that sparked a "massive number of iPod accessories" (Enderle, 2005). Compatibility with this huge market for accessories is a further hurdle to overcome for competitors.

6.3.5 Web 2.0

According to general agreement, the World Wide Web was born in 1989 when Tim Berners-Lee and the often-forgotten Robert Cailliau worked to create an information management system for in-house use within CERN, the world's largest particle physics laboratory. Since then, it has grown, changed, and developed (Berners-Lee and Fischetti, 1999; Gillies and Cailliau, 2000), and today has become one of the most important tools for information workers. Most work activity is interwoven with browsing on the Web (Brown and Sellen, 2001).

While the amount of information on the Web has grown enormously, the original concept of creating new value by linking distributed information (Berners-Lee and Fischetti, 1999; Cailliau and Ashman, 1999) has become less important. The Web became centralized as Web sites offered specific information or services and users were happy to consume (Koiso-Kanttila, 2003); this went along with a development of Web clients to *browsers* that are used only to access, not to share information (Quint and Vatton, 2005). However, although users were unable to create links or place pages on Web sites, many sites began to take in user input to increase the attractiveness of their services. Often, this followed the pattern set by Amazon.com with its user comments: the primary information was provided by those operating the server, and secondary information, e.g., reviews or recommendations, were added by unpaid users.

The term *Web 2.0* builds upon the original idea of a collaborative space and extends beyond it as it is used to denote business models as well as systems for ordering information. Although the version number suggests a uniform effort for consolidation or even a standardization, there exists no such movement (Shaw, 2005). The definition Tim O'Reilly[20] gives in *What Is Web 2.0* (2005) is consequently based on a variety of example applications (Table 6.8).

---

[20] Being somewhat of a Web 2.0 celebrity, O'Reilly was involved in coining the term (which has recently been reserved as a service mark for CMP, a company hosting a Web 2.0 conference series together with O'Reilly publishers).

Table 6.9 Defining the Web 2.0 phenomen (O'Reilly, 2005)

Web 1.0	Web 2.0
DoubleClick	Google AdSense
Ofoto	Flickr
Akamai	BitTorrent
mp3.com	Napster
Britannica Online	Wikipedia
personal websites	blogging
evite	upcoming.org and EVDB
domain name speculation	search engine optimization
page views	cost per click
screen scraping	web services
publishing	participation
content management systems	wikis
directories (taxonomy)	tagging ("folksonomy")
stickiness	syndication

While O'Reilly continues with a number of terms that are connected to the phenomenon he tries to describe (Fig. 6.38), many of these terms seem to address specific applications or, at best, individual developments in the Web, rather than creating a unified definition for a Web 2.0—while some aspects such

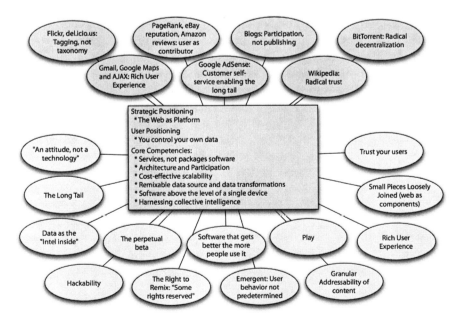

Fig. 6.38 Reproduction of Tim O'Reilly approaching a definition of qualities of the Web 2.0 (comp. O'Reilly 2005)

as "the perpetual beta" or "rich user experience" will apply to most other software as well (comp. Orlowski, 2005). The term Web 2.0 is defined as an umbrella term for all new developments on the Web—a wide definition of the term even includes a range of dynamic behavior of Web pages, namely the use of AJAX technologies.[21]

After even this superficial examination, evidence suggests that the term Web 2.0 is not well defined. Its translation as "The New New Age" (Carr, 2005) suggests that the term is used to capture all the hopes that were already connected with the original Word Wide Web. For companies, it is a convenient marketing term, suggesting modernity and technical proficiency.

6.3.5.1 Analysis

Nonetheless, the term Web 2.0 is used for this discussion, although the scope will be limited to a single development within the World Wide Web: the novelty shared by most of the companies profiting from the Web 2.0 hype is the unselfish provision of data to other services and the intake of data from other sites. The "First Web" used links to connect information archives, the "Second Web" uses links to connect applications. Consequently, the following analysis will focus on the aspect of increasing interaction of individual applications.

Compared to traditional desktop applications, the typical Web 2.0 application is functionally very much reduced. An often-cited example is Basecamp, a project-management tool provided by 37 Signals, which is built around a shared to-do list. Basecamp is simple,[22] agile (it was built in four months with 2.5 programmers, Fried, 2004), and a visually attractive interactive Web application. However, Basecamp is also closed, allowing little to no data export—and although it features less functionality than, e.g., Microsoft Project, all functionality for managing the project comes from the Basecamp site.

By contrast, other popular Web 2.0 sites, such as 43things.com, del.icio.us, digg.com, flickr.com and Google Maps deliver only partial functionality. These applications do not only use the Web as a technical platform, their usefulness increases with the integration of other services: 43things allows you to input plans for your future, which becomes interesting as it connects you to other people and their websites. Del.icio.us is an online bookmarking service that files your bookmarks under free-form tags that also allow you to access the

---

[21] This is yet another fashionable term describing the combination of manipulating a documents document object model (DOM) using JavaScript with the XMLHttpRequest method that is capable of streaming data. This allows Web pages to be updated after they are loaded, requesting additional information from the server side on demand—creating a much more dynamic behavior than possible before. (Garrett, 2005)

[22] Jason Fried describes similarities of 37signals's philosophy to *functional minimalism*: "All of our products are about doing a few simple things well and leaving out the rest. We like to solve the easy fifty to eighty percent of people's problems and forget about the rest. You'll never make those people happy, you'll never totally nail that solution. Everyone always needs something a bit different and we don't go after that." (Fried, 2004)

bookmarks of other users. Digg.com is a technology news website that combines social bookmarking with non-hierarchical editorial control; additional value is delivered as users import stories from Digg.com into their own blog with the keypress of a button. Flickr.com is an online digital photo sharing service that also allows you to create picture sets, tag pictures and image areas, and access other people's photographies; it became extremely popular as it is very easy to use Flickr to host your pictures and integrate them in your own Web site or blog. Google Maps is a service that serves maps and satellite images to other sites, allowing the generation of localized services; simple examples are "memory maps" that import Google imagery into Flickr to collect childhood memories of neighborhoods,[23] and overlaying a rising sea level with satellite imagery to simulate global warming effects.[24]

The value delivered by these applications comes through their interaction with other Web services. Many small applications that interface to each other are thus able to deliver functionality that is not provided by a single service. This is so easily done that many an individual's Web page springs into life delivering yet another combination of different services—a phenomenon that has become popular under the name *mashup*. Vint Cerf explains: "There are creative people all around the world, hundreds of millions of them, and they are going to think of things to do with our basic platform that we didn't think of. So the mashup stuff is a wonderful way of allowing people to find new ways of applying the basic infrastructures we're propagating. This will turn out to be a major source of ideas for applying Google-based technology to a variety of applications" (Perez, 2005).

6.3.5.2 Discussion

The notion of *Web 2.0* is still very young and not clearly defined. If it is understood as the functionality created by the interaction of Web applications, it presents a case for *architectural minimalism*—the multitude of services, and enthusiastic users indicate that a combination of individual functions promises great power. Technically, the Web 2.0 is dependent on a multitude of open standards, and financially, the majority of Web 2.0 application depends on individuals or companies providing their Web services without a monetary compensation. The question of who is paid how much for what functionality is not yet decided. An example is the multitude of services that build upon Google Maps—while Google currently provides their service free of charge, they are evaluating whether they will eventually switch to an ad-supported scheme, charge money for their services, or can make enough money on the data gathered from the requests (Sixtus, 2006).

---

[23] The memory maps group collects examples at http://www.flickr.com/groups/memory-maps/.

[24] http://flood.firetree.net/

This marks one of the problems of the Web 2.0 that are also applicable to architecturally minimal systems in general: as functionality is closely intertwined, data has to be exchanged between individual tools. In the Web, this currently works by giving one service the password for an account on another service; this requires very trusting users.

Table 6.10 Minimal Aspects highlighted in the notion of Web 2.0

Functional Minimalism	Structural Minimalism	Architectural Minimalism	Compositional Minimalism

6.3.5.3 A Minimal Assessment

- *Functional Minimalism*: A typical, but not obligatory attribute of "Web 2.0" applications is their focus on a limited set of features (e.g., bookmarking, sharing photographs). While this focus is partly grounded in the early status of many applications, functionality is often distributed between different applications, making a specialization possible.
- *Structural Minimalism*: The Web 2.0 is marked by a fragmented interface—it is a challenge in its own right to keep track of the different evolving applications and find out which best suits the task at hand. Once a user has decided which service he/she needs, that service's access structure can benefit from the *tool-character* of Web applications.
- *Architectural Minimalism*: An integral part of the Web 2.0 definition is its integrated nature. Applications draw on the functionality and on the data, of other applications to together provide sophisticated interfaces to the user. This allow the individual applications to concentrate on a single functionality (e.g., delivering pictures for flickr or maps for Google Maps), and places the burden of integration to the author of mashups. Through individual combination of services, users can quickly create new applications by combining existing services in the form of mashups. A peculiarity of these Web 2.0 interfaces is, however, that although the application can be quickly generated and reconfigured and users can choose between a large number of possible combinations to find the one catering to their individual tastes, the original services are often no longer identifiable to the end user.
- *Compositional Minimalism*: The Web 2.0 does no longer only provide ready-to-use applications that one finds, personalizes, and uses. Instead, the metaphor of the application is at least partially replaced by that of the service, and users are gradually beginning to create their own applications using the functionality provided by others. The service provider thus only concentrates on providing a very specific functionality and does not determine the context of its use. It is still questionable whether a transfer of this concept to non-computer-savvy end users can be managed or whether the phenomenon is to stay with the geeks.

6.3.6 Word Processing

A small german company, Brüning and Evert Softwarepartner GmbH, produced in 1986 one of the first word processing applications for the German
market, running on Apple Macintosh computers. Already in 1989, this software
integrated office and publishing tools: Ragtime 3, as it was now called, quickly
captured a share of also the French market. In 1999, Ragtime 5 was released for
Microsoft Windows and in 2003, a version for Mac OS X became available
(Ragtime, 2005).

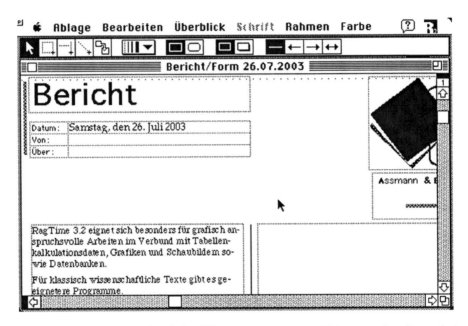

Fig. 6.39 Ragtime 3 introduced the different content types still in use today. Screenshot
Courtesy Ragtime.de

6.3.6.1 Analysis

Ragtime never aimed to compete directly with Microsoft Office, unlike other
products such as StarOffice/OpenOffice.org, KOffice, or Abiword.[25] What
makes it an interesting example here is its very different philosophy: it does
not try to accumulate features from domains, such as spreadsheets, drawing
applications, or DTP layout software, and integrate these into a simple word-
processing software. Instead, the basis for integration is not the continuous text
but the layout of the page: In Ragtime, frame elements are positioned on the

---

[25] http://www.openoffice.org, http://www.koffice.org/, http://www.abisource.com/

page. A frame's type defines both its rendering and applicable tools—there are frames for word processing, frames for spreadsheets, for diagrams, for bitmap and vector graphics, and for movies, pictures and sounds. When a frame is selected, the accessible functionality is adapted to the content of the frame: click and selection semantics change, context menus contain only useful commands (some general and some content-specific), and toolbars are exchanged to provide useful functionality.

Ragtime exemplifies the combination of different tools within a single application. Each single tool is much simpler than its competitors, e.g., the spreadsheet tool cannot create diagrams by itself like, e.g., Excel, and the word processor cannot create tables. This is compensated by a close integration of the tools. Ragtime's basis is the spatial layout of content areas on the virtual page. Each area is assigned a content type (Fig. 6.39, 6.40) that determines the tool responsible for rendering and manipulation.

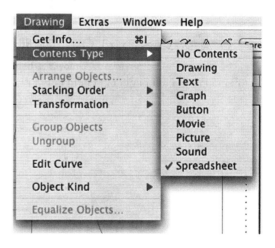

Fig. 6.40 Content type selection in Ragtime 5

The data in individual tools can be linked to create sophisticated renderings: the graphing tool takes numerical input from a spreadsheet, automatically updating the graph when the numbers are changed. The layout functionality uses direct manipulation for the content areas, much as special DTP programs do. This makes it possible to graphically combine, e.g., a spreadsheet table with text (Fig. 6.41). Each tool is responsible for strictly delimited tasks and can thus be functionally very simple.

In its latest version, Ragtime 6, some of the unique design decisions are watered:[26] the word processing component of Ragtime was redesigned for greater compatibility with the market leader, Microsoft Word. Consequently,

---

[26] Ragtime also canceled the unique distribution model that allowed for free copies for private use. (Ragtime, 2006a)

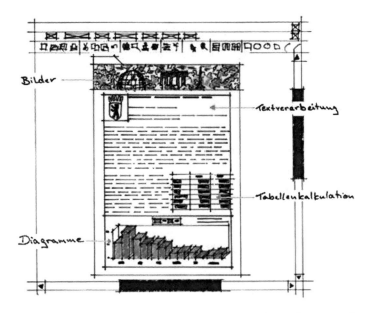

Fig. 6.41 Placement of different content types on a page. Ragtime 5 documentation

it is now possible to integrate pictures and table directly within the word processing component; although this duplicates functionality within the product and overrides the distribution of tasks between tools, the underlying motivation is clear: a greater external consistency with other word processing applications (Ragtime, 2006b).

6.3.6.2 Conclusion

Ragtime demonstrates that word processing is possible without competing with the de-facto standard Microsoft Word for feature-richness. Instead, the functionality that is highly redundant within Microsoft's Office suite—with Excel and Word both being able to create tables, graphics, and stretches of formatted text—is distributed over a number of tools. These tools have a fixed, and very limited field of responsibility and are consequently much simpler than their Microsoft counterparts.

This division of responsibility is communicated throughout the user interface: the user has first to choose the type of content (defaulting to text) before he/she can start manipulating it. For this, he/she is rewarded with a concise interface providing a set of functionality that is tailored to the content type. The contextual tabs of Microsoft Word 2007 is a step in the same direction, yet in Ragtime, the entire interface is based upon the provision of different tools for different tasks. As the tools are chosen based on the type of area focused, the change between tools does not create a cognitive burden for the user.

Ragtime 7 dissociates itself somewhat from this clear-cut approach; a possible reason is that to persist in a commercial environment, compatibility with the Word file format is a vital issue. As Word is able to mix tables, graphs and text in the layout flow, Ragtime might have been forced to comply.

6.3.7 Refining the Notion of Architectural Minimalism

Architectural minimalism can refer to the interaction level, SketchUp being an example; it is here closely connected to structural minimalism. It can also refer to the interaction of specific, functionally minimal tools. In both cases, the whole is simpler than the sum of its parts. Lego demonstrates a further, important aspect—complexity is created by the combination of simple building blocks; this example, however, lacks a good demonstration of the interaction of different tools as most Lego pieces are very similar.

While Sketchup and Ragtime seem to lie worlds apart, they are at two ends of a line that is completely covered by the term architectural minimalism: In Sketchup, atomic actions are applicable to parts of the drawing. Combined, they allow complex manipulations. In Ragtime, the tools are much more powerful, yet the combination of the functionality of individual tools through placement on a page is still what delivers value. In both cases, the functionality is deconstructed in a manner that lets the user perceive less complexity than hiding in the individual tools taken together: the whole seems simpler than the sum of its parts. Somewhere in the middle of that line lies object-oriented drawing software, such as Adobe Illustrator or OmniGraffle,[27] where individual objects can be manipulated by different tools; some of these are dependent on the type of object (e.g., font selection), others apply to all types of drawing objects (e.g., manipulation of size or orientation). Full object oriented environments, such as the Smalltalk-based Squeak (Ingalls et al., 1997), also draw part of their attractiveness from the fact that a multitude of simple tools exist that can be applied to objects and combined to deliver complex functionality.

The tools in an architecturally minimal design are visible to the user. If their use is linked to the type of object being manipulated, the functionality provided by the interface is changed as an object is selected. Usually, modes have been used to allow the user to change functionality: in a drawing program, the user could either move objects, or change their color. Modal interfaces have been heavily criticized as they can cause handling errors when the user does not remember which mode he is in (Raskin, 2000b). Coupling the functionality with the selection of objects can, for some applications, replace modal behavior as

---

[27] Information about Illustrator is provided by Adobe at http://www.adobe.com/products/illustrator/, OmniGraffle is described at http://www.omnigroup.com/applications/omni graffle/.

the outcome of an action is not determined by a system state that is difficult to discern, but by the focus of activity—of which the user generally is aware of.

Architectural Minimalism, and the resulting focus on creating visible tools is reflected in Züllighoven's "tools and materials" approach (Züllighoven et al., 1998; Züllighoven, 2004) to object-oriented software construction that has been implemented in the form of the Java framework JWAM (Breitling et al., 2000). Underlying this approach is a desire to create useful and useable software by relying on the existing distribution of work in an office environment: "the software product should represent the main concepts of the application area" (Lilienthal and Züllighoven, 1997, 36). Lilienthal et al., aim to create a "close relationship between the tasks and concepts of the application domain and the components of a software system. This relationship allows the users to recognize their specific means and objects of work and enables them to fulfill their tasks by *individually organizing work as the situation demands it*" (ibid., 36, italics mine). This demonstrates that Lilienthal et al. aim to support the user's interpretation of a task by providing separate tools at his/her disposal. The "tools and materials" approach tries to identify materials to separate functionality accessible to the user from "'pure' application domain functionality" (ibid., 37). Tools then try to bundle functionality in meaningful—and universal—units: a tool's quality depends, among other factors, on the number of contexts in which it can be applied (Züllighovern, personal communication).

In a minimal architecture, the overall functionality is decomposed and distributed between tools. When the user is allowed to change the visibility of these tools, the user interface of an application can be *configured* by users to better meet their task requirements—Eclipse.org is an example for a popular IDE that also allows users to add third-party tools in the form of plug-ins, an increasingly popular concept. When these tools are exposed not only to direct manipulation, but also offer a scripting interface, the added value created by combining the individual tools can be automated and new tools created. Although this *end-user programming* is not as widely spread, Automator is an interesting approach that builds upon Apple's functionally simple applications and their common APIs to create a graphical editor for use patterns.

A continuous spectrum is spanned between the loose coupling of applications via import and export functionality, drag and drop, and copy and paste mechanism, integration of services in another application, and the deep interconnectedness created by linking existing applications. The combination of different tools can also work on the level of interaction, as demonstrated by the SketchUp application—and the integrated use of different tools can be pursued even further as the selection of tool and application to a graphical object are parallelized using two hands, e.g., with the tool glass concept, whose practicability has been demonstrated in a free graphical Petri net editor (Beaudouin-Lafon, 2000).

The application of architectural minimalism has its limits: Whatever the reason was for Ragtime to integrate duplicate functionality in their text component, it is obvious that a division of functionality becomes more difficult as the individual tools are developed and acquire additional features; eventually, overlap of functionality will occur. UNIX operating systems can serve as an example for some pitfalls for architecturally minimal systems: Traditionally, UNIX systems have employed a multitude of different tools with a very focused functionality to solve complex tasks by composition: the complexity is reduced by identifying subtasks that can be handled by simple tools, such as grep, sed or awk, and then these tools are combined by pipe-lining the output from one tool to another for further processing. Thus, repeated actions that would require many commands can be automatized; this *shell scripting* has become a synonym for harnessing the power of the command line (Robbins, 1999).

However, the number of UNIX tools is huge and to apply the right tool to the task, one has to learn "why each one is there, how to use them by themselves and in combination with the other [tools]" (Robbins, 2005), a typical task for expert users. Furthermore, the tools themselves have changed to incorporate functionality previously reserved for other tools and introduced inconsistencies between different flavors of UNIX. As Robbins and Beebe (2005) put it in *Classic Shell Scripting*, "with shell scripts, you can combine the fundamental Unix text and file processing commands to crunch data and automate repetitive tasks. But beneath this simple promise lies a treacherous ocean of variations in Unix commands and standards". This functional overlap is potentially a critical problem for architectural minimalism—if taken to an extreme, each individual tool becomes very complex in itself, thus making the system of tools that a user needs even more complex than a single all-purpose tool would need to be.

6.4 Compositional Minimalism

The three previous notions of minimalism focus on doing more to create less, on the designer's work of selecting, structuring and partitioning functionality in a design. Compositional minimalism poses the question where a designer can do less to let users do more—how tools must be created that will be usable in many different situations. This paradoxical requirement is illustrated using two examples from everyday life: the appropriation of architecture and the ubiquitousness of the Post-It note illustrate the different aspects of compositional minimalism, namely that products will always be changed by their use and that concepts can be so successful that they appear in contexts where they were never expected.

6.4.1 Old Buildings Learn

Architecture is a favorite place for software engineers or software "architects", to visit in search of helpful analogies; the most famous analogy resulted in various pattern movements, first in software engineering and later in usability engineering. Another school of thought has not (yet) found its way from the realm of architecture to the design of interactive systems: Humans have, for a long time, created their own dwellings and only comparably recently, the profession of architects has formed to plan and engineer buildings (Kostof, 1977). But even now, home owners are not content to simply live in their houses, they are prone to change plans. Architecture has fittingly been described as "the relation between an object and its occupant" (Hill, 1998, i). As Steward Brand (1995) put it, buildings *learn*; after they are built, they are adapted and then adopted—through modifications, minor or major, they become what their "users" want them to be. A 1935 photograph of Johnstown, Pennsylvania (Fig. 6.42) illustrates that "backyards are where the action is: ... nearly every house shows signs of additions and changes in the back" (ibid., 197; Fig. 6.42). Adaption and visible change is the rule, not the exception.

Fig. 6.42 "Backyards are where the action is": residents usually modify and adapt their houses; Wikimedia Commons Photograph of Royal Crescent, Bath, England

According to Brand (ibid.), buildings can be separated into different layers. Although these layers are interdependent—a change in services might make necessary changes in structure, inner layers can often be modified decisively with only minor modification to the outer layers. He notes, however, that specifically the *services* layer of houses is very expensive to change afterwards and, if planned in an inflexible way, can interfere with useful modifications (Fig. 6.43).

Fig. 6.43 The structure of
buildings can be examined—
and changed—at different
levels. Kind permission of
Brand

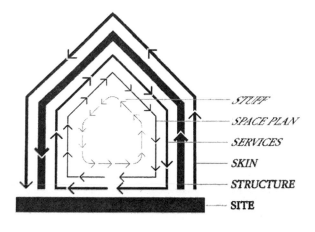

STUFF

SPACE PLAN

SERVICES

SKIN

STRUCTURE

SITE

As an example for a well-planned house that allows many different uses, he does not pick a stylish or modern building—his example is the standard American municipal building from the 1960s. Through standardized design, equal spacing, and free-standing walls on the inside, the space plan could be changed almost at will and houses originally planned as municipal offices now often serve as a library or kindergarten (see Fig. 6.44).

Fig. 6.44 The "universal" public American building of the 1950s. (Brand, 1995, 154)

As the architect refrained from making too many assumptions about the use of the building—the chimneys are at the side of the building, as are all supporting walls—and as the focus of possible uses was very broad from the beginning, the unassuming architecture of municipal buildings has helped to create a space with many uses for its inhabitants and visitors.

Moreover, adaption is so much a part of dwelling that it has become an indicator of coziness and thus turned into a streak of fashion—and there are houses being built that look as if they had been added to by generations (Fig. 6.45). However, houses that are made complicated by artificial "additions" do not only fake adaption but also hinder real adaption from taking place: as the structure is unnecessarily made complicated by bays and dormers that serve no obvious function, it becomes more difficult to serve emerging needs by adding further spaces to the house (ibid., 201).

Fig. 6.45 An artificially complicated building with a vintage look. (Brand, 1995, 201)

6.4.2 A Sticky Story: The Post-it Note

A short digression might clarify the nature of the two following examples, E-mail and Microsoft PowerPoint: tools developed for a very specific purpose can gain wide acceptance and their use can spread exponentially into ubiquitousness. Perhaps the best example for this is related to interactive systems only insofar as it sticks on most computer screens: the Post-It note.[28]

Post-it notes may be considered as literally "God-sent". In the early 1970s, Art Fry was in search of bookmarks for his church hymnal that would neither damage it nor fall out. Fry worked at 3 M. He noticed that a colleague, Dr. Spencer Silver, had developed an adhesive that left no residue after removal and could be repositioned. Fry took some of Silver's adhesive and applied it along the edge of a piece of paper. This solved his church hymnal problem. Fry soon realized that his "bookmarks" had other potential uses. As he began to leave notes on work files, coworkers started dropping by, seeking "bookmarks" for their offices. These "bookmarks" were a new way to communicate and to organize. 3 M Corporation crafted the name Post-it note for Fry's bookmarks and began production in the late 1970s for commercial use (BBC, 2000).

---

[28] The name "Post-It Note" is a trademark of 3 M Inc. patent.

In 1977, test-markets failed to show consumer interest. However in 1979, 3 M implemented a massive consumer sampling strategy, and the Post-it note took off. Today, Post-it notes and their copies are scattered across files, computers, desks, and doors in offices and homes. The church hymnal bookmark has changed the way most information workers everywhere on this planet work every day.

6.4.2.1 Discussion

Buildings are changed as their owners change; they also change as their function shifts, e.g., when kids arrive. Allowing for this change is a necessary quality in architecture that tries to support humans in their lives. Adaptation of buildings is supported by a layered architecture that differentiates those parts that cannot be changed easily (e.g., load-bearing walls) from those that are modified more easily. The design of the more static layers then tries to maximize the possible arrangements of the more dynamic layers. For architects, it is vital to consider the context of a building, yet it is impossible to foresee the use of a building in dozens of years from now; the longevity of architecture renders ineffective approaches that try to define all requirements before a building is in use. For software, by contrast, future legacy issues are often not even considered in the initial design—while the software complexity exceeds that of buildings and the accumulated experience for building materials in software engineering is much less.

The Post-It note makes a case for designs that target very specific requirements. Although it was designed for a single user, and a single task, it has gained world-wide acceptance. Almost unchanged, it can be used for a church hymnal and for business communication. Rare case. Simplicity of its design—the removable adhesive being its only feature. That is marketed now even without the paper, effectively allowing anything light enough to be turned into a Post-It.

6.4.3 E-mail

One of *the* most fundamental revolutions that computing has caused is what E-mail has done to communication: instead of sending handwritten or -typed letters or facsimile copies of the same letters to companies we trade with or people we deal with, e-mail has taken on the function of communication for most of us in many situations (for an early analysis, compare Denning, 1982)—it has become ubiquitous (Berghel, 1997b; Ducheneaut and Bellotti, 2001; Tassabehji and Vakola, 2005), created new social spaces (Parks and Floyd, 1996), and grown so important that understanding e-mail communication turned into a research topic by itself (e.g., Wilson, 2002, 126).

6.4.3.1 Description

E-mail use has changed over time and as use scenarios broadened, the nature of communication has diversified. Initially, the cost of disk space prevented e-mail from being saved and, although some users treated it like written correspondence, closing messages with "sincerely", or "yours truly", users quickly developed an informal writing style; most early e-mail mimicked oral conversation, with heavy use of exclamation points, repeated question marks, and capitalized words (comp. Lovejoy and Grudin, 2003); John Seely Brown in his plenary address at the first CHI conference in 1983 even told the story of a Xerox executive who was embarrassed about his spelling and presented his solution: "We'll build a spelling de-corrector!" (Brown, 1983, cited after (Lovejoy and Grudin 2003)). This informality caused suspicion in management, even for technology companies (Perin, 1991), and fear of productivity losses (Pickering and King, 1992).

However, tools were invented that fixed spelling and grammar and e-mail has long become widely accepted for more formal correspondence (Tassabehji and Vakola, 2005). While it is still used for private communication, it has become an irreplaceable work tool for many. Moreover, as e-mail is so easily accessible, users started to employ e-mail as a tool for tasks it was never designed for, e.g., task management and personal archiving (Mackay, 1988; Whittaker, and Sidner, 1996). And users are inventive—they use the sorted table e-mails are usually presented in to manage contacts and to-do lists, send themselves reminders or found Web URIs (Jones et al., 2001) that can be read from different computers and use the archived e-mails as a big, searchable information storage. Although this demonstrates that few technical restrictions are placed upon users by e-mail and that, for many, it seems to fulfill their tasks better than dedicated tools, it also creates the problem of *e-mail overload* (Whittaker and Sidner, 1996) that has led to many research efforts trying to devise clever replacements for traditional e-mail tools that are tailored to deal with the added task inventory under the label of *personal information management* (PIM) (for a comprehensive overview, see Boardman, 2004, 40–48).

These efforts can be classified in those that aim to reintroduce specific tools with specific workflows to support specific tasks and those that try to better support the appropriation of existing mechanisms by users. As the notion of compositional minimalism highlights, the latter approach builds upon the strengths demonstrated by E-mail as a tool. It is also likely that the efforts users already invest to tailor their tools to their task environment can be built upon; e.g., Bellotti and Smith (2000) report that E-mail takes not only a central role in personal information management but also that users appropriate features of their E-mail tools, thus building embedded mechanisms to manage complexity.

E-mail is far from being an average application. It was one of the first computer applications making use of networks (Hardy, 1996) and is still the most important electronic medium to connect individual people. In its long history, it has been used for many different purposes—and for this been named not only "the killer application of the Internet" but also "a serial-killer application!" (Ducheneaut and Bellotti, 2001). Through the central role it already occupied in daily work (Fig. 6.46), it attracted new tasks. As Whittaker et al. (2004) state, "Email's role as de facto task manager arises in large part out of its role as information conduit"—both incoming and outgoing information are often routed through e-mail. Ducheneaut and Bellotti (2001) suggest, "The network effect ensures that this tendency is infectious across a community or organization. Thus, personal information management is then embedded where it is most needed and accessible, that is, in the knowledge workers' new electronic habitat: e-mail." E-mail is used for managing tasks, often by reminders (Malone, 1983; Barreau and Nardi, 1995; Whittaker and Sidner, 1996), and for archiving information (Kaye et al., 2006; Whittaker and Sidner, 1996; Whittaker et al., 2006)—users know e-mail as a stable, time-ordered and searchable form of information and they also know they will use their e-mail very frequently. Full-text search, sequential ordering and association with important contacts provide powerful access mechanisms that can be combined with manual categorization (Malone, 1983; Barreau and Nardi, 1995). E-mail is even used to keep contact information (Whittaker et al., 2004).

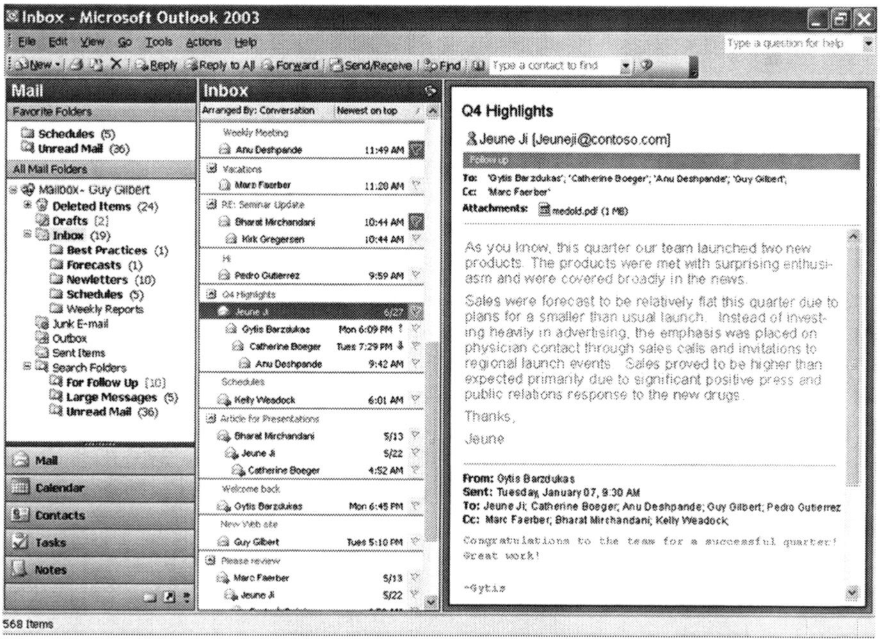

Fig. 6.46 E-mail client with folders used for information management (MS product screenshot)

The broad field of tasks that e-mail is used for is often seen as critical. Problems include fragmentation, e.g., duplicate storage in e-mail and file system that makes it difficult for users to locate information (Whittaker et al., 2006) and lack of dedicated support mechanisms for users' tasks, e.g., for contact management or time management (ibid.). However, from a minimalist standpoint, it is interesting to note that there is a discrepancy between research and use: On the one hand, many research prototypes try to provide sophisticated personal information management aids (e.g., Bellotti et al., 2003; Bergman et al., 2003; Dumais et al., 2003). On the other hand, even in software that provides much of the proposed functionality, much of it is left unused: "The results from 33 Outlook users suggested that even our technologically savvy lab members often did not use the more sophisticated features of Outlook (e.g., only just over half use the Tasks feature and far less than half use Categories to organize their mail). Our less tech savvy lab members (a small minority) were especially unlikely to use these features or even to know about them" (Bellotti et al., 2002).

6.4.3.2 Discussion

E-mail seems to work well enough for most people; replacing e-mail by dedicated PIM tools is made difficult by e-mail's central position in the workflow. Boardman and Sasse (2004) inferred from an empirical study that the everyday use of e-mail discourages users from reflecting on their own behavior. They concede that many users will continue to use only basic functionality and follow that "Future design work must take account of the variation in strategies by providing the flexibility to manage different types of information in distinct ways. For instance, tools should give users the ability to organize information as required, whilst not penalizing those users who do not want to organize." (ibid.)

A possible enhancement for e-mail clients should thus adopt the form of optional tools; these tools must not create unnecessary, additional tasks for the user (Whittaker et al., 2006). Examples include both approaches that enrich the folder structure that exists in e-mail clients through searching, sorting and tagging, and automatically categorizing e-mail and providing alternative views (e.g., Bellotti et al., 2003; Rohall et al., 2004; Danis et al., 2005; Whittaker et al., 2006), or the closer integration of external tools with the mail client. The latter approach is taken by Apple in MacOS 10.5 where the Address Book, iCal and the Notes application are being integrated into Mail 3 (Apple, 2006b).

Recent developments in electronic communication indicate that real-world use of a concept, such as E-mail, is also influenced by the public opinion that originates with its use. E-mail has lost some of the informality associated with it because it has acquired a central role in the office workflow and has thus turned into an archival medium. *Instant messaging* (IM) has begun to replace it in some contexts and for some users (Lovejoy and Grudin, 2003; Grudin et al., 2005). This demonstrates that the adoption of software is not only difficult to plan for, but that it must also be considered a self-influencing dynamic system.

Table 6.11 Dimensions of minimalism in E-mail

Functional Minimalism	Structural Minimalism	Architectural Minimalism	Compositional Minimalism

6.4.3.3 A Minimal Assessment

- *Functional Minimalism*: E-mail has but a single function: that of delivering a message (basically an ASCII file with title, sender, and date information) to a recipient address over a network. It was later extended to transport binary files, first via uuencoding and later using MIME (Levinson, 1998).
- *Structural Minimalism*: Due to the functional simplicity and the similarities with postal mail, e-mails are easily understood as a concept. E-mail clients, however, are generally less simple as they add different filtering and structuring mechanisms to the base functionality. Structuring e-mails in folders, sometimes with marking facilities, has become a very popular way of dealing with incoming and archived information and generates a user-specific, yet often rather sophisticated ordering structure.
- *Architectural Minimalism*: As E-mail is technically very simple, many other tools interface with E-mail as an outlet, either locally by starting the E-mail application with a set recipient, title and text, or by sending out e-mail, e.g., from Web applications, to signify, e.g., status changes. E-mail is scarcely used as an inlet, further adding to its central position within the daily workflow.
- *Compositional Minimalism*: Although, or perhaps because E-mail is technically very simple, it has become the pivotal center of information management for most of today's information workers. As it is a permanently used and, almost always, accessible tool, and as most information flows are anyways routed through e-mail, it took on responsibilities that were never planned to be implemented using mail: information management and storage, contact management, time scheduling, note-taking, project management, and a multitude of other important tasks are carried out using the simple means that e-mail clients provide. This is *not* a bad thing. Instead, it shows how a versatile information tool can cleverly be adopted by competent users. Thus, it should not be first priority to replace E-mail as a tool for these tasks, but rather to intelligently interface to the existing practices as new tools are developed that try to solve the existing problems with E-mail.

6.4.4 *PowerPoint*

> *It is a structure for following your intuition and your obsessions.*
> *It is the hyperfocused scribblings of the mad and the gifted.*
>
> David Byrne, Learning to love PowerPoint (Byrne, 2003)

PowerPoint, originally *Presenter* for the Apple Macintosh, was created in the early 1980s by Bob Gaskins (Parker, 2001). Since then, it has been bought and marketed by Microsoft and risen to what is one of the most successful business software products to date. Experts who follow trends in presentation techniques estimate that PowerPoint is used to make an estimated 20 to 30 million presentations every day and has between 250 and 400 million users around the globe (Schwartz, 2003; Zielinski, 2003; Simons, 2004).

This vast number of users includes not only the manager who depends on PowerPoint slides to carry him through meetings, but also the private citizen who designs slideshows for her son's wedding. Pupils prepare PowerPoint slides for school and even church masses increasingly adopt the software to flash hymn lyrics or accompany preaching (Parker, 2001). Public, the mechanics of scientific face-to-face exchange depend so heavily on PowerPoint that it seems not disproportional a conference was interrupted to thank Gaskins personally as the organizers learned that the creator of PowerPoint was in the audience (ibid.). Even the icons included with the software, androgynous silhouette stick figures, have become omnipresent as PowerPoint is also used for layout tasks (ibid.)—to create signs, web sites and printed material.

6.4.4.1 Description

PowerPoint is an application with a fairly limited functionality—at least, if one compares it with other office applications. By design, the application domain is fixed to slide shows and thus all functionality is grouped around the slide view; with a simple outline editor, a structural perspective is provided in addition to the layout view of the slide. PowerPoint can thus be considered an untypical mixture of functionality for text layout, object-oriented drawing and animation—it is possible to find many different uses for PowerPoint, yet in most areas, it has rather basic functionality (Fig. 6.47).

It seems, however, that PowerPoint's functionality is enough for most users—it has become an immensely popular multipurpose tool. Because it is so easily mastered, some users actually prefer to use PowerPoint to create not slides, but text documents, drawings, signs—and even art (Byrne, 2003): "PowerPoint is a hybrid: it does many things moderately well. Because it is a single program that allows you to combine simple layouts with diagrams and prose, it is both an ideal tool and ripe for misuse." (Brown, 2002).

Although it has a fairly complicated menu structure, introductions to Power-Point suggest that users use the toolbars to easily access functionality (Haddad and Haddad, 1999; Finkelstein, 2003). With a multitude of different tool palettes that partly appear on demand, PowerPoint can be said to adapt itself to the users tasks, e.g., when the drawing palette or the image palette appear as the users selects a graph or image object. Many common tasks are automatized, e.g., text is reformatted as content is added or deleted to optimally fit on the slide—this culminates in the implementation of an auto-content generator, which had originally been just an internal joke for management (Parker, 2001).

PowerPoint's functionality is often not sufficient for the task. However, it is still used as an outlet, with other applications delivering different types of content. For the task of creating slideshows, for example, Johnson and Nardi (1996) found that applications like PowerPoint are often not used in isolation. As its functionality is not sufficient to create, e.g., different types of formulas for engineers, mathematicians, or chemists, or specialized drawings, many other tools are involved in creating a presentation.

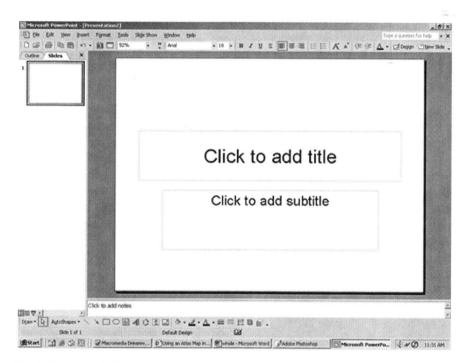

Fig. 6.47 Microsoft PowerPoint

Due to the multitude of presets that PowerPoint provides, it has a flat learning curve. It provides a skeleton for implementing the task of delivering a talk that is useful for many users as it enables them to do a fairly professional job without having special training: it helps structuring the material, suggests form and amount of presentation, maintains a clear layout, and ensures compatibility to most presentation environments (Mertens and Leggewie, 2004).

Yet the provision of default layouts for slides that, e.g., fit only 4–6 bullet points, and limit the title to about 3 words, has repeatedly been criticized. Critics find fault with "slide designs [that] have become more standardized, in large part because PowerPoint itself is used so pervasively" (Alley and Neeley, 2005). PowerPoint has even been made responsible for negatively influencing presentation style and (scientific and business) communication as a whole (Brown, 2002; Tufte, 2006). Edward Tufte found a concise slogan for critique "Power corrupts. Powerpoint corrupts absolutely" (Tufte, 2003). Some research actually targets the question how the communication style that has been "damaged" by PowerPoint could be changed for the better. Alley and Neeley proposed the use of pictures and sentence-long headlines (2005) to avoid the need to create 3-word headlines for all slides. Although some doubt remains that their alternative approach will cater to a wider audience and improve scientific exchange as a whole, it is certainly worthwhile to notice that the defaults in PowerPoint have had an immense influence on the design of both business and scientific communication—a composition that was originally conceived for a single context has influenced interpretations in different fields.

6.4.4.2 Discussion

The concept of composition implies that a design might be more or less strictly composed for a task. It is thus tempting to think that applications could be judged according to their specificity: a presentation application would be more specific than a word processor and less specific than an application to draw chemical formulas for molecules. More specific applications would rate as less compositionally minimal and vice versa. However, Johnson and Nardi found even in 1996 that "the task specificity/genericness of an application program ... depends on several fairly independent software design issues. We (1) conclude that developing application software that supports all aspects of a task well is extremely difficult and (2) suggest an alternative approach that may be more fruitful: providing collections of interoperable tools and services"(Johnson and Nardi, 1996).

Johnson and Nardi come to the conclusion that no single application can deliver a functionality that is as diverse as that needed for the generation of presentation slides. Instead, they suggest that "collections of interoperable tools and services" (ibid.) should be used to combine the necessary functionality. This highlights that in the case of an ubiquitous use of an application, it is difficult to meet the growing and diversifying demand for functionality with a monolithic architecture, and thus illustrates the link between architectural and compositional minimalism.

Table 6.12 Dimensions of minimalism in Microsoft PowerPoint

Functional Minimalism	Structural Minimalism	Architectural Minimalism	Compositional Minimalism

6.4.4.3 A Minimal Assessment

- *Functional Minimalism*: PowerPoint is a hybrid application, it offers minimal functionality in many different fields: it can be used to manipulate text, diagrams, and graphics—and it provides limited support for (interactive) animation. In each of these fields, more sophisticated applications exist, but PowerPoint is unique due to its combination.
- *Structural Minimalism*: PowerPoint is both structurally very complex, e.g., in its rather unorganized menu structure and very reduced as tool palettes offer rapid access to the rather limited functionality responsible for, e.g., text formatting.
- *Architectural Minimalism*: PowerPoint combines different tools and each tool has only a limited functionality. In contrast to object-oriented drawing applications and, more specifically, to SketchUp, there is little functional overlap in PowerPoint, i.e., few functions are applicable to different types of content. The combination is thus not on the level of interaction but lies within the creation of a collage to create the visual experience of a presentation slide.
- *Compositional Minimalism*: Due to its basic and general functionality, PowerPoint is used for a multitude of tasks very different from presentation. When used for presentation, however, its functionality is often not sufficient for generating very specific expert content. In these cases, it functions as a vehicle for presentation of context generated in other tools and is never used in isolation.

6.4.5 WikiWikiWebs

In the original proposal for the World Wide Web (Berners-Lee, 1989), the Web was envisioned as a place to share information, accessible to anyone. This was not going to happen—as Berners-Lee reflects a decade later, "although browsers were starting to spread, no one working on them tried to include writing and editing functions. . . . Without a hypertext editor, people would not have the tools to really use the Web as an intimate collaborative medium. Browsers would let them find and share information, but they could not work together intuitively" (Berners-Lee and Fischetti, 1999, 57).

Although the Web that emerged in the 1990s turned out to be site-centric, consisting of few major players who contributed information and assigned a passive role as consumer of information to the user, the vision of everyone contributing to a world-wide information web has repeatedly returned to the stage: Whether it was called *authoring hypertext* (Carr et al., 1995), *collaborative writing* (Hughes et al., 1998), *global editability* (Iorio and Vitali, 2005), or *The Writable Web*, it is still a prominent force in hypertext research—and as a topic, it also appears at the World Wide Web conference series (e.g., Miles-Board et al., 2003; Uren et al., 2003). As Bouvin (1999) summarizes various efforts for enhancing the Web, "the purpose of such ... tool[s] is [to] help users organise, associate, or structure information found on the Web ... by a single user or in collaboration with others". However, all approaches that required users to install additional tools on their computers were unable to attain a critical mass of users or reach a state of satisfactory stability.[29] So, until today, the Web of most users is still pretty much "unenhanced".

More successful was the approach of server-side applications: here, not only in research, but also in practice has authoring returned to the Web. One important genre of user-writable sites are Web logs, or Blogs (Blood, 2002). A Blog is usually published by a single author, with reader being able to refer to individual articles, thus creating a Web of comments. While this describes the current state, "the original weblogs were link-driven sites. Each was a mixture in unique proportions of links, commentary, and personal thoughts and essays. Weblogs could only be created by people who already knew how to make a website" (Blood, 2000). Today, sites such as blogger.com, blogspot.com or LiveJournal.com offer free opportunities for anyone to set up her own Web log. Blogs can acquire a community of readers who are able to subscribe to articles (using RSS technology) and can often add their own comments directly. Rebecca Blood, one of the most noted authorities on blogging, notes, "I strongly believe in the power of weblogs to transform both writers and readers from 'audience' to 'public' and from 'consumer' to 'creator'" (ibid.).

Although blogs are considered a medium for users writing the Web, they are usually centered around a single author. Also, the form of blogs is fairly fixed: entries have a heading, some article text, not extending the size of a single page, and usually some links to external information. This limits the uses of a blog to active participation in someone's reflection of the world's situation—collaboration is only possible when multiple Weblog authors reflect upon one another. By contrast, *Wikis* (Leuf and Cunningham, 2001) have been conceived as collaborative authoring spaces and received much attention as a simplistic alternative of providing a writable section of the World Wide Web to a specific user group—largely by avoiding fixed syntax limiting the discourse within the Wiki (Obendorf, 2004).

6.4.5.1 Description

A *Wiki* is a web site where every page is editable by anybody using a normal Web browser. This is achieved by adding an edit command to every page and by defining a simplified markup syntax that is converted to HTML by the Web

[29] Apart from the academic prototypes that often were not suited for productive use, there used to be some smaller companies trying to sell annotation tools for the World Wide Web (e.g. Third Voice (Weinreich et al., 2001)). Thus far, they seem to have had little economical success and have quietly disappeared. Even Microsoft pulled back their annotation mechanism "Smart Tags" (Obendorf, & Weinreich, 2003) when public protesters feared a harmful concentration of annotation services—and thus, of advertisement sources (Mossberg, 2001).

server. Links are authored using WikiWords,[30] words containing a second large letter and new pages can be created simply by mentioning them on other pages. A Wiki thus provides a very simple and very general way of "writing the Web". It has become very successful—the oldest Wikis date back to 1995 and have been used to form, e.g., the pattern movement in software engineering[31] or the Wikipedia as an alternative to traditional encyclopedias. As is noted on Cunningham's Wiki front page, "The beauty of Wiki is in the freedom, simplicity, and power it offers" (Cunningham, 2006; Fig. 6.48).

In contrast to the previous examples that provide a unifying function, where simplicity and a central position in everyday work combine to trigger the use of one application for tasks it was not meant for, Wikis are intentionally designed without a specific task in mind—the understanding of what a Wiki consists of is located at a conceptual level.

Welcome Visitors

Welcome to the WikiWikiWeb - also known as WardsWiki, or even just "Wiki". A lot of people have their first wiki experience here. This community has been around since 1995 and consists of many people. We always accept newcomers with valuable contributions. If you haven't used a wiki before, be prepared for a bit of CultureShock. The beauty of Wiki is in the freedom, simplicity, and power it offers.

The primary focuses are PeopleProjectsAndPatterns in SoftwareDevelopment. However, it is much more than just an Informal History Of Programming Ideas. It started there, but the theme has created a culture and DramaticIdentity all its own. All Wiki content is WorkInProgress. Most of all, this is a forum where people share ideas! It changes as people come and go. Much of the information here is subjective. If you are looking for a dedicated reference site, try WikiPedia.

- Feel free to add your name in RecentVisitors (consider setting yourself a UserName).
- Browse from various StartingPoints, or use the search facility, also known as FindPage.
- Bookmark RecentChanges and watch how things change.
- Please pay attention to the tone of articles. See WelcomeToWikiPleaseBePolite.
- If you have beginner questions, you can see NewUserQuestions.
- If you have any other questions, ask the WikiHelpDesk, and be patient.
- The WikiEngines page provides a reference to wiki implementations.
- You can also select one of the RandomPages, so with some luck, you start on a good point.
- People should know a little WikiHistory.

Please read widely on this Wiki before adding new Wiki pages. This helps to reduce unnecessary clutter.

WikiSquatting (using Wiki as personal Web space), WalledGardens (a series of self-contained pages within a larger wiki), ChatMode (ThreadMode without cleanup), and especially WikiSpam (commercial advertising) are all frowned upon. We have several related SisterSites - religious debates or similar material are better suited to TheAdjunct; purely artistic or whimsical stuff goes to GreenCheese.

If you like the wiki concept and want to use a wiki for your own purposes (such as discussing topics other than those mentioned above), please consider other PublicWikiForums, or look at the RunningYourOwnWikiFaq. Or you can host your own. There are many WikiWikiClones and WikiEngines available. You can get help on ChoosingaWiki if you are overwhelmed by the big list of options.

CategoryWikiHelp

EditText of this page (last edited May 25, 2006)
FindPage by searching (or browse LikePages or take a VisualTour)

Fig. 6.48 Front page of Ward Cunningham's Wiki at http://c2.com

---

[30] Newer dialects often allow the definition of arbitrarily named link anchors using bracket markup. This allows external links to be integrated seamlessly within the text.

[31] The *Portland Patterns Wiki* was created by Cunningham & Cunningham, and through its intense discussions has led to well-known publications, such as *Design Patterns* (Gamma et al., 1995).

The actual technology is developed for a specific use case: consisting of a bunch of Perl scripts, the initial WikiWiki software was hacked to provide a working solution for Cunningham's own needs (Leuf and Cunningham, 2001). The general concept was taken up by others, yet interestingly, the first adopters who set up their own sites often created software by themselves; still today, new Wiki dialects continue to be developed. Although this is partly owing to the nature of the application (being server-sided, it is often set up by programmers) and its first adopters, the many different extensions of the basic concept—access rights, hierarchy, versioning, features for discussions of changes—point towards a different conclusion: although the general idea is appropriate for different users' needs, often a specific extension or adaption of functionality is necessary.

In the case of e-mail, different clients are very similar and have almost an identical feature set, they even look like one another. PowerPoint is a single application. The design of Wikis, however, can be uniquely customized. Yet, they never become unrecognizable; their similarity lies within the concept of use and in basic core features. This demonstrates that a differentiation whether compositional minimalism applies to products or to concepts is difficult. The *composition* of Wikis defines a core feature set. Every application providing these features is considered a Wiki.

On the one hand, Wikis thus do not easily qualify as a "design". On the other hand, they most closely resemble the work of the minimalist artists that later lead to concept art—an idea is taking the place of the physical work. There is an important difference: every instantiation of this idea—every Wiki—is potentially unique.

This identifies a weakness in some current research: in many studies of the use of Wikis, no differentiation is made between Wikis on the basis of additional features; their development, on the other hand, shows that they were desirable in many contexts. Thus, they are probably important factors for the actual use of the software, possibly more important than what made different systems be considered as Wikis. Ignoring this, some studies are based on the assumption that they analyze the "use of Wikis" as a concept (comp., e.g., Désilets et al., 2005). An outstanding example is the generation of Wikipedia—which is arguably more than software: it is a movement, a bureaucracy, a process, and a sociological phenomenon (Ciffolilli, 2003; Bryant et al., 2005; Wales, 2005)—and it runs on a Wiki software.

6.4.5.2 Discussion

Wikis are an example not for a system but for an idea. Including this example among other, more concrete products illustrates that concepts are here understood as possible products of design. For concepts, an evaluation using traditional methods of HCI must fail, as it is impossible to measure the effectiveness of "a Wiki" or the satisfaction it creates. Wikis are, however, rather successful and it is important to understand the reasons behind their success. Minimalism is capable of explaining the fascination of Wikis: their strength lies within their universality and the extreme ease with which they integrate with heterogeneous environments. This interpretation of compositional minimalism highlights that analysis of designs must therefore not be limited to the design of interactive systems alone but that the organizational and social context have become increasingly important too.

Table 6.13 Dimensions of minimalism in Wiki Webs

Functional Minimalism	Structural Minimalism	Architectural Minimalism	Compositional Minimalism

6.4.5.3 A Minimal Assessment

- *Functional Minimalism*: The original idea of the Wiki is extremely simple: making Web content editable and providing a simplistic Way of creating new hypertext nodes and links using a naming convention. However, unlike the concept of E-mail, the Wiki idea has seen a diversification that has created a multitude of Wikis with different and very specific competencies, which offer fairly sophisticated functionality, such as access control, versioning, integration of external services, addition of structural views, etc.
- *Structural Minimalism*: Seen as Hypertexts, Wikis can be extremely complex in structural terms. Understood as applications, the access structure of Wikis is fairly simple, from the ubiquitous search field to the aforementioned conventions for creating and linking pages. However, the many varieties of Wikis each add individual functionality and access to this functionality is seldom consistent; consequently, users need to learn how to use each Wiki dialect separately—if the use extends beyond the Wiki's basic functionality.
- *Architectural Minimalism*: Wikis support the integration with other functionality—they can be used as parts within a more complex system, e.g., as part of a content management system and they can also form the basis for sophisticated additional functionality, e.g., as Wikipedia adds versioning and discussion functionality. The Wiki concept focuses on providing simple means to link information and create new information units. As the Web demonstrated, this is a very universal concept.
- *Compositional Minimalism*: The Wiki idea is an outstanding example for an idea whose use is almost universal. With only Hypertext as the more general notion of hyperlinked texts having received similar attention, Wikis are currently a class of applications that are being put to use for almost every imaginable context, from private Web sites to commercial ventures and across all industries. This is possible as the Wiki idea does neither limit the form of content or use of a WikiWeb nor inhibit additional functionality—it is almost universally combinable.

6.4.6 Word Processing

When computing was still in its infancy, word processing was considered not to count among the "serious" applications: "At first, the WP product was ... limited with the idea being 'those WP folks [the users] can't handle anything else'. The side effect in this KISS approach was the production of user-friendly software before it became fashionable" (Dorsey, 1983). Yet, soon word processing grew into a synonym for computer-supported work (comp., e.g., Xerox, 1983) and today has become ubiquitous. When job applications mention "software skills", word processing is included without mention. It became a basic ICT (information and communication technology) skill—the one application (but for the Web and E-mail) that most students command (Hoffman and Vance, 2005)—and it has been taught in school and universities since the late 1970s (Rickman et al., 1979; Secrist, 1980). Word processing users range from pre-school children to the elderly, from the skilled professional writer to the first-time computer user. The success of word processing in mass markets can be retraced to the use of the WYSIWYG (what you see is what you get) principle (Press, 1993; Myers, 1998), and, on a related note, to the paper metaphor.[32] As a blank sheet of paper, a word processor can be used to produce almost any document—it places few restrictions on its users.

6.4.6.1 Description

Learning to use word processing tools has always been difficult—even when there were (by today's standards) less sophisticated applications in use; Mack et al. noted in 1983, "Computer text editors are powerful, but complex, tools. Particularly in the early stages of learning, the complexity of these tools can cause serious problems for users who are not experienced with computers" (Mack et al., 1983). A suggestion taken up in Carroll's training wheels approach is that the many features of word processors inhibit learning (ibid.).

As the discussion of word processing in terms of *functional minimalism* demonstrated, only a few features are actually used by the majority of users— even expert users. As long as features directly manipulate visible attributes of the generated text, they are easily learned. Other features, such as styles, become useful only when a certain way of working is assumed—e.g., when formatting instructions must be followed (Gadomski and Kral, 1990). Many of such advanced features are hidden in word processors—the most popular word processing software today is Microsoft Word; in itself, hardly a minimal application—neither are its competitors, as competition is often used synonymously

---

[32] The 'paper metaphor' refers here to the ability of word processing software to determine the layout (placement and direction) of text using a representation of a page, much resembling the resulting output when the text is sent to a printer. A more verbatim interpretation of the 'page', without the ability to flow text to next 'pages' to make room for insertions, did not find commercial acceptance (Fatton et al., 1993).

with feature comparison. Jensen Harris of Microsoft, however, reports that "In reality, the programs themselves weren't 'bloated.' At least, the miles-long list of feature requests from customers indicated that, if anything, people expected us to do more in this space" (Harris, 2006d).

How could this seemingly paradox situation—only a few used but many requested features—stabilize? Harris' explanation is that people seemingly use different functions (ibid.). Examining simpler word processing tools, such as Abiword, Mellel, Nisus Writer, or Papyrus Office, these are successfully used in very different contexts and all have found a specific niche where they build their strength. Yet, they are unable to gather users from diverse contexts, let alone capture a majority of the market.

The creation of compositionally minimal word processing software seems to disqualify functional minimalism. Yet, the question remains whether Word was designed to minimize composition or whether the addition of features is a silver bullet to seize new markets. The notion of *compositional minimalism* does not help much to clarify why a specific word processing software has become successful: how would one prove that an attribute of a software allows users to use it in different ways? It can, however, be used to reflect about the inverse: what do successful word processing applications miss that would hinder their use in other contexts.

Much of the discussion on the success of PowerPoint is applicable here as well. However, while PowerPoint is (comparatively) simple in functional terms and often used without modification, Word is a very complex application. Consequently, evidence suggests that users tend to customize their word processor—Page et al. (1996) found 92% of their 101 users had changed the appearance of their application. Tailoring activities can be triggered as general purpose software is put to use for specific tasks. In a sense, some users then take on a designer's role (Lave et al., 1991); often, these customizations are a collaborative effort and consequently, a systemization of tailoring (e.g., in organizations) tends to emerge (Trigg and Bødker, 1994).

6.4.6.2 Discussion

Microsoft Word, a software that probably no one would link with minimality, is successfully used in a wide variety of contexts. By contrast, "simpler" word processing software is unable to cater to the majority of users as it lacks the one or other feature that is absolutely necessary for a given potential customer— software with a *minimal functionality* or a tendency towards *structural minimalism* often targets a specific market: Apple's *Pages* was developed for novice users, packages like *Nisus Writer* or *Mellel*[33] cater to the professional writer's needs. There are specific niches for applications that specialize on competencies that general purpose software does not achieve; desktop publishing, for

---

[33] http://www.nisus.com, http://www.redlex.com

example, is still a domain that is dominated by special-purpose applications. *Minimal functionality* here often coincides with maximal adaption to specific tasks, which can hinder the software's use for other tasks.

Especially in corporate environments, communities of practice (comp. Wenger, 1999) can emerge that share tasks that are not well supported—even though the functionality exists, the interface is not capable of providing an easy access. Thus, some users take the role of translators (Mackay, 1990, 1991), tinkerers (MacLean et al., 1990), or local developers (Gantt and Nardi, 1992) and tailor the software according to the community's needs.

6.4.7 Refining the Notion of Compositional Minimalism

Learning buildings demonstrate that human users will always change their surroundings, even things considered as immobile and everlasting as buildings. It is impossible to fully anticipate all these changes. It is also futile to build as if adaption had already taken place as this prevents real adaption. It might be possible to plan the construction of few restraints, allowing easier adaption. The history of the Post-It Note demonstrates that it is more commonplace to build for the specific, and find wide adaption without planning.

Contrasting PowerPoint with the examples of Wiki and word processing, it seems on the one hand possible to support a wide variety of uses with a very intuitive and simple application while, on the other hand, the use of an underlying idea generates more and more specific functional requirements, disabling functionally minimal products to serve the needs of a majority of users. These products are found in specific niches, while a standard is set by the functional giant Microsoft Word.

The amount of customization Word is subjected to is both dependent on the technical prowess of users and the cost and time trade-off involved with adapting a complex application. Although Page et al. (1996) report that 92% of the 101 users in their field study customized their word processor to some degree, they do not report a customization anywhere as dramatic as the examples shown here; their "surprising 92% of participants" often made only small changes to the interface (e.g., a change in zoom setting, or displaying the ruler bar was considered customization, and only 4% of all users made any changes to the application's pull-down menus. Furthermore, Microsoft found that only 2% of all sessions reported to them by their user feedback tools had a customized appearance[34]—not counting additional buttons added by add-ins or

---

[34] Microsoft's numbers are based on the data of users who participated in the *Customer Experience Improvement Program*, an effort to provide quantitative data on what functionality is used in which context (Harris, 2006e). Although the CEIP collected data from millions of users, it is limited by the fact that many power users disapproved of any program that would send data back to Microsoft without their knowledge. Thus, the sample is bound to be heavily biased towards non-expert and non-corporate users.

templates (Harris, 2006c). As Pipek notes, customization is difficult to analyze and support: "In the evaluations, the general usefulness of these ideas could be established, but the framing conditions (especially the subordinated nature of appropriation activities compared to 'productive' work) pose serious challenges to the design" (Pipek, 2005, 88).

The design problem connected with compositional minimalism might be compared to what architects have to deal with when designing buildings: designs become finished only after they have been put in use (Brand, 1995). In a seminal paper on the subject, Henderson and Kyng (1991) described that other activities (learning, documenting, communicating) are crucial for the process of changing tool usages in the context of changing organizational requirements. It follows that compositional minimalism will often not be designed into a product, but that it is as much a quality of the development process that needs to support appropriation of tools. Pipek even demands that design projects should "maintain a social or collaborative approach to the appropriation activity they support" (Pipek, 2005, 89). A multitude of different perspectives exist that aim to enable personalization, customization, or appropriation of tools, from the purely social to the distinctly technical (comp. Galloway et al., 2004).

The example of learning buildings adds two aspects to this discussion: (1) A layered design might be a useful approach for designers. (2) A design is not finished as it is delivered. The first insight is mirrored in Brenda Laurel's comparison of design with script-writing—designers have to leave enough room for users to act (Laurel, 1993). Fabio Sergio, an Italian professor for interaction design and former industrial designer, puts it as follows, "Designers should strive to create relationships and structure but leave composition to the user" (Sergio, 2001).

It can be useful to make the unfinished nature of designs transparent to the user, as it is done in WikiWebs—and as the Web is perceived by David Weinberger, "On the Web, perfection is scary ... The imperfection of the Web isn't a temporary lapse; it's a design decision ... the designers weighed perfection against growth and creativity, and perfection lost. The Web is broken on purpose" (Weinberger, 2002, 79). As compositionally minimal design will want to invite the user into the design process, "an important aspect of design is the degree to which the object involves you in its own completion. Some work invites you into itself by not offering a finished, glossy, one-reading-only surface"—as Brian Eno noted about old buildings (Brand, 1995). The visibility of what is happening and how the user can affect it will encourage users; this is also reflected in Matthew Chalmers notion of "seamful systems (with beautiful seams)" (Chalmers et al., 2004; see also Chalmers and Galani, 2004; Bell et al., 2006). Sengers and Gaver stress that multiple interpretations must be allowed for a design (Sengers and Gaver, 2006), the designer is no longer autocrat, he becomes an enabler for the user. For buildings, Brand however warns that "making services external"—as was done for the Centre Pompidou in Paris—is not a good idea as it immensely increases maintenance costs (Brand,

1995; Fig. 6.49). Dan Hill (2002) lists three suggestions for designers: "1. Design simple inter-relating systems, which can be removed and replaced like components ... [and] don't have to coexist to make useful product. 2. Open standards allow many people to add their minor creative addition to the mix—inspiring in turn subsequent developments. 3. [Provide the] Ability to generate something functional with the most limited set of instructions or components."

Fig. 6.49 A building turned inside out—the services (heating, water) of Centre Pompidou

Along these lines, an alternative to traditional customization support might be presented by architectural minimalism—separating the functionality and providing individual tools can aid users appropriating technology. This is not an entirely new concept—in 1996, Johnson and Nardi came to a similar conclusion when they investigated the tools used to create slide presentations. Their initial assumptions were that one could differentiate between software that is task generic and software that is task specific; the latter type of software being better suited for creating slides but the former being used for reasons of convenience. Instead, they found that many small tools were used in interaction—and as a consequence, they "conclude that developing application software that supports all aspects of a task well is extremely difficult and ... suggest an alternative approach that may be more fruitful: providing collections of interoperable tools and services" (Johnson and Nardi, 1996).

Interfacing to existing tools is a central requirement for compositional minimalism; from the Post-It adhesive to the generic nature of the Wiki Web ideal, it is a hallmark of simple and widespread ideas that they easily interface with existing—and especially with competing—technology.

6.5 Reflections on the Four Notions of Minimalism

The previous four sections have examined selected examples for their minimal qualities. As a first result, finding these (and more) examples was really simple, as many designs are complimented for their simplicity—it was only a matter of finding out in what respect a design could be considered minimal. The classification preceding each example indicates that this was more difficult. Most designs do not exemplify a single dimension of minimalism—in the actual designs, several and sometimes antagonizing forces are often at work. Although this complicated the presentation in this chapter, the analysis of an individual design was much aided by the different perspectives created by the four notions of minimalism. It also makes sense to restrict the analysis of minimalism to the function, structure, architecture and composition *of the interface*—not of the underlying service layer. Although the two are often closely linked, taking the interface as a starting point allowed the analysis to take a use-centered perspective—while often, the interface is dictated by the functionality of the back-end, the implementation of the example tools is here interpreted as resulting from the interface design.

Minimalism and its four different forms focusing on function, structure, architecture and composition have been useful tools to examine real-world designs. But the examples examined in this chapter have also helped to clarify the notions of minimalism. Before the individual refinements are summarized, an aspect of design that has been deliberately omitted from the discussion requires discussion: the aesthetics of minimalism.

6.5.1 A First Assessment of Suitability for the Analysis of Products

> *Less isn't more; just enough is more.*
> —attributed to Milton Glaser, designer

Using a multitude of different examples, this chapter has tried to illustrate the interpretation of the four notions of minimalism and their usefulness for assessing qualities of a design. Examples for the different aspects of minimalism were easy to find, demonstrating their discriminatory power—"simplicity" in designs can quickly be differentiated using the four notions. The individual discussion of each example, however, explicated that a design is not simple due to adherence to a single notion of minimalism—and that it will be difficult to create good designs by following a single path to minimalism.

Functional minimalism is already a well-established concept as it matches the established notion of information appliances. Perhaps, surprisingly, if one applies the strict definition given here (Section 3.3.1), most designs do not meet the criteria. Even simple technology is embedded in technological contexts that create complex interactions. Also, reduction of functionality has proven to be not enough in itself—a focus on the whole gestalt of a design is necessary to effect increased perception of simplicity using functional reduction.

Structural minimalism is often difficult to identify as, by definition, it is not noticeable. Structurally minimal products are often very successful in interfaces that open up new markets, such as the Palm, remote controls, or a mass market cell phone. When it comes to desktop applications, structural minimalism becomes harder as applications usually burst with features that demand users access them. The example of MS Office 2007 demonstrates the superiority of a task-oriented approach: even more functionality can look like less. However, a minimal access structure must not always result in a better interface: simplicity, like most elements of design, needs to be evaluated in context; if the application demands complexity, a dense presentation of information may be required.[35]

Architectural minimalism is a surprisingly popular concept in more distributed environments—only for the domain of classic desktop application software, monolithic programs are the rule. This suggests, on the one hand, that it is possible and useful to follow this concept and, on the other hand, that domains more open to the concept that are, by definition, both more heterogeneous and interdependent to a higher degree and thus bound to require a more complex and partitioned infrastructure. The practical examples stressed the importance of a visible distribution[36] of responsibilities across tools.

Compositional minimalism has shown itself to be the least palpable notion. As it, by definition, evades application barriers, the examples discussed here have—with the exception of the Post-It and PowerPoint—more the character of services or application concepts. This indicates that flexible use is supported by a system architecture that allows the user to choose his/her tools and his/her time, and that for many specific task concepts, configuration or customization of functionality is helpful for a tool's appropriation. Some architects use incremental design and build footpaths where people step. Designers could do the same.

6.5.2 Design Advice

To make the lessons that can be learned from the failures and successes of the different designs more accessible, guidelines for designing are extracted from the examples presented in this chapter (Table 6.14). Each guideline

---

[35] Comparisons like the one between Google and Yahoo's front page fail to include the context (5.2.6). Google is a search engine. Yahoo is a directory and should be densely packed with information.

[36] Google, the figurehead of online simplicity, made a rare acknowledgment: sometimes in product design, more is more. The distribution of functionality across a growing number of tools was part of Google's self-understanding, as Marissa Mayer noted, "Google has the functionality of a really complicated Swiss Army knife, but the home page is our way of approaching it closed. It's simple, it's elegant, you can slip it in your pocket, but it's got the great doodad when you need it. A lot of our competitors are like a Swiss Army knife open -and that can be intimidating and occasionally harmful." (Tischler & Mayer, 2005). After users of Google Video did not buy products, Mayer admitted an extra link would have helped people find the required functionality (Post-Intelligencer, 2006).

consists of three parts: a design suggestion, a list of examples relevant for the suggestion, and a note that illustrates limitations of the guideline. The individual guidelines may seem to contradict each other, e.g., prioritization of access according to frequency versus use, as they describe alternative approaches that have been pursued to create minimal designs. Even in

Table 6.14 Guidelines resulting from the analyzed designs

Functional Minimalism

Identify the core functionality of the design. Define whether the design aims to be a simple tool.	GarageBand, CommSy, SO4K (Sections 5.1.2, 5.1.3, 5.1.4), iPod Shuffle (Section 5.3.4)	Use whenever not targeting the geek.
Take a holistic perspective: define the responsibilities of the design as a whole.	GarageBand (Section 5.1.2), CommSy (Section 5.1.3), Palm (Section 5.2.2), iPod (Section 5.3.4)	Don't over-reduce, identify core competencies.
Discuss the trade-offs involved with extending functionality. Keep track of the initial vision and its changes.	CommSy (Section 5.1.3)	This becomes more difficult as your user base grows.
Assess the feasibility of providing multiple interfaces using a single platform (optionally: let users select).	GarageBand (Section 5.1.2), SO4K (Section 5.1.4)	Assess whether different product lines are a feasible option.

Structural Minimalism

Prioritize access to functionality.	All.	Trade-off speed vs. balance
Prioritize access according to frequency.	Palm (Section 5.2.2), Nokia 3310 (Section 5.2.3), Word 97–03 (Section 5.2.5)	Use if use situations can be identified. Task over tool.
Prioritize access according to activity.	Harmony RC (Section 5.2.1), Word 2007 (Section 5.2.5)	Use if activities can be identified. Tool over task.
Translate prioritization into appropriate modalities.	HyperScout (Section 5.2.4), Word 2007 (Section 5.2.5)	Use non-intrusive, contextualized media

Architectural Minimalism

Examine your interface architecture at different levels: Building blocks can be gestures or interaction techniques, or manifest themselves as visible tools.	Automator (Section 5.3.2), SketchUp (Section 5.3.3), iPod (Section 5.3.4), Web 2.0 (Section 5.3.5)	Work at multiple levels to maximize reduction.
Modularization or division in tools bears the danger of fragmentation—the whole design must remain visible.	Web 2.0 (Section 5.3.5), Google Apps (Section 5.3.7)	Carefully integrate all tools in one design.

Compositional Minimalism

Designs should not be generic but generalizable. Do not try to plan for the future, but support "misuse".	E-mail (Section 5.4.3), PowerPoint (Section 5.4.4), Word Processor (Section 5.4.6)	Design increments, balance fit to task.
Functionally minimal designs are one approach towards design support for appropriation.	E-mail (Section 5.4.3), WikiWikiWebs (Section 5.4.5)	Use functional minimalism.
Modularize functionality in your design—form "building blocks". The resulting "use patterns" can be "interpreted" in different use situations by users.	Web 2.0 (Section 5.3.5), PowerPoint (Section 5.4.4), WikiWikiWebs (Section 5.4.5)	Use architectural minimalism.

these cases, however, thoughtful reflection will find a way of combining different approaches if that is necessary for the design.

Functional minimalism is created reducing functionality. To still design a useful tool, it is crucial to identify the tool's core competency first and the core functionality that is key to the design solution. There is some danger of over-reducing in the wrong places—if the resulting design feels restrictive, it is not minimal, but defective (Sections 5.1.2–5.1.4). It is therefore necessary to focus on the design as a whole. Extending a design for a second version of a product must keep this focus and, at the same time, find ways to optimize details of the design. Differences to the initial vision that are introduced by the addition or change of features should be reflected upon and either the vision be changed accordingly or the feature be put to the question. Finally, for specific designs, multiple interfaces—or multiple product lines based on a single platform—can be useful to fine-tune the amount of functionality for customers.

Structural minimalism is created as the access structures are adopted to the task. If more functionality needs to be accessible than is to be visible for practical reasons, this often involves a prioritization, and a contextualization of individual functionality. Different approaches to prioritization include assessing the frequency of use, or the user activity (Sections 5.2.2–5.2.3 vs. 5.2.1, 5.2.5). The former is most useful when use situations can be identified and analyzed easily. Both approaches are not exclusive, yet the latter carries the risk of ignoring the effects of a changing interface on the user. It is therefore most important to consider to which modalities the identified prioritization should be translated (Sections 5.2.4–5.2.5).

Architectural minimalism can present a possible way of achieving structural simplicity. It is important that the idea of modularized tools be considered on different levels of the interface—from connecting applications (Section 5.3.2) to interaction techniques (Section 5.3.3), and from interacting devices (Section 5.3.4) to interconnected services (Section 5.3.5). The modularization created by the distribution of responsibility across different tools must be made transparent to the user; fragmentation should be avoided, and the whole of the design should remain visible (Section 5.3.7).

Compositional minimalism, finally, can be achieved by supporting appropriation as a parallel process to development: if users choose to solve tasks that a tool was not conceived for, instead of immediately trying to replace this tool, designers should first consider those design qualities that made a misuse feasible and carefully reflect if they can be linked with the design's responsibility in a way that better supports the misuse (Sections 5.4.3, 5.4.4, 5.4.6). One way of supporting misuse is trying to devise a minimal functionality as this will often allow the user to adopt the tool for his/her own needs (Sections 5.4.3, 5.4.5). Another approach is to try to provide a design's functionality in the form of smaller building blocks that can be interpreted differently in different use situations—an architecturally minimal system (Sections 5.3.5, 5.4.4, 5.4.5).

References

Alley, M., and Neeley, K. A. (2005). Rethinking the design of presentation slides: a case for sentence headlines and visual evidence. *Technical Communication*, 52(4), 417–426.

Apple. (2005). Apple Introduces iPod shuffle: First iPod Under $100. http://www.apple.com/pr/library/2005/jan/11shuffle.html Accessed 20.7.2008

Apple. (2001). Apple Presents iPod. *Press Release* http://www.apple.com/pr/library/2001/oct/23ipod.html Accessed 20.7.2008

Apple. (2006b). Mail. You've got more. http://www.apple.com/macosx/leopard/mail.html Accessed 8.8.2008

Apple. (2002). Apple Acquires Emagic. http://www.apple.com/pr/library/2002/jul/01emagic.html Accessed 17.7.2008

Barreau, D., and Nardi, B. A. (1995). Finding and reminding: file organization from the desktop. *SIGCHI Bull*, 27(3), 39–43.

Baumert, J. (2004). *StarOffice 4 Kids – Mitwachsende Software im Einsatz*. Mensch & Computer 2004, Allgegenwärtige Interaktion, München, 199–208.

Baumert, J., and Meiners, F. (2003a). Auswertung des Probeeinsatzes von "StarOffice 4 Kids". http://www.joachimbaumert.de/downloads/Auswertung_Probeeinsatz.pdf Accessed 13.10.2008

Baumert, J., and Meiners, F. (2003b). *StarOffice 4 Kids – Mitwachsende Software für den Grundschulunterricht*. Mensch & Computer 2003, Interaktion in Bewegung, Stuttgart, 385–386.

Bay, S., and Ziefle, M. (2003). Performance in mobile phones: does it depend on a proper cognitive mapping? In Dea Harris (Ed.), *Human Centred Computing*. 170–174. Lawrence Erlbaum.

BBC. (2004). iPod helps Apple triple profits. http://news.bbc.co.uk/2/hi/business/3627425.stm Accessed 20.7,.2008

BBC. (2000). Sticking around – the Post-it note is 20. http://news.bbc.co.uk/1/hi/uk/701661.stm Accessed 10.10.2008

Beaudouin-Lafon, M. (2000). *Instrumental Interaction: An Interaction Model for Designing Post-WIMP user Interfaces*. CHI '00: Proceedings of the SIGCHI conference on Human factors in computing systems, New York, NY, USA, 446–453.

Bell, M., Chalmers, M., Barkhuus, L., Hall, M., Sherwood, S., Tennent, P., Brown, B., Rowl, D., and Benford, aS. (2006). *Interweaving Mobile Games with Everyday Life*. CHI '06: Proceedings of the SIGCHI conference on human factors in computing systems, New York, NY, USA, 417–426.

Bellotti, V., Ducheneaut, N., Howard, M., and Smith, I. (2003). *Taking Email to Task: The Design and Evaluation of a Task Management Centered Email Tool*. CHI '03: Proceedings of the SIGCHI conference on Human factors in computing systems, New York, NY, USA, 345–352.

Bellotti, V., Ducheneaut, N., Howard, M., Smith, I., and Neuwirth, C. (2002). *Innovation in Extremis: Evolving an Application for the Critical Work of Email and Information Management*. DIS '02: Proceedings of the conference on Designing interactive systems, New York, NY, USA, 181–192.

Bellotti, V., and Smith, I. (2000). *Informing the Design of an Information Management System with Iterative Fieldwork*. DIS '00: Proceedings of the conference on Designing interactive systems, New York, NY, USA, 227–237.

Bentley, R., Horstmann, T., and Trevor, J. (1997). The World Wide Web as enabling technology for CSCW: The case of BSCW. *Computer-Supported Cooperative Work: Special issue on CSCW and the Web, 6*.

Beocentral. (2005). Beo 4. http://www.beocentral.com/products/beo4 Accessed 10.10.2008

Berghel, H. (1997a). Cyberspace 2000: dealing with information overload. *Communications of ACM*, 40(2), 19–24.

Berghel, H. (1997b). Email – the good, the bad, and the ugly. *Communications of ACM, 40*(4), 11–15.

Bergman, E., and Haitani, R. (2000). *Designing the PalmPilot: A Conversation with Rob Haitani. In Bergman: Information Appliances and Beyond.* Morgan Kaufmann.

Bergman, O., Beyth-Marom, R., and Nachmias, R. (2003). The user-subjective approach to personal information management systems. *Journal of American Society for Information Science and Technology*, 54(9), 872–878.

Berners-Lee, T., and Fischetti, M. (1999). *Weaving the Web : the Original Design and Ultimate Destiny of the World Wide Web by its Inventor* (1st ed ed.). San Francisco: HarperSanFrancisco.

Berners-Lee, T. J. (1989). Information Management: A Proposal. CERN CERN-DD-89-001-OC. http://www.w3.org/History/1989/proposal.html

Blood, R. (2002). *The Weblog Handbook: Practical Advice on Creating and Maintaining Your Blog.* Jackson, TN: Perseus Books Group.

Blood, R. (2000). Weblogs: A History and Perspective. *Rebecca's Pocket* http://www.rebeccablood.net/essays/ weblog_history.html Accessed 20.7.2008

Boardman, R. (2004). *Improving Tool Support for Personal Information Management.* Imperial College, London. Available online at http://www.iis.ee.ic.ac.uk/~rick/thesis/boardman04-thesis.pdf

Boardman, R., and Sasse, M. A. (2004). *Stuff Goes into the Computer and Doesn't Come Out: A Cross-Tool Study of Personal Information Management.* CHI '04: Proceedings of the SIGCHI conference on human factors in computing systems, New York, NY, USA, 583–590.

Boddie, J. (2005). Has apple hit the right disruptive notes? *HSBP Newsletter: Strategy and Innovation*, 3(4).

Bouvin, N. O. (1999). *Unifying Strategies for Web Augmentation.* HYPERTEXT '99: Proceedings of the tenth ACM conference on hypertext and hypermedia: Returning to our diverse roots, New York, NY, USA, 91–100.

Bødker, S. (1990). *Through the Interface – a Human Activity Approach to User Interface Design.* Hillsdale, NJ: Lawrence Erlbaum Associates.

Brand, S. (1995). *How Buildings Learn: What Happens After They're Built.* Penguin (Non-Classics).

Breen, C. (2006, April). GarageBand 3. *Macworld.*

Breitling, H., Lilienthal, C., Lippert, M., and Züllighoven, H. (2000). *The JWAM Framework: Inspired By Research, Reality-Tested By Commercial Utilization.* Proceedings of OOPSLA 2000 Workshop: Methods and tools for object-oriented framework development and specialization.

Brown, B. A. T., and Sellen, A. (2001). Exploring Users' Experiences of the Web. *First Monday*, 6(9).

Brown, D. (2002). Understanding PowerPoint: Special Deliverable #5. *Boxes and Arrows* http://www.boxesandarrows.com/view/understanding_powerpoint_special_deliverable_5 Accessed 13.6.2008

Brown, J. S. (1983). *When User Hits Machine, or When is Artificial Ignorance Better than Artificial Intelligence?* CHI'83 plenary address, Boston, Massachusetts.

Bryant, S. L., Forte, A., and Bruckman, A. (2005). *Becoming Wikipedian: Transformation of Participation in a Collaborative Online Encyclopedia.* GROUP '05: Proceedings of the 2005 international ACM SIGGROUP conference on supporting group work, New York, NY, USA, 1–10.

BSCW. BSCW Client Extensions for Windows. http://bscw.fit.fraunhofer.de/clientex.html Accessed 17.7.2008

Burrows, P. (1997, July 28). Is apple mincemeat? *BusinessWeek.*

Buskirk, Ev. (2004). Perspective: The secret of iPod's scroll wheel. http://news.com.com/The + secret + of + iPod's + scroll + wheel/2010-1041_3-5375101.html Accessed 18.7.2008

Butter, A., and Pogue, D. (2002). *Piloting Palm: The Inside Story of Palm, Handspring, and the Birth of the Billion-Dollar Handheld Industry*. Hoboken, NJ: Wiley & Sons.

Byrne, D. (2003). Learning to Love PowerPoint. *Wired Magazine*, 11.09.

Cailliau, R., and Ashman, H. (1999). Hypertext in the Web—a history. *ACM Comput. Surv,* 31(4es), 35.

Campbell, C. S., and Maglio, P. P. (1999). Facilitating navigation in information spaces: road-signs on the World Wide Web. *International Journal of Human-Computer Studies*, 50(4), 309–327.

Carliner, S., Dillon, A., Garrett, J. J., Haller, T., Jacobson, B., Quesenberry, W., Shedroff, N., Sless, D., Wodtke, C., Schriver, K., Rosenfeld, L., and Wurman, R. S. (2001). What's in a name? *Design Matters*, 4, 1–10.

Carlton, J., and Kawasaki, G. (1997). *Apple: The Inside Story of Intrigue, Egomania, and Business Blunders*. Darby, PA: Diane Pub Co.

Carr, L. A., DeRoure, D. C., Hall, W., and Hill, G. J. (1995). *The Distributed Link Service: A Tool for Publishers, Authors and Readers*. Fourth International World Wide Web Conference: The Web Revolution, (Boston, Massachusetts, USA), 647–656.

Carr, N. (2005). The amorality of Web 2.0. http://www.roughtype.com/archives/2005/10/the_amorality_o.php Accessed 28.8.2008

Chalmers, M., Bell, M., Hall, M., Sherwood, S., and Tennent, P. (2004). Seamful Games. http://www.ubicomp.org/ubicomp2004/adjunct/demos/chalmers.pdf Accessed 20.7.2008

Chalmers, M., and Galani, A. (2004). *Seamful Interweaving: Heterogeneity in the Theory and Design of Interactive Systems*. DIS '04: Proceedings of the 2004 conference on Designing interactive systems, New York, NY, USA, 243–252.

Ciffolilli, A. (2003). Phantom authority, self-selective recruitment, and retention of members in virtual communities: The case of Wikipedia. *First Monday*, 8(12).

CommSy. (2005). BenutzerInnenhandbuch. Kontext: Hochschule. http://www.commsy.de/downloads/commsy_nutzungshandbuch.pdf Accessed 10.10.

Conklin, E. J. (1987). Hypertext: An introduction and survey. *IEEE Computer*, 20(9), 17–41.

Cooper, A., and Reimann, R. M. (2003). *About Face 2.0: The Essentials of Interaction Design*. Wiley.

Critchley, S. (2005). I Want Less And I'm Willing To Pay For It. http://www.oreillynet.com/digitalmedia/blog/2005/03/i_want_less_and_im_willing_to.html Accessed 22.5.

Csikszentmihalyi, M. (1991). *Flow: The Psychology of Optimal Experience*. London: Harper Perennial.

Cunningham, W. (2006). Portland Pattern Repository. http://c2.com/cgi/wiki?WelcomeVisitors Accessed 25.5.2008

Dahm, M., Felken, C., Klein-Bösing, M., Rompel, G., and Stroick, R. (2005). Zur Gebrauchstauglichkeit von Handys – Breite Untersuchung und aktueller Stand. *i-com*, 4(1), 26–33.

Danis, C., Kellogg, W. A., Lau, T., Dredze, M., Stylos, J., and Kushmerick, N. (2005). *Managers' Email: Beyond Tasks and To-Dos*. CHI '05: CHI '05 extended abstracts on Human factors in computing systems, New York, NY, USA, 1324–1327.

de.internet.com (2004). Deutsche Konsumenten fühlen sich beim Kauf von Handys und Notebooks überfordert. http://de.internet.com/index.php?id = 2029134&section = Marketing-Statistics Accessed 20.6.2008

DeBoer, C. (2004). Harmony Remote Control Simulator, Tech Support & Conclusion. http://www.audioholics.com/productreviews/avhardware/HarmonyH688remotecontrol_5.php Accessed 10.10.2008

Denning, P. J. (1982). ACM president's letter: electronic junk. *Commun. ACM*, 25(3), 163–165.

Désilets, A., Paquet, S., and Vinson, N. G. (2005). *Are Wikis Usable?* WikiSym '05: Proceedings of the 2005 international symposium on Wikis, New York, NY, USA, 3–15.

Deutschman, A. (2001). *The Second Coming of Steve Jobs*. New York, NY: Broadway.

Dorsey, J. G. (1983). *Word Processing in an M.I.S Environment*. ACM 83: Proceedings of the 1983 annual conference on computers : extending the human resource, New York, NY, USA, 225.

Ducheneaut, N., and Bellotti, V. (2001). E-mail as habitat: an exploration of embedded personal information management. *Interactions*, 8(5), 30–38.

Dumais, S., Cutrell, E., Cadiz, J. J., Jancke, G., Sarin, R., and Robbins, D. C. (2003). *Stuff I've Seen: A System for Personal Information Retrieval and Re-use.* SIGIR '03: Proceedings of the 26th annual international ACM SIGIR conference on Research and development in informaion retrieval, New York, NY, USA, 72–79.

eco. (2005). Einfache Bedienung von Handys wichtiger als mehr Funktionen. http://www.eco. de/servlet/PB/menu/1541961_l1/index.html Accessed 20.7.2008

Eggli, L., Brüderlin, B. D., and Elber, G. (1995). *Sketching as a Solid Modeling Tool.* Proceedings of the third ACM symposium on solid modeling and applications, New York, NY, USA, 313–322.

Enderle, R. (2005). Looking Ahead to CES. http://www.technewsworld.com/story/39326. html Accessed 10.10.2008

Farhoomand, A. F., and Drury, D. H. (2002). Managerial information overload. *Communications on ACM*, 45(10), 127–131.

Fatton, A., Romberger, S., and Eklundh, K. S. (1993). *The Paper Model for Computer-Based Writing.* CHI '93: Proceedings of the SIGCHI conference on Human factors in computing systems, New York, NY, USA, 514.

Findlater, L., and McGrenere, J. (2004). *A Comparison of Static, Adaptive, and Adaptable Menus.* CHI '04: Proceedings of the SIGCHI conference on Human factors in computing systems, New York, NY, USA, 89–96.

Finkelstein, E. (2003). *How to Do Everything with Microsoft Office PowerPoint 2003 (How to Do Everything).* New York, NY: Mcgraw-Hill Osborne Media.

Franzke, M., and Rieman, J. (1993). *Natural Training Wheels: Learning and Transfer Between Two Versions of a Computer Application.* VCHCI '93: Proceedings of the Vienna conference on human computer interaction, London, UK, 317–328.

Fried, J. (2004). Web 2.0 Review: Don't forget there's another kind of scaling. http://www. 37signals.com/svn/archives/000881.php Accessed 20.8.2008

Gadomski, K. E., and Kral, K. M. (1990). *Using Macros & Style Sheets to Aid in Document Layout.* SIGUCCS '90: Proceedings of the 18th annual ACM SIGUCCS conference on User services, New York, NY, USA, 131–136.

Galloway, A., Brucker-Cohen, J., Gaye, L., Goodman, E., and Hill, D. (2004). *Design for Hackability.* DIS '04: Proceedings of the 2004 conference on Designing interactive systems, New York, NY, USA, 363–366.

Gamma, E., Helm, R., Johnson, R., and Vlissides, J. (1995). *Design Patterns: Elements of Reusable Object-Oriented Software (Addison-Wesley Professional Computing Series).* Upper Saddle River, NJ: Addison-Wesley Professional.

Gantt, M., and Nardi, B. A. (1992). *Gardeners and Gurus: Patterns of Cooperation Among CAD users.* CHI '92: Proceedings of the SIGCHI conference on Human factors in computing systems, New York, NY, USA, 107–117.

Garrett, J. J. (2005). Ajax: A New Approach to Web Applications. http://www.adaptivepath. com/publications/essays/archives/000385.php Accessed 26.8.2008

Gartner. (2004). Gartner Says Microsoft's Windows CE Surpassed Palm OS Shipments in Worldwide PDA Operating Systems Market in Third Quarter of 2004. http://www.gartner. com/press_releases/asset_113913_l1.html Accessed 20.7.2008

Gibson, B. (2005). First on TMO – Apple Exec: Shuffle Grabs 58% of Flash Player Market; What Cell Phone Threat? http://www.macobserver.com/article/2005/05/04.4.shtml Accessed 2.10.2008

Gillies, J., and Cailliau, R. (2000). *How the Web was Born: The Story of the World Wide Web.* Oxford: Oxford University Press.

Glenn, W. (2000a). Top 12 Word Tips. *WindowsDevCenter.com* http://www.windowsdevcenter. com/pub/a/oreilly/ windows/news/word2k_0900.html Accessed 25.5.2008

Glenn, W. J. (2000b). *Word 2000 in a Nutshell: A Power User's Quick Reference.* Cambridge, MA: O'Reilly Media, Inc.

Glinert, S. (2006). Google SketchUp. CNET Editors review http://reviews.cnet.com/Google_ SketchUp/4505-3633_7-31861341-2.html Accessed 28.8.2008

Grudin, J. (1994). Groupware and social dynamics: eight challenges for developers. *Communications on ACM*, 37(1), 92–105.

Grudin, J., Tallarico, S., and Counts, S. (2005). *As Technophobia Disappears: Implications for Design.* GROUP '05: Proceedings of the 2005 international ACM SIGGROUP conference on supporting group work, New York, NY, USA, 256–259.

Gwizdka, J. (2004). *Email Task Management Styles: The Cleaners and the Keepers.* CHI '04: CHI '04 extended abstracts on Human factors in computing systems, New York, NY, USA, 1235–1238.

Haddad, A. (1999). *Sams Teach Yourself Microsoft PowerPoint 2000 in 24 Hours.* Indiana-palis, IN: Sams.

Hales, P. (2006). Microsoft Wants Users to Actually use Office 2007. http://www.theinquirer. net/?article = 31960 Accessed 25.5.

Hammersley, B. (2005). *Developing Feeds with Rss and Atom.* Cambridge, MA: O'Reilly Media.

Hardy, I. R. (1996). *The Evolution of ARPANET Email.* University of California at Berkeley, Berkeley, CA. Available online at http://www.ifla.org/documents/internet/hari1.txt

Harris, J. (2006a). Grading On the Curve (Why the UI Part 8). http://blogs.msdn.com/ jensenh/archive/2006/04/ 11/573348.aspx Accessed 10.10.2008

Harris, J. (2006b). The End of Personalized Menus. http://blogs.msdn.com/jensenh/archive/ 2006/01/20/515328.aspx Accessed 10.10.2008

Harris, J. (2005). Tipping the Scale (Why the UI, Part 5). http://blogs.msdn.com/jensenh/ archive/2005/ 10/24/484131.aspx Accessed 10.10.2008

Harris, J. (2006c). Let's Talk About Customization. http://blogs.msdn.com/jensenh/archive/ 2006/06/27/648269.aspx Accessed 2006.28.6.

Harris, J. (2006d). Combating the Perception of Bloat. http://blogs.msdn.com/jensenh/ archive/2006/03/31/565877.aspx Accessed 2006.28.6.

Harris, J. (2006e). Inside Deep Thought (Why the UI Part 6). http://blogs.msdn.com/jensenh/ archive/2006/ 04/05/568947.aspx Accessed 10.10.2008

Harris, J. (2006f). No Distaste for Paste (Why the UI Part 7). http://blogs.msdn.com/jensenh/ archive/2006/ 04/07/570798.aspx Accessed 10.10.2008

Harrison, W. (2004). From the Editor: The Dangers of End-User Programming. *IEEE Softw,* 21(4), 5–7.

Henderson, A., and Kyng, M. (1991). There's no place like home: Continuing Design in Use. In J Greenbaum and M Kyng (Eds.), *Design at Work: Cooperative Design of Computer Systems.* 219–240. Hillsdale, NJ: Lawrence Erlbaum Ass.

Herder, E., Weinreich, H., Obendorf, H., and Mayer, M. (2006). *Much to Know About History.* AH 2006 4th international conference for adaptive hypermedia and adaptive web-based systems, Dublin, Ireland, 283–287.

Hightower, R., Ring, L., Helfman, J., Bederson, B., and Hollan, J. (1998). *Graphical Multi-scale Web Histories: A Study of PadPrints.* ACM Hypertext'98, 58–65. Available online at http://citeseer.ifi.unizh.ch/hightower98graphical.html

Hilgenstock, R., and Jirmann, R. (2006). Moodle in Deutschland. http://moodle.de/file.php/ 1/whitepaper.pdf Accessed 19.7.2008

Hill, D. (2002). Towards designing adaptive systems London: AIGA Experience Design forum.

Hill, J. (1998). *Occupying Architecture.* London: Spon Press.

Hoffman, M. E., and Vance, D. R. (2005). *Computer Literacy: What Students Know and from Whom they Learned It.* SIGCSE '05: Proceedings of the 36th SIGCSE technical sympo-sium on computer science education, New York, NY, USA, 356–360.

Hood, C. S., and Hood, D. J. (2005). *Teaching Programming and Language Concepts Using LEGOs\&\#174;* ITiCSE '05: Proceedings of the 10th annual SIGCSE conference on Innovation and technology in computer science education, New York, NY, USA, 19–23.

Höök, K. (2000). Steps to take before intelligent user interfaces become real. *Interacting with Computers*, 12(4), 409–426.

Hughes, J. (2005). Technica – Lego Technic Site: The Automatic Binding Brick. http://isodomos.com/technica/history/1940/1949.php Accessed 20.8.2008

Hughes, R. J., Shewmake, J., and Okelberry, C. R. (1998). *Ceilidh: Collaborative Writing on the Web*. SAC '98: Proceedings of the 1998 ACM symposium on Applied Computing, New York, NY, USA, 732–736.

Igarashi, T., Matsuoka, S., and Tanaka, H. (1999). *Teddy: A Sketching Interface for 3D Freeform Design*. SIGGRAPH '99: Proceedings of the 26th annual conference on Computer graphics and interactive techniques, New York, NY, USA, 409–416.

Ingalls, D., Kaehler, T., Maloney, J., Wallace, S., and Kay, A. (1997). *Back to the Future: The Story of Squeak, a Practical Smalltalk Written in Itself*. OOPSLA '97: Proceedings of the 12th ACM SIGPLAN conference on Object-oriented programming, systems, languages, and applications, New York, NY, USA, 318–326.

Iorio, A. D. and Vitali, F. (2005). *From the Writable Web to Global Editability*. HYPERTEXT '05: Proceedings of the sixteenth ACM conference on Hypertext and hypermedia, New York, NY, USA, 35–45.

Jackewitz, I., Janneck, M., and Strauss, M. (2004). CommSy: Softwareunterstützung für Wissensprojekte. In B Pape, D Krause, and H Oberquelle (Eds.), *Wissensprojekte – Gemeinschaftliches Lernen aus didaktischer, softwaretechnischer und organisatorischer Sicht*. 186–202. Münster: Waxmann.

Jackson, D. (1999). *Victorinox Original Schweizer Offiziersmesser*. Heel.

Janneck, M. (2006). *Softwaregestaltung für die Gruppeninteraktion im Kontext von CSCL – am Beispiel der Fallstudie CommSy*. Universität Hamburg,. Available online at http://www.sub.uni-hamburg.de/opus/volltexte/2006/3042/

Janneck, M., Obendorf, H., Finck, M., and Janneck, M. (2006). *Tying Collaborative Knowledge Nets*. Cooperative Systems Design – COOP 2006, 57–65.

Jaynes, E. T. (1992). The Gibbs Paradox. In CR Smith, GJ Erickson, and PO Neudorfer (Eds.), *Maximum Entropy and Bayesian Methods*. 122f. Dordrecht, Holland: Kluwer Academic Publishers.

Jeenicke, M. (2005). *Architecture-Centric Software Migration for the Evolution of Web-based Systems*. Workshop on Architecture-Centric Evolution (ACE 2005), ECOOP 2005, Glasgow,. Available online at http://swt-www.informatik.uni-hamburg.de/publications/download.php?id=322

Jobs, S. (2001). Apple Music Event 2001-The First Ever iPod Introductio On *Apple Music Event 2001*: San Francisco: Apple Computer.

Jobs, S. (2005). *Macworld 2005 Keynote: iPod Shuffle Introduction*. San Francisco: Apple Computers, Inc.

Jobs, S. (2004). The Seed of Apple's Innovation. *Business Week Online* http://www.businessweek.com/bwdaily/dnflash/ oct2004/nf20041012_4018_db083.htm

Johnson, J. A., and Nardi, B. A. (1996). Creating presentation slides: a study of user preferences for task-specific versus generic application software. *ACM Trans. Comput.-Hum. Interact*, 3(1), 38–65.

Jones, W., Bruce, H., and Dumais, S. (2001). *Keeping Found Things Found on the Web*. CIKM '01: Proceedings of the tenth international conference on Information and knowledge management, New York, NY, USA, 119–126.

Kang, H., Plaisant, C., and Shneiderman, B. (2003). *New Approaches to Help Users Get Started with Visual Interfaces: Multi-Layered Interfaces and Integrated Initial Guidance*. dg.o '03: Proceedings of the 2003 annual national conference on Digital government research, Boston, MA, 1–6.

Karjalainen, T. M. (2003). *Strategic Brand Identity and Symbolic Design Cues*. 6th Asian Design Conference, Tsukuba, Japan, 14–17.

Kaye, J. J., Vertesi, J., Avery, S., Dafoe, A., David, S., Onaga, L., Rosero, I., and Pinch, T. (2006). *To have and to Hold: Exploring the Personal Archive.* CHI '06: Proceedings of the SIGCHI conference on Human Factors in computing systems, New York, NY, USA, 275–284.

Keil-Slawik, R., and Baumert, J. (2004). StarOffice 4 Kids – Mitwachsende Software für den lernenden Nachwuchs. *Forschungs Forum Paderborn*, 7, 18–22.

Khemlani, L. (2004). SketchUp 4.0. AECbytes Product Review http://www.aecbytes.com/review/2004/SketchUp4.html Accessed 31.8.2008

Kiljander, H. (2004). *Evolution and Usability of Mobile Phone Interaction Styles.* Helsinki University of Technology, Espoo, Finland. Available online at http://lib.hut.fi/Diss/2004/isbn9512273209/isbn9512273209.pdf

Klassner, F. (2002). *A Case Study of LEGO Mindstorms\$^{TM}$ Suitability for Artificial Intelligence and Robotics Courses at the College Level.* SIGCSE '02: Proceedings of the 33rd SIGCSE technical symposium on Computer science education, New York, NY, USA, 8–12.

Klockar, T., Carr, D., Hedman, A., Johansson, T., and Bengtsson, F. (2003). *Usability of Mobile Phones.* Proceedings of the 19th international symposium on human factors in telecommunications, Berlin, Germany, 197–204.

Koerner, B. I. (2006, February). Geeks in Toyland. *Wired Magazine.* Available online: http://www.wired.com/wired/archive/14.02/lego.html.

Koiso-Kanttila, N. (2003). Consumers on the Web: Identification of usage patterns. *First Monday*, 8(4).

Kopetzky, T., and Mühlhäuser, M. (1999). *Visual preview for link traversal on the World Wide Web.* WWW '99: Proceeding of the eighth international conference on World Wide Web, New York, NY, USA, 1525–1532.

Kostof, S. (1977). *The Architect: Chapters in the History of the Profession.* Oxford: Oxford University Press.

Koved, L. and Scneiderman, B. (1986). Embedded menus: selecting items in context. *Communications on ACM*, 29(4), 312–318.

Laurel, B. (1993). *Computers as Theatre.* Upper Saddle River, NJ: Addison-Wesley Professional.

Lave, J., Wenger, E., Pea, R., Brown, J. S., and Heath, C. (1991). *Situated Learning: Legitimate Peripheral Participation (Learning in Doing: Social, Cognitive & Computational Perspectives).* Cambridge, MA: Cambridge University Press.

Leishman, D. (2004, January). NAMM Wrapup: The logic of NAMM. *Macworld.*

Leuf, B., and Cunningham, W. (2001). *The Wiki Way: Quick Collaboration on the Web.* Upper Saddle River, NJ: Addison-Wesley Professional.

Levine, R. (1996). Guide to Web Style. http://web.archive.org/web/19990508134652/www.sun.com/styleguide/ Accessed 10.10.2008

Levinson, E. (1998). RFC 2387: The MIME Multipart/Related Content-type.

Levy, S. (2006a). Q&A: Jobs on iPod's Cultural Impact. *Newsweek Technology* http://msnbc.msn.com/id/15262121/ site/newsweek?www.reghardware.co.uk Accessed 17.10.2008

Levy, S. (2006b). *The Perfect Thing.* New York, NY: Simon & Schuster.

Shim, R. (2001). Palm losing the revenue game to Compaq. CNet News.com Available online: http://www.zdnetasia.com/news/hardware/0,39042972,20087809,00.htm

Lilienthal, C., and Züllighoven, H. (1997). Application-oriented usage quality: the tools and materials approach. *Interactions*, 4(6), 35–41.

Lindholm, C., and Keinonen, T. (2003). *Mobile Usability: How Nokia Changed the Face of the Mobile Phone.* London: McGraw-Hill Professional.

Lipson, H., and Shpitalni, M. (1996). Optimization-based reconstruction of a 3D object from a single freehand line drawing. *Computer-aided Design*, 28(8), 651–663.

Lithgow, A. (1987, July 26). The ghost that is haunting lego land. *The Mail on Sunday.*

Lok, L. T. T. (2004). *A Critical Survey of Software Packages for Use by Interior Designers.* Unpublished MSc Thesis, University of Wales, Aberystwyth. Available online at http://

www.aber.ac.uk/compsci/Dept/Teaching/ MSc_dissertations/2004/Lynda_Lok.pdf#search =
%22lynda%20lok%20%20sketchup%20interior%20design%20architecture%22
Lovejoy, T., and Grudin, J. (2003). *Messaging And Formality: Will IM Follow in the Footsteps of Email?* Human Computer Interaction – Interact 2003, 817–820.
Lynch, P., and Horton, S. (1999). Web Style Guide : Basic Design Principles for Creating Web Sites. http://web.archive.org/web/20000816062833/http://www.info.med.yale.edu/caim/manual/, originally at http://info.med.yale.edu/caim/manual/ Accessed 10.10.2008
Macjams.com (2004a). Interview with GarageBand expert Francis Preve. http://www.macjams.com/article.php? story = 20041115062201549 Accessed 23.5.
Macjams.com (2004b). GarageBand Tutorial: Built-in Audio Unit Effects. http://www.macjams.com/article.php? story = 20040329063101758 Accessed 17.7.2008
Mack, R. L., Lewis, C. H., and Carroll, J. M. (1983). Learning to use word processors: problems and prospects. *ACM Transactions on Information System*, 1(3), 254–271.
Mackay, W. E. (1988). *More than Just a Communication System: Diversity in the Use of Electronic Mail.* CSCW '88: Proceedings of the 1988 ACM conference on computer-supported cooperative work, New York, NY, USA, 344–353.
Mackay, W. E. (1990). *Patterns of Sharing Customizable Software.* CSCW '90: Proceedings of the 1990 ACM conference on Computer-supported cooperative work, New York, NY, USA, 209–221.
Mackay, W. E. (1991). *Triggers and Barriers to Customizing Software.* CHI '91: Proceedings of the SIGCHI conference on human factors in computing systems, New York, NY, USA, 153–160.
MacLean, A., Carter, K., Lövstr, L., and Moran, T. (1990). *User-Tailorable Systems: Pressing the Issues with Buttons.* CHI '90: Proceedings of the SIGCHI conference on human factors in computing systems, New York, NY, USA, 175–182.
Macminute.com (2004). GarageBand Community Web Sites Ready to Launch. http://www.macminute.com/2004/01/09/ garageband Accessed 23.5.2008
Maeda, J. (2005b, September 7). Simplicity: The Goldilocks Rule. *BusinessWeek.* McGraw Hill Companies Inc.
Malone, T. W. (1983). How do people organize their desks? Implications for the design of office information systems. *ACM Transactions on Information Systems*, 1(1), 99–112.
Martell, D. (2006, July 19). Apple profit rises 48 pct, helped by iPod sales. *Washington Post.*
McGrenere, J. (2002). *The Design and Evaluation of Multiple Interfaces: A Solution for Complex Software.* Univ. of Toronto, Toronto. Available online at http://www.cs.ubc.ca/~joanna/papers/JMcGrenere_Thesis_DoubleSided.pdf
McGrenere, J., Baecker, R. M., and Booth, K. S. (2002). *An Evaluation of a Multiple Interface Design Solution for Bloated Software.* CHI '02: Proceedings of the SIGCHI conference on Human factors in computing systems, New York, NY, USA, 164–170.
McGrenere, J., and Moore, G. (2000). *Are We All In the Same "Bloat"?* Graphics Interface, 187–196. Available online at citeseer.ist.psu.edu/685361.html
Mertens, M., and Leggewie, C. (2004, May 28). Technologisches Kokain. *Freitag – Die Ost-West-Wochenzeitung,* Zeitungsverlag 'Freitag' GmbH.
Metafacts, I. (2003). Roadblocks on the Information Highway: Barriers to adoption of technology products.
Microsoft. (2006c). Microsoft Robotics Studio Provides Common Ground for Robotics Innovation. http://www.microsoft.com/presspass/press/2006/jun06/06-20MSRoboticsStudioPR.mspx Accessed 20.8.2008
Miles-Board, T., Carr, L., Kampa, S., and Hall, W. (2003). *Supporting Management Reporting: A Writable Web Case Study.* WWW '03: Proceedings of the 12th international conference on World Wide Web, New York, NY, USA, 234–243.
Mitchell, J. and Shneiderman, B. (1989). Dynamic versus static menus: an exploratory comparison. *SIGCHI Bull, 20*(4), 33–37.

Morgan, C. (2005, March). GarageBand 2. *Computer Music*. 88–89. Future Publishing Ltd.

Mossberg, W. S. (2001, June 7). New Windows XP Feature Can Re-Edit Others' Sites. *Wall Street Journal,*. Dow Jones & Company, Inc.

Myers, B. A. (1998). A Brief History of Human Computer Interaction Technology. *ACM interactions*, 5(2), 44–54.

Myers, B. A., Ko, A. J., and Burnett, M. M. (2006). *Invited Research Overview: End-user Programming*. CHI '06: CHI '06 extended abstracts on Human factors in computing systems, New York, NY, USA, 5–7.

Myers, B. A., Weitzman, D. A., Ko, A. J., and Chau, D. H. (2006). *Answering why and why not Questions in User Interfaces*. CHI '06: Proceedings of the SIGCHI conference on Human Factors in computing systems, New York, NY, USA, 397–406.

Nagel, D. (2005). Apple GarageBand 2: Home studio audio and MIDI software. http://www. macaudiopro.com/articles/ viewarticle.jsp?id = 31007 Accessed 22.5._

Nanno, T., Saito, S., and Okumura, M. (2002). *Zero-Click : a System to Support Web Browsing*. International World Wide Web Conference, Honululu, Hawaii, 90–91.

Nardi, B. A. (1993). *A Small Matter of Programming: Perspectives on End User Computing*. The MIT Press.

Nardi, B. A., and Miller, J. R. (1990a). *An Ethnographic Study of Distributed Problem Solving in spreadsheet development*. CSCW '90: Proceedings of the 1990 ACM conference on Computer-supported cooperative work, New York, NY, USA, 197–208.

Nardi, B. A., and Miller, J. R. (1990b). *The Spreadsheet Interface: A basis for end user programming*. INTERACT '90: Proceedings of the IFIP TC13 third interational conference on human-computer interaction, 977–983.

Noirhomme-Fraiture, M., and Serpe, V. (1998). *Visual Representation of Hypermedia Links According to Their Types*. AVI '98: Proceedings of the working conference on Advanced visual interfaces, New York, NY, USA, 146–155.

Nokia. (2002). Vertu Launches the World's Most Exclusive Instrument for Personal Communication. http://press.nokia.com/PR/200201/845684_5.html Accessed 1.10.2008

Norman, D. A. (2004b). Activity-Centered Design: Why I like my Harmony Remote Control. http://jnd.org/dn.mss/activitycentere.html Accessed 13.8.2008

Norman, D. A. (2004c). The Truth About Google's so-Called "Simplicity". http://www.jnd. org/dn.mss/the_truth_about.html Accessed 8.10.2008

Norman, D. A. (1999). *The Invisible Computer: Why Good Products Can Fail, the Personal Computer Is So Complex, and Information Appliances are the Solution*. Cambridge, MA: The MIT Press.

Norman, D. A. (2005). Do companies fail because their technology is unusable? *Interactions*, 12(4), 69.

Norman, D. A. (1989). *The Psychology of Everyday Things*. Jackson, TN: Basic Books.

Norman, D. A. (2002). Home theater: Not ready for prime time. *Computer*, 35(6), 100–102.

Norman, K. L. (1991). *The Psychology of Menu Selection: Designing Cognitive Control at the Human/Computer Interface (Human/Computer Interaction)*. New York, NY: Ablex Publishing Corporation.

O'Reilly, T. (2005). What is Web 2.0? Design Patterns and Business Models for the Next Generation of Software. http://www.oreillynet.com/pub/a/oreilly/tim/news/2005/09/30/ what-is-web-20.html Accessed 10.10.2008

Obendorf, H. (2003). *Einsatz elektronischer Medien zur Unterstützung der universitären Lehre: Ein Erfahrungsbericht*. Mensch & Computer 2003, Stuttgart, 356–357.

Obendorf, H. (2004). The Indirect Authoring Paradigm – Bringing Hypertext into the Web. *Journal on Digital Information*, 5(1). Available online: http://jodi.tamu.edu/Articles/v05/ i01/Obendorf/

Obendorf, H., and Weinreich, H. (2003). *Comparing Link Marker Visualization Techniques – Changes in Reading Behavior*. Proc. of 12th International World Wide Web Conference – WWW 2003, New York, NY, USA, 736–745.

Obendorf, H., Weinreich, H., Herder, E., and Mayer, M. (2007). *Web Page Revisitation Revisited: Implications of a Long-term Click-stream Study of Web Browser Usage.* CHI 2007, 597–606.

Orlowski, A. (2004, 6.1.). Jobs caps snoozathon with cut-down Emagic, iPod. *The Register.*

Orlowski, A. (2005). Web 2.0: It's. Like Your Brain on LSD!. http://www.theregister.co.uk/2005/10/21 /web_two_point_nought_poll/ Accessed 28.8.2008

Page, S. R., Johnsgard, T. J., Albert, U., and Allen, C. D. (1996). *User Customization of a Word Processor.* CHI '96: Proceedings of the SIGCHI conference on Human factors in computing systems, New York, NY, USA, 340–346.

Pape, B., Bleek, W-G., Jackewitz, I., and Janneck, M. (2002). *Software Requirements for Project-Based Learning – CommSy as an Exemplary Approach.* Proc. HICSS 2002.

Parker, I. (2001). Absolute PowerPoint. *The New Yorker*, 76–87.

Parks, M. R., and Floyd, K. (1996). Making Friends in Cyberspace. *Journal of Computer Mediated Communication*, 1(4) .

Paul, M., and Rob, B. (2000). Intermediaries personalize information streams. *Communications on ACM*, *43*(8), 96–101.

Perez, J. C. (2005). Q&A: Vint Cerf on Google's Challenges, Aspirations. http://www.computerworld.com/developmenttopics/development/story/0,10801,106535,00.html Accessed 20.8.2008

Perin, C. (1991). Electronic social fields in bureaucracies. *Commun. ACM*, 34(12), 75–82.

phpBB. (2006). phpBB.com: Creating Communities. http://www.phpbb.com/ Accessed 17.7. 2008

Pickering, J. M., and King, J. L. (1992). *Hardwiring Weak Ties: Individual and Institutional Issues in Computer Mediated Communication.* CSCW '92: Proceedings of the 1992 ACM conference on Computer-supported cooperative work, New York, NY, USA, 356–361.

Pipek, V. (2005). *From Tailoring to Appropriation Support: Negotiating Groupware Usage.* University of Oulu, Oulu, Finland. Available online at http://herkules.oulu.fi/isbn9514276302/

Pogue, D. (2004). *GarageBand: The Missing Manual (Missing Manuals).* Sebastopol, CA: O'Reilly & Associates.

Pogue, D., and Story, D. (2006). *iPhoto 6: The Missing Manual (Missing Manual).* Cambridge, MA: O'Reilly & Associates.

Press, L. (1993). Before the Altair: the history of personal computing. *Communications on ACM*, 36(9), 27–33.

Preve, F. (2004). *Power Tools for GarageBand: Creating Music with Audio Recording, MIDI Sequencing, and Loops.* San Francisco, CA: Backbeat Books.

Quint, V., and Vatton, I. (2005). *Towards Active Web Clients.* DocEng '05: Proceedings of the 2005 ACM symposium on Document engineering, New York, NY, USA, 168–176.

Ragtime. (2005). Etwas Einzigartiges schaffen. http://www.ragtime.de/Content/firmen-geschichte/index.html Accessed 5.10.2008

Ragtime. (2006a). Die RagTime GmbH stellt RagTime Privat ein. http://www.ragtime.de/link.cgi?presse_mitteilung&anc = rt6privat&pg = presse_mitteilung.html Accessed 8.10. 2008

Ragtime. (2006b). Neu in Ragtime 6. Ragtime GmbH. Available online at: http://www.ragtime.de/content/preview/Neu_in_RagTime_6.pdf

Raskin, J. (2000b). *The Humane Interface: New Directions for Designing Interactive Systems.* Upper Saddle River, NJ: Addison-Wesley Professional.

Rickman, J. T., Sunkel, M. J., and Hobbs, J. (1979). *Word Processing and Data Entry Computing Services.* SIGUCCS '79: Proceedings of the 7th annual ACM SIGUCCS conference on User services, New York, NY, USA, 68–72.

Robbins, A. (1999). *Unix in a Nutshell: A Desktop Quick Reference for SVR4 and Solaris 7 (3rd Edition).* Cambridge, MA: O'Reilly Media, Inc.

Robbins, A. (2005). *Unix in a Nutshell, Fourth Edition.* Cambridge, MA: O'Reilly Media, Inc.

Robbins, A., and Beebe, N. H. F. (2005). *Classic Shell Scripting*. Cambridge, MA: O'Reilly Media, Inc.

Rohall, S. L., Gruen, D., Moody, P., Wattenberg, M., Stern, M., Kerr, B., Stachel, B., Dave, K., Armes, R., and Wilcox, E. (2004). *ReMail: A Reinvented Email Prototype*. CHI '04: CHI '04 extended abstracts on Human factors in computing systems, New York, NY, USA, 791–792.

Rosenfeld, L., and Morville, P. (2002). *Information Architecture for the World Wide Web*. Cambridge, MA: O'Reilly.

Rosenthal, H. (2006). *Discovering Automator*. South Carolina, SC: BookSurge Publishing.

RPO. (2005, 23.12.). Moderne Technik überfordert häufig. Rheinische Post Online.

Board, RSSA. (2006). Really Simple Syndication. http://www.rssboard.org/rss-specification Accessed 10.6.2008

Rubin, C. (1999). *Running Microsoft Word 2000 (Running)*. Microsoft Press.

Schumacher-Rasmussen, E. (2004). Review: Apple GarageBand. http://www.eventdv.net/ Articles/ReadArticle.aspx?CategoryID = 52&ArticleID = 8707 Accessed 23.5.

Schwartz, J. (2003, 28 September). The level of discourse continues to slide. *The New York times*, p. 12 col. 1.

Sears, A., and Shneiderman, B. (1994). Split menus: effectively using selection frequency to organize menus. *ACM Transaction on Computer – Human Interactions*, 1(1), 27–51.

Post-Intelligencer, S. (2006). Google Admits Online Stumble. http://seattlepi.nwsource.com/ business/257040_googlestore26.html Accessed 13.10.2008

Secrist, L. J. (1980). *Should We Get Involved in Word Processing?* SIGUCCS '80: Proceedings of the 8th annual ACM SIGUCCS conference on user services, New York, NY, USA, 60–61.

Sellers, D. (2005). 'Macsimum News' Interviews Creator of iPhoto, iMovie, Bubbler. http:// www.macsimumnews.com/ index.php/archive/macsimum_news_interviews_creator_of_i-photo_imovie_bubbler/ Accessed 25.5.2008

Sengers, P., and Gaver, B. (2006). *Staying Open to Interpretation: Engaging Multiple Meanings in Design and Evaluation*. DIS '06: Proceedings of the 6th ACM conference on Designing Interactive systems, New York, NY, USA, 99–108.

Sergio, F. (2001). FreeGorifero. http://www.freegorifero.com/weblog/2002_11_01_weblo-g_archive.html Accessed 10.10.2008

Sharon, T., Lieberman, H., and Selker, T. (2003). *A Zero-Input Interface for Leveraging Group Experience in Web Browsing*. IUI '03: Proceedings of the 8th international conference on Intelligent user interfaces, New York, NY, USA, 290–292.

Shaw, R. (2005). Web 2.0? It doesn't exist. http://blogs.zdnet.com/ip-telephony/?p = 805 Accessed 9.10.2008

Shedroff, N. (2001). *Experience Design 1*. Waite Group Press.

Shneiderman, B. (2003). *Promoting Universal Usability with Multi-Layer Interface Design*. CUU '03: Proceedings of the 2003 conference on Universal usability, New York, NY, USA, 1–8.

Sievers, D. (2004). Say NO by default. \http://www.oreillynet.com/pub/wlg/5384 Accessed 17.7.2008

Simons, T. (2004). Does PowerPoint Make You Stupid? *Presentations Magazine*, 24–31. VNU Business Media.

Siracusa, J. (2001). Macworld Expo San Francisco 2001. http://arstechnica.com/reviews/ 01q1/macwldsf/mwsf-7.html#itunes Accessed 21.7.2008

Sixtus, M. (2006, 10). Jenseits von gut und böse: Der unheimliche Erfolg von Google. *c't Magazin für Computertechnik*, 162–167. heise.

SketchUp. (2006). SketchUpdate 04.27.06. http://de.sketchup.com/index.php?id = 1444

Smith, T. (2005). Apple Sued Over iTunes – again. *The Register* http://www.theregister.co.uk/ 2005/ 06/21/apple_sued_over_itunes/ Accessed 13.10.2008

Steinberg. (2006a). Cubase SL 3. http://www.steinberg.de/34_1.html Accessed 2.10.

Steinberg. (2006b). Feature Comparison. http://www.steinberg.net/552_1.html Accessed 2.10.2008

Strauss, M., Pape, B., Adam, F., Klein, M., and Reinecke, L. (2003). CommSy-Evaluations-bericht 2003: Softwareunterstützung für selbstständiges und kooperatives Lernen. *Berichte des Fachbereichs Informatik der Universität Hamburg, FBI-HH-B-251/03.*

Sutherland, I. E. (1963). *Sketchpad: A Man-Machine Graphical Communication System.* MIT,. Available online at http://www.cl.cam.ac.uk/TechReports/UCAM-CL-TR-574.pdf

Tassabehji, R., and Vakola, M. (2005). Business email: the killer impact. *Communications on ACM,* 48(11), 64–70.

Terdiman, D. (2005). IPod Shuffle Sparks Stampede. *Wired Magazine.*

Tessler, F. (2006). Keynote 3: Presentation software keeps improving with age. *Macworld* http://www.macworld.com/ 2006/01/reviews/keynote3/index.php Accessed 17.7.2008

Tischler, L., and Mayer, M. (2005). The Beauty of Simplicity. *Fast Company,* 100, 52.

Trigg, R. H., and Bødker, S. (1994). *From Implementation to Design: Tailoring and the Emergence of Systematization in CSCW.* CSCW '94: Proceedings of the 1994 ACM conference on Computer supported cooperative work, New York, NY, USA, 45–54. Available online at citeseer.ist.psu.edu/trigg94from.html

Tsandilas, T., and schraefel, mc. (2005). *An Empirical Assessment of Adaptation Techniques.* CHI '05: CHI '05 extended abstracts on human factors in computing systems, New York, NY, USA, 2009–2012.

Tufte, E. (2003). PowerPoint is evil: Power corrupts. PowerPoint corrupts absolutely. *Wired Magazine,* 11.09.

Tufte, E. R. (2006). *The Cognitive Style of PowerPoint: Pitching Out Corrupts Within,* Second Edition. Cheshire, CO: Graphics Press.

Uren, V., Shum, S. B., Li, G., Domingue, J., and Motta, E. (2003). *Scholarly Publishing and Argument in Hyperspace.* WWW '03: Proceedings of the 12th international conference on World Wide Web, New York, NY, USA, 244–250.

Voida, A., Grinter, R. E., Ducheneaut, N., Edwards, W. K., and Newman, M. W. (2005). *Listening in: Practices Surrounding iTunes Music Sharing.* CHI '05: Proceedings of the SIGCHI conference on human factors in computing systems, New York, NY, USA, 191–200.

Wales, J. (2005). *Wikipedia in the Free Culture Revolution.* OOPSLA '05: Companion to the 20th annual ACM SIGPLAN conference on Object-oriented programming, systems, languages, and applications, New York, NY, USA, 5–5.

Weinberger, D. (2002). *Small Pieces, Loosely Joined: A Unified Theory of the Web.* Cambridge, MA: Perseus Pub.

Weinreich, H., Buchmann, V., and Lamersdorf, W. (2003). *Scone: Ein Framework zur evaluativen Realisierung von Erweiterungen des Webs.* Tagungsband Kommunikation in Verteilten Systemen – KiVS 2003, 31–42.

Weinreich, H., Obendorf, H., Herder, E., and Mayer, M. (2006a). *Der Wandel in der Benutzung des World Wide Web.* Mensch & Computer 2006.

Weinreich, H., Obendorf, H., Herder, E., and Mayer, M. (2006b). *Off the Beaten Tracks: Exploring Three Aspects of Web Navigation.* WWW '06: Proceedings of the 15th international conference on World Wide Web, New York, NY, USA, 133–142.

Weinreich, H., Obendorf, H., and Lamersdorf, W. (2004). HyperScout: Linkvorschau im World Wide Web. *i-com: Zeitschrift für interaktive und kooperative Medien,* 1(3), 4–12.

Weinreich, H., Obendorf, H., and Lamersdorf, W. (2001). *The Look of the Link – Concepts for the User Interface of Extended Hyperlinks.* Proceedings of the 12th ACM Conference on Hypertext and Hypermedia, University of Aarhus, Århus, Denmark, New York, NY, USA, 19–28.

Weiser, M. (1993). Some computer science issues in ubiquitous computing. *Communications of the ACM,* 36(7), 75–84.

Weiser, M. (1991). The computer for the twenty-first century. *Scientific American,* 94–104.

Weiser, M., and Brown, J. S. (1997). The coming age of calm technolgy. *Beyond Calculation: The Next Fifty Years.* 75–85. Copernicus New York, NY, USA.

Wenger, E. (1999). *Communities of Practice: Learning, Meaning, and Identity (Learning in Doing: Social, Cognitive & Computational Perspectives S.)*. Cambridge, MA: Cambridge University Press.

Whittaker, S., Bellotti, V., and Gwizdka, J. (2006). Email in personal information management. *Communications of ACM*, 49(1), 68–73.

Whittaker, S., Jones, Q., Nardi, B., Creech, M., Terveen, L., Isaacs, E., and Hainsworth, J. (2004). ContactMap: Organizing communication in a social desktop. *ACM Transactions on Computer – Human Interactions*, 11(4), 445–471.

Whittaker, S., and Sidner, C. (1996). *Email Overload: Exploring Personal Information Management of Email*. CHI '96: Proceedings of the SIGCHI conference on Human factors in computing systems, New York, NY, USA, 276–283.

Wilkinson, S. (2002). uDrive Me Crazy. http://www.popsci.com/popsci/printerfriendly/automotivetech/e0633bcc2eb84010vgnvcm1000004eecbccdrcrd.html Accessed 10.10. otherNames

Wilson, E. V. (2002). Email winners and losers. *Communications of ACM*, 45(10), 121–126.

Witt, R. J., and Tyerman, S. P. (2002). *Reducing Cognitive Overhead on the World Wide Web*. CRPITS '02: Proceedings of the twenty-fifth Australasian conference on Computer science, Darlinghurst, Australia, 311–320.

Wollenweber, F. (2004). *Kollaborative Nutzung des World-Wide-Web*. Unpublished Diploma Thesis, University of Hamburg, Hamburg. Available online at http://vsys-www.informatik. uni-hamburg.de/getDoc.php/thesis/132/FrankWdiplomarbeit-final-070104.pdf

Wurman, R. S. (1991). *Information Anxiety*. New York, NY: Bantam Books.

Wurman, R. S., and Bradford, P. (1996). *Information Architects*. New York, NY: Graphis Inc.

Xerox. (1983). Xerox Star and the Professional : Promotional video for the Xerox Star.

Zeleznik, R. C., Herndon, K. P., and Hughes, J. F. (1996). *SKETCH: An Interface for Sketching 3D Scenes*. SIGGRAPH '96: Proceedings of the 23rd annual conference on Computer graphics and interactive techniques, New York, NY, USA, 163–170.

Ziefle, M. (2002). The influence of user expertise and phone complexity on performance, ease of use and learnability of different mobile phones. *Behaviour and Information Technology – BIT*, 21(5), 303–311.

Zielinski, D. (2003). Power has always been the point. *Presentations Magazine*, 2, 4(6) VNU Business Media.

Züllighoven, H. (2004). *Object-Oriented Construction Handbook*. Heidelberg: dpunkt Verlag.

Züllighoven, H., Bäumer, D., and Bleek, W-G. (1998). *Das objektorientierte Konstruktionshandbuch. Nach dem Werkzeug- und Materialansatz*. Heidelberg: dpunkt Verlag.

Chapter 7
Designing the Minimal

Almost no one seems to be able to recognize good design.

—Theodor Holm Nelson (1990, 236)

While understanding simplicity can be difficult, systematically designing for simplicity is more difficult. Thankfully, this is not true for minimalism alone—HCI, in general, needs to incorporate practices from more constructive disciplines: "The field of usability design takes root in the cognitive sciences—a combination of psychology, computer science, human factors, and engineering. These are all analytical fields. The discipline prides itself on its scientific basis and experimental rigor. The hidden danger is to neglect areas that are not easily addressed in the framework of science and engineering." (Norman, 2002)

As the last chapter illustrated, functional, structural, architectural and compositional minimalism together establish a minimalist standpoint that has proven useful for *analyzing* designs and explaining their simplicity. While that is useful for those interested in examining the success of existing designs and find good examples necessary to build upon, this chapter seeks a more openly constructive approach, evaluating different applications of minimalism in the activity of designing. Having a software background, I will be concentrating on software development and highlight aspects of minimalism useful for implementation in software development processes.

This chapter starts out with an argument for systematically adapting or changing the development process to incorporate reduction; only through changes in the interpretation of process patterns can a sustainable impact on design be made. Then, both a direct and an indirect approach are illustrated on how development can be changed: the minimal design game is a technique that explicitly aims to reduce the design space, to extract the core of a design, and to make visible the interrelationships of other parts to this core. It is a formalization of the design advice taken from the last chapter and will require a deep understanding and identification with the different notions of minimalism for full effect.

Changing the development process by choosing and providing a background for existing techniques, however, allows a more subtle focus on reduction that might succeed even where not all partaking stakeholders start with an

H. Obendorf, *Minimalism*, Human-Computer Interaction Series,
DOI 10.1007/978-1-84882-371-6_7, © Springer-Verlag London Limited 2009

understanding of minimalism or, at least, a shared interpretation of simplicity: Personas and scenarios are used as examples to highlight the effect of focus in scope on users and their tasks. A discussion of agile development techniques points at iterative development techniques as a means for creating comparatively simple systems and the results of a continued use of values in participatory design processes suggest that the focus of design must extend over more than only the initial conception phase into what is usually left to maintenance crews.

7.1 Process Matters

In this chapter, changing the design process is presented as the method of choice for changing the resulting design. Although, in the end, the quality of design— like anything—depends on the people implementing it and great designers will be able contribute good designs in almost any environment, this argumentation relies on the belief that values and methods used in development processes have a dramatic and sustainable effect on all participants, the subjective quality of work and the resulting products.

A short historical sketch of the rapidly changing field of information technology provides some background for the bias towards iterative and agile development expressed here. In the early days of computer science, applications were considered an appendage to the physical systems that did the computing.[1] However, the importance and cost of production of software have long outgrown that of hardware (Boehm, 1975)—and in the 1970s, the field realized that it had a crisis: projects became unmanageable, over budget, late and delivered poor quality. In one word, complexity had grown too large to be manageable (Dijkstra, 1972).

This "software crisis" resulted in the call for controlling methods and led to the systematical attempt of introducing engineering methods to software design and implementation, influencing corporate culture and approaches to developing interactive products until today. Plans and processes were created that support the analysis of requirements, the design, implementation, roll-out and maintenance of software. Their objective was the on-time, in-budget creation of monolithic blocks of well-defined features. With time, these blocks grew larger and larger as systems (and programming languages) grew—and processes were optimized to deal with managing this increasing complexity.

From a minimalist perspective, even if perfect engineering would be able to create increasingly complex software, this would not necessarily benefit the user. If engineering would restrict itself to the execution of design orders and to the realization of given requirements, the result of complex requirements would

---

[1] The predominance of the physical aspects of computing is illustrated by the names of the older scientific organizations dealing with information technology, such as the Association for Computing Machinery or the British Computer Society—explicit reference is made to the physical equipment.

clearly be a complex product. Apart from the feature overload from which the user would have to suffer, the internal complexity of the software is dramatically increased with the number and complexity of requirements.[2] Consequently, complexity in software engineering is not only defined in terms of computing; algorithmic and programmatic complexity are supplemented by *domain complexity*. As especially for complex use domains, some complexity is unavoidable, *essential complexity* is usually discerned from *incidental complexity* and software engineering techniques aim to reduce the latter and structure the former.

From all the lessons learned in software engineering, two are picked here to serve as motivations for the design of development processes: First, making plans for all eventualities, and providing a conceptually clean solution was a frequent reason for software failure as unnecessary complexity was introduced. Gabriel (1991) described the successful strategy of UNIX and C as "worse-is-better"—taking a more flexible approach proved often to be more successful than doing "the-right-thing". Second, the experience of thousands of software projects tells that, for various reasons, a sizable part, if not a majority of the requirements arrive or change after development has begun (comp. e.g. Jones, 1995).

The resulting form of development are iterative approaches that do not try to sequentially follow process phases but instead interleave different activities and enable the development team to slowly grow the software from a functional and manageable core, integrating customer and client feedback (Floyd, 1987). As the need for interaction with stakeholders and iterative design surfaced, design activities were attributed to the developer's role and replaced the rigor of engineering to some degree; software construction was understood as a creative activity. If software construction is neither pure design nor pure engineering but also understood as more than a craft, engineering methods are necessary to plan: if not design, then, at least, programmer behavior can be projected. To some degree, the process determines the product and methods determine their results.

As it presents an interface between the different disciplines and a way to introduce the minimalist perspective into design, the design process is thus, here, an object of discussion; when a design or development process is discussed in the following, it is assumed that this process denotes a number of correlated activities over a period of time. These activities can, but need not, formally be grouped into phases that follow a linear sequence. While the start of this process is often fixed, in practice, the end tends to follow less strict rules as many projects take longer than assumed or result in follow-up projects. What can be defined is the time from the start of design to the first shipment; in a waterfall

---

[2] The study of software architecture is, in large, part a study of software structure. Edsger Dijkstra (1976) pointed out the importance of how software is partitioned and structured, as opposed to simply programming so as to produce a correct result. David Parnas contributed to the field with his seminal publications on information-hiding in modules (1972) and software structures (1974).

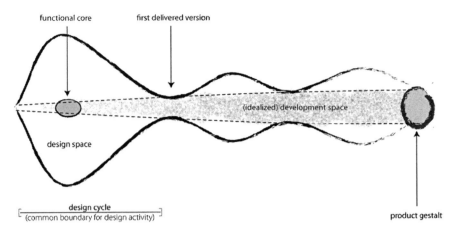

Fig. 7.1 Idealized design process without gaps between design and development

process, the latter can coincide with the end of a project (comp. Fig. 7.1). Through development, deployment and use, it is assumed, can a product gestalt be identified that defines the responsibilities and limits of a design—and thus, a potential limit for feature expansion within a single tool.

Some aspects of development processes are not visible in Fig. 7.1: Although product maintenance is usually not considered part of the design process, this discussion will argue that design and maintenance need to be coupled to cultivate reduction. Further, the activities of design and implementation will be considered as integrated; in practice, you will rather find design and development in different parts of an organization. Although both design and development may be iterative, the necessity for communication and documentation limits this quality to some extent. The visualized process relates but to a single design; development of a use environment will comprise several interdependent design processes. A process is also considered open-ended here as follow-up projects are associated with the initial design and interpreted as continuations.

Two different approaches are sketched in the remains of this chapter: the first is a direct invocation of minimalist design heuristics in the form of the minimal design game. The design game is based on the results of the previous chapter and aims to make trade-offs explicit and identify critical areas where reduction can help improve a design. Within the logic of this book, it seems a consequent solution; experience with real-world projects has shown, however, that it is difficult to introduce a new technique that only aims to reduce. Therefore, existing techniques are examined for their reductive qualities—more easily implemented and practice-proven, these methods can help to change a process if reduction is explicitly defined as an objective of their use.

7.2 A Direct Approach: Reduction as a Design Activity

> The ability to simplify means to eliminate the unnecessary
> so that the necessary may speak.
>
> —Hans Hofmann, painter

In the last chapter, *functional, structural, architectural* and *compositional minimalism* have been applied to the analysis of finished designs. A constructive application in the form of a design technique is manifest as these notions of minimalism demonstrated their value for design criticism. The technique described here defines reduction as an explicit activity in the design of interactive systems. It draws on industrial design practice and has only approximate equivalents in HCI methodology; while Usability techniques, e.g., expert reviews (Molich and Nielsen, 1990), focus on the human-computer interface of a design, the scope of the reduction activity is deliberately kept broad and the whole design is criticized in the tradition of *design crits* (comp. Wolf et al., 2006).

Design crits play an important role in *creative design activity*, which, unlike HCI methodology that traditionally either aims to identify requirements or evaluate effects of designs, tries to explore the design space through the creation of many parallel ideas and concepts, and subsequent selection. Löwgren (1995) sketched a consciously over-generalized picture as he contrasted *engineering design* that "is amenable to structured descriptions and seen as a chain of transformations from the abstract (requirements) to the concrete (resulting artifact)" with *creative design* that "is seen as a tight interplay between problem setting and problem solving ... [and] is inherently unpredictable" (ibid.).

Typical design games support the expansion of the design space and focus on inspiration, on creativity and on divergent thought—the nature of design aiming at innovation is determined by divergent and expansionist motives. On the other hand, an important part of design is the convergence through reduction and refinement. Reduction requires criteria: A filter capable of capturing essential use activities is necessary, often the projected need for functionality is used as one. The *Minimal Design Game* described below tries to focus the designer's attention to this need for reduction, for thoughtful selection—and the trade-offs involved with necessary complexity. The central idea is to use the informal frame of a game to lower the barrier to reflection about design in terms of minimalism. The game thus tries to bridge the gap between the theoretical discussion of the nature of minimalism and actual design practice; the four principles identified above can be directly applied to practical design.

Design games have a tradition in participatory design where they are used to construct a "collaborative design laboratory" that makes it possible to "play around" with the design. Data from field studies is sometimes used to prepare material to be used in the design process (Brandt and Messeter, 2004; Donovan and Brereton, 2004; Brandt, 2006). Exploration is encouraged by the ease of putting up "what if" questions; the manipulation of tangible artifacts clearly indicates the current design focus. Rules governing the game can be employed to structure the discussion, e.g., the definition of a common goal could increase the involvement of participants or introducing a turn-taking rule might force everyone into an active role—appropriate when end users are part of the design team. Design games are typically used in the beginning of a (participatory) design session and try to encourage lateral thinking processes, increase the designers' sensibility towards certain aspects of the context, or simply increase the feeling of a common vision within the group. Design games can also be applied when design is not progressing swiftly and uncommon alternatives are sought.

The Minimal Design Game is a deliberate counter-design to typical design games trying to call out creativity or lateral thinking in the player. Here, the design game is used differently, as a form of *design crit*, and as a "thought experiment". It tries to enhance analytic and synthetic qualities in the player, using a simple 2 × 2 grid of interpretations of reduction to encourage experimentation with dissection. The Minimalist Design Game, as described here, is a reflective game; it requires an existing design vision, and several different design ideas that might normally be minted into a single design. Playing the game should invite the designers to take a step back and look at the different aspects of a design to analyze where and how they match, ultimately resulting in a design that is not a combination created by adding different ideas but one that follows a consistent vision.

One goal for the design of the game itself was simplicity—following the belief that the design of user interaction works best when simple materials are used that stress the prototypical character of design work, e.g., in paper prototyping (Rettig, 1994; Snyder, 2003). Also, the tangibility of physical artifacts simplifies collaboration and reduces distraction, as the medium of design is well known (Scaife et al., 1997)—without sacrificing realism (Virzi et al., 1996). For involving several designers already working with paper on tables, a board game (see Fig. 7.2) promises seamless design interaction. The playful nature of the

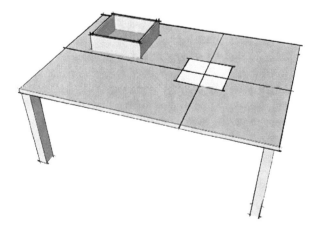

Fig. 7.2 Table layout with playing board extended by strings and "leftovers" box

game might also make reflection about the minimalist nature of the design artifact seem less daunting a task.

7.2.1 The Minimal Design Game

In the following, a short account of how a Minimal Design Game might be played is given, what is needed for preparation and what can be the end product (Fig. 7.2).

The game proceeds in two phases: an *analysis phase* and a *synthesis phase*. In preparation, the game board is placed on a table and then the design artifacts (sketches, prototypes, functional definitions, etc.) are placed on the table. The game logic prefers design artifacts with small granularity, so a preparation by 'copy and cut' can ease dissection of the available material. Now, the design team can use the grid as an encouragement to think about aspects of the design that could be reduced to yield something better where less could be more. This could mean that some functionality seems not essential or that by omitting reference to information, the interaction complexity can be reduced. It could mean that reorganizing the design around smaller, less-complex building blocks could increase transparency or that the envisioned use situations should be freed from nonessential activities.

Table 7.1 The spatial layout of the four aspects of minimalism on the table

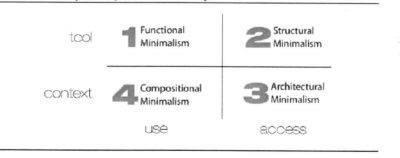

The spatial layout (compare Table 7.1) echoes the model that represents the interactions between the different notions of minimalism (Section 3.3.5): functional minimalism and structural minimalism focus on the design of a single tool, compositional and architectural minimalism highlight the interaction between different tools; the use aspect is dominant in functional and compositional minimalism, while structural and architectural minimalism center on access structure. To complement these abstract dimensions of minimalism, concrete design questions such as those that follow might be used to encourage thinking about the different ways of reduction that are possible:

1. What is the primary function, what is it that we really want to be able to do? What are important but less central functions? Which functions are motivated by the context, which are motivated by technology?
2. How is that purpose of the artifact conveyed to the user? How is information presented, what are the structures used in interaction? What are the choices for the user at a given point? What model of the application will she/he develop?
3. Can the system be simplified by splitting it up into parts? Does the user identify and understand the simple (or already well known) parts of the design? How do they combine?
4. What is the initial use context? Did we draw any conclusions from it that limit use in other contexts? Did we introduce limitations to combine tools in our application and if so, why?

While it is not uncommon for these questions to be asked in product design, the combination and context of their asking is new—a similar relationship than that of the notions of minimalism and HCI lore (see Section 4.3). As the purpose of the game—reflection on the previous design with a special focus on options for reduction, finding out where "less is more"—was made explicit, they act together to question design aspects, probing for the essential.[3]

Whenever a possible reduction is identified, the relevant design artifacts are placed on the board within the appropriate analytic dimension, and the reduction is added using Post-it notes, or physically cut out of the artifact. The eliminated features, interaction methods, structural features or use situations are placed in the leftovers box. When the design team agrees that no more reduction is possible, and all aspects of the design are represented in their minimal, essential form somewhere on the grid, the first phase ends. In the second phase, the leftovers box is revisited and its contents are put in relation to the "core" visible on the table. This ensures that migration paths to more complex designs are held open. Whenever possible, a path to integration of the design idea is considered before finally burying the design idea; however, strict preference is given to the integrity and compactness of the resulting design: what does not fit the picture will be left out. This is no strict rule but its violations will make clear the trade-offs involved with increasing complexity.

Designing an information artifact that is, in some sense, minimal is already a difficult task, the design of a second version of that artifact is even more demanding. Commonly, in second versions, more features are expected resulting in more structure. If this eventual need for expansion is not considered in the initial design, it will be very difficult to find a migration path. Examples where this proved detrimental to the product's sustained success include the Palm

---

[3] Bill Buxton explained the designers' call for a "green light process", with an up-front design phase preceding software engineering (Buxton, 2003) to be motivated by the same dilemma: development often follows functional specifications, adding more and more functionality, without an understanding of the overall design vision.

Pilot series and its lack of affordable extensions. An assumption in the *Minimal Design Game* is that it might help to plan ahead for extensions: within a minimal design strategy, first, an overall vision must be found that will incorporate both the essential design and paths for expansion. This is easier where the design artifact does not need to compete with traditional personal computers, but even there, success is possible when a niche market is targeted—as perhaps the Tablet PC might prove.

7.2.2 First Experiences

The *Minimal Design Game* was evaluated with a small number of students that voluntarily applied the technique to a design problem. No explicit explanation of the notions of minimalism was given before the test and only the questions reproduced above were presented as a guide for the game, as this was considered a preliminary evaluation designed to find out how well the questions were phrased and how much explanation would be necessary.

While this informal procedure cannot replace a more realistic evaluation, it yielded a few interesting results: most participants immediately understood the notions of *functional* and *structural minimalism*, and had no difficulties producing advice that related to these notions. They were able to identify a significant amount of functionality and of structure that was unnecessary for themselves; consequently, a layered approach was sought by most. Some, however, had problems interpreting *architectural* and *compositional minimalism*—although they later indicated understanding after the terms had been discussed with them. Although the pre-test conditions[4] may be partially to blame, architectural and compositional minimalism are not obvious in their interpretation of simplicity—as this book speculated during the analysis of products in Chapter 6 and also when minimalism was put in relation to HCI lore in Chapters 4 and 5. Both architectural and compositional minimalism are unusual and more difficult notions; and they both make use of terms that are already in use in computer science and specifically in software development. The misunderstandings that surfaced during the pre-test support the last argument as some participants confused software architecture with the architecture of the interface, and service composition—the developer's task—with user interpretation.

A second result from the test setting became clear in informal post-interviews: most participants felt that a truly minimal solution would not necessarily be a good solution. This critical stance was welcome as it underlines a proposed value of minimalism: the use of minimalism in design critique establishes a perspective that is in itself a possible object of critique. Unlike "simplicity", minimalism will not be pursued blindly. Extreme models have been very successfully used as a design method (comp. Djajadiningrat et al., 2000; Dix et al., 2006) to remove unnecessary design blocks—and often, the most simple solution is the hardest to come by, as it is difficult to believe that it could work being so simple.

7.2.3 Discussion

In the pre-test setting, students had to criticize a design they were not completely familiar with, although they had previously seen it. A realistic design setting
would allow design judgments of the context and make the game a more useful
tool. Still, an application of the *Minimal Design Game* in a real design setting
must carefully consider how much training is necessary to clearly understand
the different notions of minimalism, and to enable an informed choice about
which reductions to apply. It also seems to be inherently more difficult to use a
game for design analysis in *architectural* and *compositional* terms, as these
perspectives require a focus encompassing more than "just" the design artifact.

The immediate transfer of the defined notions of minimalism as values to
design practice is possible only after their meaning has been negotiated and
defined. Drawing on this experience, subtler modes of using minimalism to
enhance design processes are demonstrated in the following sections: First,
design techniques using scenarios are analyzed and reducing effects which are
obscured from the more immediate function of scenarios are identified. This
allows the implementation of a design process that aims to support architectural
minimalism. On a more abstract level, a real development process is analyzed
from a minimalist standpoint, providing suggestions for optimization and
discovering the use of a technique to support compositional minimalism.

7.3 The Indirect Approach: Changing the Process

> *I used to walk head first into brick walls.*
> *Only over time, I acquired an important skill: first look for the door.*
> — Anonymous

When trying to change the course of design, the direct route is not always the
shortest path to success. While the results of using a technique such as the
minimal design game are immediately connected to minimalism—and would
help to prove value in the minimalist standpoint for design, from a practitioner's perspective, there are many circumstances in which a more subtle
approach is necessary. Instead of advocating reduction directly, minimalism
can help to choose from existing and well-proven techniques from the HCI
field—and guide their application. As background knowledge, minimalism will
help understand what is to be achieved with the implementation of Usability
techniques and consequently enable to make better use of them—it is crucial to
not only understand the technique and how to apply it but also why.

While most methods will affect more than one notion of minimalism, associations with functional, structural, architectural and compositional reduction
are simplified here in order to create a small taxonomy that might be helpful in
choosing techniques. Example techniques discussed here include personas,
scenarios, requirements negotiation from agile development, and the explicit
introduction of values into software development.

7.3.1 Scoping Reduction

Choosing usability techniques will often be based on experience and on the kind of data that might be available or seem necessary. Here, a different approach is suggested: different techniques can help to reduce the design and so, from the four notions of minimalism, four different types of reduction—in terms of a design activity—are derived that motivate the choice of techniques in the discussion of individual techniques.

7.3.1.1 Functional Reduction

Without a clear understanding of the specific quality that a design should expose to the world, finding a core of functionality is impossible. At the heart of the question for the *minimal necessary functionality* is thus the definition of "what it is" that is to be designed—or in the words of David Kelley, CEO of IDEO, "If I'm trying to design a tape recorder, I can create one that's yellow that you can dunk in water; I can create one that's highly precise; I can create one that has 27 heads or scads of features—that's what I mean by 'deciding what it is'" (Kelley in a highly readable interview in Winograd, 1996, Chapter 8).

The question of "what it is" thus comes down to the question of what is missing—suggesting a focus on two design activities: the analysis of competing products, and of the future users. Together, these form the background from which the new design must stand out, and although they do not define any specific new quality, they determine and limit possibilities. As analysis of future users is typically a part of user-centered design, the discussion here will center on defining users for the purpose of design—a function that is fulfilled by the popular persona technique.[4]

7.3.1.2 Structural Reduction

Reducing the observed complexity of access structures requires a firm understanding of the ways in which the activities are structured that require users to depend on delivered functionality. Usability failures are often caused by a mismatch of the access structures, or underlying use models, of Users and the software. It can thus be said that many Usability techniques deal in one way or another with this mismatch problem.

To take the most basic Usability techniques, both expert reviews and the results of user testing deal with potential use problems from the perspective of users—many of the problems detected are related to the difficulties of accessing

---

[4] As discussed later, it is sometimes difficult to decide what exactly the core functionality of a design might be—due to changing requirements, changing environments, novelty or an interaction of design with use. Iterative and agile development can thus also help to define core functionality.

functionality and the expected "solutions" are usually incremental improve-ments. The more the expert and the test users know about the work of the target users, the better the results. At the other end of the range of methods are design metaphors that try to transfer knowledge about existing artifacts into soft-ware—or build upon common knowledge about the source of a metaphor. Context beyond the single task is used by another set of Usability techniques that tries to support modeling the design context, with its communication to users often being a secondary function. This chapter will use scenarios as an example technique.

7.3.1.3 Architectural Reduction

Techniques for reducing the architecture of a design are less easily marked out: design usually focuses on a single product, and evaluation methods also tend to try to isolate factors. Further, architectural reduction goes beyond interface design, including both interaction and systems design.

However, as the identification of "tools" that can be communicated to users and the distribution of responsibility across tools depends as much on context as structural or functional reduction, methods that identify core functionality and help understand the grouping of functionality based in the use domain are equally useful for reducing architecture. The need for considering more technical aspects such as given constraints or possible interfaces with other tools can be met as techniques from software and usability engineering move together. Techniques that help to iteratively gather feedback help to detect early on where boundaries between tools may be crossed or new units of functionality can be detected.

7.3.1.4 Compositional Reduction

Reducing the composition of a design does not mean that unintended use should be planned for. Rather, it means the removal of obstacles for unintended use or creating loosely-coupled units of functionality presenting a fair enough ratio of simplicity and power.

Methods for compositional reduction need thus to increase the flexibility of designs by removing attachments to specific procedures and by decoupling feature and function, concentrating on communicating and optimizing the effect of a feature rather than that of the intended function. Perhaps even more, as in the other notions of reduction, user feedback is key when unin-tended use needs to be gauged—who else can designers turn to for guidance if not to users? Methods that help to include users, and specifically new users, in design,[5] and methods that support the cultivation of reduction over the time of several product life-cycles seem most suited to aid compositional reduction.

---

[5] Tupperware seems to have implemented a very successful process that combines user research with marketing with distribution. Unfortunately, very little research data has found its way into usability.

7.4 Defining Scope: Using Personas

Personas are descriptions of fictitious users, often complete with representative pictures, description of families and personal interests. They can be defined on the basis of data from user research, and are used to convey a sense of the target audience to the design team. Clearly, they do not bring about a revolution in methodology: Since long before the publication of the personas technique, industrial design included techniques for market segmentation, user profiling and the definition of user roles—activities helping designers to focus on who their prospective customers would be and what they would be needing (comp. "target customer characterizations" in Moore, 1991).

Still, personas have developed quite an impact on the design of interactive software, they are widely applied in industry and have been described in books and numerous how-tos and scientific articles: their most extensive description was written by Cooper in 1999 (1999) and they have been advocated by Cooper's company ever since (comp. e.g. Brechin, 2002). Others have picked up the method as well and incorporated it into their design process (e.g. Perfetti, 2002), often using it in addition to other methods, such as contextual design (Holtzblatt, 2002) or more qualitative methods (Pruitt and Grudin, 2003).

7.4.1 Personas and Notions of Minimalism

The basic idea that stands behind personas is simple: design should be based on *empirical data* describing users, but raw data is not inherently useful and neither are many reports. *Knowledge transfer* between those who collect the data and those who approach the task of designing a product can often be improved upon as much is lost in translation. Personas focus and bundle empirical data and interpret the data in an immediately accessible format.

But there is another function for personas that is often overlooked: personas *focus* on *very few* user archetypes. The *format* of personas is *highly compressed*; months of data collection can result in one or two persona descriptions (Fig. 7.3). This is necessary for personas to fulfill their communicative function (no one will read extensive reports), but, as the argumentation will unfold, it also inherently restricts the design space.

Personas can be driven by data; advocates of this approach argue that quality increases with data (Goodwin, 2002), and that credibility is key for the acceptance of personas, and that credibility is "associated with methodological rigor and data" (Pruitt and Adlin, 2005, Chapter 1). In their great book on personas, Pruitt and Adlin link the persona technique to image diagrams (comp. Mello, 2003), a technique from marketing that extracts very few key image statements from "hundreds (if not thousands)" of statements recorded in user interviews to "facilitate deep understanding of what it is to be a customer" (ibid). While other marketing approaches could easily take the place of Mello's

Daisy Bead Company Persona - Sara Locke (Primary)

Computer Savvy
∗∗∗

Web Savvy
∗∗∗

Online Shopping Savvy
∗∗

Background

Sara is a 25 year old, single woman living in the University District of Seattle Washington. She of average height and build, fairly athletic and has brown hair and green eyes. She is unmarried but has a boyfriend of 2 1/2 hears and they are starting to think about tying the knot. She lives with her roommate, Katie, and has 2 cats, Bob and Rufus. She working in the marketing department of a high volume airplane parts manufacturer in Everett, 20 some miles north of Seattle. Her hobbies include dancing, mountain biking and snowboarding. She loves going to the movies. She also loves to shop.

Web usage

Her Internet usage is limited mainly to work related functions and E-mail. She has a hotmail account for her personal correspondence and uses it almost every day at lunch and sometimes on weekends or eves. He has shopped online but only a few times, she often finds the process confusing. Because of how she needs to use the Web at work she has a pretty good grasp of how most things work, she considers herself fairly savvy as she uses a mailing list program and spends a bit of time on marketing type sites. She doesn't enjoy spending a whole lot of time on the computer, so she prefers to get on and off quickly, and likes those sites that help her do that. Sara likes it simple and straightfor-ward.

Online shopping

As far as shopping sites goes, she likes Amazon, and Nordstroms, but doesn't have a whole lot of experience with others. She uses these mainly for gifts and would prefer to hit the mall or downtown before resorting to shopping online. Often times she may look for some information about a particular product online and then go pick it up (or not) at the store. Most of her shopping experiences have been limited to research and information gathering. When she has made a purchase she finds that sometime the process is a bit overwhelming.

Fig. 7.3 An example persona (with kind permission from Todd Zaki Warfel@messagefirst)

technique (Fig. 7.4), this illustrates Pruitt and Adlin's argumentation that design needs to be based on user data and that user data must be distilled and broken down to be useful for design.

The origin of personas is not clear—but as similarities with other methods are larger than differences, a historical description of the persona technique would have little value: Kim Goodwin (2001), a colleague of Cooper, explicitly describes them as user archetypes, a concept proposed by Mikkelson and Lee (2000). Like personas, user archetypes consist of a personal description, attributes and skills. This information is enriched with a list of high-level concerns and goals, and descriptions of some activities in the use context. Their approach was not widely adopted and, indeed, both personas and user archetypes can be seen as manifestations of user profiles as Hackos and Redish described them in

"I'm disappointed with the way it looks after installation"	"My system is too touchy"	"My system is overwhelming to learn"
The bulk bass module—I didn't want to see it first thing when we walked in the room—so we moved it to the other side.	Concern over a 6-year-old using remote and messing up the	Holding out the remote control, said "Look at this thing. It has 75 buttons!"
Speaker cables draped all over doorways, laying loosely on the floor	Grabbing the processor's remote in frustration at each channel to change in order to remove annoying echoes	Wife uses TV alone with its built-in speakers
Having a tough time cleaning the system		

Fig. 7.4 Image diagram (adapted from Mello 2003)

their book, User and Task Analysis for Interface Design (1998). User profiles describe classes of users and can both be list-based and "devoid of personality" (ibid.) or include personal descriptions and narratives.

The story that Cooper tells us about their origin is valuable for the discussion here as it vividly illustrates the objectives for Personas in design (2003):

> After eating, while my computer chugged away compiling the source code, I would walk the golf course. From my home near the ninth hole, I could traverse almost the entire course without attracting much attention from the clubhouse. During those walks I designed my program.
>
> As I walked, I would engage myself in a dialogue, play-acting a project manager, loosely based on Kathy, requesting functions and behavior from my program. I often found myself deep in those dialogues, speaking aloud, and gesturing with my arms. Some of the golfers were taken aback by my unexpected presence and unusual behavior, but that didn't bother me because I found that this play-acting technique was remarkably effective for cutting through complex design questions of functionality and interaction, allowing me to clearly see what was necessary and unnecessary and, more importantly, to differentiate between what was used frequently and what was needed only infrequently.

The persona, an imaginary person based on an intuitive interpretation of real users, is used by Cooper to represent *all users* (or at least a sizable part of all future users). It is a very broad simplification of who is going to use the software. Using personas, questions regarding the necessity and priority of features can be answered in absolute terms: instead of relying on statistical relativities such as "12% of our users will need to...", design decisions are based on Kathy's needs—and thus yield either a yes or a no. Personas thus create a strong focus on example users that makes design decisions much easier.

With the increasing use of personas, their second function, the focus on scope and the resulting reduction are identified as the real function of personas in many contexts: as smaller projects need less communication between user research and design (Spool, 2006), empathic focus—the immediate understanding and identification with users (Norman, 2004) and the focusing function—personas "eliminate the elastic user" (Reichelt, 2007)—become more important.

Personas help choosing. As Schwartz (2004, 125) observed, design means "deciding which features are worth developing" and "being forced to confront trade-offs in making decisions makes people unhappy and indecisive" (ibid.). By grounding choice in personas, options are reduced, and choices are much easier as compared to a complete analysis of who might how often use what functionality.

How does this reduce the design? First of all, by choosing to consider only a small number of users, the variety of different requirements is dramatically cut. While this does not necessarily mean that the number of tasks and activities of the example users are few and simple, *fewer users* will always need *less functionality*. By concentrating on a single user, the number of features in a design is dramatically cut, and a core functionality is implicitly defined. The result of using personas is thus a design not for the average user, but for a specific user (or at least only a handful of users)—others will then decide for themselves if they like the resulting product. The limitations and advantages of this approach are obvious as is the fact that the latter often outnumber the former.

7.4.2 Reduction and the Use of Personas

Personas are an attractively simple design tool. They have very successfully been put to use by consulting agencies (Perfetti, 2002; Holtzblatt, 2002), and by usability teams within large companies, such as Microsoft (comp. Pruitt and Grudin, 2003). An immediate reason for their success might lie within their succinctness: a difficulty of many design teams that communicate with development through written deliverables is bringing across the ideas underlying design. As far as documentation goes, personas are rather easily read and understood and if they are accepted by the development team, they provide guidance on the direction of design.

Critical for acceptance is the design of appropriate personas with regard to their audience: an effort trying to involve users in participatory design will need different representations for personas than a small company where designers and developers meet daily or a large corporation where departments partaking in the same project might be distributed over continents. The design of effective personas has been subject to intensive research and several field books have been written on the technique (for an overview of research, see Nielsen, 2004; books on the subject include Pruitt and Adlin, 2005; Kuniavsky, 2003; Mulder and Yaar, 2007)—what is perhaps not so well understood is the nature of the effect created for the design activity. This effect is here interpreted in terms of reduction.

The importance of data for the persona method depends on their use: the involvement of users is considered by some critical for their believability and their success in mixed development teams (Blomqvist and Arvola, 2002;

Goodwin, 2002; Grudin and Pruitt, 2002). Cooper's initial personas, however, were based on intuition and personal interpretation—recent publications suggest that this is still common practice and works well for introducing a UCD process or consulting—or for smaller teams (Norman, 2004; Reichelt, 2007).

The main function of Personas for this examination is the provision of a common ground for discussion through *focus*. Whether or not data is the source for building personas, to this end, the *motivation for using personas* in a project must be made explicit: as personas are used to eliminate the "elastic user" (Cooper, 1999) and focus on functional reduction, an effective use of personas both for design and implementation also depends on the function in communication that stakeholders can agree upon.

The strong focus created by personas is of fundamental importance and should be chosen with deliberate care: once personas are set, the direction of design is, as well. Personas are then useful for most directions that design can take; as Pruitt and Grudin put it (2003), "Well-crafted Personas are generative: Once fully engaged with them, you can almost effortlessly project them into new situations."

Issues of implementing personas can also result from a mismatch with the design methodology that is already in place at an organization (comp. Blomquist and Arvola, 2002); fortunately, personas interface naturally with scenarios or other models for tasks and user activities, and, thus, are often used together with other UCD methods. They also match well with techniques from software engineering, e.g., Constantine and Lockwood's user roles (a set of characteristic needs, interests, behaviors and expectations) that describe user archetypes without trying to evoke the image of a real person (Constantine and Lockwood, 2002). The reductive effect of personas is thus easily combined with other forms of reduction.

7.5 Defining Use: Scenario Techniques

Scenarios play a central role in usability engineering processes—they have long been used to illustrate possible future realities (comp. Kahn, 1962) and are now widely used as tools within design for interactive systems (Rolland et al., 1998; Hertzum, 2003). Whether they assume textual (Rosson and Carroll, 2001) or graphical form (e.g. storyboards in Beyer and Holtzblatt, 1997), whether they are written by users (Kyng, 1995a, b; Chin et al., 1997), by designers (Cooper, 1999), or employed as springboards (Bødker and Christiansen, 1997) for co-design (Carroll, 2002), they are typically used to represent context as they "emphasise *some description* of the *real world*" (Rolland et al., 1998, 1, italics mine). Jarke, Bui and Carroll summarize the function of scenarios as follow: "A scenario is a description of the *world*, in a *context* and for a *purpose*, focusing on *task interaction*. It is intended as a

means of *communication among stakeholders*, and to *constrain* requirements
engineering from one or more viewpoints (usually *not complete, consistent,
and not formal*)" (Jarke et al., 1998, italics mine). Scenarios can have a variety
of functions throughout the development process (Carroll, 1995, 1–17; Kyng,
1995a). Their concreteness is often underlined as they promise accessibility by
different stakeholder groups and thus facilitation of broad participation
(e.g. Carroll et al., 1998).

In usability engineering, a scenario can be used for one or more of the
following purposes: (1) To create a model of the current state, (2) as a medium
for exploration (Bødker and Christiansen, 1997), (3) as a medium for cooperation of user and developer (Carroll and Rosson, 1992; Carroll et al., 1998) and
finally, (4) as a (functional) specification (Rosson, 1999).[6] The formality and
exactness of scenarios varies widely with the target audience. While some of
these purposes require a high level of detail, omitting detail is necessary for
other tasks (e.g. for (4) to interface with UML, use cases or XP user stories).
Finally, the granularity of activity descriptions in scenarios varies widely, and
will often be refined in consecutive series of scenarios. Although some definitions of scenarios are very broad, and include e.g. paper prototypes, or even
software prototypes (comp. ibid.), the use of the term *scenario* shall henceforth
be limited to textual forms, possibly enhanced with graphical illustrations in the
form of storyboards.

7.5.1 Scenarios and Notions of Minimalism

> *Drama is life with the dull bits left out.*
> — attributed to Alfred Hitchcock

Scenarios are commonly used to bind a design to its context and as contextualized designs are usually considered superior, this alone is sufficient to justify
their use. Scenarios, however, have other functions that are less widely discussed. Minimalism focuses on the functionality, structure, architecture and
composition of interaction design, an—d so the perspective taken here is not
how context is represented, but how the mechanics of scenario use—both in
form and contextual representation—induce reduction in designs.

Some of the uses for scenarios—regardless of the form of scenario chosen—
are connected to the different notions of minimalism: (1) When scenarios are

---

[6] Rolland et al. (1998) classify scenarios according to their role in the requirements engineering process; they distinguish *descriptive, exploratory* and *explanatory* scenarios. The first two
map to (1) and (2), respectively, while explanatory scenarios are used to mark human or
system errors, and clarify design rationale. Explanatory scenarios thus map to both (1) and (3)
here. Rolland et al. do not explicitly examine the function of scenarios as representations of a
design specification—in this article, their discussion is limited to requirements engineering and
stops short of the design activity.

used to represent context and model the current state, they create a need for focus and conciseness—only important use practices can be included as scenarios must not exceed a certain size and their number must be kept small if they shall still be manageable. (2) In contrast to open exploration, scenario-based exploration is always (re)connected to the context; the need for grounding design ideas in real-world tasks limits the design space. (3) Scenarios force users and developers to base their argumentation in the task domain—instead of arguing about features, real-world tasks are subject to design. This has a strong focusing effect on communication and co-design. (4) Again, owing to the need for conciseness, scenarios as specifications for functionality are inherently incomplete. They focus on a set of core functions that are central to the developed design.

To summarize, the hypothesis examined here is that *scenarios considerably reduce the number of design options*, that they act as a *filter for design*. Whether they are used to represent activities from the application domain, present design solutions, facilitate communication, or guide the implementation, scenarios focus the design activity on an area of core functionality.

This is not due to a limited descriptiveness concerning technical innovations—everything can be imagined, while e.g., rapid prototyping tools are based on existing widget sets and command only limited functionality. Rather, the limitations of the scenario format, being textual, sequential and finite, limit the description of user interaction, effectively minimizing the described interaction. Furthermore, the strong emphasis on drawing from real-world tasks and their requirements introduces a perspective that focuses on the provision of solutions for existing problems. Finally, the use of scenarios in the process as a catalyst to generate a common design vision among different stakeholders limits the number of manageable scenarios and thus amplifies their focusing role.

The representation of design thoughts in the form of scenarios considerably reduces the number of design options; designs created using scenarios tend towards *functional minimalism*, if the functionality of a design is put to the question whether it can be justified within the chosen use context. Also, the form of scenarios presents a limit to feature richness—features must be represented in a very limited number of scenarios, each of which needs to be understandable and concise. The limitation of the number of scenarios that can be handled effectively concentrates attention to a limited number of use descriptions—and thus makes scenarios a tool to understand central aspects of the application context; the ability to combine different degrees of abstraction makes it possible to still represent the scope of development.

Scenarios can be used to focus on a single, specific-use context. When used in this manner, they allow the designers to adapt the access structure to this context, creating some degree of *structural minimalism*. The abundance of more formal methods—from use cases to UML "scenarios"—demonstrates, however, that more detailed accounts of user activities are necessary to successfully adapt access structures. These more formal methods can be organized more easily; thus, more descriptions of user activities and system responses can be created. They lack, however, the overview effect of scenarios and, with their potentially high number, do no longer prevent a loss of focus.

7.5.2 Scenario-Based Design

The discussion of different types of scenarios here follows their description in the literature, and draws on the experience from two courses held on Scenario-Based Design (SBD)[7] (Carroll, 1995) held at Hamburg University. Mary Beth Rosson and John Carroll (2001) base a complete usability engineering process solely on scenarios. In several successive design activities, different types of scenarios are used to develop the initial design vision into a prototypical implementation of the interactive system. To illustrate the different stages in this process, the four types of scenarios used are first described here.[8]

1. The first type of scenarios used, *problem scenarios*, tells the story of current practice, carefully tailored to reveal aspects of the stakeholders and their activities that influence design. In spite of their name, problem scenarios do not talk about current problems; their function is to ground the design in current practice in the "problem domain" (ibid., 64f). 2. The designer first introduces ideas about new functionality, new ways of thinking about users' needs and how to meet them in *activity scenarios*. Their function is to describe the future use of the design artifact, thus binding the design to concrete tasks. A more concise *vision statement* complements the scenarios, providing a more general representation of the motivation for design. 3. When the activities have been refined and confirmed upon, *information design scenarios* are used to specify representations of a task's objects and actions that will help users perceive, interpret, and make sense of what is happening. 4. Finally, *interaction design scenarios* specify the mechanisms for accessing and manipulating the task information and activities. Here, concrete interaction techniques used to manipulate information are specified, resulting in a detailed description that can easily be turned into a first prototype.

The order of scenario types demonstrates the perspective taken by scenario-based design as a methodology—design is based on current practice, and re-design first targets user activities. While other processes, such as *Contextual Design* (Beyer and Holtzblatt, 1997) do not suggest a sequence of information and interaction design[10], SBD bases the choice of interaction techniques on the

---

[7] In this approach to usability engineering, scenarios are employed in different stages of the design process to describe both the current and envisioned work context, facilitate communication between user and designer, and serve as a medium for exploration. Although this focus on scenarios as a medium might seem -academic, the design process illustrates the different uses that scenarios can have in real processes.

[8] The documentation of design rationale in the form of "claims", lists of trade-offs implied by design decisions, is omitted here for brevity, although it forms an important part of the SBD process (ibid., 72).

choice of an information model and thus also on the resulting data model. Constraints in SBD are passed from scenario to scenario, and the later, much more detailed design steps are consequently linked to the basic assumptions defined in the initial system vision and the problem and activity scenarios.

Each type of scenario introduces a new layer of constraints, the whole process is a form of iterative refinement. While this allows swift progress, fundamental changes in designs create the need to repeat several design steps and update the different types of scenarios.

From a minimal perspective, SBD focuses first on defining a core functionality, and later on devising an appropriate access structure. Problem and activity scenarios in conjunction describe the difference a design will make for work practice, and narrowly define the exact role it will play within the work context. User activities are described in concrete steps, and the design is embedded as a tool in the users' tasks. This not only forces designers to closely observe the necessities within the application domain, but it also facilitates the elaboration of essential functionality through communication with users. As Carroll et al., (Carroll et al., 1998) put it, the focus on "human activity promotes focused reflection on the usefulness and usability of an envisioned design intervention". This shifts the focus of design in an early phase of development to the consideration of use, and of the context of use—and "mitigates the temptations and distortions of technology-driven development." (ibid.)

7.5.3 Reduction and the Use of Scenarios

Scenarios, specifically when used in iterative and cyclical development, are tools that can be very effective in eliminating high-flying ideas and carve out the essential tasks for a design. The aspect of *functional minimalism* is strengthened by two properties of scenarios, content and form:

The content of scenarios—contextual descriptions of real or realistic use situations—forces designers to base their design on practice instead of technical feasibility, or "cool" functionality. Instead of *Requirements Analysis*, scenarios further *Requirements Development*: starting off from a very limited set of functionality in a single scenario, a sophisticated system is developed through iterative and interactive extension of requirements in cooperation with users. Writing additional scenarios is a way of learning about additional requirements; Carroll et al., (ibid.) report, "The client's original functional requirements ... were radically and continuously transformed. We have called this process requirements development—it progresses through a series of stages; through the course of these stages, qualitatively different requirements become accessible or salient; the work of prior stages is often prerequisite to the possibility of succeeding stages." This does not necessarily mean that the initial vision is changed—high-level goals often stay the same during a project. Yet, by representing the redesign of workplace practice in scenarios, new requirements are detected—"Scenarios encourage designers to envision outcomes before attempting to specify outcomes, and thereby, they help to make requirements more proactive in system development" (ibid.).

The *form* of scenarios also contributes to the direction of design. Functionality that seems less important is left out with less regret when a story has to be written that needs to provide justification than when a list of features allows the addition of items at no or low initial cost. As both the reader's and the writer's attention span is limited and long stories that include a large number of similar activities quickly tend to get boring, finding prototypical activities—and matching prototypical functionality—is a main concern in scenario design. Basing design on scenarios creates an informal and incomplete specification of the design artifact. A major benefit of good scenarios is therefore that they describe an essential design kernel that will eventually grow into the final application. The "patterns" described by a scenario "seed" the development, containing much of what will emerge by addition and combination of scenarios from the beginning.

Any story—as any formal model—is created from an individual perspective. But unlike a physical model (e.g. a paper prototype), stories will often contain a moral and thus hint at the underlying assumptions. Scenarios are, therefore, good tools for defining a common ground (Bødker and Christiansen, 1997) that can be used to start off design. Consistent with the minimal focus on the whole design, scenarios can also be used to understand design ideas that extend not only beyond the current tool, but also *beyond the current project* (Bødker and Christiansen, 2004). This becomes increasingly important as designs are embedded in a technical and social context that is ubiquitous.

In commercial projects, scenarios often lack the explicit focus on exemplary activities, yet they are still employed as a focal point for the overall design vision (Hertzum, 2003), and as a basis for concentrating the design on a core competency (Greenwood, 2002; Pape et al., 2004, 9). While this conflicts with the use of scenarios as experimental tools, when they must capture not just the essential and typical, but the specific and unique (comp. Grudin, 1994), scenarios also excel at describing the context of a solution. Without the need for specific details, exemplary practices can be included in envisioned solutions. However, only those vision scenarios allow the extrapolation of details that are created with a consideration for both the whole context, and the specific functional core of a design.

While scenarios do not force the designer to create systems that are structured as a combination of simple tools, they *can* facilitate the development of such systems: Scenarios are usually short stories. The need for conciseness and clarity of scenarios favors simple solutions. When different tasks will need similar features, the resulting reuse of scenario elements becomes obvious— and the different combinations that features appear in. This can be used to group the features and form categories. The scenarios' orientation on tasks can be used to identify these categories with "tools" that have some function with regard to the task. If scenarios are used in this manner, they work as tools towards an architectural minimalism of the resulting design.

As the analysis identified several points where scenarios and minimalism meet, it might be useful to revisit the notion of minimalism in the context of computer documentation (Section 3.2.4). While Carroll's minimal approach to documentation was here initially dismissed as being too different from the minimalist standpoint in art and music, Carroll's use of scenarios can be assumed to be based on his experience with minimal documentation. Carroll himself notes that "Design iteration was always the process touchstone for minimalism. ... The shift in our technical work toward the more complex domain of programming and software design had more strongly encouraged our interests in psychological design rationale. Building explicit theories about how designs are expected to impact situations of use, as illustrated earlier for training wheels interfaces, constrains and focuses the interpretation of formative evaluation data. This is the same hypothetico-deductive logic as in the scientific method" (Carroll et al., 1992, 254–255).

Documentation minimalism was (among others) based on the premise that "working on a realistic task provides the learner with an appropriate framework for integrating and applying learning experiences" (Carroll, 1997). This quality of realistic tasks is part of what makes scenarios so attractive; as in minimal literature, much can be said with few words, because the task and the work situation add much of the unspecified information. Documentation minimalism used a minimal amount of information to describe possible strategies for recovering from error; much as compositional minimalism focuses on the interpretation of the user, and values unanticipated "misuse" of functionality, documentation minimalism tried to remove unnecessary context information from the documentation to allow the learner to make the most use of the provided textual help while trying to solve real tasks.

7.6 Defining Architecture: Small Steps and Agile Methods

The notion of minimalist architecture emphasizes the possibility of creating non-monolithic products. The option of breaking a design in parts, and distributing responsibility for requirements among these parts enables each part to be more focused—on specific user groups or some of their tasks, and thus simplifies the overall design for the individual user. Often, this is a design decision that determines all further design activity, and difficult to introduce into existing systems with their existing interrelationships. Knowledge about scope and use can aid designers in making this decision—techniques such as personas and scenarios can thus also be used not to optimize a focused part, but to find focus for the parts of a design.

A design architecture, however, is easy to get wrong and changes can be costly. The approach that is sketched in the following therefore aims to first create a single, core part of a design. Iterative methods and, most specifically, agile methods, can support the designer in finding a good balance—between cost and benefit for the customer but also between adding functionality and adding a new part to the puzzle.

Interactive systems are not only created through design—this is true for standard software, but even for innovative, non-standard devices; a large part in their making breaks down to the engineering of the underlying hardware, and, more importantly, software. Adaptation of a design to the needs of users often requires efforts that transcend the surface and create requirements for the internal architecture of a system. From the four notions of minimalism, architectural minimalism, the distribution of functionality among different parts of a design is most closely connected to the underlying technicalities.

7.6.1 Simplicity in Software Engineering

> *There can be no right method; Design Simply*
> — attributed to Peter Naur

Simplicity is an important goal not only for human-computer interaction; software engineering, the discipline that aims to introduce engineering methodology to the process of constructing software, has long tried to achieve *simplicity in design*. However, the mapping of terms such as design in software engineering needs some clarification.

Balzert gives some more details about the elements of software engineering that he describes as "goal-oriented provision and systematic application of *principles*, *methods*, and *tools* for the development and application ... of complex software systems" (Balzert, 2000, 36, translation mine). According to Balzert, *principles* form the basis of engineering as they are used as a theoretical foundation; they are extracted from, and validated by experience (Balzert, 1985, 2).

Among the *201 principles of software engineering* that Davis (1995) outlines is a very prominent principle that reads "minimize complexity". This often-cited principle is commonly interpreted in terms of abstraction reducing the *internal* complexity—parting the inner workings of a computer program from its application as is exemplified by a saying attributed to Edsgar W. Dijkstra, "The art of programming is the art of organizing complexity." However, the IEEE standard 610.12 defines complexity as "The degree to which a system or component has a design or implementation that is difficult to understand or verify. Contrast with: simplicity" (IEEE, 1990). Complexity must thus be understood here as *cognitive complexity* (comp. Fenton and Pfleeger, 1996, 245), or as the effort that a user must summon up to understand the workings of a computer program. It is consensus amongst many authors that there exists an *essential complexity* that cannot be avoided as it is part of the problem domain (Brooks Jr., 1987).

Software engineering thus aims to reduce additional or *accidental complexity*. As cognitive complexity is difficult to measure quantitatively, or to identify and optimize using methods and tools from engineering, structural complexity is a popular target for reduction—and thus structural simplicity a groundlaying quality of software: "Of all the principles ... simplicity is the broadest and perhaps the most fundamental" (Clements, 1999). Abstraction, hierarchy and modularization are used to create a conceptual model of the application domain[9]—the latter is used as a means of eliciting different views of different users and providing a basis for informed discourse, thus enabling compromise (see e.g. Hirschheim et al., 1995; Mylopoulos et al., 1999, 33f; Johnson and Henderson, 2002).

Analogously, *usability engineering* can be defined as a systematic, disciplined, quantifiable approach that applies *principles*, *methods* and *tools* from the usability practice to create usable and useful software systems. As software engineering, usability engineering has often been understood in technical terms (Nielsen, 1993)—as a "technical discipline for developing computer-user interfaces that can be readily comprehended, quickly learned, and reliably operated. Its replicable techniques reduce the risk of failure" (Butler, 1996); this view is often connected to psychological analysis and measurement, and usability activities are often summative, i.e., evaluate different designs to measure improvements. The understanding of software development that is used in the following sections draws on both disciplines.

7.6.2 Minimalism in Agile Development

Keep it small and simple
—the KISS principle[10]

In the last years, a fairly new school of software development has rapidly gained attention and spread from small companies to almost all major corporations: the Agile movement. There exist a number of different software development processes that are addressed by the label Agile, and although they differ quite dramatically in detail, they share values listed in the *agile manifesto* (Beck et al., 2001). Twelve principles were defined that underlie this manifesto, and the one

---

[9] A number of sub-disciplines of computer science have influenced the development of more or less formal conceptual models: Databases (ER-diagrams), AI and programming languages contributed to this research area. (For an early account of the different disciplines, see Brodie et al., 1984).

[10] The acronym KISS is often translated to "keep it small and simple", or the less politically correct "keep it simple, stupid". The term was coined long before it was used to describe simplicity in agile processes. Example uses include the description of software functionality (Dorsey, 1983), and the formulation of slogans in marketing and articles in the press; links to Ockham's razor (1654) illustrate the KISS rule's ancient history.

that immediately seems to connect to minimalism is "Simplicity—the art of maximizing the amount of work not done—is essential" (ibid.).

However, the connection is a bit more indirect. Agile methods were developed by people whose job is software development. They were troubled that projects failed, quality decreased, and work, in general, became dissatisfying as a result. That is, agile methods are first and foremost a collection of techniques that help programmers and project managers organize their work. Simplicity is essential, but it is understood as simplicity in the work lives of developers. Minimalism in design as defined in this book is nonetheless supported by another trait of agile methods. To counter one of the most common frustrations of programmers, the poor quality of requirements, and the time and frustration that it takes to discover that something planned for might have to be realized differently—or not be needed at all, agile methods place a strong focus on iterative development. Whether they are called sprints (in Scrum) or iterations, the division of project time into small units, where a focused part of requirements are evaluated, designed and realized, helps to prioritize features, and thus to quickly build usable systems.[11] The first principle behind the agile manifesto consequently reads: "Our highest priority is to satisfy the customer through early and continuous delivery of valuable software"(Beck et al., 2001).

The resulting need for a decomposition of a design is central to agile development. From a minimal perspective, it supports reduction in two different ways. First, the need to describe the functional core of a system, start development with this core, and then adding functionality *can* be used to limit the amount of functionality. If this is made an explicit goal of development, management techniques such as the planning game can be used for reduction: together, customers and developers decide what is going to be implemented in the next iteration; this forces customers to reflect on priorities and decide what is important. This reflected planning can be very helpful to reduce less necessary requirements (Beck, 1999) and thus minimize functionality.

Second, the negotiation process, and the necessarily small units of work present a chance to make visible the separation of concerns of different parts of the design. Although these parts can be defined in technical terms (e.g. web design vs. database access), ideally, also the use relation to different stakeholders becomes obvious, and sub-systems or *tools* within a design can be defined that cater to the needs of these stakeholders, thus increasing either structural or architectural minimalism.

Examples for how agile development can create minimal applications can be found in some of the Web services that are rendered to the user of the Web 2.0: products such as Flickr for managing photos, or Basecamp for project management were developed using early releases and incorporating user feedback

---

[11] It also helps to react to change—either induced by the introduction of the software itself, or because the customer environment changed during development. This is a frequent problem: In 8,000 large software projects, about 40 percent of requirements arrived after development had begun. (Jones, 1995)

(Section 6.3.5); through integration with other web applications, their functional scope has been kept fairly focused and, consequently, they are simpler if compared to desktop applications. Clearly, the contribution that agile methods made is difficult to measure but their focus on renegotiating the necessity of requirements and their incremental approach to development can help to identify not only unnecessary requirements, but also those that don't well fit into the initial design vision for the product. Breaks in the design space can thus become more visible.

However, agile methods were not developed with a strong emphasis on usability: The projects where agile techniques were developed were typically in-house applications that were aiming to cut costs rather than to generate revenue, designed for users who would be forced to use the software in their jobs rather than opting in, for example, on a web service (Fig. 7.5). Agile methods thus focus on negotiating and implementing given requirements. As a consequence, they often have difficulties of generating or upholding a consistent vision for a product—simplicity in agile development processes refers first to qualities of the process, and second to technical qualities of the software, while the use quality of the designed product is often not mentioned explicitly.

From a minimalist perspective, this lack of overview can easily lead to feature congestion: if there is no consensus what a design aims to be, or how and in what context it is going to be used, the basis for deciding whether a

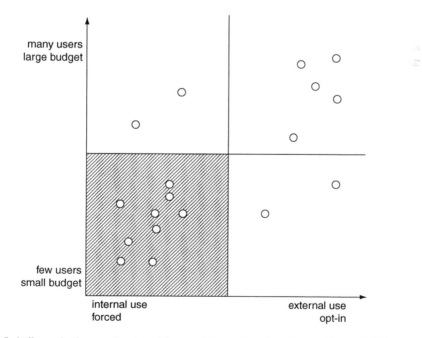

Fig. 7.5 Agile methods were developed for small internal projects (comp. Patton, 2008)

feature is really required and correctly allocated to a part of the software, becomes difficult. Yet, agile methods organize the development process by adding feature to feature. This is perhaps best illustrated by *feature-driven development* (FDD), a process model that predates the Agile Manifesto (Beck et al., 2001), but has repeatedly (Coad et al., 1999; Highsmith, 2002; Palmer and Felsing, 2002) been propagated as an agile process along with Scrum (Schwaber and Beedle, 2001; Schwaber, 2004) and Extreme Programming (XP) (Beck, 1999; Beck and Andres, 2004).

7.6.2.1 Feature-based Negotiation and Design in Agile Methods

FDD was developed to "enable the reliable delivery of working software in a timely manner with highly accurate and meaningful information to all key roles inside and outside a project" (Ltd., 2005, 4). The process starts with the conception of an *object model* that is "more shape than content" (ibid., 6), and the building of a *feature list* describing in detail the planned functionality of the system. Development is then planned, and the software is finally designed (in an engineering sense) and built *by feature*, iteratively updating the object model (de Luca, 2002; de Luca, 1998; Fig. 7.6).

FDD places its focus on the timely delivery of contracted functionality. Its main stated benefit is a reduction of the workload of its key actor, the chief architect (ibid.). It does not explicitly mention participation of users, and although it also does not forbid participation, the dominating role of the chief

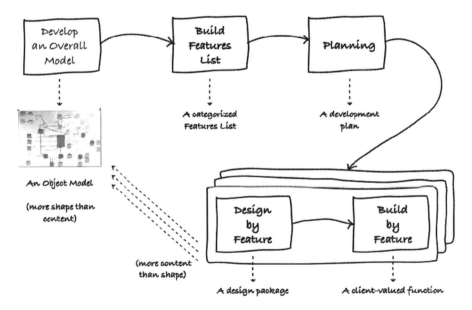

Fig. 7.6 The FDD process. (deLuca, 2002)

architect and the focus on delivery demonstrate that FDD mainly tries to reduce the risks of fixed-price projects and optimize communication between client and development team, with users taking a secondary role.

No effort is made to reduce functionality of information structure of the developed software, the design is either left to the experienced chief architect, or seen as the responsibility of the client. As the software is consequently developed feature by feature, the demands on the responsible designer are tremendous as the process nowhere makes an effort to establish a general vision for development, or connect individual features to user tasks. Due to the iterative nature of (technical) design, efforts to sketch "the big picture" are sacrificed for an increase of the reliability of development cost planning. This carries the implicit dangers of features that, only after completion, turn out to be unnecessary and that do not lead to a consistent access structure as application designers are often driven by their sense of completion; Green (1989) calls such a strategy "opportunistic design". He understands design as redesign and consequently asks for a modifiable notation—a poor fit with FDD's feature list.

Agile methods are designed first to support development teams to take better control of their work. The iteration (or Sprint for Scrum) as basic unit of work is much smaller than e.g. milestones in less agile processes, and thus methods for estimating and controlling are much easier to implement. The iteration (or Scrum) meeting is used to negotiate which steps are to be taken in the next iteration; this ensures to some degree that, instead of over-planning iterations, features are selected according to their importance for the client. The underlying assumption is thus that not everything that is planned must necessarily make it into a design. Still, the accumulation of features is not necessarily always a good method to create a coherent, useful, whole Design.

This is no problem with FDD alone: other agile processes, such as XP, also shy the reconception of work practice. This has several reasons; two important factors are a fear of "big up-front designs", and an economical interest in negotiation project contracts: The cost of change increases with the investment made in the conception phase. As experience has shown that changing requirements are a natural part of software development (Floyd, 1987), agile methods propagate to start with small designs and continuously change the project to fit the developing needs—this approach is described as *refactoring* (Fowler et al., 1999). As the reconception of work practice is a difficult and extensive process, the predictability of generated costs is limited. While in traditional, fixed-price methods, this risk is taken by the developers—hurting either the developers' profits or product quality, agile methods tend to limit the risk by accepting only concrete requests for functionality (Beck et al., 2001). As a consequence, organizational change is often not part of the developers' mandate, and no financial resources are allocated.

7.6.2.2 Walking Small Steps: Interaction Design and Agile Development

From the point of minimalism, agile processes still have many positive traits: technology is not developed without need (Jeffries, 2001), reducing the danger that investments in technology drive the direction of design. Further, in some agile processes such as XP, collaboration with users is an implicit part, and immediate feedback loops encourage the incremental development of requirements (Beck et al., 2001). The key question is how to keep this agility alive while still creating an overall design that guides the allocation of features by defining the core of what is designed.

The integration of agile methods and usability engineering is currently an intensively debated topic. A number of different approaches exist that have been implemented with varying success in both small and large commercial development efforts and usually combine a number of usability techniques with an iterative approach, interleaving usability and development activities (Sy and Miller, 2008; Patton, 2008). These mixed projects are often the first implementations of agile processes in these companies and thus Scrum, as a very low-impact process, is usually the basis for iterative development. A short design cycle, "sprint zero", precedes actual development and after each sprint (iteration), design concepts and code are exchanged between interaction designers and developers.

While this is certainly an improvement over processes where the result of implementing a sketched design would be seen only in the next milestone release, sometimes as long as a year in the making, the approach introduces some difficulties that may not be necessary: First, documentation becomes more important as the end of an iteration is the only defined time where information is exchanged between the interaction designers and developers. Second, the time pressure on designers is increased as they must deliver a complete set of requirements and also test the implementation of features created in the last iteration. This has been addressed by using longer iterations. Third, agility is reduced as an iteration now no longer holds all activities necessary for implementing any single feature and time from user research to design to implementation and testing will take four iterations in total, close to the 6–12 months of common non-agile development processes.

Most importantly from a minimalist perspective, however, is the continuing lack of close collaboration between interaction designers and developers in the process.[12] If a design impacts the technical architecture of a product, the chances are good that this is not a one-way relationship. Possibilities and limitations are created underneath the surface and designers need to know their material well before they can attempt to partition their design. Providing

---

[12] This does not necessarily mean that collaboration between individuals is impossible in any given project, nor will a lack of defined collaboration prevent sound designs. However, if collaboration is reduced to documents in a process, this speaks about the existing culture divide in a company.

requirements that describe meaningful units in terms of the users and their needs then enables developers to actually produce a working core early on; iterative prototyping becomes possible. A tight coupling of the technical and the use perspective is thus necessary to improve the design step by step—and collect feedback that helps to understand what forms the core for a given design.

7.6.2.3 Agile Reduction

Agile methods are somewhat lacking in the definition of an initial product vision. XP propagates an informal communication between the developers, manifested in the principle of collective code ownership (Beck, 1999): instead of assigning different specialist roles and responsibilities for software modules to members of the development team, a shared understanding of all source code is desired.[13] Extending this shared understanding to less formal representations of the system—such as scenarios or other forms of documents for interface design—adds understanding of the design gestalt and provides an interface to usability engineering methods.[14]

Using scenarios as tools in agile processes thus promises to strengthen the positive effects of agile development—taking small steps and avoiding non-requirements—while keeping the problem of creating a consistent product gestalt to a minimum. XP already uses stories as a design technique that interface very well with other forms of describing necessary features; e.g. Lauesen (2003) used scenarios as a tool for creating requirements that flow directly into stories. Defining reduction as an objective in development provides a background that can guide the application of scenarios; the following paragraphs try to recapture some lessons learned from the author's own experiences with scenarios in extreme programming projects (comp. Obendorf et al., 2005; Obendorf and Finck, 2007; Obendorf and Finck, 2008).

Integration of scenarios in agile methods is based on the need for an overview. As simply interfacing usability engineering and development teams holds the danger of losing agility due to the increased need for synchronization and communication[15], an integrative approach was sought for instead—hopefully preventing both the building of unnecessary features by first defining a product

---

[13] The second edition of *Extreme Programming: Explained* (Beck and Andres, 2004) softens this requirement with the "core practice" called "Whole Team", acknowledging specific roles, but still demanding that "all the contributors to an XP project sit together, members of one team" (Jeffries, 2001; Jeffries et al., 2000).

[14] Seffah et al. (2004) described the preconditions for integrating Usability Engineering and Software Engineering as follows: "Historically, UCD has been described as the opposite of the system-driven philosophy generally used in engineering (Norman and Draper, 1986). .... This Cartesian dichotomy that decouples the UI from the remaining system and builds a barrier between engineers and psychologists is not an engineering approach. ... usability specialists must think and work like engineers (Mayhew, 1999)."

[15] For an example, Beyer et al., (2004) had to significantly reduce their *Contextual Design* method to make it more lightweight. Still, the design and the development team need to interact, and in practice this interaction is often limited to iteration meetings, thus introducing a need for documentation into the agile process, effectively reducing its agility.

vision and functional core and the loss of the ability to quickly react to change, enabling development to both change direction as needed and stop adding more functionality if appropriate.

More than scenarios are necessary to create an equal footing for both usability and software development concerns. When XP relies on the customer to deliver a specification, stories play a central role in the communication of client and developer (Cohn, 2004). Due to the differences in language between designers, developers and users, this is often difficult and so other methods come into play: e.g. essential use cases[16] (Constantine and Lockwood, 1999) introduce a more formal representation; Ambler (2002) proposed to use UML system models as a means of communication with the customer. Formal methods, however, are primarily employed in communication with experienced domain experts, prohibiting co-design with real end users.

Scenarios enable this communication by being comprehensible and changeable by different stakeholders, and add depth and context to stories. To enable the developers creating a more detailed picture of the application domain, we drew on Holtzblatt's and Beyer's description of contextual inquiry (Beyer and Holtzblatt, 1995) that tries to "make the work visible" (Suchman, 1995) as a basis for design. Scenarios were then used to represent the knowledge gathered and to capture the use of existing tools within the context. Other lightweight methods can be equally useful for enriching the XP process if the context of development demands that, e.g., the persona methods described before.

The resulting process pattern (Obendorf et al., 2006; Fig. 7.7) thus stands as an example of how an idealized agile design process might look: *problem scenarios* and *activity scenarios* were adapted from Scenario-Based-Engineering (Rosson and Carroll, 2001): the *requirements scenario* rooted all development efforts in the context, it was used to identify the core functionality of the

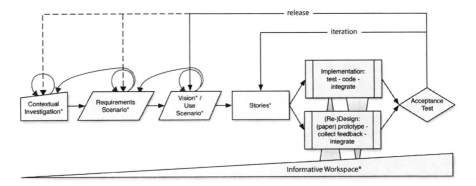

Fig. 7.7 Process pattern integrating scenarios into an XP process (Obendorf et al. 2006)

---

[16] Essential use cases are a generalized form of use cases as they are defined in the Unified Modeling Language (comp. Fowler, 2003), and try to capture essential interactions between the user and the system instead of individual steps.

proposed system. The *use scenario* is a less strict version of Rosson and Carroll's *activity scenario*, mixing activities with sketches of partial solutions within the interface; it was used to bundle the design of functionality in a single step, directly relating it to the defined problem in the *requirements scenario*. The definition of implementation activities was broadened, as well: our notion of stories includes storyboards as possible (and often necessary) elements. The tasks that are deduced from stories can lead to further contextual investigation, throw-away prototyping or the advancement of the *vision* that is used to communicate about the proposed solution with customers and end users. It was interesting to note that we could easily agree on the use of fairly standardized design techniques, such as paper prototyping or XP's test-code-integrate cycle, yet had a much harder time to define the format for representing intermediate results. As our focus on agile, iterative design forbids the continuous maintenance of e.g., scenarios as design documents or the constitution of a comprehensive archive of contextual findings, we heavily rely on informal and incomplete information stored on notes on pin boards; this "informative workspace" works both like its related XP technique, namely takes the function of organizing and visualizing progress, and like the "affinity diagram" used in *Contextual Design* (Beyer and Holtzblatt, 1997; Holtzblatt et al., 2004), as part of the workspace visualized the team's understanding of the problem domain and the projected solutions.

First tests of this process pattern were implemented both in academic settings and in industry; regardless of the differences in limitations for implementing the full process, scenarios turned out to be the key element (comp. Obendorf and Finck, 2007; Obendorf and Finck, 2008): Throughout the development process, scenarios held together the requirements voiced in single stories, often connecting technically-separated stories belonging to a single task or illustrating the interface between different tasks. Having these different levels of abstraction allowed the design team to concentrate on individual parts of a design without losing track of the sometimes complicated interplay of different parts of the software.[17] Extending the scenario techniques with a documented design vision allowed to reflect on the whole design—although the vision itself is never complete, it allows the extrapolation of the behavior of parts of the system that are not detailed in the vision.

7.6.3 Reduction in Agile Methods

Designing for architectural minimalism is more challenging than reducing functionality or access structure. There are no proven methods and we are

---

[17] In the academic setting, a student project realized a distributed calendar application, with a client-server architecture; in one industrial project, the relationship of different workflows for registering insurance records, and the necessities for interfacing with other software components were captured in scenarios.

only beginning to understand the dynamics and use patterns in software environments with distributed responsibilities, where services can be exchanged and new interaction patterns emerge. The change in the World Wide Web, where software becomes available as a service, content is shared and technical possibilities open up new ways of social interaction, is a great chance to learn more about how to design for products that do not try to be an swiss army knife but instead place their bets on sharing responsibility.

Designing a minimalist architecture requires skills that go beyond modeling the static structure used to interact with the design—creating a great information architecture is not enough. Instead, the interaction with both existing products and emerging use patterns needs to be considered to find partitions in responsibility that can help increasing the focus of design.

This chapter has argued that flexibility is a key quality to pursue in development processes as it allows to assume the core of a design will only reveal itself in the interaction with its user; while interaction design must strive to design tools for different users and tasks, agile methods can help to discover the dependency of the core to the necessary as development focuses on single parts of a design. As Freeman-Benson and Borning (2003) put it, there is even more minimalism to agile methods: as change is always an option, the software architecture resulting from agile development tends to reduce the costs for refactoring and is thus more open to change—a chance for creating compositional minimalism.

It has become clear however that configuring the development process alone cannot guarantee an architecturally minimal design: architectural units must be visible in the design. If these units are not made up by clearly different applications, the design must use other means to provide the user with clearly identifiable units. Following a tool metaphor can help doing so, as long as tools can be learned independent of one another and still work together to support the users in solving their domain problems. One way of accomplishing this is to visibly design metaphors into the system, e.g., by explicitly separating between tools and materials (comp. Züllighoven, 2004), or by providing distinct perspectives on data; visual windows (Lauesen and Harning, 2001; Lauesen, 2005) are an example for the latter approach.

7.7 Defining Growth: Using Values in Design

Understanding minimalism is difficult. Creating minimalism is more difficult. Yet, the analysis of products in the previous chapter indicated that maintaining minimalism may be the most challenging task: with a product's age, it grows and accumulates functionality, patterns of use may change both independently and because of the use of the product. Without a clear objective to keep things simple, feature-creep is inevitable.

Depending on the kind of products one looks at, fostering minimalism throughout the lifetime of a design and its evolution is thus a vital activity that is frequently overlooked. This might come as somewhat of a surprise, considering that software projects tend to live longer than planned for and maintenance becomes an increasingly important topic.[18] However, the life-cycle of the development of most products ends with their delivery, maintenance is seen as a different and separate activity.

Compositional minimalism can be generated by extreme functional minimalism, as access structures are made simple without regard to the task that is attached to the function. It is also possible to identify use patterns that are applicable universally across different types of users and tasks; patterns of use created by design, like the "desktop metaphor" or interaction idioms (comp. Cooper and Reimann, 2003) are examples for such access structures. However, more often than not, optimizing access for one user will hurt another—and while making these tradeoffs explicit can help designing a consistent product (comp. Carroll and Rosson, 1992), appropriation is often made more difficult—and as the non-intended use is not known at design time, trade-offs are frequently not made consciously.

Widening the scope of design could provide more guidance on the path to simplicity: products usually start with a fairly minimal set of functionality and will then (by initial design or based on user feedback) acquire a better fit to the tasks they are put to—in any product's life, functional and structural minimalism are possible early on. Yet, with increasing age and sophistication, functionality tends to accumulate and the user base broadens and diversifies. Attending the product through these phases helps to become aware of the implicit trade-offs and can support taking unnecessary composition from a design. The example approach reported here illustrates this by taking it one step further: a product is followed throughout its life with a participatory design approach; through the cultivation of values, a community of users is built that help improve the design—even as new users introduce non-intended patterns of use.

7.7.1 Values in Software

Conception and design will always involve values—on many different levels: values of the designer, of the users, of other stakeholders; values that apply to the technology, to the design, to the methodology, to the stakeholders' contexts, and to ethical questions concerning humanity in general. Regardless of the consequently evasive nature of the term values, no attempt is made here to rigidly define the scope of its use. Rather, differences with existing approaches are discussed to arrive at a usable, yet still fairly wide definition: as the focus

---

[18] Eastwood reports that in Fortune 1000 companies, 75% of the total IT budget goes to maintenance. (for further figures see Koskinen, 2003)

here lies on the manner of use of values in the development process, values on different levels can coexist—as long as they guide design.

Ethical issues play an important role as computers increasingly affect our work and lives and many different projects concentrate on an important value to promote its use in technology, e.g., autonomy, informed consent or trust. For some values, such as universal usability, new areas for research have been established (Shneiderman, 2000). Values also played an important role in the creation of some approaches to design, e.g., equality and democratic participation in *participatory design* (Bjerknes and Bratteteig, 1995). However, the use of these values in concrete design is not well defined.

To fill the need for an overarching framework, Batya Friedman proposed to explicitly integrate human values in the design process for computer technology through *Value-Sensitive Design* (Friedman, 1997; Friedman, 1996). As values are influenced by design decisions, Friedman et al., (2008) propose to start with a conceptual investigation of identified values and follow with making explicit value conflicts. They argue that values need ideally to be incorporated into the organizational structure of the development project. The concrete design advice that they provide is to map the impact of design trade-offs on value conflicts, thus highlighting how it affects different groups of stakeholders.

A number of other approaches use *personal values* to provide the background for design (e.g. Voida and Mynatt, 2005; Leitner et al., 2008). Values are here taken from the users' conceptual system and design is optimized in order to increase the impact on positive values such as "social recognition" or "family security".

Values are also often used to describe *non-functional requirements* that shall be communicated by a design to the users:[19] Dalsgård and Halskov term this distinction value vs. intention, for them, a value could be "instil a solemn mood" or "inspire exploration" (Dalsgård and Halskov, 2006).

The direct translation of value to economical worth is often overlooked in design theory, although it takes an important role in actual design processes. *Worth-centered development*,[20] an approach championed by Gilbert Cockton (2004b, a, 2005; Gilmore et al., 2008), tries to bring a more realistic perspective into design and include economical aspects in evaluation criteria by changing the underlying value system (Cockton, 2007). Cockton poses that computing, psychology and sociology have all failed to deliver value to customers and that, "Value can take many forms. It is not solely a question of capitalist profits and

---

[19] If values only pertain to qualities of a design, values in this sense are coming close to the psychological term "hedonic quality" that was defined to measure non-functional qualities of a design, e.g. "innovative" or "exciting".(Hassenzahl et al., 2000; Hassenzahl and Ullrich, 2007).

[20] Worth-centered development started out as value-based development. The name change was made to highlight the importance of delivering worth, "focusing on specific arenas of value", and broadens the focus of design factors to include "'needs', 'quality', 'values' and 'wants'" (Cockton, 2006).

sales. It can be political, personal, organizational, cultural, experiential or spiritual. Our role should be to understand what is valued by a system's stakeholders and support them in delivering this value" (Cockton, 2004b, 155).

The main focus of *value-based development* in this chapter is exactly this explicit negotiation of values: A *shared understanding of values* helps to create designs valuable for the user. Value-based design extends this understanding to the development of existing systems, where values have been established both within the existing use community and within the development team. Here, it is no longer possible to extract values from users and try to cater to their needs. Instead, the negotiation of shared interests becomes a central issue for development processes. If a form of minimalism—or the easier-to-understand simplicity—is accepted by all stakeholders, the maintenance of existing systems can be changed into a cultivation of the design, adapting it for new use practices, refactoring it into meaningful tools and removing barriers for unintended use.

Value-based development is here introduced using a case study for an example; it is not to be taken as a proven, polished development process. Instead, the case study demonstrates that the need to extend the focus of design to maintenance—the need for *software cultivation*—can be filled by explicitly making negotiating values in the design process. As this chapter tried to illustrate so far, traditional HCI techniques support the design of structurally and, to some extent, functionally minimal product. The change in evaluation criteria brought about by incorporating other values in the design and consequently the basis for its assessment extends this support beyond structural minimalism.

7.7.2 Case Study: CommSy—Designing with Values

Starting in 1999, a software development project at the University of Hamburg aimed to provide a web-based platform for the exchange of information and documents. CommSy, the resulting product, is today an open source platform that serves more than 25,000 users from mainly non-academic settings.[21] CommSy started as a student project, then became a part of the Wisspro research project, and is now maintained and cultivated by a startup company.

The fact that the first users were the developers themselves, together with the perspective on software development promoted by Christiane Floyd (1987, 1989, 1993; Floyd and Piepenburg, 1993) installed a tradition of participatory design for the project. In the Scandinavian tradition, the design process is considered as both organization and software development. This is echoed in the interests of the developers who tried during the Wisspro phase to not only design better software support for university courses but to also find a methodology for courses that would fit better with the underlying concept of knowledge projects.

---

[21] CommSy is available from http://www.commsy.net

Frequent *Development Workshops* were held to analyze requirements and develop designs for future developments. The form of workshops was a mix of the *future workshop* (Greenbaum et al., 1991) and *priority workshop* (Braa, 1995) techniques, addressing new work practice as well as resource planning. As developers, developer-users and users partook, and every important change was discussed, often until a consensus was reached, a close cooperation with users was maintained. New developments were often first implemented using paper prototypes (cf. Snyder, 2003) to involve non-technical users in the development process and collect early feedback. Using online questionnaires or semi-structured interviews, usage feedback was gathered as background rationale for future designs, reaching a large proportion of CommSy users.

7.7.2.1 Functional and Structural Minimalism

As the development team grew and temporarily became distributed over several locations, a need arose to formalize the vision underlying the project. To this end, a number of principles or *values* were codified that consequently guided the direction of development. This marks a change in the communication with users: internal use was no longer dominant and users were no longer seen as a natural part of the development team. Instead, the defined values were used with a "sense of mission" (Floyd et al., in Pape et al., 2004, 394) to communicate the "CommSy philosophy" (ibid.); part of the project's mission was inducing a change in the way users work with the software.

The three values that the development team arrived at were *simplicity*, integration into a *media mix*, and the ideal of *responsible use* (comp. Jackewitz et al., 2002). *Simplicity* was interpreted mostly in terms of functional minimalism[22]—it was often used in discussions to question the addition of a new feature in answer to a user request. However, simplicity was also used as an argument to support the *addition* of a new feature—as exactly this feature would make the life of some users simpler and obliterate the need for another tool or a work-around. For the developers, this twofold—and contradictory—use of the notion of simplicity was sometimes confusing. Resolution in the process was based on a discussion where all partaking stakeholders had to agree; it was welcomed, however, to renew feature proposals (often using a new paper prototype). This "lazy" implementation policy led to a differentiation of feature requests in those that appeared only once and those that surfaced again and again in discussions. Although this procedure bears the risk that the direction of

---

[22] Jackewitz et al., (2002) expand the notion of simplicity to "clear functionality...simple structure...simple layout", and "simple access". However, unlike the simplicity of functionality, the other interpretations cease to be part of recent CommSy versions: the "simple" that here denotes a unified structure was later dropped in favor of structural minimalism, and the "simple layout" is also changing in current versions with the addition of icons. Still relevant is the "simple access" by relying on Web standards, yet this infrastructure-based understanding of simplicity is beyond the scope of this analysis.

development would be dominated by the more outgoing and better-connected users, it served well to identify a core of features that would be important to these users.

All three principles function as arguments to reduce the overall complexity of the system, mostly by providing guidelines to reduce its functionality: As CommSy was initially created for cooperative teaching in small project groups, it was assumed that no differentiation of access rights was necessary. This led to a much simpler design—access rights in file systems are inherently difficult to understand (Reeder and Maxion, 2005)—and had a positive effect on learnability, controllability and user satisfaction. To conserve the advantage thus gained, only very simple protection mechanisms were introduced (information items that are read-only except for the author) and negotiation of *responsible system use* was taken out of the system and placed into the context—giving both the users and the system more flexibility. The integration within a *media mix* describes the assumption that CommSy should not be able to cater all needs arising within even a "simple" university course. This acknowledges the installed base of tools already in use (e.g. e-mail), and focuses the functionality on areas where support by existing tools is unsatisfactory and CommSy provides a real value to users.

Intense participation of key users contributed to the software's fit to the users' tasks—extensive care was taken to optimize wording and minimize unnecessary navigation: As Carroll et al., (2000) described, key users took on important roles during the development. User meetings were held in all development phases to exchange experiences and elaborate requirements for the future development of CommSy. Users involved in these processes also started to exchange information without the developers' intervention; typical characteristics of communities of practice (Fischer, 2004; Wenger, 1999; Wenger and Snyder, 2000) developed, such as the negotiation of meaning among the members, mutual engagement in joint enterprises, and a shared repertoire of activities, symbols and artifacts.

7.7.2.2 Architectural Minimalism

Over the course of development, use of CommSy spread rapidly to include other departments and universities, secondary schools and virtual networks of freelancers. As a result, the diversification of use contexts that had already been existing from the beginning quickly gained new momentum. Thus, the development team had to deal with changing user requirements and also with less and less familiar contexts of use. *Functional* and *structural* minimalism are notions that map to well-established goals of the PD process; they are useful primarily because they support a refined and more selective analysis of what qualities distinguish a "simple" product.

The combination of the long heritage of the development project and the need for change brought about by the changing contexts required other strategies to maintain simplicity: *Functional minimalism* became more difficult to maintain as the development was continued by a spin-off company that relied on its customers to fund development—on the basis of their demand for non-existing functionality. *Structural minimalism* was much more difficult to achieve as the use context broadened and different users would have increasingly different strategies for using the software to accomplish their tasks.

Still, simplicity remained a central value for developers and most users. Two different approaches were used to resolve this mismatch between the need for keeping the design simple and the demand for new functionality: features were made *configurable* and *openness* was introduced as a new value.

Making functionality configurable is an approach often used in growing software ecosystems. A very flexible implementation for configuration is the definition of an interface for plug-ins that can then extend the functionality within, often, very generous limits. The change in architecture for CommSy was less broad, partly because defining a plug-in architecture for a mature software system is not a quick task: content within the platform was already grouped in categories, such as appointments, documents or discussions. Extensions would define a new category and the visibility of categories would be configurable by the developers (for different communities of practice) and power users (for their specific tasks). While this reduced consistency, it maintained or improved manageability for the different user groups, and contributed to keeping the interface simple.

From a perspective of architectural minimalism, the design value of using the platform within a *media mix* was a first step toward acknowledging that different tools could be used for different tasks. By extending this value to *openness* (Finck and Jackewitz, 2006), it was made explicit that these tools would not be replaced by CommSy; to enable users to make better use of their preferred combination of different tools, interfaces with existing infra-structure were implemented (e.g., for calendar software, a library catalog, course administration software and office software).

7.7.2.3 Compositional Minimalism

> *We kept the tool clean and uncluttered by letting people get creative.*
> *People figured out how to solve issues on their own.*
> —37signals (2006, ch. 6)

From the start, development was laid out as a participatory design effort. This does not only mean that users were allowed to partake in design discussions and actively involve themselves in development, it also meant that developers would be drawn into the users' application domains as they dealt with their specific needs. This, in turn, made it often possible to share the responsibility for reaching user goals between the software and the users' organization of work, thereby reducing the need for specific features.

With the shift in economical funding, not only the objectives of development but also the context for participation changed: Instead of facing a single, homogeneous group of users, the CommSy developers became increasingly involved with very different groups of users. This required a different approach to participatory design: Traditional PD focuses on support for a single *community of practice*[23], which may consist of very different stakeholders that share a common practice (comp. Wenger, 1999). Building and fostering this community of practice helps not only create a pool of participating users but also enables them to help themselves (this is retold in more scientific terms in Wenger et al., 2002). However, many of the specific requirements elaborated within these communities of practice are of *little* or *no significance* in other contexts.

This posed a problem for the development of CommSy: On the one hand, exploring new contexts of use—and thus, new customers—was vital to the commercial interests of the spin-off company. On the other hand, the development team needed to bundle resources and tried to avoid parallel implementations that would increase the complexity of software and difficulty of administration and maintenance.

With the increasing dissemination of the software in different contexts, the importance of *compositional minimalismrose*, and the development of *design principles* acquired a central role. The communication between domain experts and programmers made values useful even in the early phase of the development process, yet with the addition of different heterogeneous contexts, the design philosophy that captures the rationale for design decisions took on another role: values were used to communicate the reason for taking one design direction and consciously ignoring other options to users. The design values acquired a communication function and changes in the direction of design became visible early as the values favored in design discussions shifted. The move towards a *design philosophy* made it possible not only to discuss the inherent design values with users, but also to develop them further and assess their validity. Some methods used in this effort are sketched in the next section.

7.7.3 Sharing Explicit Values in Communities of Interest

During the development of the CommSy software, a need for catering to different contexts arose and the methods for participation were adopted to address this need. Although it was not planned in advance, the use of *design principles* turned out to provide a good basis for discussing design when stakeholders span several very different contexts: while traditional PD methods suffice to work within a *singular* context of use or *community of practice*, the

---

[23] *Communities of practice* were already used by John Seely Brown, "They are peers in the execution of 'real work'. What holds them together is a common sense of purpose and a real need to know what each other knows. There are many communities of practice within a single company, and most people belong to more than one of them." (Brown, 1990), and made popular by Etienne Wenger who defined them as "a group of people informally bound together by shared expertise and passion for a joint enterprise." (Wenger and Snyder, 2000)

newly formed methodology was successful in establishing a manifold *community of interest*.

The aim of **PD** is, in minimalist terminology, the creation of a software whose fit to a single context is optimal—often, structural minimalism is sought. For multiple contexts, it is necessary to establish a common base of experiences first and consequently develop sensitivity for different perspectives among the users to enable them to reflect on *software use as tool appropriation*. The notion of *compositional minimalism* is thus highly relevant when designing for multiple contexts.

The experiences from the CommSy case study can be generalized based on the distinction between the different levels of involvement that coexisted during the development process (see Fig. 7.8): communication with individual user representatives, with members from a single community of practice, and with representatives from several different communities of practice that should form a community of interest.

Communication with user representatives took the form of personal one-to-one links of key users and individual members of the development team; the nature of this participation could be described as feature-based—design requests often concerned a single feature and were based on immediate task

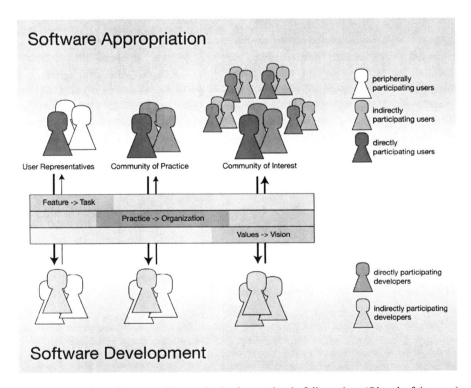

Fig. 7.8 Extension of scope and increasingly abstract level of discussion. (Obendorf, in press)

requirements. Both *communication with a single community of practice* and *communication with representatives from several communities of practice* happened in workshops and the *commented case studies* were used to document the discussion within the community of interest. The participation was based on organizational practice and design principles, or a vision of use, respectively.

7.7.3.1 Techniques Developed and Analyzed

To meet this new challenge of pooling the interests of different communities and the development team, new ways of bringing users from different contexts together had to be established to balance their respective needs and upcoming requirements. The goal was to establish a community of interest (O'Day et al., 1996) across the different communities of practice, united less through common practices in their respective work context but rather through a shared interest in CommSy use. *Communities of interest*, defined as "communities of communities" (Brown and Duguid, 1991), do not share a common practice. They are instead defined by a shared interest (Fischer, 2001; Fischer, 2006). For software development, this means that if one can build and foster a community of interest (in this case in the developed software), chances are high that a mode of communication with users can be established that allows to draw conclusions about shared values and similarities in the requirements for software use—even if the individual work practices are dramatically different. Thus, a shared perspective or vision, could be formed and "a joint development without overly neglecting specific use contexts" (Obendorf et al., in press) might become possible.

Building such a community of interest would allow—at least to some extent—a joint development, reducing the risk of neglecting specific use contexts. To this end, two techniques were developed to create and nurse a community of interest: *intercontextual user workshops* and *commented case studies:* Intercontextual user workshops are very similar in appearance to user workshops traditionally found in PD practice. The only visible difference is that users come together from different use contexts—and thus have difficulties communicating with each other. Instead of discussing shared individual work practices, values are used to introduce suggestions and problems, thus building a bridgehead that can spark interest and understanding in other users. Commented case studies try to persist this experience in written form; an introduction by the design team forms the basis for use descriptions sent in by real users, complete with their issues and proposed solutions. Conflict with existing values is often referred to as difficulties are named and solutions are proposed. The case studies close with a written answer from the developers, where they try to justify some design decisions and describe changes brought about by participation in the next release (for further details, see Finck et al., 2006).

Reflection on system usage and design happens both on a concrete level of use practices and tasks within specific communities and an abstract level of design philosophy and underlying viewpoints and values within the different contexts. By means of addressing values on an abstract level, users from different contexts succeed in clarifying their requirements without having to share details of their daily work routines and practices. An example: The demand for highly differentiated access rights, which was expressed by several users, boiled down to a discussion of trust, hierarchies, and authority and the value of equality that is inherent in the design.

It must be borne in mind, however, that even dedicated value negotiations do not guarantee the success of cooperation; in this case study, the participative development with one virtual network had difficulties due to a mismatch of proposed values and concrete requests for functionality (Janneck et al., 2006); it turned out that the network's self-conception—which was a good match with the software's design principles—did not relate to the actual work practice within the network.

7.7.4 Reduction in Value-Based Development

In the discourse of practitioners, a dichotomy is often present between "design" and "construction" (Berkun, 2005), or "creative design" and "engineering design" (Löwgren, 1995), with the former referring to an explorative approach of solution-finding, and the latter of implementing according to specifications. Perspectives based on this dichotomy are restricted as they do not realize that design requires construction and construction requires context. Industrial design has many logical elements, construction is often a creative activity (Gedenryd, 1998). The case study is an example for a process where design and construction are intertwined to the point of being inseparable—development is considered an activity that can be performed by non-programmers, users are readily accepted as members of the development team, and many developers are also frequent users. Together, these conditions allowed a transformation of the "we-need" feature discussion to a reflective "what-is-the-tool" discussion, and to the formation of *design principles* early on in the development process. The shared understanding of what the design incorporates borne by the tradition of informal corridor communication and supported by regular workshops, focused development on the question of how the design could best be used in existing, and later, in new contexts.

During the early years, development was mainly focused on a single context. The meaning of "simplicity" encompassed both *functional* and *structural minimalism* in that time. This led often to open conflicts where advocates and opponents of a new feature both based their argument on "simplicity". The notions of minimalism put forward here would have allowed a disambiguation of simplicity in many of these conflicts.

When development lost its single focus and targeted new contexts and, thus, different communities of practice, *functional minimalism* became more and more difficult to follow as a value. Simplicity remained a core value, although initial design decisions based on *functional* simplicity were revised. In return for this partial loss of meaning, simplicity acquired new interpretations; the design principle *media mix* was strengthened and renamed to *openness*. The simple use of CommSy as a tool interfacing with other tools moved into the focus of development, allowing the functional core to remain relatively stable but requiring structural extensions and external interfaces.

Due to the coverage of several distinct use contexts, the aspect of *compositional minimalism* was also strengthened in the development process—appropriation had to be supported to allow a continuing development of a single software package, maintaining a relative simplicity in functionality, and still cater for a wide variety of different uses. A *community of interest*, enabling users from different contexts to communicate with each other and the development team, had to be established to allow further participation of users in the development process. *Value-based participation* used the existing principles to shift the design cooperation to a new level that allowed the comparison and categorization of practices from different contexts.

Based on the different levels of abstraction that we find in both the workshops and the case studies (Fig. 7.8), we distinguish three levels where our software development process benefited from the methods described here (see Table 7.2): on the first level, users' acceptance of development decisions is increased as they learn about the rationale behind design. Reciprocally, developers obtain legitimation as their underlying values are being confirmed by users. On the second level, empowerment of users comes along with a deepened understanding of the respective domain on the developers' side. Building upon this, on the third level, users are enabled to integrate the software into their work practice, while developers can form a consistent vision spanning the different use contexts.

Table 7.2 Benefits of value-based participation

Users	Development Team
Increased Acceptance	Legitimation for design
Empowerment	Domain understanding
Use vision	Software vision

Lifting the communication to a more abstract level risks introducing new sources of misunderstandings. It is thus crucial for the communicating stakeholders to negotiate the meaning of the values that communication is based upon. A differentiated understanding of minimalism reduces the risk of misunderstanding simplicity—as the previous discussion demonstrated, the number of different interpretations is high. Minimalism is an important tool to raise the awareness of what simplicity means and when a shift in its meaning takes place. This refined understanding of simplicity can help to implement the proposed technique of value-based design successfully.

Using values in design does not only promise to increase the abstraction of communication in participatory design—and thus the consistence of a shared vision, it can also be helpful to explicitly root design in desired values. Making these values visible can increase the acceptance of the process itself if the values create worth for potential customers. As Friedman et al., put it, in some cases, "[the] process by which the design was produced is equally important for the legitimacy of the result" (Friedman et al., 2008).

For many applications, it makes sense to assume that the software development process is complemented by a software appropriation process on the users' behalves. If one accepts that the designers' power to determine the software does not extend into the users' application domain, it becomes an important aspect of development processes to learn from the users how they actually use the functionality that was intended for a specific purpose.

The idea of giving values a guiding role for implementing a design and matching the product to a vision determined by values[24] has recently attracted strong interest from researchers and practitioners alike (Miller et al., 2007; Cockton, 2007, 2004b; Henderson et al., 2006; Henderson and Bradt, 2006; Bolchini et al., 2008; Dalsgård and Halskov, 2006; Flanagan et al., 2005; Voida and Mynatt, 2005; Light et al., 2005; Law et al., 2007), and first experiences are reported as applications are developed on the basis of negotiating values. The case study reported here suggests that values do not only allow to enrich the basis for design and evaluation by rooting quality criteria in the user domain, but are also useful for sustaining communication with users even as the user base broadens and task-based analysis becomes increasingly difficult.

While without feedback from users, appropriation of use is difficult to design for, the channels for collecting user feedback are more diverse than described here: market research, the analysis of previous models or products from the competition can all yield important information that can enable designers to reduce compositional complexity in their designs. It is important to understand possible "mis"-use to be able to support it well; compositional minimalism is thus more than cultivating a communication culture in a community of interest and the path described only stands for an example of how to integrate the concept of compositional minimalism in your design process.

7.8 Engineering Simplicity? A Reality Check

> *However beautiful the strategy, you should*
> *occasionally look at the results.*
> —attributed to Sir Winston Churchill

This chapter lists several approaches to create better development processes using the notions of minimalism developed in this book. The preconditions for

---

[24] Values are here again used in the broadest sense, limited neither to the design itself as in the case study nor to software costs (comp. Boehm, 2003).

writing this chapter differed from all preceding parts of this book: there was little to build upon and evidence is hardly sufficient to substantiate the claims made herein—it's stepping on much thinner ice. While the use of minimalism for the analysis of existing designs could build upon existing research and the experience of others and the definition of minimalism for the design of interactive systems relies on the scholarly discourse on minimalism in art and music, the approaches brought forward in this chapter should be taken as suggestions and as stimulus to perhaps take some of the presented ideas forward.

The structure developed in this discussion for understanding and modifying methods that can support the creation of minimalism is more universal: From a definition of minimalism (or even of simplicity), it is straightforward and clearly possible to introduce new design activities that reduce a design to increase its focus. The first approach tries to formalize and make more accessible the minimalist standpoint in the form of a design game. This was successful for discerning *functional* and *structural minimalism* but the concepts of *architectural* and *compositional minimalism* were not immediately understood by the students who served as designers in the informal study. As the game is restricted to use design prototypes and other material available in the form of paper, these notions were difficult to integrate even by more experienced designers as they are, by definition, determined by design context external to the system. It, thus, seems to be more feasible to restrict the use of the game to differentiate between structure and functionality, and find other means to address the contextual forms of minimalism.

It is also obvious that while this might work well in product design with time and resources allocated for extensive design sessions, it is difficult to implement in more restricted environments (namely in those where agile development methods are typically used): convincing management to invest time to do less needs a strong position and determination. Therefore, and to include those not explicitly interested in keeping the design minimal—to customers who voice requirements and calculate costs and users who often see only a part of the whole design, implicitly putting existing methods to the task of reducing complexity feels like a promising approach.

For the reduction of functionality, the persona method has excellent references; although its main use is the provision of a broadcasting medium for results from user research, an implicit limitation is its greatest strength for providing focus on scope: the necessary fidelity of working personas and their representation in written form restricts the number of different personas that can be used in a design process to only very few. As a result, many possible users will be ignored in the design process. From the point of view of functional minimalism, this is often very constructive as fewer requirements will have to be dealt with and a simple design will be much easier to accomplish.

Reducing the observable access structure is possible with many design techniques: everything that creates a better fit to task has the potential of reducing structure. Scenarios are especially well suited to combine this reduction with a focus on core use due to their informal nature. Due to their incomplete representation of context, good scenarios tend to capture prototypical interaction—allowing for an optimal structural fit where it is most important. Again, restrictions resulting from their written form limit the number of features described within a scenario and help to identify core functionality. Scenarios thus act as a *filter for design*, reducing *functionality* and *structure*. If applied to this end, they can also support the partitioning of functionality and be used to identify the building blocks for an *architecturally minimal system*.

A short digression on Carroll's minimalism can help explain the closeness of functional and structural minimalism with the scenarios that Carroll's later work concentrates upon. Documentation minimalism reduced not the design of a system and not descriptions of its use. The reduction of documentation minimalism focused on instructions and help sheets. In their reduced form, they could be used as real work was done and errors surfaced. In "Making errors, making sense, making use" (1992), Carroll laid down the theoretical framework underlying the rules that documentation minimalism would create: with real use, and through making errors, design improves. In his work with scenarios, the conception of design underlying the making of the concrete techniques is the same.

Personas and scenarios are often used together and they are easily integrated in different development contexts. Both methods are very versatile, which in turns means that they can fulfill very different functions in a development process—providing focus is just one possibility. Minimalism provides a background for planning the type of reduction that is expected from using these techniques and helps to intentionally use personas or scenarios in design discussions—using the questions identified in the design game:

1. What is the primary function, what is it that we really want to be able to do?
2. How is that purpose of the artifact conveyed to the user?
3. Can the system be simplified by splitting it up into parts?
4. Did we draw any conclusions from it that limit use in other contexts?

Following the general direction of these suggestions might help to create less complex and less bloated designs and resist feature-bloat, whereas simply keeping simplicity on the design agenda would not suffice. However, with increasing age, functionality will nonetheless tend to accumulate and structure might be difficult to adjust to different use contexts as the product is increasingly successful—*functional* and *structural minimalism* are not enough.

In search of methods that help focus on the latter forms of minimalism, agile methods are examined as iterative development promises to limit feature congestion by implementing user feedback and constantly negotiating and prioritizing requirements with customers. From a usability perspective, however, agile methods tend to forgo the understanding of the design gestalt as they focus on this negotiation, the responsibility for the design is returned to the customer—not an ideal solution if simplicity is a set goal for development. Based on the author's personal experience, scenarios are put to the test in an integrated development process that is a blend of extreme programming and usability engineering. While different usability techniques are used in the process, scenarios fulfill the function of distilling the requirements gathered into a minimal form, helping to identify different responsibilities in the design and to generate a design solution that solves the formulated problem and is extensible to include more conventional features. Judging from the first results, this challenge is met with some success by the adopted scenarios. Again, Carroll's early focus on iterative development (comp. Carroll 1992) can explain why agile methods and scenarios are a good match.

As growth and age of a design create dynamics that tend to make it more complicated as features accumulate and tasks change and diversify, the last part of this chapter discusses how simplicity can be cultivated in the development process.[25] Value-based participatory design is presented as a possibility to integrate users in the design process and to deal with the challenge of emerging use contexts and resulting changes in the requirements for a design. The CommSy case study illustrates these dynamics of the development process, as a shift from functional and structural to architectural and compositional minimalism was induced by growth of the user base. Although this resulted in a somewhat increased complexity of the product, in some areas *architectural minimalism*, exemplified by placing functionality into optional modules, and a turn towards openness to other tools, also reduced the overall complexity of the system. As new contexts were constantly being added to the user base, it became clear that not all use situations could be planned for. Instead, support for appropriation became central, both for individual communities of practice and for a community of interest centered around the product. To this end, value-based development evolved as a methodology that enabled community building and participatory design for different fields of use—*minimizing composition* within the design.

The minimalist standpoint can be considered a versatile tool for analyzing and modifying development processes—even as the nature of applying the notions of minimalism displays a large variation in the presented approaches. Although the empirical basis is far less broad than in the last two chapters, and what is presented should be understood as suggestions rather than rules—the exemplary use of minimalism to identify and influence dynamics in development processes demonstrated the value of a constructive use of minimalism.

---

[25] The inclusion of use in product design and development can also help better estimate acceptance—software development methods often relate little to customers and do not connect the product to its use (comp. Forlizzi, 2008; Rainey, 2005, 482) and marketing approaches consider customer satisfaction as a static after-market result(comp. Vanalli and Cziulik, 2003).

References

37signals (2006). Getting Real. https://gettingreal.37signals.com/toc.php _q?_4

Ambler, S. W., and Jeffries, R. (2002). *Agile Modeling: Effective Practices for Extreme Programming and the Unified Process.* New York, NY: Wiley.

Balzert, H. (1985). Allgemeine Prinzipien des Software Engineering. *Angewandte Informatik,* 1, 1–8.

Balzert, H. (2000). *Lehrbuch der Software- Technik 1/2. mit 3 CD-ROMs. Band 1 (2. Auflage, 2000), Band 2 (1. Auflage, 1998) Software- Entwicklung / Software-Management, Software-Qualitätssicherung, Unternehmensmodellierung.* Berlin: Spektrum Akademischer Verlag.

Beck, K. (1999). *Extreme Programming Explained: Embrace Change.* New York, NY: Addison Wesley.

Beck, K., and Andres, C. (2004). *Extreme Programming Explained: Embrace Change (2nd Edition).* New York, NY: Addison-Wesley Professional.

Beck, K., Beedle, M., van Bennekum, A., Cockburn, A., Cunningham, W., Fowler, M., Grenning, J., Highsmith, J., Hunt, A., Jeffries, R., Kern, J., Marick, B., Martin, R. C., Mellor, S., Schwaber, K., Sutherland, J., and Thomas, D. (2001). Agile Manifesto. www.agilemanifesto.org Accessed 2.7.2008

Beyer, H., and Holtzblatt, K. (1997). *Contextual Design: A Customer-Centered Approach to Systems Designs (The Morgan Kaufmann Series in Interactive Technologies).* San Fransisco, CA: Morgan Kaufmann.

Beyer, H. R., and Holtzblatt, K. (1995). Apprenticing with the customer. *Communications of ACM,* 38(5), 45–52.

Beyer, H. R., Holtzblatt, K., and Baker, L. (2004). *An Agile Customer-Centered Method: Rapid Contextual Design.* Extreme Programming and Agile Methods – XP/Agile Universe 2004, 50–59. Available online at http://www.incontextdesign.com/resource/pdf/XPUniverse2004.pdf

Bjerknes, G., and Bratteteig, T. (1995). User participation and democracy: a discussion of Scandinavian research on systems development. *Scandinavian Journal of Information Systems,* 7(1), 73–98.

Blomquist, Å., and Arvola, M. (2002). *Personas in Action: Ethnography in an Interaction Design Team.* NordiCHI '02: Proceedings of the second Nordic conference on Human-computer interaction, New York, NY, USA, 197–200.

Boehm, B. (1975). *The high cost of software.* Addison-Wesley.

Boehm, B. (2003). Value-based software engineering. *SIGSOFT Software Engineering Notes,* 28(2), 4.

Bolchini, D., Garzotto, F., and Paolini, P. (2008). *Value-Driven Design for "Infosuasive" Web Applications.* Beijing, China, 745–754. Available online at http://doi.acm.org/10.1145/1367497.1367598

Bødker, S., and Christiansen, E. (1997). Scenarios as springboards in the design of CSCW. In Be al. (Ed.), *Social Science Research, Technical Systems and Cooperative.* 217–234. Mahwah, NJ: Erlbaum.

Bødker, S., and Christiansen, E. (2004). *Designing for Ephemerality and Prototypicality.* DIS '04: Proceedings of the 2004 conference on Designing interactive systems, New York, NY, USA, 255–260.

Braa, K. (1995). *Priority Workshops: Springboard for User Participation in Redesign Activities.* Proc. COOCS 1995, New York, NY, USA, 246–255.

Brandt, E. (2006). *Designing Exploratory Design Games: A Framework for Participation in Participatory Design?* Participatory Design Conference, Trento, Italy, 57–66.

Brandt, E., and Messeter, J.,rn. (2004). *Facilitating Collaboration Through Design Games.* PDC 04: Proceedings of the eighth conference on Participatory design, New York, NY, USA, 121–131.

Brechin, E. (2002). Reconciling market segments and Personas. http://www.cooper.com/journal/2002/03/ reconciling_market_segments_an.html

Brodie, M. L., Mylopoulos, J., and Schmidt, J. W. (1984). *On Conceptual Modelling: Perspectives from Artificial Intelligence, Databases, and Programming Languages (Topics in Information Systems)*. Berlin: Springer-Verlag.

Brooks, Jr. F. P. (1987). No silver bullet – Essence and accidents of software engineering. *IEEE Computer*, 20(4), 10–19.

Brown, J. S., and Duguid, P. (1991). Organizational learning and communities-of-practice: toward a unified view of working, learning, and innovation, organization. *Science*, 2(1), 40–57.

Brown, J. S. (1990). Research that reinvents the corporation. *Harvard Bus. Rev*, 68(1), 102.

Butler, K. A. (1996). Usability engineering turns 10. *Interactions*, 3(1), 58–75.

Buxton, B. (2003). *Performance by Design: The Role of Design in Software Product Development*. Proceedings of the second international conference on usage-centered design, Portsmouth, NH, 1–15.

Carroll, J. M, (1992). Making errors, making sense, making use. In C Floyd (Ed.), *Software Development and Reality Construction*. 155–167. Berlin Heidelberg New York: Springer.

Carroll, J. M. (1995). *Scenario-Based Design: Envisioning Work and Technology in System Development*. New York, NY: John Wiley & Sons.

Carroll, J. M. (1997). *Reconstructing Minimalism*. SIGDOC '97: Proceedings of the 15th annual international conference on computer documentation, New York, NY, USA, 27–34.

Carroll, J. M. (2002). *Scenarios and Design Cognition*. IEEE joint international conference on requirements engineering (RE'02), Essen, 3. Available online at http://doi.ieeecomputer-society.org/10.1109/ICRE.2002.1048498

Carroll, J. M., Chin, G., Rosson, M. B., and Neale, D. C. (2000). *The Development of Cooperation: Five Years of Participatory Design in the Virtual School*. DIS '00: Proceedings of the conference on designing interactive systems, New York, NY, USA, 239–251.

Carroll, J. M., and Rosson, M. B. (1992). Getting around the task-artifact cycle: how to make claims and design by scenario. *ACM Transactions on the Information Systems*, 10(2), 181–212.

Carroll, J. M., Rosson, M. B., Jr., George, C., and Koenemann, J. (1998). Requirements Development in Scenario-Based Design. *IEEE Transactions On the Software Engineering*, 24(12), 1156–1170.

Carroll, J. M., Singley, M. K., and Rosson, M. (1992). Integrating theory development with design evaluation. *Behavior & Information Technology*, 11, 247–255.

Chin, G. J., Rosson, M. B., and Carroll, J. M. (1997). *Participatory Analysis: Shared Development of requirements from scenarios*. CHI '97: Proceedings of the SIGCHI conference on Human Factors in computing Systems, New York, NY, USA, 162–169.

Clements, P. C. (1999). *Constructing Superior Software (Software Quality Institute Series)*. Indianapolis, IN: Sams Publishing.

Coad, P., Lefevre, E., and DeLuca, E. (1999). *Java Modeling in Color with UML: Enterprise Components and Process*. New Jersey, NJ: Prentice Hall.

Cockton, G. (2004a). *From Quality in Use to Value in the World*. CHI '04: CHI '04 extended abstracts on Human factors in computing systems, Vienna, Austria: ACM Press.

Cockton, G. (2004b). *Value-centred HCI*. NordiCHI '04: Proceedings of the third Nordic conference on Human-computer interaction, New York, NY, USA, 149–160.

Cockton, G. (2005). *A Development Framework for Value-Centred Design*. CHI 2005 Extended Abstracts, 1292–1295, Portland, OR: ACM Press.

Cockton, G. (2006). *Designing worth is worth designing*. Oslo, Norway, 165–174. Available online at http://doi.acm.org/10.1145/1182475.1182493

Cockton, G. (2007). Putting Value into E-valu-ation. In E Law, E Hvannberg, and G Cockton (Eds.), *Maturing Usability: Quality in Software, Interaction and Value*. Berlin: Springer.

Cohn, M. (2004). *User Stories Applied: For Agile Software Development*. New Jersey, NJ: Addison Wesley.

Constantine, L. L., and Lockwood, L. A. D. (2002). Usage-centered engineering for web applications. *IEEE Software*, 19(2), 42–50.

Constantine, L. L., and Lockwood, L. A. D. (1999). *Software for Use: A Practical Guide to the Models and Methods of Usage-Centered Design (Acm Press Series)*. New Jersey, NJ: Addison-Wesley Professional.

Cooper, A. (1999). *The Inmates Are Running the Asylum : Why High Tech Products Drive Us Crazy and How To Restore The Sanity*, Indianapolis, IN: Macmillian Publishing.

Cooper, A. (2003). The Origin of Personas. http://www.cooper.com/journal/2003/08/the_origin_of_personas.html

Cooper, A., and Reimann, R. M. (2003). *About Face 2.0: The Essentials of Interaction Design*. New York, NY: Wiley.

Dalsgård, P., and Halskov, K. (2006). *Real life Experiences with Experience Design*. Oslo, Norway, 331–340. Available online at http://doi.acm.org/10.1145/1182475.1182510

Davis, A. M. (1995). *201 Principles of Software Development*. Columbus, OH: McGraw-Hill.

de Luca, J. (1998). Original FDD Processes. http://www.nebulon.com/articles/fdd/original-processes.html Accessed 2.7.2008

de Luca, J. (2002). Latest FDD Processes. http://www.nebulon.com/articles/fdd/download/fddprocessesA4.pdf Accessed 2.7.2008

Dijkstra, E. (1976). A Discipline of Programming.

Dijkstra, E. W. (1972). The humble programmer. *Communications of the ACM*, 15(10), 859–866.

Dix, A., Ormerod, T., Twidale, M., Sas, C., Gomes da Silva P., and McKnight, L. (2006). *Why Bad Ideas are a Good Idea*. Proceedings of HCIEd.2006-1 Inventivity, Ballina/Killaloe, Ireland,. Available online at http://www.comp.lancs.ac.uk/computing/users/dixa/papers/HCIed2006-badideas/

Djajadiningrat, J. P., Gaver, W. W., and Fres, J. W. (2000). *Interaction Relabelling and Extreme Characters: Methods for Exploring Aesthetic Interactions*. DIS '00: Proceedings of the conference on Designing interactive systems, New York, NY, USA, 66–71.

Donovan, J., and Brereton, M. (2004). *Meaning in Movement: A Gestural Design Game*. Extended Abstracts PDC2004 Artful integration: Interweaving Media, Materials and Practices, Toronto, Canada.

Dorsey, J. G. (1983). *Word Processing in an M.I.S Environment*. ACM 83: Proceedings of the 1983 annual conference on computers : Extending the human resource, New York, NY, USA, 225.

Fenton, N. E., and Pfleeger, S. L. (1996). *Software Metrics: A Rigorous and Practical Approach*. Boston, MA: International Thomson Computer Press.

Finck, M., and Jackewitz, I. (2006). Flyer zur Software CommSy. http://service.commsy.net/downloads/commsy_flyer_produkt.pdf Accessed 13.10.2008

Finck, M., Janneck, M., Obendorf, H., and Gumm, D. (2006). *CCS – eine Methode zur kontextübergreifenden Softwareentwicklung*. Mensch & Computer 2006: Mensch und Computer im StrukturWandel, München, 93–102.

Fischer, G. (2001). *External and Sharable Artifacts as Sources for Social Creativity in Communities of Interest*. Computational and cognitive models of creative design V: Reprints of the fifth international roundtable conference on computational and cognitive models of creative design, Sydney, 67–89.

Fischer, G. (2004). *Social Creativity: Turning Barriers into Opportunities for Collaborative Design*. PDC 04: Proceedings of the eighth conference on Participatory design, New York, NY, USA, 152–161.

Fischer, G. (2006). Beyond binary choices: Understanding and exploiting trade–offs to enhance creativity. *First Monday*, 4(11).

Flanagan, M., Howe, D. C., and Nissenbaum, H. (2005). *Values at Play: Design Tradeoffs in Socially-Oriented Game Design*. Portland, Oregon, USA, 751–760.

Floyd, C. (1987). Outline of a Paradigm Change in Software Engineering. In Be al. (Ed.), *Computers and Democracy – A Scandinavian Challenge, 253–350, Avebury, England: Avebury.*

Floyd, C. (1993). STEPS – A Methodical Approach to PD. *Commun. ACM*, 36(6), 83.

Floyd, C., and Piepenburg, U. (1993). *STEPS – ein softwaretechnischer Projektansatz und seine arbeitswissenschaftliche Begründung.* GI Jahrestagung, 145–150.

Floyd, C., Reisin, F-M., and Schmidt, G. (1989). *STEPS to Software Development with Users.* ESEC '89, 2nd European Software Engineering Conference, 48–64.

Forlizzi, J. (2008). The Product Ecology: Understanding Social Product Use and Supporting Design Culture. *International Journal of Design*, 2(1), pp. 11–20.

Fowler, M. (2003). *UML Distilled: A Brief Guide to the Standard Object Modeling Language, Third Edition.* New Jersey, NJ: Addison-Wesley Professional.

Fowler, M., Beck, K., Brant, J., Opdyke, W., and Roberts, D. (1999). *Refactoring: Improving the Design of Existing Code.* New Jersey, NJ: Addison-Wesley Professional.

Freeman-Benson, B., and Borning, A. (2003). *YP and Urban Simulation: Applying an Agile Programming Methodology in a Politically Tempestuous Domain.* Agile Development Conference, Salt Lake City, Utah.

Friedman, B. (1996). Value-sensitive design. *Interactions: New Visions of Human-Computer Interaction*, 3(6), 17–23.

Friedman, B. (1997). *Human Values and the Design of Computer Technology.* Stanford: CSLI publications.

Friedman, B., Kahn, P. H., Jr., and Borning, A. (2008). Value sensitive design and information systems. In KE Himma and HT Tavani (Eds.), *The Handbook of Information and Computer Ethics.* 69–101. Hoboken, NJ: John Wiley & Sons, Inc.

Gabriel, R. P. (1991). Lisp: Good news, bad news, how to win big. *AI Expert* 6, pp. 31–39. Available online: http://www.dreamsongs.org/WIB.html

Gedenryd, H. (1998). *How Designers Work (Lund University cognitive studies).* Unpublished PhD Dissertation, Lund University, Lund. Available online at http://www.lucs.lu.se/People/Henrik.Gedenryd/HowDesignersWork/

Gilmore, D. J., Cockton, G., Churchill, E., Kujala, S., Henderson, A., and Hammontree, M. (2008). *Values, Value and Worth: Their Relationship to hci?* Florence, Italy, 3933–3936.

Goodwin, K. (2001). Perfecting your Personas. http://www.cooper.com/journal/2001/08/perfecting_your_personas.html

Goodwin, K. (2002). Getting from Research to Personas: Harnessing the Power of Data. http://www.cooper.com/journal/2002/11/getting_from_research_to_perso.html

Green, T. R. G. (1989). Cognitive dimensions of notations. In A Sutcliffe and L Macaulay: People and Computers v 443–460. Cambridge: Cambridge University Press.

Greenbaum, J., Kyng, M., and King, M. (1991). *Design at Work: Cooperative Design of Computer Systems.* Hillsdale, NJ: Lawrence Erlbaum Associates Inc, US.

Greenwood, W. (2002). Product complexity driving you crazy? Learn where to cut. http://www.cooper.com/newsletters/2002_06/product_complexity-learn_where_to_cut.htm Accessed 13.10.2008

Grudin, J., and Pruitt, J. (2002). *Personas, Participatory Design and Product Development: An Infrastructure for Engagement.* Participatory Design Conference, Malmö, Sweden.

Grudin, J. (1994). Groupware and social dynamics: eight challenges for developers. *Communications of ACM*, 37(1), 92–105.

Hackos, J., and Redish, J. (1998). User and task analysis for interface design. *Sciences, 4*, 515–526.

Hassenzahl, M., Platz, A., Burmester, M., and Lehner, K. (2000). *Hedonic and Ergonomic Quality Aspects Determine a Software's Appeal.* CHI '00: Proceedings of the SIGCHI conference on Human factors in computing systems, New York, NY, USA, 201–208.

Hassenzahl, M., and Ullrich, D. (2007). To do or not to do: Differences in user experience and retrospective judgments depending on the presence or absence of instrumental goals. *Interacting with Computers*, 19(4), 429–437.

Henderson, A., Anderson, L., Ashley, J., Heuman, P., and Rohn, J. (2006). *The Route to the Sea for User Value*. MontrÈal, QuÈbec, Canada, 53–56.

Henderson, A., and Bradt, A. (2006). *Building User Value into the Business Case*. MontrÈal, QuÈbec, Canada, 25–27.

Hertzum, M. (2003). Making use of scenarios: a field study of conceptual design. *International Journal on Human-Computer Studies*, 58(2), 215–239.

Highsmith, J. (2002). *Agile Software Development Ecosystems*. Addison Wesley.

Hirschheim, R., Klein, H, K., and Lyytinen, K. (1995). *Information Systems Development and Data Modeling: Conceptual and Philosophical Foundations (Cambridge Tracts in Theoretical Computer Science)*. Cambridge, MA: Cambridge University Press.

Holtzblatt, K. (2002). Personas and Contextual Design. http://www.incent.com/community/design_corner/02_0913.html

Holtzblatt, K., Wendell, J. B., and Wood, S. (2004). *Rapid Contextual Design: A How-to Guide to Key Techniques for User-Centered Design (The Morgan Kaufmann Series in Interactive Technologies)*. San Fransisco, CA: Morgan Kaufmann.

IEEE. (1990). *610.12-1990: IEEE Standard Glossary of Software Engineering Terminology* (610.12). IEEE.

Jackewitz, I., Janneck, M., and Pape, B. (2002). *Vernetzte Projektarbeit mit CommSy*. Mensch & Computer 2002: Vom interaktiven Werkzeug zu kooperativen Arbeits- und Lernwelten.

Janneck, M., Finck, M., and Obendorf, H. (2006). *Grenzen bei der Verwendung von Leitbildern – ein Fallbeispiel*. Mensch & Computer 2006: Mensch und Computer im StrukturWandel, München, 73–82.

Jarke, M., Bui, X. T., and Carroll, J. M. (1998). Scenario management: An interdisciplinary approach. *Requirements Engineering Journal*, 3(3–4), pp. 155–173.

Jeffries, R., Anderson, A., Hendrickson, C., and Jeffries, R. E. (2000). *Extreme Programming Installed*. Addison-Wesley Professional.

Jeffries, R. (2001). What is Extreme Programming? http://www.xprogramming.com/xpmag/whatisxp.htm#whole Accessed 6.8.2008

Johnson, J., and Henderson, A. (2002). Conceptual models: Begin by designing what to design. *Interactions*, 9(1), 25–32.

Jones, C. (1995). *Patterns of Software Systems Failure and Success*. Boston, MA: International Thomson Computer Press.

Kahn, H. (1962). *Thinking the unthinkable*. London: Weidenfeld and Nicolson.

Koskinen, J. (2003). Software Maintenance Costs. http://users.jyu.fi/~koskinen/smcosts.htm

Kuniavsky, M. (2003). *Observing the User Experience: A Practitioner's Guide to User Research*. San Fransisco, CA: Morgan Kaufmann.

Kyng, M. (1995a). Creating contexts for design. *Scenario-Based Design: Envisioning Work and Technology in System Development*. 85–107. New York, NY: John Wiley & Sons, Inc. New York, NY, USA.

Kyng, M. (1995b). Making representations work. *Commun. ACM*, 38(9), 46–55.

Lauesen, S. (2003). Task descriptions as functional requirements. *IEEE Software*, 20(2), 58–65.

Lauesen, S. (2005). *User Interface Design: A Software Engineering Perspective*. Boston, MA: Addison-Wesley Longman Publishing Co., Inc.

Lauesen, S., and Harning, M. B. (2001). Virtual windows: Linking user tasks, data models, and interface design. *IEEE Software*, 18(4), 67–75.

Law, E. L-C., Hvannberg, E., and Cockton, G. (2007). *Maturing Usability: Quality in Software, Interaction and Value (Human-Computer Interaction Series)*. Secaucus, NJ: Springer-Verlag New York, Inc.

Leitner, M., Wolkerstorfer, P., Sefelin, R., and Tscheligi, M. (2008). *Mobile Multimedia: Identifying User Values Using the Means-End Theory*. Amsterdam, The Netherlands, 167–175. Available online at http://doi.acm.org/10.1145/1409240.1409259

Light, A., Wild, P. J., Dearden, A., and Muller, M. J. (2005). *Quality, Value(s) and Choice: Exploring Deeper Outcomes for HCI Products.* Portland, OR, USA, 2124–2125.

Löwgren, J. (1995). *Applying Design Methodology to Software Development.* New York, NY, USA, 87–95.

Mayhew, D. J. (1999). *The Usability Engineering Lifecycle: A Practitioner's Handbook for User Interface Design (The Morgan Kaufmann Series in Interactive Technologies).* San Fransisco, CA: Morgan Kaufmann.

Mello, S. (2003). *Customer-Centric Product Definition: The Key to Great Product Development.* PDC Professional Publishing.

Mikkelson, N., and Lee, W. O. (2000). *Incorporating user archetypes into scenario-based design.* UPA 2000.

Miller, J, K., Friedman, B., and Jancke, G. (2007). *Value tensions in design: the value sensitive design, development, and appropriation of a corporation's groupware system.* Sanibel Island, Florida, USA, 281 290.

Molich, R., and Nielsen, J. (1990). Improving a human-computer dialogue. *Communications of ACM,* 3, 338–348.

Moore, G. A. (1991). *Crossing the Chasm.* New York, NY: Harper Collins Publishers.

Mulder, S., and Yaar, Z. (2007). *The User Is Always Right: A Practical Guide to Creating and Using Personas for the Web.* Indianapolis, IN: New Riders.

Mylopoulos, J., Chung, L., and Yu, E. (1999). From object-oriented to goal-oriented requirements analysis. *Communications of the ACM,* 42(1), 31–37.

Ltd. N (2005). FDD overview.

Nelson, T. H. (1990). The right way to think about software design. In B Laurel and D Mills (Eds.), *The Art of Human-Computer Interface Design.* Ontario: Addison-Wesley Publishing Company Inc.

Nielsen, J. (1993). *Usability Engineering.* Boston: Academic Press.

Nielsen, L. (2004). *Engaging Personas and Narrative Scenarios.* Copenhagen: Copenhagen Business School.

Norman, D. A. (2004). Ad-Hoc Personas & Empathetic Focus. http://www.jnd.org/dn.mss/adhoc_personas_em.html

Norman, D. A. (2002). Emotion & design: attractive things work better. *interactions, 9*(4), 36–42.

Norman, D. A., and Draper, S. (1986). *User Centered System Design: New Perspectives on Human-Computer Interaction.* Hillsdale, NJ: Lawrence Erlbaum Associates.

O'Day, V. L., Bobrow, D. G., Hughes, B., Bobrow, K. B., Saraswat, V. A., Talazus, J., Walters, J., and Welbes, C. (1996). *Community designers.* Proceedings of the PDC'96, 3–13.

Obendorf, H., Schmolitzky, A., and Finck, M. (2006). *XPnUE – Defining and Teaching a Fusion of eXtreme Programming and Usability Engineering.* HCI educators workshop 2006: HCIEd.2006-1 inventivity: Teaching theory, design and innovation in HCI, Limerick, Ireland,. Available online at http://www.idc.ul.ie/hcieducators06/Procs

Obendorf, H., Finck, M., and Janneck, M. (in press). Intercontextual Participatory Design: Communicating Design Philosophy and Enriching the User Experience. *Prepared for Scandinavian Journal on Information Systems (SJIS).*

Obendorf, H., and Finck, M. (2007). *Szenariotechniken & Agile Softwareentwicklung.* Mensch & Computer. pp. 19–29. München: Oldenbourg Verlag.

Obendorf, H., and Finck, M. (2008). *Scenario-Based Usability Engineering Techniques in Agile Development Processes.* CHI '08: ACM Conference on Human Factors in Computing Systems, Florence.

Obendorf, H., Finck, M., and Schmolitzky, A. (2005). Teaching balance and respect: HCI Group & Software Technology Group at the University of Hamburg. *Interactions,* 12(5), 36–37.

Palmer, S., and Felsing, M. (2002). *A Practical Guide to Feature Driven Development.* New Jersey, NJ: Prentice Hall PTR.

Pape, B., Krause, D., and Oberquelle, H. (2004). *Wissensprojekte: Gemeinschaftliches Lernen aus didaktischer, softwaretechnischer und organisatorischer Sicht.* Münster [u.a.]: Waxmann.

Parnas, D. L. (1972). On the criteria to be used in decomposing systems into modules. *Commun. ACM*, 15(12), 1053–1058.

Parnas, D. L. (1974). *On a 'Buzzword': Hierarchical Structure.* In Software pioneers: contributions to software engineering (2002), pp. 429–440, New York, NY: Springer.

Patton, J. (2008). Twelve Emerging Best Practices for Adding UX Work to Agile Development: How Experienced UX Practitioners have Adapted to Work Happily in Agile Environments. http://agileproductdesign.com/blog/emerging_best_agile_ux_practice.html

Perfetti, C. (2002). Personas: Matching a Design to the Users' goals. http://www.uiconf.com/uie-7/goodwin_article.htm

Pruitt, J., and Grudin, J. (2003). *Personas: Practice and Theory.* CHI 2003 Extended Abstracts.

Pruitt, J., and Adlin, T. (2005). *The Persona Lifecycle: A Field Guide for Interaction Designers. Keeping People in Mind Throughout Product Design.* San Fransisco, CA: Morgan Kaufmann.

Rainey, D. L. (2005). *Product Innovation: Leading Change through Integrated Product Development.* Cambridge, MA: Cambridge University Press.

Reeder, R. W., and Maxion, R. A. (2005). *User Interface Dependability through Goal-Error Prevention.* DSN '05: Proceedings of the 2005 International Conference on Dependable Systems and Networks (DSN'05), 60–69. Available online at http://www.cs.cmu.edu/afs/cs.cmu.edu/user/maxion/www/pubs/ReederMaxionDSN05.pdf

Reichelt, L. (2007). Yes, you should be using personas.

Rettig, M. (1994). Prototyping for tiny fingers. *Communications of the ACM*, 37(4), 21–27.

Rolland, C., Ben Achour, C., Cauvet, C., Ralyté J., Sutcliffe, A., Maiden, N. A. M., Jarke, M., Haumer, P., Pohl, K., Dubois, E., and Heymans, P. (1998). A Proposal for a Scenario Classification Framework. *Requirements Engineering Journal*, 3(1), 23–47.

Rosson, M. B. (1999). Integrating development of task and object models. *Communications of the ACM.*, 42(1), 49–56.

Rosson, M. B., and Carroll, J. M. (2001). *Usability Engineering Scenario-based Development of Human Computer Interaction.* San Fransisco, CA: Morgan Kaufmann Publishers Inc,US.

Scaife, M., Rogers, Y., Aldrich, F., and Davies, M. (1997). *Designing for or Designing with? Informant Design for Interactive Learning Environments.* CHI '97: Proceedings of the SIGCHI conference on Human factors in computing systems, New York, NY, USA, 343–350.

Schwaber, K. (2004). *Agile Project Management with Scrum (Microsoft Professional).* Washington, DC: Microsoft Press.

Schwaber, K., and Beedle, M. (2001). *Agile Software Development with SCRUM.* New Jersey, NJ: Prentice Hall.

Schwartz, B. (2004). *Paradox of Choice.* New York, NY: Harper Perennial.

Seffah, A., and Metzker, E. (2004). The obstacles and myths of usability and software engineering. *Communications of the ACM*, 47(12), 71–76.

Shneiderman, B. (2000). Universal usability. *Communications of the ACM*, 43(5), 84–91.

Snyder, C. (2003). *Paper Prototyping: The Fast and Easy Way to Design and Refine User Interfaces (The Morgan Kaufmann Series in Interactive Technologies).* San Fransisco, CA: Morgan Kaufmann.

Spool, J. M. (2006). When Should You Use Personas? http://www.uie.com/brainsparks/2006/12/26/when-should-you-use-personas/

Suchman, L. (1995). Making work visible. *Communications of the ACM*, 38(9), 56–ff.

Sy, D., and Miller, L. (2008). *Optimizing Agile User-Centred Design.* Florence, Italy, 3897ñ3900.

Vanalli, S., and Cziulik, C. (2003). *Seven Steps to the Voice of the Customer.* International Conference on Engineering Design (ICED) 2003, Stockholm.

Virzi, R. A., Sokolov, J. L., and Karis, D. (1996). *Usability Problem Identification Using Both Low- and High-Fidelity Prototypes.* CHI '96: Proceedings of the SIGCHI conference on human factors in computing systems, New York, NY, USA, 236–243.

Voida, A., and Mynatt, E. D. (2005). *Conveying user values between families and designers.* Portland, OR, USA, 2013–2016. Available online at http://doi.acm.org/10.1145/1056808. 1057080

Wenger, E. (1999). *Communities of Practice: Learning, Meaning, and Identity (Learning in Doing: Social, Cognitive & Computational Perspectives S.).* Cambridge, MA: Cambridge University Press.

Wenger, E., McDermott, R. A., and Snyder, W. (2002). *Cultivating Communities of Practice: A Guide to Managing Knowledge.* Cambridge, MA: Harvard Business School Press.

Wenger, E. C., and Snyder, W. M. (2000). Communities of practice: The organizational frontier. *Harvard Business Review,* 78(1), 139–145.

Winograd, T. (1996). *Bringing Design to Software.* New York, NY: ACM Press.

Wolf, T. V., Rode, J. A., Sussman, J., and Kellogg, W. A. (2006). *Dispelling "Design" as the Black Art of CHI.* CHI '06: Proceedings of the SIGCHI conference on human factors in computing systems, New York, NY, USA, 521–530.

Züllighoven, H. (2004). *Object-Oriented Construction Handbook.* Heidelberg: Dpunkt Verlag.

Part V
Reflections on Minimalism

Chapter 8
Minimalism Revisited

Bad artists copy. Good artists steal.

— attributed to Pablo Picasso

The previous chapters establish a minimalist standpoint for the design of interactive systems: an analytic perspective of existing values and processes in human–computer interaction based on four notions of minimalism, combined with a preference for the simple. It is now time to question what benefits and limitations the preceding discussion managed to identify. Has something new been generated by the transfer of the notions of minimalism into the realm of interaction design? And has something else been lost, or become less visible? This chapter tries to give an account of how the notions of minimalism influence the perspective of analysis.

Minimalism is an extreme and potentially powerful concept, a radical approach evoking strong emotional impressions. In art and music, patterns developed by minimalist artists and musicians are still influencing current works. It has been difficult to transfer this strong standpoint into other domains, such as cooking—although it has certainly been tried more than once. The design of interactive systems, however, with the increasingly popular notion of simplicity is an obvious candidate for minimalism: we want our meals to be complex and delicate, while interactive systems should often simply support us dealing with more important matter than technology—rather than trying to be surprising, absorbing and emotionally moving. Still, the touchstone of a minimalist perspective must be whether design techniques can be better understood (or modified) and put to use to create simplicity.

The Palm, the Apple iPod Shuffle and the Post-it note are examples that demonstrate it is possible to design simplicity in complex systems. To create simplicity, design must go beyond the surface, it will never suffice to only put over a deceptively simple cover. The difficulties simplifying Microsoft Word only by changing the interface and hiding functionality might be enough evidence (Chapter 6), yet a simple dishwasher story might do more convincing job:

H. Obendorf, *Minimalism*, Human-Computer Interaction Series,
DOI 10.1007/978-1-84882-371-6_8, © Springer-Verlag London Limited 2009

In a small church community, the task of cleaning dishes was usually carried out by women, many of them already retired, from the neighborhood. Until a new, ultra-silent dishwasher was delivered. The General Electrics engineers had given their best to create the ultimately simple interface – no distracting displays, only two buttons. However, as a result, the women are now no longer washing the dishes. The main button, labeled Start/Reset, would set the machine in motion. As the machine is ultra-silent, this would take very good ears to detect, and as the users were often not sure whether they had hit the button, so they would hit it again. And thus reset the washing procedure, so that the machine would be ready for new commands after more or less two minutes. However, until then, they would have hit the button too often to remember it being an even or an odd number...

(Tognazzini, 2003).

The immediate bottom line is that simplicity may be deceptive, feedback may be necessary and mapping complexity should be avoided. Taken a step further, the story collects many claims of the minimalist standpoint: the scope of design must be broadened to include the whole system (including its internal architecture), and the context of use and users.

8.1 The Minimal Perspective on Design

A beautiful program's way of doing things is so close to your own that creative symbiosis develops, a thought-amplifying feedback loop.
—David Gelernter (1998, 25)

The complexity gap, the chasm between the desired ease of use and the necessary complexity of use environments, or, more precisely, the reduction of the gap, is an aim of numerous methodological approaches to the design of human-computer interaction. Yet, while design practice is busy trying to build bridges spanning the complexity gap, a reflective treatment of the values and motivations that underlie these approaches is rare. Instead, a shared belief that simplicity is desirable forms the basis for manifold design decisions and suggestions. The meaning of simplicity, however, differs from author to author, and even from application to application, and the phrase "less is more" is used wherever it serves an illustrating function.

Minimalism, closely connected with the "less is more" motto, has not been defined as a term within human-computer interaction before. Its definition bears the promise of a deeper understanding of simplicity, and of a differentiation between different notions of simplicity that overlay and obstruct each other in the literature. Using the term minimalism in design can be both useful and dangerous: it easily engages members of diverse background into discussion, yet negotiations of meaning must precede almost every discussion of minimalism if incompatible meanings are to be excluded.

Before a successful definition, however, stands the transfer from the liberal arts, spiritual home of the term, to the interdisciplinary field concerned with the design of interactive systems. A proposal for this transdisciplinary undertaking is made in this book, introducing a minimalist perspective to the science of design.

The roots of minimalism lie within painting and sculpture. Conceived of by critics, the term minimalism was used to identify a group of artists in the U.S. that started to appear during the 1960s and concentrated on experimenting with different means of reduction (Section 2.1). They tried to reduce their *means*, the *meaning* of their works, the structure in their works, and the constructional effort by using *patterns*; different approaches alternatively tried to minimize actions of the spectator, delivering total control, and creating *freedom* through involvement, turning the onlooker's interpretation into an important part of the artwork. Minimalism as a term was so successful that its use spread to music (Section 2.2), where different artists created modern "classical" music, opposing Serialism, and creating a new musical language that reintroduced tonality, and employed different forms of repetition. Although minimal music itself never became part of popular culture, its influence extends to current pop and electronic music.

Minimalism was also taken up to describe trends in literature, typography, and architecture (Section 2.3). While each discipline had its individual interpretation of the term, and fierce battles were fought defining the artistic merit of reduction, almost all protagonists agreed on the listed aspects. The subsequent transfer of the notion of minimalism to the design of interactive systems is thus based on a shared, although not univocal, understanding of the term (Section 2.4).

Four notions of minimalism are defined (Sections 3.3.1, 3.3.2, 3.3.3, 3.3.4), and their interactions are discussed (Section 3.3.5). All four notions of minimalism refer to the interface seen from a user's perspective; although the definition uses the terms structural and architectural, which are conventionally connected with the internal construction of a system, the focus of this book lies on the interaction with a design, examining the construction of a system only as it becomes determinant of the perceivable interface. Minimalism is explicitly more than superficial, yet it deduces requirements for the system architecture from the architecture of the interface, not otherwise.

Functional Minimalism denotes the reduction in accessible functionality. A functionally minimal system focuses on its core competency and presents only few key features to the user.

Structural Minimalism denotes the reduction in perceived access structure. This involves trade-offs as important functionality is made more directly accessible—at the cost of making unimportant functionality harder to access. The success of this strategy depends on the ability to determine this importance; adaptive approaches must consider the negative effects of changing access structures.

Architectural Minimalism denotes the reduction of perceived complexity through a transparent distribution of responsibility across tools. The combination of simple tools creates the necessary functional complexity for the user.

Compositional Minimalism denotes the reduction of a design's specificity for planned tasks. A compositionally minimal system makes fewer assumptions about its use and places fewer restrictions upon its users. This extends the notion of user control beyond the individual task.

Although there is some conceptual overlap, the different notions of minimalism focus on different aspects of the design: functional and structural minimalism highlight aspects of the concrete design, while architectural and compositional minimalism point towards more transient aspects of the design that are determined by the construction method and the introduction into the work context (Fig. 8.1). Functional minimalism and structural minimalism both affect the system's *user interface* directly, while architectural and compositional minimalism work at different levels, namely the inner construction of the system and the users' "interface" to the system, or the integration with other tools.

Structural and architectural minimalism both focus on adapting the tool to the task, modifying the structure by which functionality is accessed, while functional and compositional minimalism stress the connection between the use of the tool and the context of use.

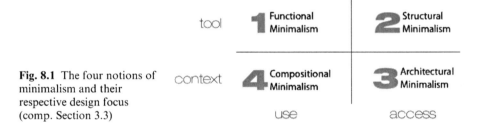

Fig. 8.1 The four notions of minimalism and their respective design focus (comp. Section 3.3)

Together, these four notions of minimalism form a perspective on existing, experience-based, expert knowledge that allows to group and categorize design heuristics that have been found to support the design of simple interactive systems. By differentiating between qualities of an interface that in combination create a simpler use experience, a more constructive understanding of interaction is defined.

Compared with existing standards and norms, a new perspective on existing HCI lore is created that groups and categorizes often-cited guidelines without aspiring to provide a complete theoretical framework (Chapter 4). Minimalism also provides some direction in understanding the links between common rules and values of design (Chapter 5).

8.2 Minimalism as an Analytic Tool

> Things should be as simple as possible. But no simpler.
>
> — attributed to Albert Einstein

The analysis of design products is responsible for much of the physical weight of this book (Chapter 6): the four notions of minimalism are each introduced with an "exotic" example that highlights peculiarities of the respective notion before real-world examples are introduced and discussed. In total, twelve examples are examined for their minimal qualities, with different application for word processing providing the background for an encounter of the different perspectives on a single domain.

Each product was chosen as it can be considered special in its simplicity, and the four notions of minimalism are used to discuss how this simplicity relates to the different perspectives on reduction. Although each example is simple in more than one way, the four perspectives allow a differentiation of the minimal aspects that combine to create the design's simplicity. It is also possible to speculate about design priorities that led to the development of the individual product.

The discussion suggests that building functionally minimal products—such as Apple's iLife applications—can help to reach a mass market as a subset of the functionality that professional software needs to deliver is often useful enough to motivate new users to start e.g., editing video or making computer music. The resulting simplicity more than makes up for missing features—if the presented product feels "whole" and does not openly advertise that it is "only" a restricted version, creating a shareware feeling (e.g., by advertising missing functionality). However, the examples also demonstrate that functional minimalism in software is difficult as features tend to accumulate.

Structural minimalism is responsible for the simplicity and consequently the popularity of many designs that underwent intensive user testing. However, the initial success and the current stagnation of the Palm Pilot, and the historical episode of Nokia building explicitly simple mobile phones (Section 6.2.3) illustrates the difficulties of keeping pace with the feature frenzy. The analysis suggests that a distinction can be made between inflexible and flexible minimal structures, depending on the generalizability of the tasks or activities that the structure is adopted for. The new 2007 Microsoft Office suite is an example for grouping functionality according to activity, introducing easily visible modes for the toolbar-like ribbon.

Architectural minimalism is analyzed on the level of tools interacting within an application through direct manipulation, using SketchUp as an example. Yet, also the more common distribution of functionality across different applications (as in Apple's Automator) or services (as in the Web 2.0 platform) is put forward for analysis.

The necessity of including the appropriation of products by users as a parallel process during development to be able to achieve some compositional minimalism is highlighted as successful products are explored that allow its users to freely choose the use context, e.g., presentation software and WikiWebs.

The discussion demonstrates that it is possible—and that it can be very profitable—to build minimal interfaces, even if customers demand tools for complex and diverse tasks. The examples focus on specific qualities of existing designs and relate these to the notions of minimalism, identifying minimal traits in the examined designs.

But the examples serve not only an illustrating function, they are also used to question and improve the abstract definitions of the notions of minimalism. As a consequence, the minimal terminology is further sharpened, allowing a shift towards the constructive to be introduced that enables not only the abstract designation of minimal attitudes, but also the identification of matching minimal "best practices". These design heuristics are extracted and assigned to one

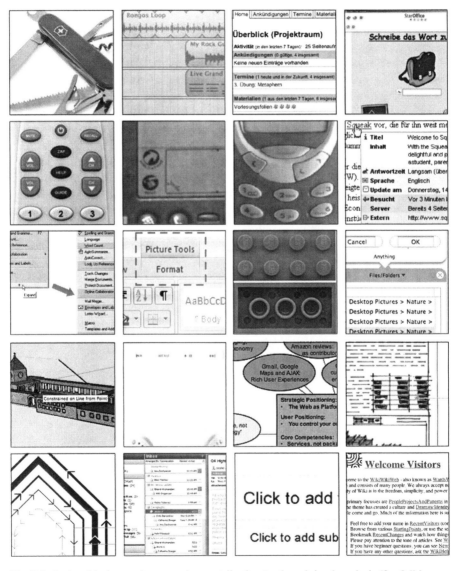

Fig. 8.2 A visual index to the examples contributing to the minimal analysis (for full images see Chapter 6)

of the four notions of minimalism, in the hope that they could be helpful for new designs (Section 6.5.2).

Figure 8.2 displays an overview of the products examined in the sixth chapter. *First row:* 6.1.1 Cutting edges, 6.1.2 Apple GarageBand, 6.1.3 CommSy, 6.1.4 Functionally minimal word processors. *Second row:* 6.2.1 Remote controls, 6.2.2 Palm Handheld, 6.2.3 Nokia 3110 series, 6.2.4 HyperScout. *Third row:* 6.2.5 Structural minimalism in Word 2000 and 2007, 6.3.1 Lego bricks, 6.3.2 Apple Automator. *Fourth row:* 6.3.3 SketchUp, 6.3.4 Apple iPod, 6.3.5 Web 2.0, 6.3.6 Architectural minimalism in Ragtime. *Fifth row:* 6.4.1 Learning Buildings, 6.4.3 E-mail, 6.4.4 Powerpoint, 6.4.5 WikiWikiWebs.

An abbreviated overview of the minimal design heuristics is given in Table 8.1. The listed heuristics are not understood to be imperative. Rather, it is obvious that heuristics assigned to a single notion of minimalism contradict each other, e.g. suggest that a structural reduction could be reached by prioritized access according to frequency, or activity. This is no fault—instead, the heuristics describe alternative approaches to attaining an effect that is covered by the respective definition of structural minimalism. A designer must therefore take the design context of the given examples into account, and individually weigh trade-offs for a specific design problem.

Table 8.1 Summary of Minimal Design Heuristics (compare Chapter 6.5.2, Table 6.13)

Functional Minimalism
- Identify the *core functionality* of the design. Define whether the design aims to be a simple tool.
- Take a holistic perspective: define the responsibilities of the design *as a whole*.
- Discuss trade-offs involved with extending functionality. Keep track of the initial vision and its changes.
- Assess the feasibility of providing multiple interfaces using a single platform (optionally: let users select).

Structural Minimalism
- Prioritize access according to *frequency*.
- Prioritize access according to *activity*.
- Translate prioritization into appropriate modalities.

Architectural Minimalism
- Examine your interface architecture at different levels: Building blocks can be gestures or interaction techniques, or manifest themselves as visible tools.
- Modularization, or division in tools risks fragmentation—the *whole design must remain visible*.

Compositional Minimalism
- Designs should not be generic, but generalizable. Do not try to plan the future, support "misuse".
- Functionally minimal designs are one approach towards design support for appropriation.
- Modularize functionality in your design—form "building blocks". The resulting "use patterns" can be "interpreted" in different use situations by users.

8.3 Minimalism as a Constructive Tool

The successful application of the four different notions of minimalism in the analysis of design products created an immediate motivation to give them a more constructive role in the designs of interactive systems. As they could be used to differentiate and prioritize aspects of "simplicity" in designs, an immediate idea was to use the same language in system construction like in system analysis; the resulting technique was the Minimal Design Game. To enable a more subtle integration in existing development processes, existing techniques can be analyzed and selected with regard to their minimal qualities; different existing techniques are assigned to the four notions of minimalism ranging from personas and scenarios to agile development methods and value-based design approaches.

8.3.1 A Minimalist Design Method: The Minimal Design Game

The Minimal Design Game (Fig. 8.3; Section 7.2) is a paper-based set of methods that tries first to analyze an existing design for possibilities of reduction. In a second step, it revisits the reduced design ideas and assesses their suitability for integration with the core idea that was uncovered by stripping away the unnecessary.

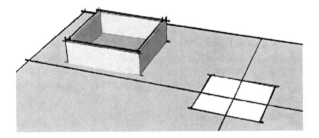

Fig. 8.3 The Minimal Design Game Setup: Ready for Reduction?

By laying out the "design space" on the table surface, and by asking the following questions, a design is challenged for its coherence, and parts that might be reduced or refactored become visible:

1. What is the primary function, what is it that we really want to be able to do?
2. How is that purpose of the artefact conveyed to the user?
3. Can the system be simplified by splitting it up into parts?
4. Can adaptation that limits use in other contexts be reduced?

In a preliminary evaluation of the Minimal Design Game, most participants immediately understood the notions of *functional* and *structural minimalism*, and produced promising results using the provided guiding questions. Interpreting *architectural* and *compositional minimalism*, however, was more difficult; these notions are not obvious and present a new perspective, they both make use of terms that are already in use in computer science, and specifically in software development. As a second consequence from the evaluation, it became clear that the demonstrative focus on minimal designs encourages critical assessment about how minimal a solution should be.

8.3.2 Indirect Minimalism in Existing Methods

It is certainly valuable to have techniques at hand that focus on reducing a design. However, there are many reasons that will prevent such "destructive" activities in real projects, beginning with the differences in definitions for simplicity, and going beyond the need to extend the focus on creating the minimal beyond the initial design to maintenance and redesign. The least resistance is to be expected if the existing development process can be continued with only small twists—and chances are good that this is possible: existing methods have proven to be able to produce simplicity, and having a firm understanding in how they reduce choices for design can help to strengthen this effect. Understanding the minimalist perspective might thus help you to make better use of your existing tools.

8.3.2.1 Minimalism through Focus on User Scope

A frequent cause of feature frenzy is the consideration "it seems somehow useful, I can imagine someone might need that". Limiting requirements to real users is thus the first step towards a reduction in functionality. Reduction is even stronger if the number of users is kept artificially small—the risk of not satisfying some users is put against the chance of creating a better design for the remaining majority.

Functional reduction is discussed using the well-known, but not necessarily well-defined method of personas. Fictional characters that represent actual users might not seem useful for every project if only the communication function of personas is taken into consideration. But there is more to personas: they have a strong focusing effect for the design scope: if but a few personas are used to contextualize design, it will be much easier to decide what is important, and thus identify a functional core for development.

8.3.2.2 Minimalism through Focus on Tasks

The reduction of perceived access structures is a common objective of usability techniques—whether setting out to implement the formative modeling of user tasks or a summative evaluation through user tests with end users, the aim is a better fit of access structures to user tasks. To prevent the introduction of inflexibility by optimizing the structure to tasks specific to only a part of the possible users, some overview is necessary, complementing the more focused information collected on users' tasks.

Scenarios promise to deliver this focus-and-context through their informal nature: the level of abstraction that is used to describe tasks is up to their author; if written well, core functionalities are set in context and provide both important information about structure and more general information about the interaction of different tasks. Scenarios thus act as a *filter for design*, reducing *functionality* and *structure*. They can also support the partitioning of functionality and be used to identify the building blocks for an *architecturally minimal* system.

8.3.2.3 Minimalism through Iterative and Agile Development

Going beyond functional and structural minimalism requires a deeper under-standing of the use context. The approach taken in this book assumes that iterative development using evolutionary prototypes eases the design task by incorporating realistic user feedback as early as possible in the process—design can be based on empirical results rather than deduction and hypothesis build-ing, and technological design decisions are reviewable early on. Agile processes are used to illustrate the mechanics of iterative development, partly because they are becoming increasingly popular in the industry, partly because they propose simplicity as an explicit value for development.

Yet, although agile development processes explicitly aim to reduce, reduc-tion in agile processes focuses on the construction of a system, and the con-struction process. By avoiding the development of unnecessary components, incrementally advancing and minimizing the necessity for process documenta-tion, a lightweight process is created. Its agility helps reacting to requirement changes, and thus supports the development of software where a formal speci-fication is not possible in advance—most interactive systems would fall under this category. However, agile methods strongly focus on individual features to negotiate and prioritize product design. While this approach promises to minimize risks for both developer and customer, the lack of a holistic focus as maintained by a minimalist standpoint risks the fragmentation and over-diversification of the design.

As an example for overcoming these weaknesses, a combination of extreme programming with scenario techniques is described (Fig. 8.4) where the process is kept as agile as possible and scenarios supply an overview of the design gestalt and bring contextual grounding to the stories used for developing individual features.

8.3.2.4 Minimalism in Application Growth

Finally, the identification of shifts from focus on functional and structural to architectural and compositional minimalism in an example development process demonstrates that the minimalist standpoint helps to cultivate simplicity in aging and growing applications. A case study illustrates the need for a shift from func-tional and structural minimalism to architectural and compositional minimalism.

Value-based participatory design is proposed as an example process that includes users in design activities across several generations of a product, and

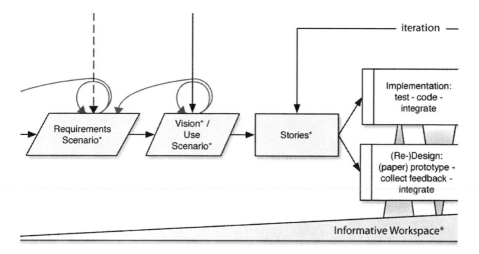

Fig. 8.4 The XPnUE process pattern introduces scenario techniques to Extreme Programming

thus helps to better judge the trade-offs implicit in design decisions introducing new functionality and adding to access structure, and identify shifts in usage practice. Values are used to support the communication with users from different contexts, and to support fostering a community of interest growing from several communities of practice.

Using values in design made it possible to envision a system that is more than structurally minimal—as there is no single-use case that it could be optimally fit to, but instead to identify blocks of functionality that can be made into tools for specific audiences—shifting towards a more architecturally minimal interface, and to examine where the software inhibits "creative misuse", thus reducing unnecessarily strict composition in the design (Fig. 8.5).

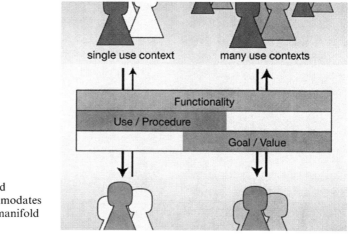

Fig. 8.5 Value-based development accommodates diverging needs of manifold contexts

8.4 Refining the Definition of Minimalism

This book introduced minimalism as a perspective on design. Although not aspiring to form a design theory, it approached a formal definition of four notions of minimalism in Chapter 3 based on the discourse on minimalism in art and music: *functional, structural, architectural* and *compositional minimalism*. Each dimension is loaded with implicit propositions, some of which might have become more obvious in its following application. To improve on the original definitions, limitations and interactions of the four notions of minimalism are summarized here, hoping to provide a better background for their application.

8.4.1 Functional Minimalism Revisited

Straightforward, if not simple, functional minimalism comes first to mind when looking for reduction in a design. However, although it is most easily implemented—by omitting functionality—it is difficult to get right, and challenging to maintain: Definitions of what is minimal change as *users or tasks change*. What is minimal for one may be too little for another, or too much, or both. As any design decision, functional reduction requires trade-offs; what makes it more difficult than the usual decision is that no single stakeholder can be identified to stand for non-inclusion of a certain feature. Instead, it is the *whole* of the design that needs to be considered to keep functionality lean. As this *design gestalt* is completely abstract, it is difficult to embody in the design process—and often, a strong designer is needed to withstand the temptation of pleasing just this one user who really needs just this one feature. And the next.

Another problem is brought with the nature of product development itself: the *2.0 syndrome*. While, for example, furniture design classics might sell for a decade, or even longer, eventually becoming valued antiques, software ages quickly, and new software is not often sold on the grounds of improved quality, but because of added features. Imagine an advertisement that says a product did exactly the same, but differently (and perhaps, better), or even the announcement of a new version that does not any longer include a given feature (maybe exactly the one you always needed) in order to be less distracting—it sounds too risky, and not spectacular enough.[1] Further, resisting the introduction of new features—or extending an ideally minimal set of functionality without disturbing its balance is inherently difficult.

The discussion of the different types of minimalism, and the analysis of the design products has shown that functional minimalism is closely connected to other forms of minimalism. Structural minimalism *hides functionality*; it

---

[1] Even when designers create a functionally more minimal device, advertisements will often focus on its features; a good example is the iPod Shuffle—it did not say "no display, fewer buttons, less hassle" but "shuffle!".

therefore helps to make designs *appear* more minimal. In effect, structural minimalism is often used as a replacement for functional minimalism. As the principle of functional minimalism is more and more violated, however, it becomes increasingly difficult to maintain the illusion of simplicity.

Architectural minimalism leads directly to functional minimalism in the tools that are part of the architecturally minimal toolbox—each individual tool has fewer responsibilities, and can therefore focus on fewer functions. The two forms of minimalism coexist and require each other—without reduction in tools, a toolbox is difficult to characterize as minimal, and the distribution of responsibilities underlies many design decisions that lead to the reduction of functionality (the statement that a function is omitted is made far more easy if there is something that can be relied on to fill that need).

Finally, compositional minimalism is often easier to achieve with functionally minimal tools, because they tend to be easier to master, and are, like the proverbial hammer, not adapted to a specific task, thus supporting creative misuse.

Functional Minimalism denotes the reduction in accessible functionality. A functionally minimal system focuses on its core competency and presents only few key features to the user.

Functional Minimalism can define *a simple and powerful product*, or an *ideal for the product gestalt* (a long-term vision) that guides development.

Functional minimalism

- eases the creation of minimal-access structures (structural minimalism), its usefulness in turn depends on the absence of accidental complexity;
- will often create products that do not stand by themselves. Usefulness will come through interaction with other tools, functional focus helps to provide interfaces to other tools (architectural minimalism);
- can be but cannot remain successful without continuing design—adaptation and product cultivation are necessary ingredients.

8.4.2 Structural Minimalism Revisited

In a world where all software is functionally minimal, there would be no need for structural minimalism—there is no need to differentiate between actual and perceived minimality of choices. However, our failure to create functionally minimal products leaves ample room for structural approaches to minimalism. Structural minimalism was defined as minimal perceived access structures for functionality. In other words, it equals *immediate* access to functionality in users' work.

Access structures can be defined *statically* by the designer, possibly according to user research and following some plan of what tasks they will be used for. This is usually associated with the information architecture, or information design. Different strategies can be followed to create well-adapted, or, to emphasize the manual work involved, well-tailored systems. Following a simple frequency strategy (ordering functions according to their expected use frequency) is surprisingly powerful, especially when the input channel of the product is a limiting factor (true, e.g. for mobile phones and PDA). However, the resulting access structures are created without insight into the reasons for coherence, and can be fragile—the better they are adapted to specific tasks, the more prone they are to age and eventually fail. This explains the emergence of interaction patterns, and eventually standards that develop a strong attraction and reduce change in task execution.

It is also possible for the end-user, or a specially empowered administrator-user, to *manually* adapt access structures to the needs. Often, this simply means configuration or customization, but end-user programming could be included as an extreme of the adaptive agency of the user. This is not only a very convenient solution for the designer, it is also a very democratic solution as every user is responsible for the simplicity of his/her own interface. However, there are several issues associated with adapting access structures: Even configuration is so costly that few users undertake the effort to acquire and execute the skills necessary to adapt their interface—and only for those applications that are used extremely frequently. Configuration, customization, and end-user programming are activities separate from, and often on top of the normal work activities, and can thus be an expense that is difficult to justify. Interfaces changed by customization isolate users in that they lose the option of calling to colleagues and coworkers for help. Customized, and especially pre-tailored interfaces also have a social dimension—who would like to be named a novice after years of specific use of a complex software, and who would reject being an expert? This makes it especially difficult to gain acceptance for those approaches that aim to simplify the complexities of customization by providing increasingly complex (expert) layers of access structures.

Although in theory not only convenient but also close to optimal, *automatically* minimizing access structures by some program logic has yet to be proven to deliver value to the end user. Adaptive systems are a very active area for research, and very popular with those developing algorithms; the use context is however only seldom taken into account, and even without context, adaptivity can create disorientation when it equals a loss of stability (Gajos et al., 2008).

Different techniques of not only arranging but also visibly grouping functionality according to task have proven value. These are not necessarily new techniques, as for example, toolbars have been around for quite some time. However, tools such as Microsoft's ribbon combine the tool—within-a-software— with modes, and thus effectively render a complex software with many random-access tools into a number of more single-purposed interfaces sharing a common application envelope. This is a clear step towards architectural minimalism in that the architecture of a software landscape is grouped into clearly discernible tools. Maintaining structural minimalism in the resulting, much smaller groups of functions becomes much easier. Architectural minimalism can thus be interpreted not as something completely different, but rather as defining structure on another level: structural minimalism refers to the task level associated with one tool, architectural minimalism to a level where activities determine the interaction of complementing tools.

Limitations of structural minimalism have become clear as functionality is acquired over time: traditional approaches, such as hiding the complexity in menus and sub-menus, don't scale well—at least if functionality keeps to accumulate in products over time. The Palm example demonstrated that limiting your focus on structural minimalism might provide an ideal tool—but only for a limited target group, and for a limited time, because inflexibility is introduced as a side effect. Other methods for reducing the access structure are then necessary.

When structural minimalism creates this inflexibility, the ability for adopting a tool for non-intended use is decreased; compositional minimalism might thus be interpreted as the antithesis of structural minimalism. However, an obscure or complex access structure does also complicate the adoption of functionality. Structural minimalism is thus neither "good" or "bad"; some adaptations trade off simplicity for one user with complexity for another—this happens as the structure used for shaping access is not generalizable across users. In other words, inflexibility is introduced, as consistence on the level of the application, and between differing user groups is violated—sometimes this may be necessary. Use patterns and Cooper's idioms are examples of attempts at finding more general truths, or establishing standards that procreate generalizable truths as they are adopted.

Structural Minimalism denotes the reduction in perceived access structure. This involves trade-offs as important functionality is made more directly accessible—at the cost of making unimportant functionality harder to access. The success of this strategy depends on the ability to determine this importance; adaptive approaches must consider the negative effects of changing access structures.

Effectiveness, efficiency, and satisfaction are often indirect results of structural minimalism as Usability methods focus on tuning the access structure to the needs of users.

Structural Minimalism can create flexible and versatile tools if it *groups universally applicable units of functionality* or creates *interaction patterns* gaining broad acceptance, but it can also introduce *inflexibility* into products as highly specialized tasks are supported.

Structural minimalism

- helps to hide complexity; can be harmful in case of failure;
- is often specific to users (scope) and depends on their tasks (use);
- can be dangerous if it introduces inflexibility;
- must therefore ideally be generalizable;
- should not exist in isolation.

8.4.3 Architectural Minimalism Revisited

Architectural minimalism extends the scope of design: instead of creating a single product, the focus of design is placed on the environment of the future product; while the *use context* was important before, the *use environment* includes all other tools that will be used alongside, or together with the design. These can already exist, and thus be beyond the direct reach of design, or they can be part of what is to come—given enough time and energy, it is possible to design a complete use environment (as Apple has done for OS X).

There is a close relationship between the usefulness of a functionally minimal part and its use environment: at first sight, the perspective of architectural minimalism is not necessary if a design is functionally so simple that the need to define parts within the design does not exist. But the utility of functionally minimal tools is strongly determined by the availability of other tools that supplement their functionality: a chisel needs a hammer, and the iPod Shuffle would be of little use without the iTunes software. Simple tools become powerful only because, on a larger scope, other tools exist. It is not a prerequisite that these other tools are actively designed, but understanding them helps to place the focused functionality in context: architectural minimalism often coexists with functional minimalism on different levels of abstraction.[2] The initial notion of architectural minimalism is thus expanded to include non-self-designed tools.

While the definitions of structural and functional minimalism are clearly distinguishable, the former relating to a single tool and its "perceived access structure", the latter to the "distribution of responsibility across tools", their shared focus on grouping functionality requires a clarification of differences and similarities that have surfaced in the discussion of designs and approaches to designing minimality: For the user, *tools* are access structure that is applied to solve a task at hand. But there is more to tools than to, say, the ordering of menu items: they create manageable and touchable manifestations of structure that present users with a descriptive model for their coherence—all functions ascribed to a tool need to belong there. Access structures defined in interaction patterns (e.g. a shopping cart) or idioms (e.g. a context menu) work on a different level: they remain conceptual and less graspable than tools that are directly connected to user tasks (e.g. the spreadsheet or text editor). The notion of architecture implies that different parts can be analyzed in isolation—they are functionally complete even if they would need other tools to be useful.

For architectural minimalism to work, the *division of responsibility* that forms the basis of the design architecture must be understood by the user—at least in so far as he/she will need to make use of the defined parts. Architectural

---

[2] It is not required for architecturally minimal use environments to hold only functionally minimal parts.

minimalism thus requires keeping the *whole use environment visible*; this is true both for the designer and for the user of a product. If designs are built by adding part to part, the risk of fragmentation is great—tools might be distributed, but access should remain not only easily possible, but also visible. Google experienced what happens as this fails when different services were not visible on their home page: removed from sight, they failed to add to the use environment.

Creating architectural minimalism involves deciding where to draw a line between different parts of a design entrusted with different functions. Technical considerations can be the source for this demarcation as tasks are distributed across different modalities, e.g. differentiating roles of a PDA or music player and a computer. To support choice regarding the use of different parts of a design, responsibility can also be defined along different activities, effectively allowing the designation of coherent groups of functionality that can then be bundled in explicitly visible tools. As in structural minimalism, this allows appropriation: different users can choose the tools they need for their specific tasks—without requiring these tasks to be defined in entirety.

To enable interaction between different designs, there must be a match in both conceptual and technical interfaces.[3] As the notion of architecture suggests, reduction must go beyond the user interface in architectural minimalism. A technical basis is necessary to allow for a separation of concerns. Conceptual interfaces are often defined by convention, for the technical interfaces, standards, and especially the rising popularity of open standards, allow use of different tools in conjunction. It is difficult, however, to reach the level of openness that the Post-it note demonstrates: no technical solution is in sight that connects to as many environments as the glue invented by the 3M engineer (Section 6.4.2). However, the monolithic application slowly becomes a thing of the past as interfaces between different services gain importance: from Hypertext, the idea of connecting different types of documents has evolved to connecting different types of applications and services on the Web, on the desktop, and in service-oriented enterprise architectures.

Architectural minimalism implies that different parts of a design create different perspectives that can be simple. Understanding their interaction, however, can be complex, and designing for the use environment is no trivial task. Choosing a process that delivers immediate and realistic feedback from use can help designers to create minimal architectures: while each part iteratively grows to a sound whole, responsibility can be distributed across the developing parts—the complex use environment needs not to be created in a big up-front design, but is built up from small pieces, based on technological spikes and a stepwise evolution of the design gestalt.

---

[3] The distribution of functionality bears the risk of increasing overall complexity due to inconsistency, both for the maintainer (in the role of designer, manufacturer or administrator), and for the user.

Architectural Minimalism denotes the reduction of perceived complexity through a transparent distribution of responsibility across tools. The combination of simple tools creates the necessary functional complexity for the user.
Architectural minimalism can generate complex functionality built upon the interaction of simple, often functionally minimal, tools.

Architectural minimalism

- needs to be considered on a more abstract level than the single tool;
- requires some degree of functional and structural minimalism;
- conflicts with inflexibility introduced through structural minimalism;
- touches both technical aspects and visual design;
- increases the need for incremental design;

8.4.4 Compositional Minimalism Revisited

Although we all misuse tools on a daily basis, we tend not to think of that. If you are not convinced, think of all the objects that you have used to open a bottle, crack a nut or get someone's attention (comp. Westrum, 1991; Penley and Ross, 1991). Designing for creative misuse, however, seems self-contradictory: how could you intentionally design something for an unintended use? The answer to this question is: Of course, you can't. Yet, compositional minimalism is not about intending the unintended, but about inviting the creativity of end-users through reducing the fixation on a problem that is perhaps only limited to a small target group, or a personal fancy of the designer, and about putting trust into the abilities of end users to make use of tools for their own ends. To encourage them, they will, in turn, have to place trust in the tools provided to them, and it also helps if they understand and master their use.

A designer must thus provide functionality, create relationships and structure, possibly even define responsibilities for parts of his/her design—but leave part of the composition to the user. This is a dramatic change in the role attributed to designers and HCI practitioners: the *autocrat* must become the *enabler*.

Although closely related, in contrast to the perspective on appropriation taken by architectural minimalism, compositional minimalism focuses on the user and the use of a design in context. While it is clearly possible to create great, compositionally minimal designs based on intuition (or even accident), it might help to include the user and his/her experience with the product in the design. Extending the design process to include actual use is thus central to the idea of compositional minimalism—reducing composition can not only focus on a state of design, it must also become a process. This calls for a dramatic departure from current practice, where a design is handed off to development, and reaches the deployment stage long after design is finished.

For compositional minimalism, the evolution of a design and the changes in the use of the resulting product series are parallel and interacting processes that must be viewed in conjunction. For the life-cycle of a design, this means that the design of a successful product must evolve, or at least, include knowledge about existing predecessors as the user base broadens. Mechanisms for including new users in the design process need to be established to learn about their ways of using a product, and removing barriers that might keep them from adoption. Value-based design was shown to be an example for including users in the design process, and sustaining communication with new users from different use contexts.

Creative misuse is prevented by tightly determining possible uses for functionality. The inversion of this argument yields that the principle that makes creative misuse possible is loose coupling of functionality (cf. Weick, 2001, 43f). Consequently, manifestations from all other definitions of minimalism can help to encourage the appropriation denoted by compositional minimalism: functionally minimal designs will often clearly communicate their use, and if the technical conditions are met, users might start to change the intended context of use. Structural minimalism can help with transferring functionality from one domain to another if it is not reached by adaptive "intelligence" or inflexible adaptation to specific tasks as it accentuates the functionality of a tool.

Architectural minimalism, however, is probably the most promising approach for supporting compositional minimalism: it deconstructs complex functionality into smaller, more manageable tools that can consequently be combined in unplanned contexts of use—parts of the functionality can be unbundled.

> *Compositional Minimalism* denotes the reduction of a design's specificity for planned tasks. A compositionally minimal system makes fewer assumptions about its use and places fewer restrictions upon its users. This extends the notion of user control beyond the individual task.
>
> Compositional Minimalism might be the most useful form of minimalism for the user as it empowers her/him to freely choose and employ tools. For design, it is most difficult to implement as it, by definition, cannot be planned, only supported.
>
> **Compositional minimalism**
>
> - implies that appropriation can be *encouraged* but never *determined;*
> - requires to extend the focus of design to product families and maintenance;
> - attributes the designer with the role of an *enabler;*
> - matches well with iterative development as the *change of use* and the *evolution of the design* progress in parallel.

8.5 Implications of a Minimalist Standpoint for Design

> *Perfection is reached, not when there is no longer anything to add,*
> *but when there is no longer anything to take away.*
>
> — Antoine de Saint-Exupéry

Design is commonly understood as an act of creation, opening up possibilities by defining new problems and introducing matching solutions; design is associated with addition, growth and augmentation. Metaphorically, reduction seems unfitting in a design context. Yet, reduction is part of all design processes, every choice between different design options reduces the design space, the result of a design process is only one of a multitude of possibilities. Reduction in itself is part of design.

Minimalism changes the perception of design by making reduction a central, conscious activity, and, perhaps more importantly, by changing the value system to include the thought that well less may be more. By defining different forms of minimality, and thus different paths to simplicity, each with its benefits and limitations, reduction is given scope and direction. Minimalism presents the chance for designers to become more aware of the implications of their choices.

The value system of design is adjusted as a minimalist standpoint is assumed: with *functional minimalism*, focus shifts from individual features to the whole of a design, defining a gestalt and measuring its coherence. With *structural minimalism*, flexibility is introduced as not the single task but the whole-use context forms the base for design, and with *architectural minimalism*, the use environment replaces the single product as the matter of design. *Compositional minimalism* finally widens the boundaries of design to include more than a single cycle, and aims at sustainable development instead of disposable products.

With the definition of architectural and compositional minimalism, wide-reaching consequences manifest themselves for interaction design—as users' needs are included and negotiated over several product generations, iteratively converging on a design gestalt for a tool, a shift from product to process becomes necessary (comp. Grønbæk et al., 1993), and as the single product becomes part of a use environment, static information architecture must become dynamic *interaction architecture*. These extensions of the field would help to understand and influence many current trends, from the Web 2.0 phenomenon to the ubiquitous dissemination of contextualized interactive devices. The same is true in reverse; more experience with these developments will also help to better understand minimalism and its implications.

For the author, the most valuable discovery related to minimalism was the complexity of the discourse on its meanings, and the resulting chance to reflect the understanding of interaction design as a discipline, to question the motivation and the very procedures used in human-computer interaction. The definition of minimalism for interaction design might have added a new standpoint to view accumulated knowledge from. And perhaps, this brings with it not only the chance for a fresh look at design, but also practical value in creating more simple products, generating better value for both users and designers.

References

Gajos, K. Z., Everitt, K., Tan, D. S., Czerwinski, M., and Weld, D. S. (2008). Predictability and Accuracy in Adaptive User Interfaces. CHI 2008, Florence, Italy, 1271–1274. Available online at http://doi.acm.org/10.1145/1357054.1357252

Gelernter, D. (1998). *The Aesthetics of Computing*. Quezon: Phoenix House.

Grønbæk, K., Grudin, J., Bødker, S., and Bannon, L. (1993). Achieving cooperative system design: shifting from a product to a process focus. *Participatory Design: Principles and Practices*. 79–96. Mahwah, N.J.: Lawrence Erlbaum Associates.

Penley, C., and Ross, A. (Eds.). (1991). *Technoculture*. Minneapolis: University of Minnesota Press.

Tognazzini, B. (2003). Multiple Mistakes Drown Interface (with a Letter from Joe Moran). http://www.asktog.com/columns/055Dishwasher.html Accessed 3.8.2008.2008

Weick, K. (2001). *Making Sense of the Organization*. Hoboken, NJ: Blackwell.

Westrum. (1991). *Technologies & society: The Shaping of People and Things*. Belmont, California: Wadsworth Pub. Co.

Chapter 9
Minimal Aesthetics

Simplicity carried to the extreme becomes elegance.
—Jon Franklin (1994)

Minimal design will never affect only functionality; it is bound to invoke an aesthetic impression. Whether it is a knife with a single function or a remote control with a single button, minimal artifacts are bound to create an aesthetic experience. Gelernter (1999) stresses that simplicity combined with effective power creates a forceful sense of satisfaction and equals beauty. However, while the function of an interface will influence its visual design, it does not completely determine its appearance; neither will the perception of functionality completely determine the aesthetic experience.[1] Two important aspects of product design have so far been omitted from the discussion: the purposeful excitement of aesthetic experiences, and the visual (or superficial) design of interfaces.

In the liberal arts, theory is often used synonymously with aesthetics, and consequently, minimalism is understood as an aesthetic notion. In HCI, usability is usually defined as a measurement of effectiveness and efficiency of a tool, combined with user satisfaction (ISO9241, 1998). For much of the twentieth century, aesthetic judgement in art was based upon formal properties like color, rhythm, and harmony (Eaton, 1998). Eaton suggests that affect on the observer is a more expressive measure as aesthetic value changes according to context. Gadamer (1998) further proposes a cognitive element in aesthetics, where the observer's interaction with art is "playful", and joy comes from learning about the world and oneself. While aesthetics was traditionally only considered of indirect influence as part of the "graphic design experience" (Tullis, 1988, 378), or the "visual look" (Marcus, 1995), it is now recognized as an important factor for the perceived usability, or "goodness" of a design (Hassenzahl, 2004), and efforts are currently made to connect usability with "joy of use", and measure hedonistic qualities (Hassenzahl et al., 2000), create heuristics for designing

---

[1] While it has been suggested that a usable design would be perceived as more attractive (Karvonen, 2000), experimental studies so far only found evidence that the visual appearance influences perceived usability (Tractinsky, 1997; Hassenzahl, Burmester, and Koller, 2003).

enjoyment (Malone, 1984; Monk et al., 2002) or define levels of design to induce emotions (Norman, 2004b). There are, however, few rules on how to create aesthetic designs, and no models that explain why designs are considered to be aesthetic. Heller (2005, 49) provides an explanation: while industrial design could develop rules for shapes, color, weight, type, volume and space out of long experience, interaction design is a young discipline. More importantly, "Interaction forms but one part of a whole solution; moreover, it is skeletal in nature, hidden under our more tangible and sensory details." (ibid.)

As the focus of this book is on designing *interactive* systems, it seems to be useful to differentiate the interaction design from "superficial" visual design; in semiotical terms, this differentiation translates to the denotative and the connotative function of design (Eco, 1986). Packaging can play an important role and influence the perception of a product, although design often follows a primarily functional, and only secondarily a communicative intention. When industrial products are considered, a form of "minimalist" design is currently en vogue that extends beyond minimalist functionality and minimalist structure: minimalism often evokes an aesthetic reaction, and thus influences the connotative aspect of design. Fewer functions often means fewer buttons, less visible structure equals less visual clutter. Both allow designers to extend on the created feeling of clarity. How important product design is for the success of products is illustrated by a user quote collected by Norman: "After plunking down $400 for an iPod I almost wouldn't have cared about the product after having unwrapped the packaging, it was that nice." (user cited in Norman, 2004b, 214) Here, not even the outer appearance of the tool itself, but even the disposable shell used to package it on the way to the customer became an aesthetic event. This demonstrates that it is possible to add to, or change, the perception of a tool without changing the tool itself.

"Form follows function" is a motto often connected with the Bauhaus design movement. Bauhaus grew out of the German Werkbund, a group advocating a closer alignment of the arts and industry. Following Walter Gropius' (1919) *Bauhaus Manifesto*, artists working within the design school made a conscious design decision to shun purely ornamental elements that detracted from an object's primary function. This decision was directed against the contemporary Arts and Crafts movement, and its celebration of elaborate ornamentation. The Bauhaus focused on designing highly practical objects, and on bringing good design to everyday life. It stressed the properties of material and experimented with reduction. This was mainly directed against ornamentation: while craftsmen would spend effort to paint flowers on a vase or cut patterns into a cupboard, straight lines and primitive forms were propagated by Bauhaus designers.

It might seem that this demonstrates design has only to communicate the function of an object, and that decoration is an evil in itself. The 1924 Bauhaus chess pieces by Josef Hartwig (Fig. 9.1), however, stand as proof for the difficulty in drawing a strict line to decoration: in the tradition of Bauhaus, the chess pieces were made out of industrial material, and they were stripped of all superfluous ornamentation (Bobzin, 2004). This included getting rid of the symbolism of

Fig. 9.1 Josef Hartwig: Bauhaus chess set (1924) with kind permission of Bauhaus-Archiv Museum für Gestaltung Berlin.

knights, queens, kings and pawns. Instead, the pieces' tops were formed to indicate the possible movement. The Bauhaus chess pieces were not a commercial success. Although they literally communicated the function of each piece, this was not what chess players were interested in. Chess players usually know how to move their pieces, but they like to think of them as knights, queens, kings, and pawns. In a way, the decoration of chess pieces had become part of their function.

How much aesthetic "packaging" is subject to Zeitgeist is illustrated by Mijksenaar and Westendorp (1999) using the example of radios: the different designs shown in Fig. 9.2 demonstrate the differences of designs for a device playing music. Mijksenaar and Westendorp maintain that designers "try hard to make products instantly comprehensible to us, but they can't keep up with the electronics engineers and software programmers who develop . . . more features"; their example shows, however, that existing functionality can be exposed (in the 1970s and 1980s) to demonstrate technical superiority, or hidden (in the 1990s) to appeal to the customers' appetite. Also, the five early models clearly show the development from a technical gadget to a piece of furniture.

The evolution of tastes for visual appearance can be verified looking at current Web designs that show a trend towards the reduction of visual clutter. As Fig. 9.3 illustrates, navigation elements are becoming visually simplified on most sites. Although primarily a matter of taste, there is also a connection to functionality: early Web design employed many visual cues to create realistic affordances. This indicated possible activities, e.g. the 3-dimensional buttons conveyed their "clickability". As use conventions, such as the placement of a navigation area, were established, the need for such communication became less pressing, and the visual appearance of interface elements was gradually simplified (Wroblewski, 2005, 3rd principle).

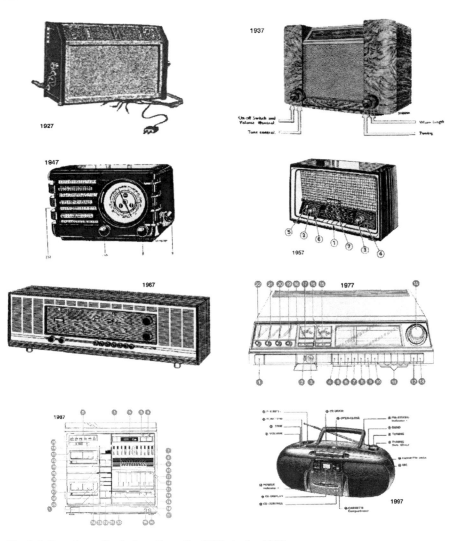

Fig. 9.2 Popular radio designs from the 1920s to the 1980s

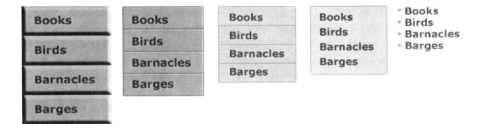

Fig. 9.3 Navigation elements on Web sites becoming visually simpler in the last years

Above evolution of graphic design could also be interpreted as a development of visual language that increasingly resembles visual design for paper media. As the display of options for interaction becomes less important, the rules of traditional design apply. Edward Tufte crafted the "$1 + 1 = 3$" rule (Tufte, 1986, 111) to illustrate that unnecessary visual clutter can suggest information that is not really there, e.g. two lines can cause visible interaction in moiré patterns or optical vibration.

The reduction of visual clutter must not necessarily lead to visually simpler designs. Tufte advocates a high data density—for him, an interface is good if it displays a high amount of information in a small space. Many examples[2] that Tufte presents in *The Visual Display of Quantitative Information* (1986) and *Envisioning Information* (Tufte, 1990) demonstrate how highly complex patterns can be detected using information visualization. A reproduction of one of his examples, Charles Joseph Minard's famous map of the Russian march by Napoleon Bonaparte (Minard, 1869), is shown in Fig. 9.4; this map displays all the qualities that Tufte values in information displays: there is little visual clutter, no extra lines or borders detract attention, and all elements of the map are meaningful. The information displayed is very dense as many different information perspectives are overlaid: geographic location, troop strength, direction, and temperature are all visualized in a complex composition. Thus, this single map illustrates much of the story and the reasons behind Napoleon's march to Russia, and illustrates the great losses on the way back. Tufte demands similar qualities from information systems[3]; he consequently proposes that screen space should be devoted primarily to content, shying even windows and menus (Wilchins, 1998) and preferring information-dense designs.

For Tufte, more *information* in the same space is preferable. He actually did count the number of links on a home page: the more links, the better the design. While this might contradict the minimalist standpoint—and Tufte in fact argues against the Google approach to access to functionality, preferring the portal functionality that e.g. Yahoo provides (compare Section 6.2.6)—it highlights the interaction of structural and compositional minimalism: as the example of the Minard map demonstrates, it is important for Tufte that information presents itself to interpretation; the more, the better. Pre-selection of data allows fewer interpretations, and produces less "rich" interaction. This is a position echoed by Don Norman, who insists "Why are Yahoo! and MSN such complex-looking places? Because their systems are easier to use. Not because they are complex, but because they simplify the life of their users by letting them see their choices on the home page: news, alternative searches, other items of interest." (Norman, 2004a).

---

[2] The outstanding quality of Tufte's books was reason enough to use a reference rather than a reproduction of his graphs here. If you don't already know them, please do have a look.

[3] By contrast, this book tries to differentiate information and interaction design.

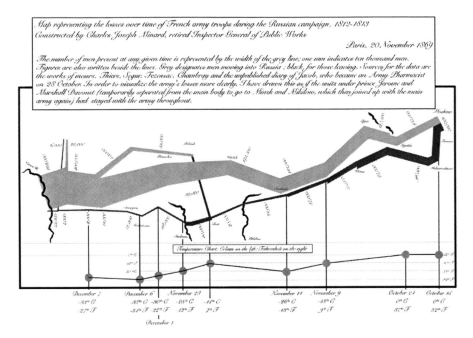

Fig. 9.4 Reproduction of Minard's map of Napoleon's march to Russia, drawn by the author.

However, he repeatedly refers to a "reduction of noise" (Tufte, 1986), and proposes that the signal-noise ratio be taken as a measure for quality.[4] The interpretation of information depends on its status as "signal" or "noise", as "function" or "decoration". For those seeking information on the Web, Yahoo thus puts forward much noise. Minimal designs can thus actually display a better signal-noise ratio, and allow a richer interaction—it depends on the *context of use*. According to Löwgren (2006), aesthetic qualities, or "use qualities" of a design differ depending on *genre*. Use qualities are "properties of digital designs that are experienced in use and the designer is in a position to influence" (ibid., 384). In other words, they define agreeable values for users and designers, and can consequently be used to guide design—Löwgren, for example, defines what is here denoted as functional minimalism as "(technical) elegance" (ibid., 396).

As compositional minimalism is difficult to design using conventional techniques of HCI, aesthetics could be used to aid design where traditional evaluation fails—it widens the design perspective to account for appropriation of technology (e.g. Petersen et al., 2004; Shusterman, 1999; Bertelsen and Pold, 2004). Bertelsen and Pold (ibid.) give the example of using notions from art

---

[4] The concept of signal-noise ratio appeals to Web designers and has been taken up as a basis for design argument by different individuals; 37signals even started a Weblog on the topic (http://37signals.com/svn/).

history, such as "baroque" to be used for criticizing design; they aim to capture use qualities that are not focused upon by traditional usability methods. For Bertelsen, basing design upon aesthetics enables reconsideration of the dilemma between "curriculum for use" and "unanticipated use" (Light, 2005; Bertelsen, 2006). Minimalism could present a perspective for design critique based on aesthetic understanding to supplement the analysis demonstrated in this chapter. When using such an aesthetic approach, however, care must be taken to differentiate between a systematic and a folk understanding of minimalism, lest the critique be based purely on personal taste.

References

Bertelsen, O. W. (2006). Tertiary Artifacts at the Interface. In P Fishwick (Ed.), *Aesthetic computing*. 357–368. Cambridge, MA: MIT Press.

Bertelsen, O. W. and Pold, S. (2004). *Criticism as an Approach to Interface Aesthetics*. NordiCHI '04: Proceedings of the third Nordic conference on human-computer interaction, New York, NY, USA, 23–32.

Bobzin, A. (2004). *Das Bauhaus-Schachspiel von Josef Hartwig: Entstehungs- und Rezeptionsgeschichte*. Fachhochschule Berlin, Berlin.

Eaton, M. M. (1998). Locating the aesthetic. In C Korsmeyer (Ed.), *Aesthetics: The Big Questions*. 84–91. Malden, MA: Blackwell.

Eco, U. (1986). Function and sign: Semiotics of architecture. In M Gottdiener and AP Lagopoulos (Eds.), *The City and the Sign*. New York, NY: Columbia University Press.

Franklin, J. (1994). *Writing for Story: Craft Secrets of Dramatic Nonfiction*. New York, NY: Plume.

Gadamer, H. G. (1998). From "Truth and method". In C Korsmeyer (Ed.), *Aesthetics: The Big Questions*. 91–97. Malden, MA: Blackwell.

Gelernter, D. (1999). *Machine Beauty: Elegance and the Heart of Technology (Repr ed) (Masterminds)*. New York, NY: Basic Books.

Gropius, W. (1919). The Bauhaus Manifesto. http://www.dmoma.org/lobby/Bauhaus_manifesto.html Accessed 23.7.2008

Hassenzahl, M. (2004). The interplay of beauty, goodness and usability in interactive products. *uman-Computer Interaction*, 19, 319–349.

Hassenzahl, M., Burmester, M., and Koller, F. (2003). *AttrakDiff: Ein Fragebogen zur Messung wahrgenommener hedonischer und pragmatischer Qualität*. Mensch & Computer 2003. Interaktion in Bewegung, Stuttgart, 187–196.

Hassenzahl, M., Platz, A., Burmester, M., and Lehner, K. (2000). *Hedonic and Ergonomic Quality Aspects Determine a Software's Appeal*. CHI '00: Proceedings of the SIGCHI conference on Human factors in computing systems, New York, NY, USA, 201–208.

Heller, D. (2005). Aesthetics and interaction design: some preliminary thoughts. *Interactions*, 12(5), 48–50.

ISO9241. (1998). ISO 9241: Ergonomic requirements for office work with visual display terminals (VDTs).

Karvonen, K. (2000). *The Beauty of Simplicity*. CUU '00: Proceedings on the 2000 conference on universal usability, New York, NY, USA, 85–90.

Light, A. (2005). Report: Aesthetic Approaches to HCI. http://www.usabilitynews.com/news/article2174.asp Accessed 20.7.2008

Löwgren, J. (2006). Articulating the use qualities of digital designs. In P Fishwick (Ed.), *Aesthetic Computing*. 383–403. Cambridge, MA: MIT Press.

Malone, T. W. (1984). Heuristics for designing enjoyable user interfaces: lessons from computer games. *Human Factors in Computer Systems*. 1–12. Ablex Publishing Corp. Norwood, NJ, USA.

Marcus, A. (1995). Principles of effective visual communication for graphical user interface design. *Human-computer interaction: toward the year 2000*. 425–441. Morgan Kaufmann Publishers Inc. San Francisco, CA, USA.

Mijksenaar, P. and Westendorp, P. (1999). *Open Here: The Art of Instructional Design*. New York, NY: Joost Elffers Books.

Minard, C. J. (1869). Carte figurative des pertes successives en hommes de l'armée française dans la campagne de Russie. 1812–1813.: ENPC: Fol 10975, 10974/C612.

Monk, A., Hassenzahl, M., Blythe, M., and Reed, D. (2002). *Funology: Designing Enjoyment*. CHI '02: CHI '02 extended abstracts on Human factors in computing systems, New York, NY, USA, 924–925.

Norman, D. A. (2004a). The truth about Google's so-called "simplicity". http://www.jnd.org/dn.mss/the_truth_about.html Accessed 8.10.2008

Norman, D. A. (2004b). *Emotional Design: Why We Love (Or Hate) Everyday Things*. New York, NY: Basic Books.

Petersen, M. G., Iversen, O. S., Krogh, P. G., and Ludvigsen, M. (2004). *Aesthetic Interaction: A Pragmatist's Aesthetics of Interactive Systems*. DIS '04: Proceedings of the 2004 conference on designing interactive systems, New York, NY, USA, 269–276.

Shusterman, R. (1999). Somaesthetics: A disciplinary proposal. *Journal of Aesthetics and Art Criticism*, 57.

Tractinsky, N. (1997). *Aesthetics and Apparent Usability: Empirically Assessing Cultural and Methodological Issues*. CHI '97: Proceedings of the SIGCHI conference on Human factors in computing systems, New York, NY, USA, 115–122.

Tufte, E. R. (1986). *Visual Display of Quantitative Information*. Cheshire, CT: Graphics Press.

Tufte, E. R. (1990). *Envisioning Information*. Cheshire, CT: Graphics Press.

Tullis, T. S. (1988). Screen design. In M Helander (Ed.), *Handbook of Human-Computer Interaction*. 377–411. Amsterdam: Elsevier.

Wilchins, D. (1998, April 17). Getting inside design. *Yale Herald*, Yale, CT. Available online at www.yaleherald.com/archive/xxv/4.17.98/exclusive/index.html.

Wroblewski, L. (2005). 9 Lessons from 9 Years of Interface Design. http://www.lukew.com/ff/entry.asp?209 Accessed 22.6.2008

Chapter 10
Unconnected Ends

Truly, you have a dizzying intellect.
—Man in Black, The Princess Bride

Minimalism as a perspective, and the analysis in this book have limitations, some of which are listed here; this is combined with an agenda for further research where future investigations might help clarify the role of minimalism. This chapter is not named *Unconnected Ends* for nothing—if you are willing to add, please connect to the author or the companion web site of this book at http://smplct.org.

Mathematicians dislike computer-assisted proofs—correct and verifiable as they may be, they don't transport the spark of intuition that seems to be required from scientific mathematical practice. Computer scientists like concepts-of-proof to demonstrate scientific progress, while art historians claim that science must take the form of well-documented arguments. While transdisciplinary work is often called for, the different understandings of how science works can make it difficult to transfer concepts. In this book, the transdisciplinary approach, aiming at the transfer of the notion of minimalism from art and music history to the field of human-computer interaction, made necessary some unusual 'design decisions': there is no single interpretation for minimalism, there is no measurement of degree, and there is no constructed (read artificial) prototype system demonstrating the meaning of minimalism. Instead, this book has tried to preserve the inherently discursive character of the notion of minimalism in the transfer to prevent a loss of meaning.

An inherent limitation comes from the underlying definition of minimalism, which in the arts never acquired a canonical state—it is frequently used, but with slightly different meanings; it is given as a label, but often not welcomed. What I have learned in reading the literature, however, is that this very unde-cidedness, the space for interpretation left open by the scholarly discourse, motivates the formation of a self-conceived definition. This book would there-fore prefer to start a discourse about the meaning of minimalism rather than persist on exactly following the propositions made herein: the notion of minim-alism must be open to new interpretations in HCI. The four aspects of

H. Obendorf, *Minimalism*, Human-Computer Interaction Series,
DOI 10.1007/978-1-84882-371-6_10, © Springer-Verlag London Limited 2009

minimalism proposed here were chosen as they form a solid foundation for the
analysis of designs, and can to some degree be clearly differentiated. They
should by no means be understood as the only possible interpretations of
minimalism or as the only meanings of simplicity.

The discussion of existing literature from the fields of design and interaction
design indicated that the four aspects of minimalism form a useful basis for
discussing many topics that repeatedly surface in human-computer interaction.
Care should be taken with the words that we use to describe our disciplines: the
understanding of *simplicity* deserves a better definition, and an application not
only as a label, but as a tool, or a value set underlying design or evaluation. To
this end, different understandings of simplicity must be found, and its purely
positive connotation must be subjected to revision. In short, the limits of
simplicity must be mapped out—an undertaking that will take a joint effort.

In this book, minimalism was used and understood as an extreme example
for reduction and as a tool for understanding design. No theory for interaction
design was proposed here, and the focus on the transfer of the conceptions
underlying minimalism in art and music has drawn attention from links to
minimalist theories such as the minimalism in mathematics, Chomsky's language minimalism or Carroll's documentation minimalism. A more rigorous
examination of these connections might help understand the design posture
taken by reduction based on the four notions of minimalism proposed here.

Regarding methods for analyzing and constructing minimalism, this book
offered opinionated and empirically informed suggestions rather than trying to
be a practice-proven handbook. The observed base for the discussion of designs
and processes is necessarily limited; specifically, more detailed analyses of
designs—this book chose breadth over depth here as internals of designs are
not easily accessible[1]—need to be examined in order to confirm or confute the
practical value of minimalism. Further research is also necessary to evaluate the
practical value of the minimalist background for applying existing techniques
and modifying software development processes. It is, however, perhaps not
overly optimistic to expect more data to be available in the future: the current
trend towards simplicity, and most notably the distribution of responsibility in
current web and application developments suggest that more insights into the
construction of architecturally and compositionally minimal systems will be
published in the near future.

For *human-computer interaction* as a discipline, the focus on context and
process needs to be widened. Effects of minimalism for the development of
standard software require further research as, here, reduction will not come
easily. The field of configuration and end-user development (Sections 5.3, 5.4)
will become increasingly important. The process of appropriation needs further
integration in the reflection of usability methods. To encourage the transfer of

---

[1] In this book, sources from the Web have been cited where no 'scientific' source was available
as designers usually do not reflect on their practice using conference articles. Weblogs and
press releases were used instead.

minimalism to *design practice*, more examples, and more experiments are necessary, transforming the minimalist standpoint in a set of practical tools.

Software engineering must find answers for its relation to usability engineering, and face the focus on the whole that is promoted by architectural and compositional minimalism. The analysis in this book indicated that although both disciplines aim to improve software quality by attaining simplicity, the focus of reduction differs. The use of techniques from usability engineering in software development processes promises to allow an increased focus on the whole design, thus increasing the reflection on the necessity of features, and the forces that drive and orient development. An equitable fusion of techniques from these two disciplines might create synergies for the design of simple systems.

Finally, to demonstrate the attractiveness of these techniques for professional software development, the economical use of minimalism must be discussed and a possible role defined for minimalism as part of internally or publicly communicated company values (Jenson, 2002, 2005). Research on the function of simplicity in marketing needs to be integrated—a starting point lies in economists' discussions, the role of simplicity in management and business processes (Jensen, 2000, 31; Trout and Rivkin, 1998), and for marketing[2] (Cristol and Sealey, 2000).

References

Bittel, L. R., and Bittel, M. A. (1978). *Encyclopedia of Professional Management*. New York, NY: McGraw-Hill.

Cristol, S. M., and Sealey, P. (2000). *Simplicity Marketing: End Brand Complexity, Clutter, and Confusion*. New York, NY: Free Press.

Jensen, B. (2000). *Simplicity: The New Competitive Advantage In A World Of More, Better, Faster*. Darby, PA: Diane Pub Co.

Jenson, S. (2002). *The Simplicity Shift: Innovative Design Tactics in a Corporate World*. Cambridge, MA: Cambridge University Press.

Jenson, S. (2005). Default thinking: Why mobile services are setup to fail. In R Harper (Ed.), *The Inside Text: Social, Cultural and Design Perspectives on SMS*. 305–325. New York, NY: Springer.

Kotler, P. (1975). *Marketing for Nonprofit Organizations*. (Subsequent editions in 1982, 1986, 1991, 1996, 2003, and 2006. Alan Andreasen joined as co-author in 1986.) Englewood Cliffs, NJ: Prentice Hall.

Stone, M., and Foss, B. (2001). *Successful Customer Relationship Marketing*. London: Kogan Page Business Books.

Trout, J., and Rivkin, S. (1998). *The Power of Simplicity*. Columbus, OH: McGraw-Hill Companies.

---

[2] Minimal marketing must market the minimal; instead, it has been misunderstood as investing minimal effort in marketing, assuming that "demand will grow ... simply because they are offering it" (Kotler, 1975, 8), placing "confidence in the assumption that quality speaks for itself" (Bittel, and Bittel, 1978, 709), and, e.g. by cut-price airlines, as "focusing simply on the bare product, the price and easy booking" (Stone, and Foss, 2001, 355).

Chapter 11
Conclusion

There is always an easy solution to every human problem – neat, plausible and wrong.[1]

—Henry Louis Mencken

Beauty is Simplicity plus Power. Simplicity is desirable. And simplicity is created through reduction. Based on this understanding of design, answering the questions regarding direction and degree of reduction, and thus differentiating the meaning of simplicity, was motivation for the transfer of the notion of minimalism to the design of interactive systems that this book attempts to implement.

This book does not attempt to provide an unambiguous set of rules for design. Instead, it tries something more: The minimal standpoint introduced in this book offers a new perspective on the design of interactive systems: focus shifts from individual features to the overall gestalt of the design. This emphasis on the whole supports a holistic perspective: design evolves no longer solely around the *user*, but converges on *use*. The consequential perspective of *use-centered design* presents an alternative to focusing alternatively only on the user, or on the technical composition. The focus on *reduction* and the *modularization of design* promise to limit the expansion of complexities to human scale.

Minimalism adds constructive advice and support in choosing concrete procedures to this abstract posture. Replacing minimalism with simplicity, four values are defined in this book that can guide the design of interactive systems: *functional* simplicity, *structural* simplicity, *architectural* simplicity and *compositional* simplicity. These values differentiate the meaning of simplicity and can thus be used to analyze existing designs or make informed design choices when developing a new product. The minimal perspective was also shown to be useful for analyzing and modifying the processes that are used to install product qualities in designs, both on a literal and on a very abstract level.

---

[1] You will often find the more suggestive, albeit most probably more incorrect quote, "For every complex problem, there is an answer that is clear, simple—and wrong". The original quote appeared in the *New York Evening Mail* on November 16, 1917, The Divine Afflatus.

H.L. Obendorf, *Minimalism*, Human-Computer Interaction Series,
DOI 10.1007/978-1-84882-371-6_11, © Springer-Verlag London Limited 2009

It is my hope that minimalism has the potential of widening the perspective on interaction design, and that the transfer of a notion rooted in art and music was successful in bringing a new standpoint to design that can help both scholars and practitioners to better understand their discipline and reflect on their practice.

Perhaps, it is more than coincidence when manufacturers of some of the most complex applications today promote simplicity as a guiding design principle, or when they are successful selling their complex products with an air of simplicity. Simplicity is openly credited as an important basis for ease of use; it is possible that we are going to see more minimalism and even *more* of *less* in the future.

Index

Printed in the United States
150919LV00002B/77/P